19th Annual Conference of the European Association for Machine Translation (EAMT 2016)

Published in Special Issue of the Baltic Journal of Modern Computing (Volume 4 (2016), Number 2)

Riga, Latvia
30 May - 1 June 2016

ISBN: 978-1-5108-3185-8

Printed by Curran Associates, Inc. (2016)

For permission requests, please contact the Association for Computational Linguistics
at the address below.

Association for Computational Linguistics
209 N. Eighth Street
Stroudsburg, Pennsylvania 18360

Phone: 1-570-476-8006
Fax: 1-570-476-0860

acl@aclweb.org

Additional copies of this publication are available from:

Curran Associates, Inc.
57 Morehouse Lane
Red Hook, NY 12571 USA
Phone: 845-758-0400
Fax: 845-758-2633
Email: curran@proceedings.com
Web: www.proceedings.com

TABLE OF CONTENTS

Baltic J. Modern Computing, Vol. 4 (2016), No. 2, 99-101

Special issue

of the

Baltic Journal of Modern Computing

(Vol. 4(2016), No. 2)

Proceedings

of the

19th annual conference

of the

European Association
for Machine Translation
(EAMT)

Riga, Latvia, 2016

Foreword from the president of the European Association for Machine Translation

Mikel L. FORCADA

Departament de Llenguatges i Sistemes Informàtics,
Universitat d'Alacant, E-03690 Sant Vicent del Raspeig, Spain

mlf@ua.es

As newly-elected president of the European Association for Machine Translation (EAMT) it is a great pleasure for me to write the foreword to this special issue of the Baltic Journal of Modern Computing, which also serves as the proceedings of the first EAMT conference held under my presidency: the 19th annual conference of the EAMT in Riga, Latvia. It is also a great honour, but also a great responsibility, to be given the chance to continue the huge work done by Andy Way's during a fruitful six-year-long presidency. Taking advantage of the momentum impressed on the EAMT by Andy, I hope I can live up to the expectations of our membership and of the wider machine translation community. If I succeed, it will be thanks to the help of a hard-working Executive Committee, whose members are elected or ratified when our Association holds a General Assembly as part of each annual conference.

The EAMT started organizing annual workshops in 1996; then, these workshops have become annual conferences, and have been hosted all around Europe. In the last years, the venue has steadily moved from west to east: from Barcelona (2009) to Saint-Raphaël (2010) to Leuven (2011) to Trento (2012) and finally —after skipping one year to host the successful world-wide MT Summit 2013 in Nice— to Dubrovnik (2014), only to turn around a little bit after visiting Antalya in 2015 to come to Riga in 2016. Yes, you have guessed: EAMT 2017, our 20th annual conference, will surely be west from Riga. It will be announced at EAMT 2016 shortly after I am writing these lines. Those who miss our conference, will find out by visiting our Association's website, EAMT.org.

By the way, if you have not done so yet, please consider joining the EAMT. Our membership rates are low, particularly for students, and have not increased since the EAMT's inception. You will benefit from discounts when attending not only our conferences, but also the conferences held by our partner associations the Asia-Pacific Association for Machine Translation (AAMT) and the Association for Machine Translation in the Americas (AMTA). You will also have an exclusive chance to benefit from funding for your activities related to machine translation. And perhaps you can get even more involved and participate in serving the European machine translation community by becoming a member of the Executive Committee of the EAMT.

But let me go back to EAMT 2016. As in previous conferences, it is great to see the strong programme put together by our programme chairs: Antonio Toral, as research track chair, and Tony O'Dowd and Alexandru Ceausu, as user track co-chairs. There will also be a projects and products session which showcases the advance of machine translation in Europe. And, last but not least, I also feel very fortunate to have Alex Fraser as our invited speaker to top it all off.

EAMT 2016 would have never been possible without the generous offer to host and the hard work done subsequently by the local organizing committee at the well-known machine translation and language technology company Tilde, headed by Andrejs Vasiļjevs, and without the hospitality of the University of Latvia represented by Juris Borzovs. I warmly thank them all!

Another round of heartfelt thank-yous go to the co-editors-in-chief of the Baltic Journal of Modern Computing, and a special one to managing co-editor Evalds Ikaunieks. This is the first time that our whole proceedings are given the unique chance of becoming a special issue in an indexed, open-access journal; I hope this multiplies the impact of the advances presented in our conference.

Finally, I would like to thank EAMT 2016 attendees for coming to Riga. I hope the conference leads to new friendships and fruitful collaboration.

Mikel L. Forcada
EAMT President
May 2016

Baltic J. Modern Computing, Vol.4 (2016), No.2, 102

Preface from the Programme Chairs

Antonio TORAL[1], Tony O'DOWD[2], Alexandru CEAUSU[3]

[1]ADAPT Centre, School of Computing, Dublin City University, Ireland
[2]KantanMT, , Invent Building, Dublin City University, Ireland
[3]AMPLEXOR International, Luxembourg, Luxembourg

atoral@computing.dcu.ie, tonyod@kantanmt.com,
alexandru.ceausu@amplexor.com

It is our pleasure to welcome you to the 19th annual conference of the European Association for Machine Translation (EAMT) to be held in Riga, Latvia. We have really enjoyed serving as programme chairs for this edition of the conference. The EAMT conference has become the most important event in Europe in the area of machine translation for researchers, users, professional translators, etc. As in previous editions, the conference is organised around three different tracks: research, user and projects/products. The research track concerns novel and significant research results in any aspect of machine translation and related areas while the user track reports users' experiences with machine translation, in industry, government, NGOs, etc. Finally, the project and product track offers projects and products the opportunity to be presented to the wide audience of the conference.

This year we have received 36 submissions to the research track, 8 submissions to the user track and 25 descriptions of projects and products. Overall, submissions come from 34 different countries. Each submission to the research and user tracks was peer-reviewed by three independent members of the Programme Committee. In the research track 19 papers out of 36 (53%) were accepted for publication while 5 papers out of 8 were accepted in the user track (63%).

Aside from regular papers from the three tracks, the programme includes an invited talk by Alexander Fraser, MT Group Leader at LMU München, on the hot topic of machine translation into morphologically rich languages. We will also have a presentation by the winner of the EAMT Best Thesis Award.

We would like to thank the Programme Committee members and additional reviewers, whose names are listed below, for their high quality reviews and recommendations. These have been very useful for the Programme Chairs to make decisions. We would also like to thank all the authors for trying their best to incorporate the reviewers' suggestions when preparing the camera ready papers. For those papers that were not accepted, we hope that the reviewers' comments will be useful to improve them. Special thanks to Mikel L. Forcada, who took care of the projects and products track.

Baltic J. Modern Computing, Vol.4 (2016), No.2, 103-105

EAMT 2016 Committees

Chairs

General chair: Mikel Forcada (Universitat d'Alacant, Spain)
Research programme chair: Antonio Toral (Dublin City University, Ireland)
User programme co-chair: Tony O'Dowd (KantanMT, Ireland)
User programme co-chair: Alexandru Ceausu (Amplexor, Luxembourg)
Local organisation co-chair: Andrejs Vasiļjevs (Tilde, Latvia)
Local organisation co-chair: Rihards Kalniņš (Tilde, Latvia)
Local host: Juris Borzovs (University of Latvia)

Research Committee

Eleftherios Avramidis (DFKI, Germany)
Bogdan Babych (University of Leeds, UK)
Loïc Barrault (Université du Maine, France)
Núria Bel (Universitat Pompeu Fabra, Spain)
Nicola Bertoldi (Fondazione Bruno Kessler, Italy)
Laurent Besacier (Université J. Fourier, France)
Arianna Bisazza (University of Amsterdam, Netherlands)
Hervé Blanchon (Laboratoire d'Informatique de Grenoble, France)
Michael Carl (Copenhagen Business School, Denmark)
Francisco Casacuberta (Universitat Politècnica de València, Spain)
Helena Caseli (Universidade Federal de São Carlos, Brazil)
Mauro Cettolo (Fondazione Bruno Kessler, Italy)
David Chiang (University of Notre Dame, USA)
Marta R. Costa-Jussà (Institute For Infocomm Research, Singapore)
Jinhua Du (Dublin City University, Ireland)
Nadir Durrani (University of Edinburgh, UK)
Andreas Eisele (Directorate-General for Translation (EC), Luxembourg)
Cristina España-Bonet (Universitat Politècnica de Catalunya, Spain)
Mireia Farrús (Universitat Pompeu Fabra, Spain)
Mark Fishel (University of Tartu, Estonia)
George Foster (National Research Council, Canada)
Federico Gaspari (Dublin City University, Ireland)

Ulrich Germann (University of Edinburgh, UK)
Barry Haddow (University of Edinburgh, UK)
Christian Hardmeier (University of Uppsala, Sweden)
Yifan He (Bosch RTC, USA)
Kenneth Heafield (Bloomberg Labs, USA)
Teresa Herrmann (Karlsruhe Institute of Technology, Germany)
Hieu Hoang (New York University, Abu Dhabi, UAE)
Matthias Huck (University of Edinburgh, UK)
Gonzalo Iglesias (University of Cambridge, UK)
Jie Jiang (Applied Language Solutions, UK)
Marcin Junczys-Dowmunt (Adam Mickiewicz University, Poland)
Philipp Koehn (John Hopkins University, USA)
Qun Liu (Dublin City University, Ireland; Chinese Academy of Sciences, China)
Pavel Pecina (Charles University in Prague, Czech Republic)
Juan Antonio Pérez-Ortiz (Universitat d'Alacant, Spain)
Maja Popovic (Humboldt University of Berlin, Germany)
Raphael Rubino (Universität des Saarlandes, Germany)
Víctor Sánchez-Cartagena (Prompsit Language Engineering, Spain)
Felipe Sánchez-Martínez (Universitat d'Alacant, Spain)
Kepa Sarasola (Euskal Herriko Unibertsitatea, Spain)
Lane Schwartz (University of Illinois, USA)
Rico Sennrich (University of Edinburgh, UK)
Kashif Shah (University of Sheffield, UK)
Khalil Simaan (University of Amsterdam, Netherlands)
Michel Simard (National Research Council, Canada)
Lucia Specia (University of Sheffield, UK)
Ankit Srivastava (DFKI, Germany)
Sara Stymne (Uppsala University, Sweden)
Jörg Tiedemann (Uppsala University, Sweden)
Dan Tufis (Academia Romana, Romania)
Marco Turchi (Fondazione Bruno Kessler, Italy)
Francis M. Tyers (UiT Norgga árktalaš universitehta, Norway)
Josef van Genabith (Universität des Saarlandes, Germany)
Vincent Vandeghinste (University of Leuven, Belgium)
David Vilar (Nuance Communications, USA)
Martin Volk (University of Zurich, Switzerland)
Andy Way (Dublin City University, Ireland)
Jürgen Wedekind (University of Copenhagen, Denmark)
François Yvon (Université Paris Sud, France)

User Committee

Nora Aranberri (Euskal Herriko Uni, Spain)
Diego Bartolomé (Tauyou, Spain)
Olga Beregovaya (Welocalize, US)
James Cogley (Microsoft, Ireland)
Stephen Doherty (University of New South Wales, Australia)
Kurt Eberle (Lingenio, Germany)
Andreas Eisele (European Commission, DGT, Luxembourg)
Tatjana Gornostaja (Tilde, Latvia)
Declan Groves (Microsoft, Ireland)
Manuel Herranz (Pangeanic, Spain)
Fred Hollowood (Fred Hollowood Consulting, Ireland)
Maxim Khalilov (bmmt, Germany)
Hilário Leal Fontes (European Commission, Luxembourg)
Pedro Luis Díez-Orzas (Linguaserve, Spain)
Paul Mangell (Alpha CRC, UK)
Jay Marciano (Lionbridge, US)
Daniel Marcu (Uni Southern Calif, US)
John Moran (Transpiral, Ireland)
Antoni Oliver (Universitat Oberta de Catalunya, Spain)
Niko Papula (Multilizer, Finland)
Mirko Plitt (Modulo Language Automation, Switzerland)
Bruno Pouliquen (World Intellectual Property Organization, Switzerland)
Gema Ramírez-Sánchez (Prompsit Language Engineering, Spain)
Spyridon Pilos (European Commission, Belgium)
Gregor Thurmair (Linguatec, Germany)
Ventsislav Zhechev (Yelp, US)

Additional Reviewers

Mikel Artetxe (Euskal Herriko Unibertsitatea, Spain)
Annette Rios Gonzales (University of Zurich, Switzerland)
Sanja Štajner (University of Mannheim, Germany)
Eva Vanmassenhove (Dublin City University, Ireland)

Baltic J. Modern Computing, Vol. 4 (2016), No. 2, 106-114

Patterns of Terminological Variation in Post-editing and of Cognate Use in Machine Translation in Contrast to Human Translation

Oliver ČULO, Jean NITZKE

Fachbereich Translations-, Sprach- und Kulturwissenschaft, Universität Mainz
An der Hochschule 2, 76726 Germersheim, Germany

{culo,nitzke}@uni-mainz.de

Abstract. Post-Editing and machine translation are often studied from the viewpoint of efficiency (measured e.g. in words processed) or of quality (e.g. human judgement of fluency). Little is known, however, about how post-editing and machine translation change the linguistic profile of the texts produced in contrast to human translations. In this paper, we present a pilot study contrasting lexical profiles of a small collection of texts, focussing on two aspects: variation patterns in terminological translation in post-edited texts, and the translation of cognates in machine translation, both contrasted to purely human translations. The study was conducted for the translation direction English-German.

Keywords: Translation, Post-Editing, Terminology, Cognates

1. Introduction

Post-editing (PE) is a rather new mode of translation production which is increasingly studied from various angles. A pervasive topic is the raise in productivity which is associated with post-editing, even though to varying degrees depending on such factors as the language pair or the quality of the MT (cf. e.g. Groves and Schmidtke, 2009; O'Brien, 2011) and certainly on the complexity of the setting in which it is used (cf. e.g. Silva, 2014). Recently, there has also been growing interest in how PE differs from human translation (HT), mainly in terms of process-based research (Michael Carl et al., 2011; Elming et al., 2014; Mesa-Lao, 2014), by means of evaluating gaze behaviour and keystroke activities of post-editors.

Little is known, however, about how post-edited texts differ in their linguistic properties from human translations. For machine translated texts, Lapshinova-Koltunski (2013; 2015) provides insights on linguistic properties of texts translated by humans either manually or with the help of CAT tools, or by various machine translation systems. She analyses such features as verbal vs. nominal style and investigates whether typical translation properties such as shining-through (Teich, 2003) or explicitation (Blum-Kulka, 1986) can be observed not only in HT, but also in machine translated texts. Carl and Schaeffer (forthcoming) report that PE products exhibit less lexical variation in translation than HT products, possibly due to the priming of the machine translation output.

In the following, we present a pilot study analysing how texts may differ in terms of their lexical profiles between purely human translations and when machine translation (MT) is added to the process. We focused on two specific kinds of lexemes: terms and cognates. In the first experiment, we contrasted post-editing and human translation along the dimension of term translation within the domain of Languages for Specific Purposes (LSP). In the second experiment we compared translation choices made by humans and machine translation systems in terms of cognates, in order to understand in which other ways MT may change the lexical profiles of texts. Cognates are lexical items that have a similar form and meaning in two languages, like German *System* and English *system*, but are not always the best or preferred translation equivalents.

2. Studies

2.1. Patterns of terminological variation

The data used for the analysis in this subsection was collected in an experiment in which participants were asked to translate (HT), fully post-edit (FPE) and light-post-edit (LPE) texts from either the technical or the medical domain. The texts were of low formality level and originated from LSP texts freely available on the internet. The three technical texts selected for the experiment are parts taken from a dish washer manual, the three medical texts were taken from package leaflets ranging from a vaccine against measles to human insulin for diabetes patients and medication for treatment of cancer. All texts were about 150 words long. The data collection is a generic collection in the sense that we did not aim at studying one specific phenomenon (e.g. term translation), but it is generally aimed at contrasting the PE and HT processes and products along various dimensions.

The texts were automatically pre-translated by Google Translate for the PE tasks. A permutation scheme was set for the three sessions for each domain so that each text would be translated, fully and lightly post-edited the same amount of times, but by different participants (cf. Table 1). Participants had access to internet search facilities, including online dictionaries and term databases such as IATE[1].

The participant groups consisted of 12 advanced translation students for the technical and 9 for the medical texts, all students at FTSK Germersheim. They had at least two years of training and had passed at least one course on translating in the domain they would translate and post-edit in in the experiment. Some had minor post-editing experience, but given that PE is not part of the regular course offering at the institute, it can be assumed that all participants were better trained in HT than in PE.

The technical texts were thus translated, lightly and fully post-edited each four times, the medical texts each three times. The participants used the Translog-II editor for all three tasks, which logged the participant's key stroke activities, and eye movements were recorded using a Tobii TX 300. The eye-tracking and keylogging data were not used for the present study. The experiment data will be made available through the translation process research database (TPR-DB)[2].

---

[1] http://iate.europa.eu/
[2] https://sourceforge.net/projects/tprdb/files/

Table 1. Permutation scheme for human translation, full, and light post-editing

Participant	Text 1	Text 2	Text 3
P01	HT	LPE	FPE
P02	FPE	HT	LPE
(...)			

Participants were given instructions on how to post-edit. Part of the instructions for the full PE was to ensure terminological consistency of the post-edited texts. In general, only one term is used to describe one concept in LSP texts. Indeed, in one case where two term naming variants were used synonymously in a package leaflet – the Latin-derived term *varicella* and the equivalent English term *chickenpox*– translators would opt for one variant in human translation: either the more formal Latin-derived variant *Varizellen* or the more colloquial German variant *Windpocken* (cf. Table 5).

Carl and Schaeffer (forthcoming) observe that HT is more varied than PE in terms of lexical variation. A quick look at the number of types used for all texts produced in one translation mode (cf. Table 2) confirms this for our text collection: we counted the types for nouns, verbs adjectives and adverbs for the machine translated texts first, and then for the "bag of words" of all lightly post-edited, all fully post-edited and all human-translated texts. It is not surprising that MT has the lowest number of types, as there was only one machine translated text per source text, where there were multiple translations resp. post-edits. The numbers given in Table 2 also comply with our hypothesis that in light post-editing there would be less lexical variation than in full post-editing, where post-editors are expected to produce a translation of higher quality. For all texts together in HT, however, we get by far the highest number of types, i.e. for multiple translation vs. multiple full post-edits of a text, there seems to be more lexical variation in HT.

As ensuring terminological consistency was not part of the assignment for light PE, we ruled out these data for the analysis presented below.

Table 2. Number of lexical types (nouns, verbs, adjectives, adverbs) per translation mode for all texts of that mode combined. Note that for MT, there is only one target text per source text while there are multiple target texts for the other modes

translation mode	no. of lexical types
MT	277
LPE	330
FPE	384
HT	488

For measuring variation in lexical rendering in translation, Carl and Schaeffer (forthcoming) propose to make use of the Perplexity coefficient. The perplexity coefficient is usually used to measure decision (un)certainty for a translation model. Carl and Schaeffer test whether perplexity and production- and reading-times in translation and post-editing can be correlated. We use the perplexity coefficient as measure of variation in term translation in order to test whether Machine Translation shines through in the final post-editing product.

We manually identified term candidates in the source texts and their counterpart translations; term candidates were verified as term through the use of IATE. We chose terms that appear three times or more often in the source text and checked whether the translations of those varied or whether they were left untranslated; if a term was not translated at one point, we calculated this as variation. There was one borderline case: the phrase *where measles are common* was translated by the German compound noun *Masernvorkommen* 'measles occurrence'. Nominalisation and compounding are typical processes for translations from English to German, but as the word *measles* had been consistently rendered by the noun *Masern* as first part of the German compound, we chose not to count this as variation.

Table 3. Mapping of term variant to translation event type for translations of the term *dish washer* in two post-editing sessions

Session	term translation	term frequ.	event type
P10_FPE	Spülmaschine	2	pref.t.trans
	Geschirrspülmaschine	2	syn.1.trans
	Geschirrspüler	1	syn.2.trans
P21_FPE	Geschirrspülmaschine	4	pref.t.trans
	Spülmaschine	2	syn.1.trans

Table 3 lists the renderings and their frequencies of translations of the term *dish washer* for two specific post-editing session. One problem becomes apparent when looking at the list of terms used in the translations for one and the same concept in Table 3: As we did not define an a priori list of preferred terms for the tasks, post-editors would vary in their choice of preferred term for concepts which exhibited high terminological variation. We thus needed to map these results onto a scheme which would allow us to measure terminological variation across texts independent of the post-editors choice of preferred term.

We chose to classify term translations into types of "events" consistent with terminology theory (cf., e.g., Arntz, 2014). For each session, we defined a *preferred term* a posteriori, variations of this term were categorized as *synonymous terms*. We thus count two main types of events: translation-by-preferred-term (*pref.t.trans*) and translation-by-synonymous-term (*syn.trans*), where each different synonymous term used counts as a different subtype of event (simply numbered, i.e. *syn.1.trans*, *syn.2.trans*, etc.).[3] For participant P21, defining the preferred term was simple, as one term, namely *Geschirrspülmaschine*, was used more often as a translation of dish washer than the other. The event type syn1.trans covers all translations by means of the synonym *Spülmaschine*. For participant P10, assigning the preferred term status to one of the two synonyms *Spülmaschine* or *Geschirrspülmaschine* is arbitrary, as both appear equally

---

[3] Indeed, the classification of events could be simpler (e.g. type-1, type-2, …), and opting for one variant as preferred variant is an extra step that is not necessary for computing the perplexity value. This classification is, however, compatible with a theoretical construct well established in Translation Studies and, following the proposals made in (Čulo, 2014), represents, we believe, a mutually understandable concept for both fields (MT and Translation Studies).

frequently; as *Spülmaschine* appeared first in the translation, we chose this as the preferred term. By classifying term variants into these types of events, we were able to aggregate translation probabilities across texts (cf. Table 4). These translation probabilities are then used to calculate the perplexity value for a term over all human translation and post-editing sessions.

Table 4. Aggregated translation event type frequency for FPE of participants P10 and P21 for the translation of *dish washer*

event type	freq.	prob.
pref.t.trans	6	0.55
syn.1.trans	4	0.36
syn.2.trans	1	0.09

Table 5 lists the perplexity values for 10 terms in the MT, the full PE (FPE) and the HT. Our findings reveal levels of variation on the terminological level in the post-edited texts close, but not identical, to those of the machine translation outcomes. MT shows variation for fewer terms than HT, but in cases of variation, usually exhibits stronger variation. In PE, the variation patterns of MT were carried over even though the task description explicitly stated to correct inconsistent terminology.

A Kendall's Tau test comparing FPE and MT values from Table 5 confirms a strong correlation between the variation patterns, which is not true for the comparison between MT and HT. This result indicates a *shining through* (Teich, 2003) of the MT in the post-editing products on the terminological level.

Table 5. Perplexity value (MT) and aggregated perplexity value (FPE and HT) per translation of ST term

ST term (frequency in ST)	MT	FPE	HT
vaccine (3)	1	1	1.57
measles (4)	1	1	1
varicella (1) / chickenpox (3)	1.75	1.82	1
Protaphane (6)	1	1	1
anticancer medicine (3)	1	1	1.57
dishwasher (text 1: 5)	2.81	2.07	1.23
dishwasher (text 2: 5)	1.96	1.48	1
rinse aid (4)	1	1	1.33
filter (3)	1	1	1.42
upper filter assembly (3)	1.89	1	1.75

2.2.   Cognate translation

Following the results of the first experiment, we attempted to understand in which other ways the lexical profile of machine translated texts might differ from that human translations. In a pilot study, we compared corpus data (taken from the English-German Translation Corpus of TU Chemnitz[4]) with machine translated data (Google Translate[5])

---

[4] http://ell.phil.tu-chemnitz.de/search/
[5] https://translate.google.com/

for 13 English-German cognates that occurred more than five times in the corpus data. Cognates "are those translation words that have similar orthographic-phonological forms in the two languages of a bilingual [...]; non-cognates are those translations that only share their meaning in the two languages [...]" (Costa et al., 2000, p.1285). In the language pair English-German, *system* and *System* are for example cognates, while *government* and *Regierung* are non-cognates. *System* is not always the best translation for *system*, however; depending on the context, translations like *Anlage* (roughly 'installation') or *Verfahren* 'procedure' may be better options. So called *false friends* are different from cognates in that false friends are two words that share the same form, but not the same meaning across two languages, like the English word *actual* (real, existing) vs. the German *aktuell* (current, latest).

Table 6. Proportions of cognate translation, human vs. machine translation

Lemma	N	HT			MT		
		Cognate	Non-cog	Other	Cognate	Non-cog	Other
acceptance	25	32 %	52 %	16 %	68 %	32 %	0 %
affair	**7**	**29 %**	**71 %**	**0 %**	**29 %**	**71 %**	**0 %**
competence	25	32 %	56 %	12 %	56 %	44 %	0 %
complexity	15	93 %	0 %	7 %	100 %	0 %	0 %
compromise	**14**	**100 %**	**0 %**	**0 %**	**100 %**	**0 %**	**0 %**
fantasy	9	63 %	37 %	0 %	100 %	0 %	0 %
intelligence	14	64 %	36 %	0 %	100 %	0 %	0 %
orientation	*22*	*55 %*	*23 %*	*23 %*	*41 %*	*59 %*	*0 %*
program	10	90 %	0 %	10 %	100 %	0 %	0 %
reaction	7	71 %	14 %	14 %	86 %	14 %	0 %
routine	10	80 %	0 %	20 %	100 %	0 %	0 %
sequence	31	6 %	84 %	10 %	23 %	77 %	0 %
tendency	22	73 %	9 %	18 %	91 %	9 %	0 %

In a first step, we looked up the cognates in the corpus and counted how often the cognate was translated with the German equivalent cognate and how often with a non-cognate alternative. In the second step, the sentences from the corpus were machine translated and we counted the cognate/non-cognate translations for the data. The results are presented in Table 6. The category *Other* comprises realisations that could not be directly interpreted as cognate or non-cognate, e.g. when the cognate was not translated at all, or when the noun in the source text was verbalised in the target text, as in the following example where the noun *acceptance* is translated by means of the verb *akzeptierten*:[6]

Source: "[...] political stability rested on the <u>acceptance</u> in all classes of the legitimacy [...]"

---

[6] While this may seem counterintuitive at first, there are two reasons for this decision: First, noun and verb, though derived from the same root, may have slightly different meanings, e.g. in the current case the cognate *Akzeptanz* would – intuitively – rather mean ‚rate of acceptance' or ‚degree of willingness to accept' whereas *akzeptieren* can be translated as ‚accept' in terms of ‚not oppose a measure' in the given context. Second, we currently assume that a word class shift needs more cognitive effort (given, e.g. potential shifts in meaning) than simply taking over a cognate form within the same word class and thus do not classify cases involving word shifts as cognate translations.

Target: "[…] beruhte ihre Stabilität darauf, daß alle Klassen die Legitimität […]
      akzeptierten"
Lit.: […] *rested their stability on that all classes the legitimacy [...] accepted*

In nine instances, the cognate was translated more often with the German cognate by the MT system than in the human translation (see non-highlighted elements in Table 6), in two instances the cognate translation appeared equally often (see bold-faced elements in Table 6) and only once did the human translation data make more use of cognate translation than the MT system (see italicised elements in Table 6). A Pearson's Chi-squared test showed significance (χ^2= 10.91, p < .001) for the difference between machine translation and the corpus data considering the selection of cognate and non-cognate translation options. Conclusively, MT output and human translations show different patterns for translating cognates. The category *Other* was not needed for the MT output, highlighting that for the MT system used for translation in this case, word class shifts seem to be rarer at least in cases in which a cognate is available in the same word class in the target language.

3. Discussion

In this study, we focused on two aspects of the lexical profile of texts and how these may change when MT is added to the process of translation. We saw in one of the two studies that MT can have an influence on the outcome of PE; even in cases where participants were asked to make certain corrections, these were not made. We do not have an explanation for this, but we can offer one hypothesis: As Mesa-Lao (2014) observes in his pilot study on the differences between the human translation and the post-editing process, there seemed to be no clear initial orientation or final revision phases in most of the post-editing sessions in his study. This pattern might be disadvantageous for a sub-task like ensuring terminological consistency. Further investigation of the typing/correction patterns may reveal more on the role of these phases for terminological consistency.

The study presented here is very limited with respect of the instances investigated. A larger scale study could reveal more on the influence of MT on the lexical (and grammatical) profile of translations (here: from English to German). It should be added that the study on terminological variation presented here was guided by target language norms which hold for German certainly, but not necessarily for other languages or language pairs.

Also, it still needs to be proved whether the cognate profile of post-edited texts will be similar to that of MT. A logical follow-up question to such a finding would, however, be whether in fields, where post-edited texts make up a significant proportion of the texts produced, original language production is influenced by the linguistic profiles of the post-edited texts (e.g., if confirmed for post-edited texts, whether cognates are also used more often in more recent original language production). While the observations made may point into this research direction, the limited scope of the study cannot serve to give any indication about the answer to this question.

Last but not least, it needs to be pointed out that the changes in the lexical profile observed in MT and PE were results of the characteristics of the MT systems used on a specific text type and language pair. Of course, these characteristics may change depending on a variety of factors; from the viewpoint of translation studies, uncovering and understanding these factors is vital, both as potential feedback to MT researchers and in terms of understanding the role of MT in and its influence on translation.

4. Conclusions and future work

In further studies, the influence of the machine cognate translation on the post-editing process will be studied. We will focus on the following two questions: Do translators accept the cognate translation of the machine translation system or will they choose another solution in the post-editing process? Will the variation of cognate translation rather direct to the variation in machine translation or the variation of translation from scratch? And ultimately: Are patterns observed in post-edited texts also reproduced in original language? If the latter was the case, then MT might be seen as a driving force of language change in certain areas. We believe that understanding in which way the characteristics of a single text, and through many texts of an LSP as a whole, may change through the use of MT can – depending on which changes (e.g. higher term consistency) may be desirable or undesirable – provide important feedback for MT research and engineering.

References

Arntz, Klaus-Dirk Reiner; Picht, Heribert; Schmitz. (2014). *Einführung in die Terminologiearbeit.*

Blum-Kulka, Shoshana. (1986). Shifts of Cohesion and Coherence in Translation. In Juliane House and Shoshana Blum-Kulka (eds), *Interlingual and Intercultural Communication*, 17–35. Tübingen: Gunter Narr Verlag.

Carl, Michael, Barbara Dragsted, Jakob Elming, Daniel Hardt, and Arnt Lykke Jakobsen. (2011). The Process of Post-Editing: A Pilot Study. In Bernadette Sharp, Michael Zock, Michael Carl, and Arnt Lykke Jakobsen (eds), *Proceedings of the 8th International NLPSC Workshop. Special Theme: Human-Machine Interaction in Translation*, 131–42. Copenhagen Studies in Language 41. Frederiksberg: Samfundslitteratur.

Carl, M, and M Schaeffer. (forthcoming). Literal Translation and Processes of Post-Editing. In *Translation in Transition: Between Cognition, Computing and Technology*. Amsterdam: John Benjamins.

Costa, Albert, Alfonso Caramazza, and Nuria Sebastian-Galles. (2000). The Cognate Facilitation Effect: Implications for Models of Lexical Access. *Journal of Experimental Psychology: Learning, Memory, and Cognition* 26 (5): 1283–96.

Čulo, Oliver. (2014). Approaching Machine Translation from Translation Studies: A Perspective on Commonalities, Potentials, Differences. In *Proceedings of the Seventeenth Annual Conference of the European Association for Machine Translation (EAMT)*, 199–208. Dubrovnik, Croatia.

Elming, Jakob, Laura Winther Balling, and Michael Carl. (2014). Investigating User Behaviour in Post-Editing and Translation Using the CASMACAT Workbench. In Sharon O'Brien, Laura Winther Balling, Michael Carl, Michel Simard, and Lucia Specia (eds), *Post-Editing of Machine Translation*, 147-169. Cambridge Scholars Publishing.

Groves, Declan, and Dags Schmidtke. (2009). Identification and Analysis of Post-Editing Patterns for MT. In *MT Summit XII: Proceedings of the Twelfth Machine Translation Summit*, 429–36. Ottawa, Canada.

Lapshinova-Koltunski, Ekaterina. (2013). VARTRA: A Comparable Corpus for the Analysis of Translation Variation. In *Proceedings of the 6th Workshop on Building and Using Comparable Corpora*, 77–86. Sofia, Bulgaria.

————. (2015). Variation in Translation: Evidence from Corpora. In Claudio Fantinuoli and Federico Zanettin (eds), *New Directions in Corpus-Based Translation Studies*, 93–113. Translation and Multilingual Natural Language Processing 1. Berlin: Language Science Press.

Mesa-Lao, Bartolomé. (2014). Gaze Behaviour on Source Texts: An Exploratory Study Comparing Translation and Post-Editing. In Sharon O'Brien, Laura Winther Balling, Michael Carl, Michel Simard, and Lucia Specia (eds), *Post-Editing of Machine Translation*, 219-245. Cambridge Scholars Publishing.

O'Brien, Sharon. (2011). Towards Predicting Post-Editing Productivity. *Machine Translation* 25 (3): 197–215.

Silva, Roberto. (2014). Integrating Post-Editing MT in a Professional Translation Workflow. In: Sharon O'Brien, Laura Winther Balling, Michael Carl, Michel Simard, and Lucia Specia (eds), *Post-Editing of Machine Translation*, 24–51.

Teich, Elke. (2003). Cross-Linguistic Variation in System and Text. A Methodology for the Investigation of Translations and Comparable Texts. Vol. 5. *Text, Translation, Computational Processing*. Berlin/New York: Mouton de Gruyter.

Received May 2, 2016, accepted May 4, 2016

Graphonological Levenshtein Edit Distance:
Application for Automated Cognate Identification

Bogdan BABYCH

Centre for Translation Studies, University of Leeds, Leeds, LS2 9JT, UK

b.babych@leeds.ac.uk

Abstract: This paper presents a methodology for calculating a modified Levenshtein edit distance between character strings, and applies it to the task of automated cognate identification from non-parallel (comparable) corpora. This task is an important stage in developing MT systems and bilingual dictionaries beyond the coverage of traditionally used aligned parallel corpora, which can be used for finding translation equivalents for the 'long tail' in Zipfian distribution: low-frequency and usually unambiguous lexical items in closely-related languages (many of those often under-resourced). Graphonological Levenshtein edit distance relies on editing hierarchical representations of phonological features for graphemes (graphonological representations) and improves on phonological edit distance proposed for measuring dialectological variation. Graphonological edit distance works directly with character strings and does not require an intermediate stage of phonological transcription, exploiting the advantages of historical and morphological principles of orthography, which are obscured if only phonetic principle is applied. Difficulties associated with plain feature representations (unstructured feature sets or vectors) are addressed by using linguistically-motivated feature hierarchy that restricts matching of lower-level graphonological features when higher-level features are not matched. The paper presents an evaluation of the graphonological edit distance in comparison with the traditional Levenshtein edit distance from the perspective of its usefulness for the task of automated cognate identification. It discusses the advantages of the proposed method, which can be used for morphology induction, for robust transliteration across different alphabets (Latin, Cyrillic, Arabic, etc.) and robust identification of words with non-standard or distorted spelling, e.g., in user-generated content on the web such as posts on social media, blogs and comments. Software for calculating the modified feature-based Levenshtein distance, and the corresponding graphonological feature representations (vectors and the hierarchies of graphemes' features) are released on the author's webpage: http://corpus.leeds.ac.uk/bogdan/phonologylevenshtein/. Features are currently available for Latin and Cyrillic alphabets and will be extended to other alphabets and languages.

Keywords: cognates; Levenshtein edit distance; phonological features; comparable corpora; closely-related languages; under-resourced languages; Ukrainian; Russian; Hybrid MT

1. Introduction

Levenshtein edit distance proposed in (Levenshtein, 1966) is an algorithm that calculates the cost (normally – the number of operations such as deletions, insertions and substitutions) needed to transfer a string of symbols (characters or words) into another string. This algorithm is used in many computational linguistic applications that require some form of the fuzzy string matching, examples include fast creation of morphological and syntactic taggers exploiting similarities between closely related languages (Hana et al., 2006), statistical learning of preferred edits for detecting regular orthographic correspondences in closely related languages (Ciobanu and Dinu, 2014). Applications of Levenshtein's metric for the translation technologies and specifically for Machine Translation include automated identification of cognates for the tasks of creating bilingual resources such as electronic dictionaries (e.g., Koehn and Knight, 2002; Mulloni and Pekar, 2006; Bergsma and Kondrak, G. 2007), improving document alignment by using cognate translation equivalents as a seed lexicon (Enright, J and Kondrak, G., 2007), automated MT evaluation (e.g., Niessen et al., 2000; Leusch et al., 2003).

Levenshtein distance metrics has been modified and extended for applications in different areas; certain ideas have yet not been tested in MT context, but have a clear potential for benefiting MT-related tasks. This paper develops and evaluates one of such ideas for a linguistic extension of the metric proposed in the area of computational modelling of dialectological variation and measuring 'cognate' lexical distance between languages, dialects and different historical periods in development of languages, e.g., using cognates from the slow-changing part of the lexicon – the Swadesh list (Swadesh, 1952; Serva and Petroni, 2008; Schepens et al., 2012).

In this paper the suggestion is explored of calculating the so called Levenshtein's 'phonological edit distance' between phonemic transcriptions of cognates, rather than the traditional string edit distance (Nerbonne and Heeringa 1997; Sanders and Chin, 2009). This idea is based on the earlier linguistic paradigm of describing phonemes as systems of their phonological features, formulated in its modern form by Roman Jacobson – see (Anderson, 1985) for the development of the theory; later it was introduced into generative and computational linguistic paradigms by Chomsky and Halle (1968). The idea is that each phoneme in a transcription of a cognate is represented as a structure of phonological distinctive features, such as:

[a] = [+vowel, +back; +open; –labialised]

1.1. Distinctive phonological features: the background

In phonology, sounds of a language form a system of phonemes (i.e., minimal segments of speech that can be used in the same context and distinguish meanings in minimal word pairs, which differ only by one such segment (i.e., a phoneme). For example, English phonemes /p/ and /b/ distinguish meaning in *pull vs. bull; pill vs. bill*; phonemes /v/ and /w/ distinguish meanings of *vary vs. wary*. However, Ukrainian sounds /v/ and /w/ are positional variants, or allophones, of the same phoneme, since they are never used in the same position or distinguish meanings: /w/ is restricted to a word-final position after a vowel: *вийшов* /vyjšow/ *'entered'*). There is evidence that phonemes are not simply linguistic constructs, but have a psychological reality, e.g., for native speakers they form cognitive pronunciation targets; non-native speakers often confuse phonemes that are not separated in their first language (e.g., native Ukrainian speakers would confuse /v/ and /w/ when speaking English). In languages where writing systems and pronunciation are close to each other, e.g., Ukrainian or Georgian, the written characters usually correspond to phonemes (much less often – to allophones).

Phonemes and allophones are characterised by a further internal structure, which consists of a system of distinctive phonological features (Jakobson et al., 1958). These features are typically based on differences in their acoustic properties and the way of how they are pronounced (their articulation). For example, /v/ and /w/ are both *consonants,* i.e., they are formed with a participation of noise (unlike vowels */u, o, a/,* etc., which are formed with an unobstructed sound); both are *fricative* consonants, i.e., they are formed with a constant air friction against an obstacle in the vocal tract (unlike plosive consonants, such as */b, p, d, t, g, k/* that include a build up of air behind some obstacle during an initial silence, followed by its instant release); the difference between */v/* and */w/* is that */v/* is *labio-dental,* i.e., the air friction is created with the teeth and the lower lip, while */w/* is bilabial, i.e., the source of friction is the upper and lower lip, while the teeth are not involved.

However, not all acoustic or articulatory differences become distinctive phonological features. The necessary condition is that these features should capture *phonological* distinctions, i.e., those needed for differentiation between phonemes: e.g., *long* vs. *short* pairs of vowels in Dutch differ primarily by their length; however, they have further qualitative differences as well, which are visible on their spectrograms, but are not perceived by speakers as features that make phonemic distinctions; therefore, these qualitative differences are not part of their distinctive phonological features. Similarly, the same Ukrainian vowels in stressed and unstressed positions are very different qualitatively, but these differences are not perceived as phonological, i.e., the ones that distinguish different phonemes, so both stressed and unstressed variants have the same set of distinctive features.

Some distinctive phonological features are in *correlated oppositions*, i.e., they distinguish sets of phonemes that only differ by a single feature, e.g., *+voiced* vs *–voiced* (i.e., formed with or without the vocal cords) distinguishes */d/~/t/; /z/~/s/; /b/~/p/; /v/~/f/, /g/~/k/.* These correlated features often switch their value in positional or historical alternations, and as a result, may distinguish cognates in closely related languages.

Nowadays there are standard description of phonemes and phonological features for most languages of the world, illustrated with sound charts, e.g., by the International Phonetic Association (IPA) (Ladefoged and Halle, 1988). These charts group sounds along several dimensions of their distinctive phonological features, such as *place, manner* of articulation, *voiced/voiceless* for consonants; *high/low, back/front, roundness* for vowels, with finer-grained sub-divisions. Sound charts for individual languages can be found in standard language references. For the experiments described in this paper the systems of phonological distinctive features for Ukrainian and Russian has been adapted from (Comrie and Corbett, Eds., 1993: 949, 951, 829).

1.2. Application of phonological features for calculating the edit distance

For using phonological distinctive features in calculation of the Levenshtein edit distance, the idea is to replace the operation of substitution of a whole character by the substitution of its constituent phonological feature representations, which would be sufficient to convert it into another character: so rewriting [o] into [a] (which, e.g., is a typical vowel alternation pattern in Russian and distinguishes some of its major dialects) would incur a smaller cost compared to the substitution of the whole character, since only two of its distinctive phonological features need to be rewritten:

[o] = [+vowel, +back; +*mid;* +*labialised*]

On the other hand, the cost of rewriting the vowel [a] into the consonant [t] (the change which normally does not happen as part of the historical language development or dialectological variation) would involve rewriting all the phonological features in the representation, so the edit cost will be the same as for the substitution of the entire character:

[t] = [*+consonant; –voiced; +plosive; +fronttongue; +alveolar*]

According to Nerbonne and Heeringa (1997:2) the feature-based Levenshtein distance makes it "…possible to take into account the affinity between sounds that are not equal, but are still related"; and to "…show that *'pater'* and *'vader'* are more kindred then *'pater'* and *'maler'*." This is modelled by the fact that phonological feature representations for pairs such as [t] and [d] (both front-tongue alveolar plosive consonants, which only differ by 'voiced' feature), as well as [p] and [v] (both labial consonants), share greater number of phonological features compared to the pairs [p] and [m] (which differ in sonority, manner and passive organ of articulation) or [t] and [l] (which differ in sonority and the manner of articulation). However, the authors point out to a number of open questions and problems related to their modified metric, e.g., how to represent phonetic features of complex phonemes, such as diphthongs; what should be the structure of feature representations: Nerbonne and Heeringa use feature vectors, but are these vectors sufficient or more complex feature representations are needed; how to integrate edits of individual features into the calculation of a coherent distance measure (certain settings are not used, whether to use Euclidian or Manhattan distance, etc.).

Linguistic ideas behind the suggestion to use Levenshtein phonological edit distance are intuitively appealing and potentially useful for applications beyond dialectological modelling. However, to understand their value for other areas, such as MT, there is a need to develop a clear evaluation framework for testing the impact of different possible settings of the modified metric and different types of feature representations, to compare specific settings of the metric to alternatives and the classical Levenshtein's baseline. Without a systematic evaluation framework the usefulness of metrics remain unknown.

This paper proposes an evaluation framework for testing alternative settings of the modified Levenshtein's metric. This framework is task-based: it evaluates the metric's alternative settings and feature representations in relation to its success on the task of automated identification of cognates from non-parallel (comparable) corpora. The scripts for calculating the modified feature-based Levenshtein distance, and the corresponding graphonological feature representations (vectors and the hierarchies of features) are released on the author's webpage[1]. Features are currently available for Latin and Cyrillic alphabets, new alphabets will be added in future.

Graphonological Levenshtein distance can also be applied, calibrated and evaluated for other tasks, beyond the task of cognate identification, e.g., to robust transliteration, reconstruction of diacritics or recognition of words with distorted, non-standard or variable spelling, e.g.: the names *Osama/ Usama/ Ousamma /Осама/ Усама/ Усамма* are closer to each other in terms of their underlying phonological feature sequences than their plain character-based distances. Evaluation on these tasks may lead to alternative preferred settings and feature representations for the graphonological Levenshtein metric, compared to evaluation on the cognate identification task described here.

The paper is organised as follows: Section 2 presents the set-up of the experiment, the application of automated cognate identification; the design and feature representations for the metric and the evaluation framework. Section 3 presents evaluation results of different metric settings and comparison with the classical Levenshtein distance; Section 4 presents conclusion and future work.

---

[1] http://corpus.leeds.ac.uk/bogdan/phonologylevenshtein/

2. Set up of the experiment

2.1. Application of automated cognate identification for MT

Automated cognate identification is important for a range of MT-related tasks, as mentioned in Section 1. Our project deals with rapid creation of hybrid MT systems for new translation directions into and from a range of under-resourced languages, many of which are closely related, or 'cognate', such as Spanish and Portuguese, German and Dutch, Ukrainian and Russian. The systems combine rich linguistic representations used by a backbone rule-based MT engine with statistically derived linguistic resources and statistical disambiguation and evaluation techniques, which work with complex linguistic data structures for morphological, syntactic and semantic annotation (Eberle et al., 2012). While there is a potential in using a better-resourced pivot language for creating linguistic resources for MT and building pivot systems (e.g., Babych et al., 2007), in our project the translation lexicon for the hybrid MT systems is derived mainly via two routes:

1. Translation equivalents for a smaller number of highly frequent words, which under empirical observations of Zipf's and Menzerath's laws (Koehler, R. 1993; 49) tend to be shorter (Zipf, 1935:38; Sigurd et al., 2004:37) and more ambiguous (Menzerath, 1954, Hubey, 1999; Babych et al., 2004: 7), are generated as statistical dictionaries from sentence-aligned parallel corpora. However, as only small number of parallel resources is available for under-resourced languages, there remain many out-of-vocabulary lexical items.

2. The remaining 'long tail' in Zipfian distribution containing translation equivalents for a large number of low-frequent and usually unambiguous lexical items (as they typically have only one correct translation equivalent) is derived semi-automatically from much larger non-parallel comparable corpora, which are usually in the same domain for both languages. We use a number of different techniques depending on available resources and language pairs (Eberle et al., 2012: 104-106). For closely related languages (depending on the degree of their 'relatedness') the 'long tail' contains a large number of cognates. In the experiments described here, for Ukrainian / Russian language pair this number reached 60% of the analysed sample of the lexicon selected from different frequency bands (see Section 3).

In order to cover this part of the lexicon, the automated cognate identification from non-parallel corpora is used for generating draft ranked lists of candidate translation equivalents. The candidate lists are generated using the following procedure:

1. Large monolingual corpora (in my experiments – about 250M for Ukrainian and 200M for Russian news corpora) are PoS tagged and lemmatised.

2. Frequency dictionaries are created for lemmas. A frequency threshold is applied (to keep down the 'noise' and the number of hapax legomena.

3. Edit distances for pairs of lemmas in a Cartesian product of the two dictionaries are automatically calculated using variants of the Levenshtein measure.

4. Pairs with edit distances below a certain threshold are retained as candidate cognates (in the experiments I used the threshold value of the Levenshtein edit distance normalised by the length of the longest word <=0.36, intuitively: 36% of edits per character)

5.   Candidate cognates are further filtered by part-of-speech codes (cognates with non-matching parts of speech are not ranked).

6.   Candidate cognates are filtered by their frequency bands: if the TL candidate is beyond the frequency band threshold of the SL candidate, the TL candidate is not ranked (in the experiment I used the threshold *FrqRange* > 0.5 for the difference in natural logarithms of absolute frequencies – see formula (1), intuitively: candidates should not have frequency difference several orders of magnitude apart.

7.   Candidate cognate lists are ranked by the increasing values of the edit distance.

$$FrqRange = \frac{\min(\ln(FrqB),\ln(FrqA))}{\max(\ln(FrqB),\ln(FrqA))} \qquad (1)$$

These ranked lists are presented to the developers, candidate cognates are checked and either included into system dictionaries, or rejected. Developers' productivity of this task crucially depends on the quality of automated edit distance metric that generates and ranks the draft candidate lists.

The task of creating parallel resources and dictionaries from comparable corpora is not exclusive to hybrid or rule-based MT. Similar ideas are used in SMT framework for enhancing SMT systems developed for under-resourced languages via identification of aligned sentences and translation equivalents in comparable corpora, which generally reduces the number of out-of-vocabulary words not covered by scarce parallel corpora (Pinnis et al., 2012). In these settings, dictionaries of cognate lists can become an additional useful resource, so achieving a higher degree of automation for the process of cognate identification in comparable corpora is equally important for the SMT development. Under these settings an operational task-based evaluation for Levenshtein edit distance metrics will be the performance parameters of the developed SMT systems.

2.2. Development of Levenshtein graphonological feature-based metric

For the task of automated cognate identification a feature-based edit distance will need further adjustments, which go beyond the metric used in modelling dialectological variation. The metric is designed to work directly with orthography rather than with phonetic transcriptions; alternative ways of representing phonological features (feature vectors vs. feature hierarchies) are evaluated, and a method of calculation of rewriting cost for feature-based representations is selected.

2.2.1. Phonological distance: phonetic transcription vs. raw orthographic strings

The metric works directly with word character strings, not via the intermediate stage of creating a phonological transcription for each word. While for modelling of dialects (many of which do not capture pronunciation differences in their own writing systems) the transcription may be a necessary step, MT systems normally deal with languages with their own established writing systems. There are practical reasons for extracting features from orthography rather than phonological transcriptions: automated phonological transcription of the orthographic strings may create an additional source of errors; resources for transcribing may be not readily available for many languages; for the majority of languages very little can be gained by replacing the orthography by transcription (apart from more adequate representation of digraphs and phonologically ambiguous characters, which can be addressed also on the level of orthography).

However, there are more important theoretical reasons for preferring original orthographic representations. For instance, orthography of languages is usually based on a combination of three principles: *phonetic* (how words are pronounced), *morphological* (keeping the same spellings for morphemes – minimal meaning units, such as affixes, stems, word routes, irrespective of any pronunciation variation caused by their position, phonological context, regular sound alternations, etc.) and *historic* (respecting traditional spelling which reflects an earlier stage of language development, even though the current pronunciation may have changed; often orthography reflects the stage when cognate languages have been closer together). Example 2 illustrates the point why orthography might work better for cognate identification:

	Russian	*Ukrainian*	
Orthography	sobaka (собака) 'dog'	sobaka (собака) 'dog'	(2)
Phonological transcription	[sabaka] (с[а]бака)	[sobaka] (с[о]бака)	
Change	[o] -> [a]	[o] -> (no change)	

The pronunciation change [o] -> [a], which in some (at that time) marginal Russian dialects dates back to the 7th-8th century AD (Pivtorak, 1988: 94) (one of the explanations for this change is the influence the Baltic substratum), was not reflected in Russian educated written tradition, even at the later time when those dialects received much more political prominence and influenced the pronunciation norm of the modern standard Russian. In many cases such historic orthography principle makes the edit distance between cognates in different languages much shorter, and the phonological transcription in these cases may obscure innate morphological and historical links between closely related languages reflected in spelling. Therefore, using orthography to directly generate phonological feature representations has a theoretical motivation.

One specific issue in using the orthography-based phonological metric is dealing with digraphs – the two letter combinations denoting one sound (c.f., similarly, diphthongs need special treatment in the transcription-based metric), especially in cases when the two languages use different writing systems. This problem, however, is much smaller if the alphabets are similar or the same. On the other hand, treating historic digraphs as two separate letters with two feature sets may be beneficial in some cases, e.g., *Thomas* vs. *Хома (Homa)*, where the first letter of the Ukrainian word (*h*) is historically a closer match to one of the letters of the English digraph *th*.

In this paper the term *graphonological features* is used to refer to representations of phonological features that are directly derived from graphemes. The approach adopted in my experiment is that each orthographic character in each language is unambiguously associated with a set of phonological features, even though its pronunciation may be different in different positions.

2.2.2. Graphonological representations: feature vectors vs. feature hierarchies

Features in graphonological representations of characters can be organized in different ways. In my initial experiments the problems with structuring them as flat feature vectors became apparent. Even though in some examples there has been improvement in the rate of cognate identification caused by richer feature structures, as compared to the baseline Levenshtein metric, in many more cases (and often counter to the earlier intuition) these feature structures caused unnecessary noise and lower ranking for true cognates, while non-cognates received smaller feature-based edit distance score. This unwanted overgeneration issue has been traced back to the use of feature vectors as graphonological feature structures.

The example (3) illustrates the reason for such overgeneration. If the feature vector representations are used, the proposed graphonological metric (GrPhFeatLev) calculates that the following edit distances should be the same, which is a counter-intuitive result (especially given that the traditional Levenshtein's metric (Lev) clearly shows that the character-based edit distance is shorter):

robitnyk (робітник) 'worker' (uk) & *rabotnik* (работник) 'worker' (ru)
    GrPhFeatLev =1.2   Lev=2.0

---

robitnyk (робітник) 'worker'(uk) & *rovesnik* (ровесник) 'age-mate, of   (3)
the same age' (ru)
    GrPhFeatLev =1.2   Lev=3.0

There is a specific problem when intuitively unrelated consonants (at least among Ukrainian-Russian lexical cognates) [b] and [v], or [t] and [s] – still receive very small rewriting scores. Figure 1 and Tables 1 and 2 show overlapping graphonological features for these words. In both cases, while one of the more essential features was not matched – *manner of articulation*, but instead the smaller edit distance resulted from matching less important features: [*active* and *passive* articulation organs] and [*voice*]. The problem with using feature vector representation is that all of the features stay on the same level, there is no way of indicating that certain features are more important for cognate formation and perception.

	r(р)	o(о)	b(б)	i(і)	t(т)	n(н)	y(и)	k(к)
	0·0	1·0	2·0	3·0	4·0	5·0	6·0	7·0	8·0
r(р)	1·0	0·0	1·0	2·0	3·0	4·0	5·0	6·0	7·0
o(о)	2·0	1·0	0·0	1·0	2·0	3·0	4·0	5·0	6·0
v(в)	3·0	2·0	1·0	0·4	1·4	2·4	3·4	4·4	5·4
e(e)	4·0	3·0	2·0	1·4	0·8	1·8	2·8	3·8	4·8
s(с)	5·0	4·0	3·0	2·4	1·8	1·0	2·0	3·0	4·0
n(н)	6·0	5·0	4·0	3·4	2·8	2·0	1·0	2·0	3·0
i(и)	7·0	6·0	5·0	4·4	3·4	3·0	2·0	1·2	2·2
k(к)	8·0	7·0	6·0	5·4	4·4	3·8	3·0	2·2	1·2

Figure 1. GPhFeatLev Levenshtein: Edit distance matrix with *feature vectors* for *robitnyk* (робітник) 'worker'(uk) & *rovesnik* (ровесник) 'age-mate, of the same age' (ru)

b (б)	['type:consonant', 'voice:voiced', 'maner:plosive', 'active:labial', 'passive:bilabial']
t (т)	['type:consonant', 'voice:unvoiced', 'maner:plosive', 'active:fronttongue', 'passive:alveolar']

Table 1: Phonological feature vectors in Ukrainian word 'robitnyk' (робітник) – 'worker' overlapping features in intuitively unrelated characters are highlighted

v (в)	['type:consonant', 'voice:voiced', 'maner:fricative', 'active:labial', 'passive:labiodental']
s (c)	['type:consonant', 'voice:unvoiced', 'maner:fricative', 'active:fronttongue', 'passive:alveolar']

Table 2: Phonological feature vectors in Russian word 'rovesnik (ровесник) – 'age-mate', 'of the same age'

To address this problem, instead of feature vectors *hierarchical representations of features* are used, where a set of central features at the top of the hierarchy needs to be matched first, to allow lower level features to be matched as well (Figure 2).

Figure 2 shows that for the feature hierarchy of the grapheme [b] to match the hierarchy of the grapheme [v] there is a need to match first the grapheme type: consonant (which is successfully matched), and then – a combination of *manner* of articulation and *active* articulation organ (which is not matched, since [b] is plosive and [v] is fricative), and only after that – low level features such as voice may be tried (not matched again, because the higher level feature structure of *manner + active* did not match). Note that the proposed hierarchy applies to Ukrainian–Russian language pair, and generalizing it to other translation directions may not work, as relations may need rearrangements of the hierarchy to reflect specific graphonological relations between other languages.

Consonant feature hierarchy	**Example (pl- prefix on lower level features enforces feature hierarchy)**

Type
    {Manner+Active}
        Voice
        Passive
	[b]:
	['type:consonant',
	    {'maner:**pl**-plosive', 'active:**pl**-labial',}
	    'voice:**pl**-voiced',
	    'passive:**pl**-bilabial'

Figure 2. Hierarchical feature representations for consonants: non-matching higher levels prevent from matching at the lower levels: [**pl**-voiced] will not match before [plosive, labial] match

2.2.3. Calculating combined substitution cost for variable length feature sets

As the number of features for different graphemes may vary, the edit distance is computed between partially matched feature sets as an F-measure between Precision and Recall of their potentially overlapping feature sets, and subtracting it from 1. As a result the measure is symmetric, (4):

$$Prec = len(FeatOverlap) \, / \, len(NofFeatA)$$

$$Rec = len(FeatOverlap) \, / \, len(NofFeatB)$$

$$OneMinusFMeasure = 1 - (2 * Prec * Rec) / (Prec + Rec)$$

$$matrix[zz + 1][sz + 1] \\ = min(matrix[zz + 1][sz] + 1, matrix[zz][sz \\ + 1] + 1, matrix[zz][sz] \\ + OneMinusFMeasure) \tag{4}$$

In these settings lower cost is given to substitutions; while insertion and deletions incur a relatively higher cost. As a result, cognates that have different length are much harder to find using the graphonological Levenshtein edit distance, and in these cases the baseline character-based Levenshtein metric performs better. A general observation is that the feature-based metric can often find cognates inaccessible to character-based metrics when the main differences are in *substitution*, but it misses cognates that involve more *insertions*, *deletions* and changing *order* of graphemes, as shown in Table 3.

uk	ru	GPhFeatLev	Baseline Lev
рішення rishennia 'decision'	решение resheniye 'decision'	**Found**	Missed
сьогодні s'ogodni 'today'	сегодня segodnia 'today'	**Found**	Missed
колгосп kolgosp 'collective farm'	колхоз kolhoz 'collective farm'	**Found**	Missed
коментар komentar 'commentary'	комментарий kommentariy 'commentary'	Missed	**Found**
перерва pererva 'break'	перерыв pereryv 'break'	Missed	**Found**

Table 3. Examples of missed and found cognates for each metric

2.3. Evaluation sample

Evaluation is performed for the baseline Levenshtein metric and the proposed feature-based metric with two settings: one using flat feature vectors for graphonological representations, and the other – using hierarchically organised features. Evaluation was done on a sample of 300 Ukrainian words selected from 6 frequency bands in the frequency dictionary of lemmas (ranks 1-50, 3001-3050, 6001-6050, 9001-9050, 12001-12050, 15001-15050), Russian cognates were searched in the full-length frequency dictionary of 16,000 entries automatically derived from the Russian corpus (as described in Section 2.1). For 274 out of the 300 Ukrainian words either the baseline Levenshtein metric, or the experimental feature metric returned Russian candidate cognates (with the threshold of

$$\frac{LevDist}{max(len(W1), len(W2))} \leq 0.36$$

applied across all the metrics, as mentioned in Section 2.1. Different settings for modifications of Levenshtein edit distance can be systematically evaluated in this scenario by using human annotation of the candidate cognate lists.

3. Evaluation results

The 274 lists of cognate candidates provided by each metric were then labelled according to the following annotation scheme: Table 4:

Label	Interpretation
NC	No cognate: a word in source language (SL) does not have a cognate in the target language (TL)
0D	Zero difference: absolute cognates there is no difference in orthographic strings in the SL and TL
FF	'False friends' cognates with different meaning in the SL and TL
CL	Cognate **wins** in the *baseline* (string-based Levenshtein) – having a higher rank
CF	Cognate **wins** in the *tested* approach (feature-based Levenshtein)
WL	Cognate **looses** in the *baseline* (string-based Levenshtein)
WF	Cognate **looses** in the *tested* approach (feature-based Levenshtein)
ML	Cognate is **missed** by the *baseline* (string-based Levenshtein)
MF	Cognate is **missed** by the *tested* approach: (feature-based Levenshtein)

Table 4. Labels used for candidate cognate annotation

Counts of annotation labels for each of the categories are shown in Table 5 and Table 6.

	per cent	count
Have no cognates (*NC*)	34.31%	94
False Friends (*FF*)	1.82%	5
0 Difference cognates (*0D*)	16.42%	45
Cognates with +/– differences (existence, rank)	41.6%	114
All cognate candidates in sample	**100%**	**274**

Table 5. Parameters of evaluation sample

	Lev (baseline character-based)		*GPFeat Vectors (feature-based flat vectors)*		*GPFeat Hierarchy (feature-based hierarchical)*		*Difference: GPFeatHierarchy - Lev*
	per cent	**#**	*per cent*	**#**	**per cent**	**#**	**per cent**
correct, higher is better: *CL* **vs** *CF* **(+exclude 0 differences,** *0D***)**	47.08% (36.68%)	129 (84)	*46.72%*	*128*	**51.09%** (41.48%)	140 (95)	**+4.01%** (+4.80%)
present, but lost on rank (*WL* vs *WF*; lower better)	**2.19%**	6	*10.58%*	*29*	2.55%	7	-0.36%
cognates missing (*ML* vs *MF*; lower is better)	13.87%	38	*10.58%*	*29*	**9.85%**	27	**+4.02%**

Table 6. Comparative performance of distance measures for the task of ranking cognates

It can be seen from the tables that while the baseline Levenshtein metric (Table 6, column *Lev*) outperforms the feature-based metric that uses feature vector graphonological representations (column *GPFeat Vectors*), but the feature-based metric outperforms the baseline when hierarchical graphonological feature representations are used (column *GPFeat Hierarchy*). The improvement is about 4% (or nearly 5%, if trivial examples of absolute cognates are discounted). There is no improvement in ranking of found equivalents, which may be due to the noise related to a relatively higher cost of insertions, deletions and reordering of characters.

4. Conclusion and future work

Even though the traditional character-based Levenshtein metric gives a very strong baseline for the task of automated cognate identification from non-parallel corpora, the proposed graphonological Levenshtein edit distance measure outperforms it. Hierarchically structured feature representations, proposed in this paper, capture linguistically plausible correspondences between cognates much more accurately compared to traditionally used feature vectors. These representations are essential components of the proposed graphonological metric. Feature-based metric often identifies cognates which are missed by the baseline Levenshtein character-based metric.

Different settings of the metrics were compared under the proposed task-based evaluation framework, which requires a relatively small amount of human annotation and can calibrate further developments of the metric and refinements of the feature representation structures. This framework tests the metric directly for its usefulness for the task of creating cognate dictionaries for closely related languages.

For practical tasks both the traditional and feature-based Levenshtein metrics can be used in combination, supporting each other strengths, especially if boosting recall in the cognate identification task is needed.

Future work will include extending evaluation to other languages and larger evaluation sets, measuring improvements in MT systems enhanced with automatically extracted cognates, learning optimal feature representations and optimising feature weights for specific translation directions from data, extending character-based frameworks, such as (Beinborn et al., 2013). However, the graphonological Levenshtein distance metric may find applications beyond the task of cognate identification, e.g., for robust transliteration, identification of spelling variations or distortions, for integrating feature-based representations into algorithms for learning phonological and morphosyntactic correspondences between closely related languages and into algorithms for automatically deriving morphological variation models for automated grammar induction tasks, with a goal of building large-scale morphosyntactic resources for MT.

Acknowledgements

I thank the reviewers of this paper for their insightful, detailed and useful comments.

Bibliography

Anderson, S. R. (1985). Phonology in the twentieth century: Theories of rules and theories of representations. University of Chicago Press.

Babych, B., Elliott, D., Hartley, A. (2004, August). Extending MT evaluation tools with translation complexity metrics. In Proceedings of the 20th international conference on Computational Linguistics (p. 106). Association for Computational Linguistics.

Babych, B., Hartley, A., Sharoff, S. (2007). Translating from under-resourced languages: comparing direct transfer against pivot translation. Proceedings of MT Summit XI, Copenhagen, Denmark.

Beinborn, L., Zesch, T., Gurevych, I. (2013). Cognate Production using Character-based Machine Translation. In IJCNLP (pp. 883-891).

Bergsma, S., Kondrak, G. (2007, September). Multilingual cognate identification using integer linear programming. In RANLP Workshop on Acquisition and Management of Multilingual Lexicons.

Chomsky, N., Halle, M. (1968). The sound pattern of English. Harper & Row Publishers: New York, London.

Ciobanu, A. M., Dinu, L. P. (2014). Automatic Detection of Cognates Using Orthographic Alignment. In ACL (2) (pp. 99-105).

Comrie, B. , Corbett, G., Eds. (1993). The Slavonic Languages. Routledge: London, New York.

Eberle, K., Geiß, J., Ginestí-Rosell, M., Babych, B., Hartley, A., Rapp, R., Sharoff, S & Thomas, M. (2012, April). Design of a hybrid high quality machine translation system. In Proceedings of the Joint Workshop on Exploiting Synergies between Information Retrieval and Machine Translation (ESIRMT) and Hybrid Approaches to Machine Translation (HyTra) (pp. 101-112). Association for Computational Linguistics.

Enright, J., Kondrak, G. (2007) A fast method for parallel document identification. Proceedings of Human Language Technologies: The Conference of the North American Chapter of the Association for Computational Linguistics companion volume, pp 29-32, Rochester, NY, April 2007.

Hana, J., Feldman, A., Brew, C., Amaral, L. (2006, April). Tagging Portuguese with a Spanish tagger using cognates. In Proceedings of the International Workshop on Cross-Language Knowledge Induction (pp. 33-40). Association for Computational Linguistics.

Hubey, M. (1999). Mathematical Foundations of Linguistics. Lincom Europa, Muenchen.

Jakobson, R., Fant, G., Halle, M. (1951). Preliminaries to speech analysis. The distinctive features and their correlates.

Koehler. R. (1993). Synergetic Linguistics. In: Contributions to Quantitative Linguistics, R. Koehler and B.B. Rieger (eds.), pp. 41-51.

Koehn, P., Knight, K. (2002). Learning a Translation Lexicon from Monolingual Corpora, , ACL 2002, Workshop on Unsupervised Lexical Acquisition

Ladefoged, P., Halle, M. (1988). Some major features of the International Phonetic Alphabet. Language, 64(3), 577-582.

Leusch, G., Ueffing, N., Ney, H. (2003, September). A novel string-to-string distance measure with applications to machine translation evaluation. In Proceedings of MT Summit IX (pp. 240-247).

Levenshtein, V. I. (1966). Binary codes capable of correcting deletions, insertions, and reversals. Soviet Physics Doklady 10 (8): 707–710.

Menzerath, P. (1954). Die Architektonik des deutchen Wortschatzes. Dummler, Bonn.

Mulloni, A., Pekar, V. (2006). Automatic detection of orthographic cues for cognate recognition. Proceedings of LREC'06, 2387, 2390.

Nerbonne, J., Heeringa, W. (1997). Measuring dialect distance phonetically. In Proceedings of the Third Meeting of the ACL Special Interest Group in Computational Phonology (SIGPHON-97).

Nießen, S.; F. J. Och; G. Leusch, and H. Ney. (2000) An evaluation tool for machine translation: Fast evaluation for MT research. In Proc. Second Int. Conf. on Language Resources and Evaluation, pp. 39–45, Athens, Greece, May

Pinnis, M., Ion, R., Ştefănescu, D., Su, F., Skadiņa, I., Vasiļjevs, A., Babych, B. (2012) Toolkit for Multi-Level Alignment and Information Extraction from Comparable Corpora // Proceedings of ACL 2012, System Demonstrations Track, Jeju Island, Republic of Korea, 8-14 July 2012.

Pivtorak, H. P. (1988). Forming and dialectal differentiation of the old Ukrainian language. (Formuvannya i dialektna dyferentsiatsiya davn'orus'koyi movy – Формування i діалектна диференціація давньоруської мови). Naukova Dumka, Kyiv. (in Ukrainian).

Sanders, N. C., Chin, S. B. (2009). Phonological Distance Measures. Journal of Quantitative Linguistics, 16(1), 96-114.

Schepens, J., Dijkstra, T., Grootjen, F. (2012). Distributions of cognates in Europe as based on Levenshtein distance. Bilingualism: Language and Cognition, 15(01), 157-166.

Serva, M., Petroni, F. (2008). Indo-European languages tree by Levenshtein distance. EPL (Europhysics Letters), 81(6), 68005.

Sigurd, B., Eeg-Olofsson, M., Van Weijer, J. (2004). Word length, sentence length and frequency–Zipf revisited. Studia Linguistica, 58(1), 37-52.

Swadesh, M. (1952). Lexico-statistic dating of prehistoric ethnic contacts: with special reference to North American Indians and Eskimos. Proceedings of the American philosophical society, 96(4), 452-463.

Zipf, G. K. (1935). The psycho-biology of language.

Received May 3, 2016, accepted May 4, 2016

Baltic J. Modern Computing, Vol. 4 (2016), No. 2, pp. 129–140

Improving Phrase-Based SMT Using Cross-Granularity Embedding Similarity

Peyman PASSBAN, Chris HOKAMP, Andy WAY, Qun LIU

ADAPT Centre
School of Computing
Dublin City University
Dublin, Ireland

{ppassban,chokamp,away,qliu}@computing.dcu.ie

Abstract. The phrase–based statistical machine translation (PBSMT) model can be viewed as a log-linear combination of translation and language model features. Such a model typically relies on the phrase table as the main resource for bilingual knowledge, which in its most basic form consists of aligned phrases, along with four probability scores. These scores only indicate the co-occurrence of phrase pairs in the training corpus, and not necessarily their semantic relatedness. The basic phrase table is also unable to incorporate contextual information about the segments where a particular phrase tends to occur. In this paper, we define six new features which express the semantic relatedness of bilingual phrases. Our method utilizes both source and target side information to enrich the phrase table. The new features are inferred from a bilingual corpus by a neural network (NN). We evaluate our model on the English–Farsi (En–Fa) and English–Czech (En–Cz) pairs and observe considerable improvements in the all En↔Fa and En↔Cz directions.

Keywords: Statistical machine translation, phrase embeddings, incorporating contextual information.

1 Introduction

The process of PBSMT can be interpreted as a search problem where the score at each step of exploration is formulated as a log-linear model (Koehn, 2010). For each candidate phrase, the set of features is combined with a set of learned weights to find the best target counterpart of the provided source sentence. Because an exhaustive search of the candidate space is not computationally feasible, the space is typically pruned via some heuristic search, such as beam search (Koehn, 2010). The discriminative log-linear model allows the incorporation of arbitrary context-dependent and context-independent features. Thus, features such as those in Och and Ney (2002) or Chiang et al. (2009) can be combined to improve translation performance. The standard baseline bilingual features included in Moses (Koehn et al., 2007) by default are: the *phrase translation* *probability $\phi(e|f)$, inverse phrase translation probability $\phi(f|e)$, direct lexical weighting $lex(e|f)$ and inverse lexical weighting $lex(f|e)$.*[1]

The scores in the phrase table are computed directly from the co-occurrence of aligned phrases in training corpora. A large body of recent work evaluates the hypothesis that co-occurrence information alone cannot capture contextual information as well as the semantic relations among phrases (see section 2). Therefore, many techniques have been proposed to enrich the feature list with semantic information. In this paper, we define six new features for this purpose. All of our features indicate the semantic relatedness of source and target phrases. Our features leverage contextual information which is lost by the traditional phrase extraction operations. Specifically, in both sides (source and target) we look for any type of constituents including phrases, sentences or even words which can fortify the semantic information about phrase pairs.

Our contributions in this paper are threefold: a) We define new semantic features and embed into PBSMT to enhance the translation quality. b) In order to define the new features we train bilingual phrase and sentence embeddings using an NN. Embeddings are trained in a joint distributed feature space which not only preserves monolingual semantic and syntactic information but also represents cross-lingual relations. c) We indirectly incorporate external contextual information using the neural features. We search in the source and target spaces and retrieve the closest constituent to the phrase pair in our bilingual embedding space.

The structure of the paper is as follows. Section 2 gives an overview of related work. Section 3 explains our pipeline and the network architecture in detail. In Section 4, experimental results are reported. We also have a separate section to discuss different aspects of embeddings and the model. Finally, in the last section we present our conclusions along with some avenues for future work.

2 Background

Several models such as He et al. (2008), Liu et al. (2008) and Shen et al. (2009) studied the use of contextual information for statistical machine translation (SMT). The idea is to go beyond the phrase level and enhance the phrase representation by taking surrounding phrases into account. This line of research is referred as discourse SMT (Hardmeier, 2014; Meyer, 2014). Because NNs can provide distributed representations for words and phrases, they are ideally suited to the task of comparing semantic similarity. Unsupervised models such as *Word2Vec*[2] (Mikolov et al., 2013a) or *Paragraph Vectors* (Le & Mikolov, 2014) have shown that distributional information is often enough to learn high-quality word and sentence embeddings.

A large body of recent work has evaluated the use of embeddings in machine translation. A successful usecase was reported in (Mikolov et al., 2013b). They separately

---

[1] Although the features contributed by the language model component are as important as the bilingual features, we do not address them in this paper, since they traditionally only make use of the monolingual target language context, and we are concerned with incorporating bilingual semantic knowledge.

[2] http://code.google.com/p/word2vec/

project words of source and target languages into embeddings, then try to find a transformation function to map the source embedding space into the target space. The transformation function was approximated using a small set of word pairs extracted using an unsupervised alignment model trained with a parallel corpus. This approach allows the construction of a word-level translation engine with very large monolingual data and only a small number of bilingual word pairs. The cross-lingual transformation mechanism allows the engine to search for translations for OOV (out-of-vocabulary) words by consulting a monolingual index which contains words that were not observed in the parallel training data. The work by Garcia and Tiedemann (2014) is another model follows that the same paradigm.

However, machine translation (MT) is more than word-level translation. In Martínez et al. (2015) word embeddings were used in document-level MT to disambiguate the word selection. Tran et al. (2014) used bilingual word embeddings to compute the semantic similarity of phrases. To extend the application of text embedding beyond single words, Gao et al. (2013) proposed learning embeddings for source and target phrases by training a network to maximize the sentence-level BLEU score. Costa-jussa et al. (2014) worked at the sentence-level and incorporated the source side information into the decoding phase by finding the similarities between phrases and source embeddings. Some other models re-scored the phrase table (Alkhouli et al., 2014) or generated new phrase pairs in order to address the OOV word problem (Zhao et al., 2014).

Our network makes use of some ideas from existing models, but also extends the information available to the embedding model. We train embeddings in the joint space using both source and target side information simultaneously, using a model which is similar to that of Devlin et al. (2014) and Passban et al. (2015b). Similar to Gao et al. (2013) we make embeddings for phrases and sentences and add their similarity as feature functions to the SMT model.

3 Proposed Method

In order to train our bilingual embedding model, we start by creating a large bilingual corpus. Each line of the corpus may include:

- a source or target sentence,
- a source or target phrase,
- a concatenation of a phrase pair (source and target phrases which are each other's translation),
- a tuple of source and target words (each other's translation).

Sentences of the bilingual corpus are taken from the SMT training corpus. Accordingly, phrases and words are from the phrase tables and lexicons, generated by the alignment model and phrase extraction heuristic used by the SMT model. This means that the bilingual corpus is a very large corpus with size of $2 * |c| + 3 * |pt| + |bl|$ which $|c|$ indicates the number of source/target sentences, $|pt|$ is the size of the phrase table and $|bl|$ is the size of the bilingual lexicon.

By use of the concatenated phrases and bilingual tuples we try to score the quality of both sides of the phrase pair, by connecting phrases with other phrases in the same language, and with their counterparts in the other language. Section 3.1 discusses how the network benefits from this bilingual property.

Each line of the bilingual training corpus has a dedicated vector (row) in the embeddings matrix. During training embeddings are updated. After training, we extract some information to enrich the phrase table. First we compute the semantic similarity between source and target phrases in phrase pairs. The similarity shows how semantically phrases are related to each other. The *Cosine* measure is used to compute the similarity:

$$similarity(E_s, E_t) = \frac{E_s.E_t}{||E_s|| \times ||E_t||}$$

where E_s and E_t indicate embeddings for the given source and target phrases, respectively. We map *Cosine* scores into the [0,1] range. This can be interpreted as a score indicating the semantic relatedness of the source and target phrases. The similarity between the source phrase and target phrase is the first feature and is referred as *sp2tp*.

Among source-side embeddings (word, phrase or sentence embeddings) we search for the close match to the source phrase. There might be a word, phrase or sentence on the source side which can enhance the source phrase representation and ease its translation. If the closest match belongs to a phrase, probably that is a paraphrased form of the original phrase and if the closest match belongs to a word, probably that is a keyword which could enhance the word selection quality. We refer to this source-side similarity score as *sp2sm*.

We also look for the closest match of the source phrase on the target side. As we jointly learn embeddings, structures that are each other's translation should have close embeddings. We compute the similarity of the closest target match to the source phrase (*sp2tm*). We compute the same similarities for the target phrase, namely the similarity of the target phrase with the closest target match (*tp2tm*) and the closest source match (*tp2sm*). The source and target matches may preserve other type of semantic similarity (*sm2tm*), therefore these features should add more information about the overall quality of the phrase pair. All new features are added to the phrase table and used in the tuning phase to optimise the translation model. Figure 1 tries to clarify the relation among different matches and phrases.

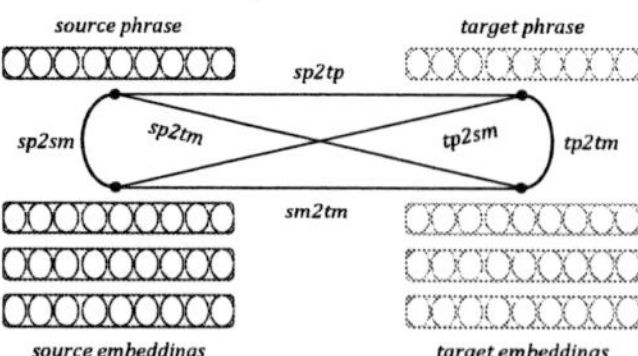

Fig. 1. *sp, tp, sm* and *tm* stand for *source phrase, target phrase, source match* and *target match*, respectively. The embeddings size for all types of embedding are the same. The source/target-side embedding could belong to a source/target word, phrase or sentence. The labels of arrows indicate the Cosine similarity between two embeddings which is mapped into the [0,1] range.

3.1 Learning Embeddings

Our network is an extension of Le and Mikolov (2014) and Passban et al. (2015b). In those methods, documents (words, phrases, sentences and any other chunks of text) are treated as atomic units in order to learn embeddings in the same semantic space as the space used for the individual words in the model. The model includes an embedding for each document which in our case may be a monolingual sentence, a monolingual phrase, a bilingual phrase pair or a bilingual word pair. During training, at each iteration a random target word (w^t) is selected from the input document to be predicted at the output layer by using the context and document embeddings. The context embedding is made by averaging embeddings of adjacent words around the target word. Word and document embeddings are updated during training until the cost is minimized. The model learns an embedding space in which constituents with similar distributional tendencies are close to each other. More formally, given a sequence of $S_i = w_1, w_2, ..., w_n$ the objective is to maximize the log probability of the target word given the context and document vector:

$$\frac{1}{n} \sum_{j-1}^{n} \log p(w_j^t | C_i^{w^t}, D_i)$$

where $w_j^t \in S_i$ is randomly selected at each iteration. D_i is the document embedding for S_i and C^{w^t} indicates the context embedding which is the mean of embeddings for m preceding and m following words around the target word.

As previously mentioned, S_i could be a monolingual sentence or phrase, in which case w^t and adjacent words are from the same language. In other words, the context includes m words before and m words after the target word. S_i also could be a concatenation of source and target phrases. In that case context words are selected from both languages, i.e. m words from the source (the side from which the target word is selected) and m words from the target side. Finally S_i could be a pair of source and target words where C^{w^t} is made using the target word's translation. The word on one side is used to predict the word on the opposite side. In the proposed model m is the upper bound.

Table 1. Context vectors for different input documents. w^t is **better** and $m = 5$. Italics are in Farsi.

D_1	know him **better** than anyone
C_1^{better}	[know, him, than, anyone]$_s$
D_2	know him **better** than anyone . *āv rā bhtr āz hrks myšnāsy*
C_2^{better}	[know, him, than, anyone]$_s$ + [*āv, rā, bhtr, āz, hrks*]$_t$
D_3	**better** . *bhtr*
C_3^{better}	[*bhtr*]$_t$

Table 1 illustrate some examples of the context window. The examples are selected from the En–Fa bilingual corpus (see Section 4).[3] In C_1 the context window includes 2 words before **better** and 2 words after. In this case the target word and all other context words are from the same language (indicated by a 's' subscript). In the second example the input document is a concatenation of English and Farsi phrases, so C_2 includes m (or fewer) words from each side (indicated with different subscripts). In the final example the input document is a word tuple where the target word's translation is considered as its context.

As shown in Huang et al. (2012), word vectors can be affected by the word's surrounding as well as by the global structure of a text. Each unique word has a specific vector representation and clearly similar words in the same language would have similar vectors (Mikolov et al., 2013a). By use of the bilingual training corpus and our proposed architecture we tried to expand the monolingual similarities to the bilingual setting, resulting in an embedding space which contains both languages. Words that are direct translations of each other should have similar/close embeddings in our model. As the corpus contains tuples of $< word_{L_1}, word_{L_2} >$, embeddings for words which tend to be translations of one another are trained jointly. Phrasal units are also connected together by the same process. Since the bigger blocks encompass the embeddings for words and phrasal units they should also have representations which are similar to the representations of their constituents.

3.2 Network Architecture

In the input layer we have an embedding matrix. Each row in the matrix is dedicated to one specific line in the bilingual corpus. During training embeddings are tuned and updated. The network has only one hidden layer. A *Softmax* layer is placed on top of the hidden layer to map values to class probabilities. *Softmax* is a vector-valued function which maps its input values to the [0,1] range. The output values from the *Softmax* can be interpreted as class probabilities for the given input. The *Softmax* function is formulated as follows:

$$P(w_j^t | C_i^{w^t} \bullet D_i) = \frac{\exp(h_j.w_j + a_j)}{\sum_{j' \in \mathcal{V}} \exp(h_j.w_{j'} + a_{j'})}$$

Intuitively, we are estimating the probability of selecting the j-th word as the target word from the i-th training document. The input for the *Softmax* layer is $h = W(C_i^{w^t} \bullet D_i) + b$, where W is a weight matrix between the input layer and the hidden layer, b is a bias vector and $\bullet$ indicates the concatenation function. w_j is the j-th column of another weight matrix (between the hidden layer and the *Softmax* layer) and a_j is a bias term. The output of *Softmax*, $V \in \mathbb{R}^{|\mathcal{V}|}$, is the distribution probability over classes which are words in our setting. The j-th cell in V is interpreted as the probability of selecting the j-th word from the target vocabulary $\mathcal{V}$ as the target word. Based on *Softmax* values the word with the highest probability is selected and the error is computed accordingly. The network parameters are optimized using stochastic gradient descent and

---

[3] We used the DIN transliteration standard to show the Farsi alphabets; https://en.wikipedia.org/wiki/Persian_alphabet

back-propagation (Rumelhart et al., 1988). All parameters of the model are randomly initialized over a uniform distribution in the [-0.1,0.1] range. Weight matrices, bias values and word embeddings are all network parameters which are tuned during training. The embedding size in our model is 200. Figure 2 illustrates the whole pipeline.

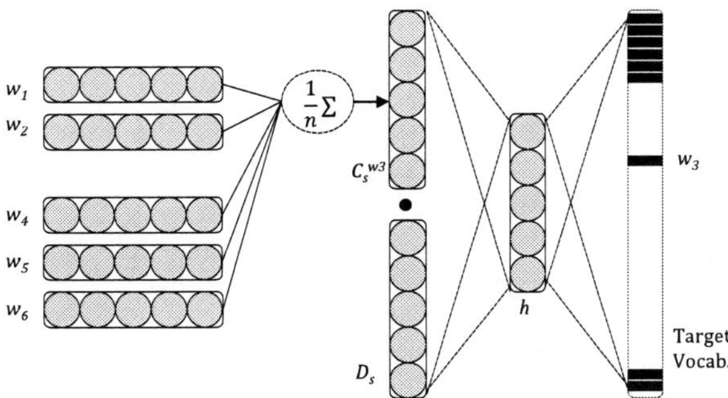

Fig. 2. Network architecture. The input document is $S = w_1\ w_2\ w_3\ w_4\ w_5\ w_6$ and the target word is w_3.

4   Experimental Results

We evaluated our new features on two language pairs: En–Fa and En–Cz. Both Farsi and Czech are morphologically rich languages; therefore, translation to/from these languages can be more difficult than it is for languages where words tend to be discrete semantic units. Farsi is also a low-resource language, so we are interested in working with these pairs. For the En–Fa pair we used the TEP++ corpus (Passban et al., 2015a) and for Czech we used the Europarl[4] corpus (Koehn, 2005). TEP++ is a collection of 600,000 parallel sentences. We used 1000 and 2000 sentences for testing and tuning, respectively and the rest of the corpus for training. From the Czech dataset we selected the same number of sentences for training, testing and tuning. The baseline system is a PBSMT engine built using Moses (Koehn et al., 2007) with the default configuration. We used MERT (Och, 2003) for tuning. In the experiments we trained 5-gram language models on the monolingual parts of the bilingual corpora using SRILM (Stolcke et al., 2002). We used BLEU (Papineni et al., 2002) as the evaluation metric. We added our features to the phrase table and tuned the translation models. Table 2 shows the impact of each feature. We also estimated the translation quality in the presence of the all features (we run MERT for each row of Table 2). Bold numbers are statistically significant according to the results of paired bootstrap re-sampling with p=0.05 for 1000 samples (Koehn, 2004). Arrows indicate whether the new features increased or decreased the quality over the baseline.

---

[4] http://www.statmt.org/europarl/

Table 2. Impact of the proposed features.

Feature	En–Fa	↑↓	Fa–En	↑↓	En–Cz	↑↓	Cz–En	↑↓
Baseline	21.03	0.00	29.21	0.00	28.35	0.00	39.63	0.00
sp2tp	21.46	**0.43** ↑	29.71	**0.50** ↑	28.72	**0.37** ↑	40.34	**0.71** ↑
sp2sm	21.32	0.29 ↑	29.74	**0.53** ↑	28.30	0.05 ↓	39.76	0.13 ↑
sp2tm	21.40	**0.37** ↑	29.56	**0.35** ↑	28.52	0.17 ↑	39.79	0.16 ↑
tp2tm	20.40	0.63 ↓	29.56	0.35 ↑	28.00	0.35 ↓	39.68	0.05 ↑
tp2sm	21.93	**0.90** ↑	29.26	0.05 ↑	28.94	**0.59** ↑	39.81	0.18 ↑
sm2tm	21.18	0.15 ↑	30.08	**0.87** ↑	28.36	0.01 ↑	39.99	**0.36** ↑
All	21.84	**0.81** ↑	30.26	**1.05** ↑	29.01	**0.66** ↑	40.24	**0.61** ↑

Results show that the new features are useful and positively affect the translation quality. Some of the features such as *sp2tp* are always helpful regardless of the translation direction and language pair. This feature is the most important feature among others. The *sm2tm* feature always works effectively in translating into English and the *tp2sm* feature is effective when translating from English. In the presence of all features results are significantly better than the baseline system in all cases. Some of the features are not as strong as the others (*tp2tm*) and some of them behave differently based on the language (*sp2tm*).

5 Discussion

Numbers reported in in Section 4 indicate that the proposed method and features result in a significant enhancement of translation quality, but it cannot be decisively claimed that they are always helpful for all languages and settings. Therefore we tried to study the impact of features not only quantitatively but also qualitatively. We mainly focus on three issues in this section. First we show how the features change SMT translations. Then we show ability of the network in capturing cross-lingual similarities and finally we discuss the way we learn embeddings.

Based on our investigation, the new features seem to help the model determine the quality of a phrase pair. As an example for the English phrase *"but I'm your teammate"* in the phrase table, the corresponding Farsi target phrase is *"āmā mn hm tymyt hstm"* which is the exact translation of the source phrase. The closest match in the source side is *"we played together"* and in the target side is *"Ben mn ānjā bāzy krdm"* (meaning *"I played in that team"*). These retrieved matches indicate that this is a high-quality phrase. By comparing the outputs we recognized that before adding our features the word *"your"* was not translated. In translation into Farsi, possessives sometimes are not translated and the verb implicitly shows them, but the best translation is a translation including possessives. The translation of *"your"* appeared in the output after adding our features.

The proposed model is expected to learn the cross-lingual similarities along with the monolingual relations. To study this feature Table 3 shows two samples. Results in Table 3 show the proposed model can capture cross-lingual relations. It is also able to model similarities in different granularities. It has word level, phrase level and sentence level similarities. Retrieved instances are semantically related to the given queries.

Table 3. The top 10 most similar vectors for the given English query. Recall that the retrieved vectors could belong to words, phrases or sentences in either English or Farsi and word or phrase pairs. The items that were originally in Farsi have been translated into English, and are indicated with *italics*.

Query	sadness
1	<*apprehension*, nervous>
2	*emotion*
3	<*ill*,sick>
4	pain
5	<*money*,money>
6	*benignity*
7	<*may he was punished*,punished harshly>
8	is really gonna hurt
9	i know tom ' s dying
10	<*bitter*,angry>

Tang et al. (2015) proposed that a sentence embedding could be generated by averaging/concatenating embeddings of the words in that sentence. In our case the model by Tang et al. was not as beneficial as ours for both Farsi and Czech. As an example if the *sp2tp* is computed using their model, it degrades the En–Fa direction's BLEU from 21.03 to 20.97 and its improvement for the Fa–En direction is only +0.11 points (almost 5 times less than ours). Our goal is not to compare our model to that of Tang et al.. We only performed a simple comparison on the most important feature to see the difference. Furthermore, according to discussions from Le and Mikolov (2014) document vectors (such as ours) work better than averaging/concatenating vectors. Our model also contains both source and target side information in word and phrase embeddings. Averaging cannot provide such rich information. Our results are aligned with Devlin et al. (2014), who showed the impact of using both source and target side information.

6   Conclusion and Future work

In this work we proposed a novel neural network model which learns word, phrase, and sentence embeddings in a bilingual space. Using embeddings we define six new features which are incorporated into an SMT phrase table. Our results show that the new semantic similarity features enhance translation performance across all of the languages we evaluated. In future work, we hope to directly include the distributed semantic representation into the phrase table, allowing on-line incorporation of semantic information into the translation model features.

Acknowledgement

We would like to thank the three anonymous reviewers and Rasul Kaljahi for their valuable comments and the Irish Center for High-End Computing (www.ichec.ie) for providing computational infrastructures. This research is supported by Science Foundation Ireland through the CNGL Programme (Grant 12/CE/I2267) in the ADAPT Centre (www.adaptcentre.ie) at Dublin City University.

References

Alkhouli, T., Guta, A., & Ney, H. (2014). Vector space models for phrase-based machine translation. *Syntax, Semantics and Structure in Statistical Translation*.

Chiang, D., Knight, K., & Wang, W. (2009). 11,001 new features for statistical machine translation. In *Proceedings of human language technologies: The 2009 annual conference of the north american chapter of the association for computational linguistics* (pp. 218–226). Boulder, Colorado.

Costa-jussa, M., Gupta, P., Rosso, P., & Banchs, R. (2014). English-to-hindi system description for wmt 2014: Deep sourcecontext features for moses. In *Proceedings of the ninth workshop on statistical machine translation, baltimore, maryland, usa. association for computational linguistics*.

Devlin, J., Zbib, R., Huang, Z., Lamar, T., Schwartz, R., & Makhoul, J. (2014). Fast and robust neural network joint models for statistical machine translation. In *Proceedings of the 52nd annual meeting of the association for computational linguistics* (Vol. 1, pp. 1370–1380).

Gao, J., He, X., Yih, W., & Deng, L. (2013). Learning semantic representations for the phrase translation model. *CoRR, abs/1312.0482*.

Garcia, E. M., & Tiedemann, J. (2014). Words vector representations meet machine translation. *Syntax, Semantics and Structure in Statistical Translation*, 132.

Hardmeier, C. (2014). *Discourse in statistical machine translation*. Unpublished doctoral dissertation.

He, Z., Liu, Q., & Lin, S. (2008). Improving statistical machine translation using lexicalized rule selection. In *Proceedings of the 22nd international conference on computational linguistics - volume 1* (pp. 321–328). Stroudsburg, PA, USA: Association for Computational Linguistics. Retrieved from http://dl.acm.org/citation.cfm?id=1599081.1599122

Huang, E. H., Socher, R., Manning, C. D., & Ng, A. Y. (2012). Improving word representations via global context and multiple word prototypes. In *Proceedings of the 50th annual meeting of the association for computational linguistics: Long papers-volume 1* (pp. 873–882).

Koehn, P. (2004). Statistical significance tests for machine translation evaluation. In *Emnlp* (pp. 388–395).

Koehn, P. (2005). Europarl: A parallel corpus for statistical machine translation. In *Mt summit* (Vol. 5, pp. 79–86).

Koehn, P. (2010). *Statistical machine translation* (1st ed.). New York, NY, USA: Cambridge University Press.

Koehn, P., Hoang, H., Birch, A., Callison-Burch, C., Federico, M., Bertoldi, N., et al. (2007). Moses: Open source toolkit for statistical machine translation. In *Proceedings of the 45th annual meeting of the acl on interactive poster and demonstration sessions* (pp. 177–180).

Le, Q. V., & Mikolov, T. (2014). Distributed representations of sentences and documents. *CoRR, abs/1405.4053*.

Liu, Q., He, Z., Liu, Y., & Lin, S. (2008). Maximum entropy based rule selection model for syntax-based statistical machine translation. In *Proceedings of the conference on empirical methods in natural language processing* (pp. 89–97). Stroudsburg, PA, USA: Association for Computational Linguistics. Retrieved from http://dl.acm.org/citation.cfm?id=1613715.1613729

Martínez, E., España Bonet, C., Márquez Villodre, L., et al. (2015). Document-level machine translation with word vector models. In *Proceedings of the 18th annual conference of the european association for machine translation (eamt)* (pp. 59–66). Antalya, Turkey.

Meyer, T. (2014). *Discourse-level features for statistical machine translation.* Unpublished doctoral dissertation, École Polytechnique Fédérale de Lausanne.

Mikolov, T., Chen, K., Corrado, G., & Dean, J. (2013a). Efficient estimation of word representations in vector space. *CoRR, abs/1301.3781*.

Mikolov, T., Le, Q. V., & Sutskever, I. (2013b). Exploiting similarities among languages for machine translation. *CoRR, abs/1309.4168*.

Och, F. J. (2003). Minimum error rate training in statistical machine translation. In *Proceedings of the 41st annual meeting on association for computational linguistics - volume 1* (pp. 160–167). Sapporo, Japan.

Och, F. J., & Ney, H. (2002). Discriminative training and maximum entropy models for statistical machine translation. In *Proceedings of the 40th annual meeting on association for computational linguistics* (pp. 295–302). Philadelphia, Pennsylvania.

Papineni, K., Roukos, S., Ward, T., & Zhu, W.-J. (2002). BLEU: a method for automatic evaluation of machine translation. In *Proceedings of the 40th annual meeting on association for computational linguistics* (pp. 311–318).

Passban, P., Hokamp, C., & Liu, Q. (2015b). Bilingual distributed phrase representation for statistical machine translation. In *Proceedings of mt summit xv* (pp. 310–318).

Passban, P., Way, A., & Liu, Q. (2015a). Benchmarking SMT performance for Farsi unisng the TEP++ corpus. In *Proceedings of the 18th annual conference of the European Association for Machine Translation (eamt)* (pp. 82–88). Antalya, Turkey.

Rumelhart, D. E., Hinton, G. E., & Williams, R. J. (1988). Learning representations by back-propagating errors. *Cognitive modeling, 5*, 3.

Shen, L., Xu, J., Zhang, B., Matsoukas, S., & Weischedel, R. (2009). Effective use of linguistic and contextual information for statistical machine translation. In *Proceedings of the 2009 conference on empirical methods in natural language processing: Volume 1 - volume 1* (pp. 72–80). Singapore.

Stolcke, A., et al. (2002). SRILM-an extensible language modeling toolkit. In *Interspeech*.

Tang, D., Qin, B., & Liu, T. (2015). Document modeling with gated recurrent neural network for sentiment classification. In *Proceedings of the 2015 conference on empirical methods in natural language processing* (pp. 1422–1432).

Tran, K. M., Bisazza, A., & Monz, C. (2014). Word translation prediction for morphologically rich languages with bilingual neural networks. In *Proceedings of the 2014 conference on empirical methods in natural language processing (EMNLP)* (pp. 1676–1688).

Zhao, K., Hassan, H., & Auli, M. (2014). Learning translation models from monolingual continuous representations.

Received May 2, 2016 , accepted May 5, 2016

Baltic J. Modern Computing, Vol. 4 (2016), No. 2, 141-151

Comparing Translator Acceptability of TM and SMT Outputs

Joss MOORKENS, Andy WAY

ADAPT Centre, School of Computing, Dublin City University, Ireland

joss.moorkens@dcu.ie, away@computing.dcu.ie

Abstract. This paper reports on an initial study that aims to understand whether the acceptability of translation memory (TM) among translators when contrasted with machine translation (MT) unacceptability is based on users' ability to optimise precision in match suggestions. Seven translators were asked to rate whether 60 English-German translated segments were a usable basis for a good target translation. 30 segments were from a domain-appropriate TM without a quality threshold being set, and 30 segments were translated by a general domain statistical MT system. Participants found the MT output more useful on average, with only TM fuzzy matches of over 90% considered more useful. This result suggests that, were the MT community able to provide an accurate quality threshold to users, they would consider MT to be the more useful technology.

Keywords: Machine Translation, Human Evaluation, Translation Memory, Confidence Estimation

1. Introduction

The role of the translator has changed considerably over the past 25-30 years, with technology playing an ever more vital role in a specialised translator's workflow. Bota et al. (2013) noted that some translation technology tools are "more highly regarded than others". Translation Memory (TM), for example, is considered acceptable and necessary (Heyn, 1998), whereas Machine Translation (MT) remains unpopular among many translators. Surveys support the first of these claims, in that while users may have problems with certain extrinsic aspects of TM tools such as pricing or user-friendliness, they have no objection to leveraging previous human translations (Lagoudaki, 2008; Kelly et al., 2012).

For those of us with longer memories, it was not always this way. When commercial TM tools were first introduced, many translators resented the imposition of this new technology. However, early adopters found that, once past the initial learning curve, they could achieve perceptible productivity gains, although the financial benefit of these gains was mitigated to an extent when discounts based on TM matches became common (García, 2006).

As regards the second claim above, a disadvantage for MT is that in exactly the same way as with the introduction of TM, translators further resent the imposition of the newer technology, especially when associated discounts are expected immediately. Translators have complained about having to make tedious repetitive corrections to MT output, lack of creativity, and "limited opportunity to create quality" when post-editing

(Moorkens and O'Brien, 2015). These complaints are exacerbated by the perishable and often poorly-written source content that is pushed towards MT in localisation workflows (Way, 2013; Moorkens and O'Brien, 2015). Despite many studies having shown that MT post-editing increases productivity, users do not always perceive this increase (Koehn, 2009; Gaspari et al., 2014). Despite the increasing incorporation of MT into translation workflows via post-editing (PEMT) or sub-segment auto-suggestion, MT does not yet appear to be widely accepted by translators (cf. Penkale and Way, 2013; Way, 2013).

While this is obvious to many, we consider it worth pointing out the main difference between TM and MT: namely that while MT attempts to translate all sentences in an input document, TM does not (except in the case of 100% matches, for which translators receive little or no remuneration in any case); TM systems merely search the source side of a set of translation pairs for the closest-matching instances above some pre-determined threshold imposed by the translator (so-called 'fuzzy matches'; Sikes (2007)). A ranked list of the said translation pairs is then presented to the translator with user-friendly colour-coding to help the user decide which parts are useful in the composition of the target translation, and which should be ignored and discarded. The addition of project-specific or historical information from the suggested TM segment metadata may help the translator with this decision (Teixeira, 2014). Accordingly, we note the different roles played by the human-in-the-loop here: when using TM, the human still *translates*, whereas with MT, the MT output is usually *post-edited*. There are exceptions here as the delineation between TM and MT has become somewhat blurred, with some tools incorporating both technologies and others adding sub-segment autosuggestions from MT output (Green et al. 2014; O'Brien and Moorkens, 2014).

Given that today's statistical MT (SMT) engines have greatly improved in terms of the quality of their output (cf. Way (2013) for a list of use-cases where MT demonstrably plays an invaluable role), it is disappointing for MT developers to learn that human translators still appear to draw greater satisfaction from slow, interactive TM tools as opposed to fully automatic, fast MT systems. For example, 75% of respondents to Moorkens and O'Brien's (2016) survey of translators agreed that TM helps with their work, whereas only 30% said the same of MT; what's more, 56% indicated that they considered MT a problematic technology. Participants in another study by Moorkens and O'Brien (2015) said that they found post-editing tiring as they are required to be "constantly vigilant … due to the absence of any confidence indication".

More positively, Koskinen and Ruokonen (2016) suggest that translators are "quite willing to adopt new technology as long as it makes their work more efficient". Consequently, we feel that some of the problems with MT reside in how it is presented. In particular, if making productivity improvements could be made demonstrable to and perceptible for users, there would be far fewer objections to MT as a technology in its own right than we have seen heretofore. Accordingly, this paper reports on an initial study that seeks to answer the following question: *Is comparative acceptability of TM over MT predicated on the user's ability to optimise the precision and usefulness of match suggestions by setting a minimum match threshold?*

We contend that the answer to this question is yes, and that:

1.   MT would be considered more acceptable to users if only those matches that required relatively small amounts of editing were presented to post-editors.

2.   TM would be less acceptable to users if matches that required large amounts of editing were presented to translators.

In other words, we suggest that translators' comparative preference of TM over MT demonstrates their preference for precision over maximum recall.

Guerberof (2012) found that the average post-editing time for English-to-Spanish MT trained on a source text-appropriate technical domain was roughly equivalent to the time required to edit an 85-94% fuzzy TM match. Not all MT output will be of this quality of course, and the translator's bugbear of repetitive mistakes to correct in MT output remains a problem, although great strides are being made to incorporate translator feedback into iterative retraining of SMT systems (cf. Du et al., 2015). However, if the ability to set an accurate threshold is one of the things that makes TM useful and acceptable to translators, this highlights the need for accurate confidence prediction of MT quality that correlates with human judgement (e.g. Specia et al. (2009); Specia (2011); Turchi et al. (2013)), the absence of which we believe to be a major stumbling block for acceptability.

This study is reported with the caveat that the research was carried out with a small number of translators for a single domain and language pair, and is intended to preface a larger-scale study that will include measures of actual post-editing effort. However, all participants have substantial translation experience (on average 11.4 years of professional translation experience and 4.5 years of professional post-editing experience) and the chosen language pair of English-German is acknowledged to be a difficult one for MT systems.

The remainder of this paper is organised as follows. In Section 2, we describe the methodology chosen to test the central hypothesis in this paper. In Section 3, we present the results of the experiments conducted, which are discussed further in Section 4. In Section 5, we conclude, and list a number of avenues for further work in this area.

2. Methodology

In this study, seven translators were asked to rate the usefulness of 60 match suggestions in German for 60 English source text segments. Source segments were taken from the documentation for the open-source computer-aided design (CAD) program FreeCAD and from the Wikipedia page for CAD.[1] Table 1 shows the homogeneity of all segments, the segments used for TM matching, and those translated using MT, which all exhibited similar characteristics (well within the standard deviation for each text) using common corpora analyses (such as the type/token ratio of lexical variation) in the WordSmith WordList tool.[2] Note that some types appear in both TM and MT corpora.

Table 1. Wordsmith statistics for source data.

	Overall	Segments for MT	Segments for TM
Types (distinct words)	447	260	268
Type/token ratio (TTR)	42.21	46.93	53.07
Mean word length (chars.)	4.82	4.87	4.76

---

[1] https://en.wikipedia.org/wiki/Computer-aided_design
[2] http://www.lexically.net/wordsmith

30 segments were translated into German using the generic Microsoft Bing SMT system[3] and 30 target segments were fuzzy match suggestions offered by the Omega-T[4] tool loaded with an English-German TM. The TM was created from the translation of documentation from a commercial CAD software tool, and contained 301,583 translation units (although 7,659 of these contained only numbers, dates, or punctuation symbols). The TM tool suggested only a few matches – there were 42 matches for 141 segments, a match rate of just 29.8% – with most of those suggestions having a low fuzzy match score.[5] For this reason, matches were not taken sequentially, but chosen to provide a reasonable variety of fuzzy match scores. The top-10 fuzzy matches ranged from 73 to 100% and the lowest 10 from 19 to 46%. The range of fuzzy matches are shown in Figure 1.

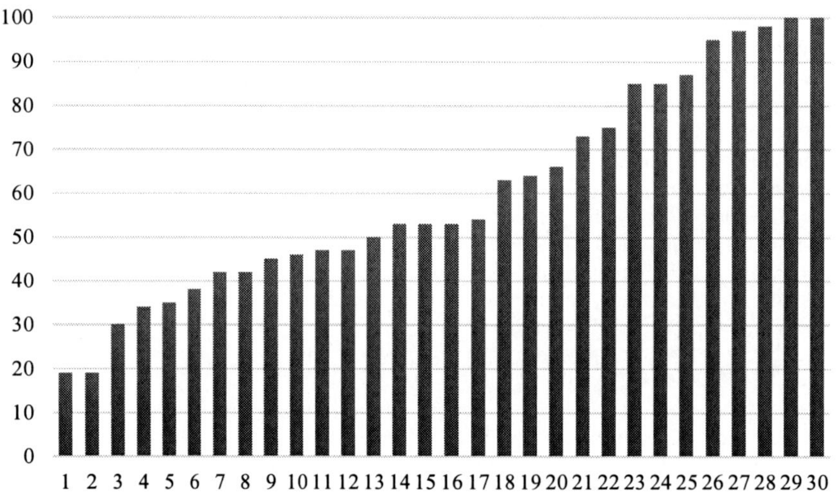

Figure 1. TM target segments' fuzzy-match percentage.

Source text segments and their associated TM or MT target segments were randomised and copied into a six-page survey,[6] where each page contained 10 target text suggestions without any indication of provenance or quality. Participants – all of whom were paid – were informed about the background of the study, and that they could withdraw at any time without penalty (although none did). They were then asked to fill in details of their translation experience, age range, and opinion of MT (all non-mandatory questions) before beginning to rate the 60 segments. Ratings were based on a decision as to whether to retain or delete the target suggestion before beginning to edit or translate from scratch, and were similar to those used by Krings (2001) and Specia et

---

[3] http://www.bing.com/translator/
[4] http://www.omegat.org/
[5] We take this as supporting evidence of our claim that TM technology is actually of little use to most translators, and certainly nowhere near as potentially useful as MT.
[6] The survey used the Limeservice platform, available at www.limeservice.com.

al. (2009), and modified from the rating descriptions used in Moorkens et al. (2015), which were found to be an inconsistent predictor of post-editing effort. The ratings chosen by participants via radio button for each segment were as follows:

1. Not usable – delete and translate from scratch,
2. Useful – editing is faster than translation from scratch,
3. Almost perfect – only requires minor edits or none at all.

This study used purposive sampling, gathering participants appropriate to the research question. Participants were requested to take part via an open call on social media and direct emails to translators with the appropriate language pair listed on the website of the Irish Translators and Interpreters Association.[7] Participants reported between one and 22 years' translation experience. Five participants had experience of post-editing of between five months and 11 years. Users' attitudes to MT tended to be positive, with one considering it "useful for repetitive texts". Users did not consider MT a threat to translators, an attitude consistent with translators in other studies (Katan, 2011). One participant suggested that they are complementary technologies and said "I highly doubt MT can ever replace HT". Another wrote: "Some think MT will replace [human] translation, but although it's getting better and better, that is not possible for the majority of content out there".[8] Another participant said that MT is an "excellent productivity tool when used for suitable content", and that its "greatest advantage is the often higher consistency in terminology and style". Two participants were less effusive, with one writing that it's only useful for "technical texts with a simple sentence structure", and another considering that he or she works faster without MT, which is "not usable for professional translations without heavy editing". We have to acknowledge the possibility that translators with a very negative opinion of MT chose not to take part on the basis of the project description in the emailed invitation to participate, although we do not consider this to be very likely.

3. Results

Participants spent on average 31.6 minutes (max. 53 minutes 14 seconds, min. 14 minutes 28 seconds) completing the rating survey, including one participant who completed the survey in two sittings on consecutive days. Inter-rater agreement was considered moderate using Fleiss' kappa, where K=0.446. Percentage agreement was 77.8% overall, with greater consistency amongst raters for TM matches (84.3%) than for MT output (71.3%), a more consistent result than in Moorkens et al. (2015), albeit with fewer participants.

On average, participants rated the MT output more positively as a basis for post-editing, with a median segment rating of 2 (where 1 is not usable and 3 is almost

---

[7] http://www.translatorsassociation.ie/

[8] It is refreshing to see well-informed translators speaking with authority on MT, owing the great strides taken by the MT community to reach out to translators on this issue. It is all the more disappointing, then, to see TAUS' recent blog "The Future Does Not Need Translators" (https://www.taus.net/blog/the-future-does-not-need-translators) which in our opinion seeks to undermine the *status quo* and unnecessarily antagonise translators.

perfect). It is interesting to note that no machine-translated segment received a rating of 1 from all participants. The median rating for TM matches without a fuzzy match threshold was 1.14. Segments were randomised and presented without any indication of fuzzy match percentage, or whether the target text came from MT or TM. Despite this, there was a very strong correlation between fuzzy match percentage and average participant rating, where r=0.838 (and p < 0.001). Table 2 shows how many times each rating was chosen by a participant for segments from MT and TM.

Table 2. Number of occurrences of each rating.

Rating	Overall	TM	MT
1	185	136	49
2	146	37	109
3	89	37	52

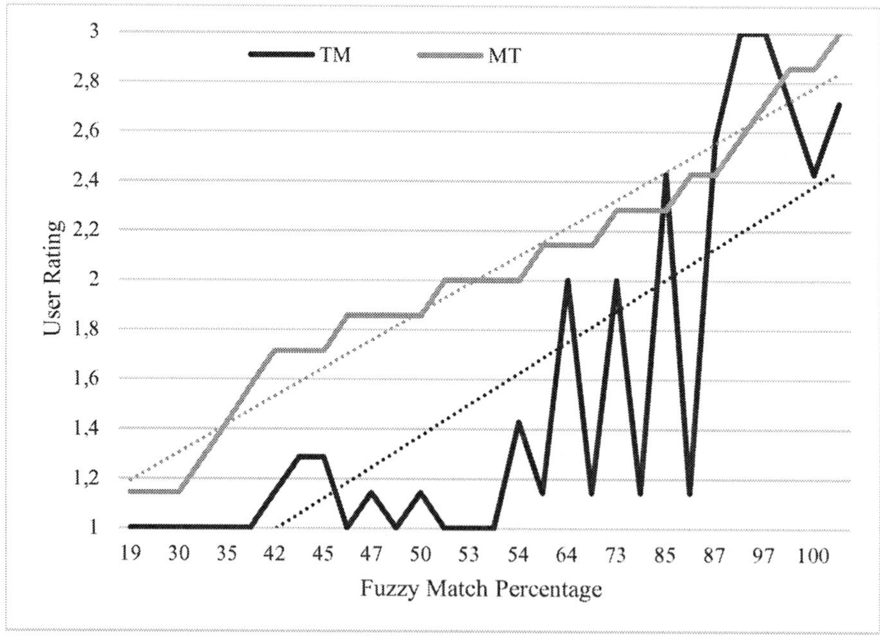

Figure 2. Relationship between average rating and fuzzy match percentage for TM. Ratings for MT output are shown for comparison, charted in order of average rating.

Figure 2 shows the relationship between fuzzy match percentage and average participant rating. Ratings for MT output are shown for comparison, charted in order of average rating (as they had no fuzzy match percentage). Trend lines for TM and MT output clearly show the comparatively higher quality of MT output amongst participants. Note too that at 70-75% fuzzy match thresholds, settings which are often applied in practice (SDL Trados Studio's default threshold is 70%), many TM matches are ranked well below equivalent MT suggestions, with many ranked as not useable at all. This further demonstrates (cf. Simard and Isabelle, 2009) that arbitrarily imposing a cut-off as is the norm in the translation industry above which TM is used and below which MT is used, harms translator performance.

Participants were presented with a free text box after every ten segments in which to make comments. One participant mentioned the amount of time required to make a quality judgement on a proposed target text segment. He wrote that "MT Output has to make some kind of general sense (syntactically) to trigger within the post-editor a positive impulse to start post-editing and not dismiss [it]". Another participant commented that "the main thing to keep in mind is that the analysis of MT output takes time and the smart decision is to dismiss such segments early." De Almeida (2013) believes that this decision-making at speed is problematic for some translators, especially for mid-ranking MT outputs. Koehn (2009), when discussing periods spent by translators pausing during the translation process, notes that "different lengths of pauses indicate the different problems which the translators are dealing with", and that for post-editors "most of the time is spent on contemplating changes, but very little on executing them". Speculating about the translator's behaviour during such pauses, Koehn (2009) intuits that the translator "is reading more of the MT output and looking for mistakes to be corrected". Mesa-Lao (2014) also stresses this focus on the target text for post-editing, noting that study participants either give the source text a cursory read or skip "straight to the target text in search of errors". In this study we found a moderate correlation between the number of mid-ranking (ranked 2: "useful – editing is faster than translation from scratch") segments on a survey page of ten and the amount of time (in comparison to the participant's median time) required for completing a survey page of ten ranking exercises (r_s=0.44141, p=0.006). We suggest that while some translators can decide quite quickly whether to accept and post-edit good MT outputs, and reject poor MT output in favour of translating themselves from scratch, those of a middling quality slow down the translators' decision-making process, exactly what we are trying to avoid by introducing technology into the translation pipeline.

11 of the 30 TM match proposals in this study received scores of 1 (not usable) from all participants, suggesting that they considered the matches wholly dissimilar to the source text, despite five of these proposals receiving match percentages of around 50%. One participant betrayed some irritation with these poor TM proposals, commenting that they contained "serious mistranslations that cannot be understood without reading the source a few times." In a small number of instances, TM match proposals were dismissed when they might have been used as a basis for editing, or might have been perceived more favourably when displayed with a high fuzzy match percentage or with sections for leverage highlighted or colour-coded within a TM tool. For example, the proposed target text for the source segment '*Cmd-1 turns the Tool Sets palette on and off.*' was '*Aktiviert und deaktiviert den Fangmodus*' [Activates and deactivates the snap mode]. Here the 'activates and deactivates' phrase could have been leveraged by users, but all participants considered the segment as a whole unusable and eschewed this option.

4. Discussion

The strong association between fuzzy match percentages and participant ratings, despite the fact that percentages were not displayed onscreen, demonstrates an advantage that TM has over MT: fuzzy matches are reasonably accurate gauges of quality that correlate with human judgement, whereas "the correlation between human judges and all [contemporary] automatic measures of MT quality" is "quite low" (Turian et al., 2003). Some progress has been made in research on MT confidence estimation without use of reference translations. Specia et al. (2009), in a study that aimed to eliminate very poor MT results, identified 84 segment-level features that could be used to estimate MT quality, with results that correlated far better with human judgements than several commonly-used automatic evaluation metrics. Accurately gauging the quality of time-consuming mid-ranking MT output will be a more onerous task. Turchi et al. (2013) noted the subjectivity of human judgements and the associated difficulty in confidence estimation using machine learning based on human annotation. Specia (2011) suggested machine-learning models based on user post-edits as a route for accurate MT confidence estimation. It is less likely that users would have accepted TM were it not possible to impose a quality threshold that users can confidently consider accurate and personalise to their own requirements based on years of experience. Once this threshold is removed, participants in this study commented on the low-quality match proposals and rated many segments poorly. For this reason, we consider the answer to the research question presented in Section 1 to be answered – at least in part – in the affirmative, such that comparative acceptability of TM over MT is indeed predicated on the user's ability to set a minimum fuzzy match threshold.

In Section 1, we mentioned users' complaints that MT output requires "constant vigilance", but results in Section 3 also highlighted the time required for manual evaluation of MT output prior to post-editing. TM tools not only provide users with accurate measures of quality, indicating words and colour-coded sub-segments that may be left untouched, but the time and effort required for manual evaluation is also removed. This suggests that the ability to set an accurate threshold for MT quality (which would be made easier if an automatic metric can be found that correlates strongly with human judgement) should lead to further productivity gains by saving the time required for manual evaluation, as well as reducing the user's cognitive effort.

Note that this is harder than it might seem, as translators are not necessarily good arbiters of MT quality, especially vis-à-vis TM quality. In their work on combining SMT and TM for optimal translation recommendation to post-editors, He et al. (2010) note in their evaluation that while end-users are not made aware of which segments come from SMT and which from TM, one post-editor "obviously mistakes MT outputs for TM outputs". They note that this indicates not only that "phrase-based SMT system[s] [are] able to produce outputs that are … grammatically acceptable enough to be recognized as human translations in the TM", but also "how much the post-editors subconsciously trust the TM [which] may be an explanation for the relatively low acceptance of MT technology in the localization industry and demonstrates the need for TM–MT integration". In a similar line of work, we note here the recent effort by STAR to combine TM and MT in an interesting way, where MT matches are used to reinforce fuzzy matching (Hofmann, 2015).

Participants in this study were reasonably satisfied with the quality of MT output despite the use of a generic engine for a difficult language pair. This suggests that, contrary to perceived wisdom in the field, quality is not the sole barrier for widespread MT acceptance. The results of Moorkens et al. (2015) showed that the addition of onscreen MT confidence indication alone does not immediately lead to behavioural changes for post-editors. Users need to learn to trust measures of quality or confidence, but also need to be presented only with proposals (as segments or sub-segments) that will be useful to them.

Participants in this study were mostly well-disposed to MT, and as such were willing to rate segments without prejudice, despite the lack of provenance metadata. They had the confidence to participate in MT research without being suspicious of the research motives. The challenge will be to convince those less well-disposed to MT that automatic translation can be perceptibly beneficial, despite the increasingly large body of evidence to support this point of view. As a move in that direction, we suggest that the ability to only display useful MT output will greatly improve acceptability.

5. Conclusions and Further Work

In this paper, we have set out to challenge the perception among translators that TM is a more useful technology than MT is. While this does not appear to be true *per se*, what is unquestionably important is the translator's ability to control the fuzzy match threshold. When low- and mid-ranking fuzzy matches are presented to translators without the accompanying fuzzy match scores, translators find the suggestions irritating, and for over 36% of such instances, useless for their purposes. In contrast, *all* of the MT matches suggested were rated as having some utility to post-editors.

Accordingly, we contend that this finding demonstrates very clearly a serious mistake that has been made by introducing MT into the PEMT pipeline. Translators are quite used – one might even say 'happy' – to not having help from CAT tools for every segment, as TM offers useful suggestions only some of the time; in this study we found fuzzy matches for 29.8% of segments, although many of these at 13-70% (see Figure 1) could not be considered useful. In contrast, MT developers have allowed the soft underbellies of their engines to be exposed 'warts and all' to translators, as MT outputs are typically provided for every source segment. What we have demonstrated in this paper is that when the constraints on fuzzy match thresholding are relaxed, translators actually find TM to be of (much) less use than SMT. This suggests to us very strongly that robust, reliable MT confidence measures need to be developed as a matter of urgency which can be used by post-editors to wrest control over what MT outputs they wish to see, and perhaps more importantly still, which ones should be withheld.

In further work, we aim to extend this study to more language pairs, and larger amounts of data translated using *both* TM and MT, assigned randomly to a wider range of translators not only for rating, but also for post-editing. We expect the conclusions drawn in this initial study to be confirmed in further research, which will, we hope, concentrate the minds of MT engine developers to develop a consistent measure of quality for each MT segment output by the system, which can be relied upon – and configured – by human translators. We expect that once translators can control what MT output they actually get to see, then MT will meet with considerably wider acceptance from the translator community.

Acknowledgements

This research is supported by the ADAPT Centre for Digital Content Technology, funded under the SFI Research Centres Programme (Grant 13/RC/2106) and co-funded under the European Regional Development Fund. The authors wish to extend their thanks to the participants in this research, and to the anonymous reviewers whose suggestions and advice were gratefully received.

References

Bota, L., Schneider, C., and Way, A. (2013). COACH: Designing a new CAT Tool with Translator Interaction. *Proceedings of Machine Translation Summit XIV,* (Nice, France), 8pp.

De Almeida, G. (2013). *Translating the post-editor: an investigation of post-editing changes and correlations with professional experience across two Romance languages.* PhD Thesis. Dublin City University, Ireland.

Du, J., Srivastava, A., Way, A., Maldonado-Guerra, A., and Lewis, D. (2015). An Empirical Study of Segment Prioritization for Incrementally Retrained Post-Editing-Based SMT. *MT Summit XV, Proceedings of the Fifteenth Machine Translation Summit*, (Miami, FL), 172—185.

García, I. (2006). Translation Memories: A Blessing or a Curse? In Pym, A., Perekrestenko, S. (Eds.) *Translation Technology and its Teaching.* Tarragona, Spain: Universitat Rovira i Virgili.

Gaspari, F., Toral, A., Kumar Naskar, S., Groves, D., and Way, A. (2014). Perception vs Reality: Measuring Machine Translation Post-Editing Productivity. *Proceedings of the 11th conference of the Association for Machine Translation in the Americas: Workshop on Post-editing Technology and Practice (WPTP3),* (Vancouver, Canada), 60–72.

Green, S., Wang, S., Chuang, J., Heer, J., Schuster, S., and Manning, C. D. (2014). Human Effort and Machine Learnability in Computer Aided Translation. *Proceedings of the 2014 Conference on Empirical Methods in Natural Language Processing (EMNLP)*, (Doha, Qatar), 1225—1236.

Guerberof, A. (2012). *Productivity and Quality in the Post-editing of Outputs from Translation Memories and Machine Translation.* PhD thesis. Universitat Rovira i Virgili, Tarragona, Spain.

He, Y., Ma, Y., Roturier, J., Way, A., and van Genabith, J. (2010). Improving the Post-Editing Experience Using Translation Recommendation: A User Study. *Proceedings of AMTA 2010: The Ninth Conference of the Association for Machine Translation in the Americas*, (Denver, CO.), 247—256.

Heyn, M. (1998). Translation Memories – Insights & Prospects. In L. Bowker, M. Cronin, D. Kenny and J. Pearson (Eds.) *Unity in Diversity? Current Trends in Translation Studies*, Manchester: St. Jerome, 123—136.

Hofmann, N. (2015). MT-enhanced fuzzy matching with Transit NXT and STAR Moses. *EAMT-2015: Proceedings of the Eighteenth Annual Conference of the European Association for Machine Translation*, (Antalya, Turkey), 215.

Katan, D. (2011). Occupation or profession: A survey of the translators' world. In R. Sela-Sheffy & M. Shlesinger (Eds.), *Profession, identity and status: Translators and interpreters as an occupational group*, Amsterdam: John Benjamins, 65-88.

Kelly, N., DePalma, D. A., and Hegde, V. (2012). Voices from the freelance translator community (Report). *Common Sense Advisory*, Boston MA.

Koehn, P. (2009). A process study of computer-aided translation. *Machine Translation* 23(4): 241-263.

Koskinen, K., and Ruokonen, M. (2016). Love letters or hate mail? Translators' technology acceptance in the light of their emotional narratives. In D. Kenny (Ed.), *Human Issues in Translation Technology: The IATIS Yearbook*. Abingdon: Routledge (to appear).

Krings, H. P. (2001). *Repairing Texts*. Kent State University Press, Ohio, USA.

Lagoudaki, E. (2008). *Expanding the possibilities of translation memory systems*. PhD thesis. Imperial College, London, UK.

Mesa-Lao, B. (2014). Gaze behaviour on source texts: An exploratory study comparing translation and post-editing. In Sharon O'Brien, Laura Winther Balling, Michael Carl, Michel Simard, Lucia Specia (Eds.), *Post-editing of Machine Translation: Processes and Applications*, Newcastle-upon-Tyne: Cambridge Scholars, 219-245.

Moorkens, J., and O'Brien, S. (2015). Post-Editing Evaluations: Trade-offs between Novice and Professional Participants. *Proceedings of the 18th Annual Conference of the European Association for Machine Translation (EAMT 2015)*, (Antalya, Turkey), 75—81.

Moorkens, J., O'Brien, S., Silva, I. A. L., Fonseca, N., and Alves, F. (2015). Correlations of perceived post-editing effort with measurements of actual effort. *Machine Translation* 29(3-4), 267-284. doi: 10.1007/s10590-015-9175-2

Moorkens, J., and O'Brien, S. (2016). Assessing User Interface Needs of Post-Editors of Machine Translation. In Dorothy Kenny (Ed.*), Human Issues in Translation Technology: The IATIS Yearbook*. Abingdon: Routledge (to appear).

O'Brien, S., and Moorkens, J. (2014). Towards intelligent post-editing interfaces. In Baur, W., Eichner, B., Kalina, S., Kessler, N., Mayer, F. and Orsted, J. (Eds.) *Man versus Machine: Proceedings of the XXth FIT World Congress (Vol. I)*, Berlin, Germany: BDÜ, 131—137.

Penkale, S., and Way, A. (2013). Tailor-made Quality-controlled Translation. *Proceedings of Translating and the Computer 35*, London, UK, 7pp.

Sikes, R. (2007). Fuzzy matching in theory and practice. *Multilingual*, 18(6):39 – 43.

Simard, M. and Isabelle, P. (2009). Phrase-based machine translation in a computer-assisted translation environment. *Proceedings of The Twelfth Machine Translation Summit (MT Summit XII)*, (Ottawa, Canada), 120 – 127.

Specia, L., Cancedda, N., Dymetman, M., Turchi M., and Cristianini, N. (2009). Estimating the Sentence-Level Quality of Machine Translation Systems. *Proceedings of the 13th Annual Conference of the EAMT*, (Barcelona, Spain), 28–35.

Specia, L. (2011). Exploiting objective annotations for measuring translation post-editing effort. *Proceedings of the 15th conference of EAMT*, (Leuven, Belgium), 73–80.

Teixeira, C. S. C. (2014). The handling of translation metadata in translation tools. In Sharon O'Brien, Laura Winther Balling, Michael Carl, Michel Simard, Lucia Specia (Eds.), *Post-editing of Machine Translation: Processes and Applications*, Newcastle-upon-Tyne: Cambridge Scholars, 109—125.

Turchi, M., Negri, M., and Federico, M. (2013). Coping with the Subjectivity of Human Judgements in MT Quality Estimation. *Proceedings of the 8th Workshop on Statistical Machine Translation (WMT'13)*, (Sofia, Bulgaria), 240—251.

Turian, J. P., Shen, L., and Melamed, I. D. (2003). Evaluation of Machine Translation and its Evaluation. *Proceedings of MT Summit IX*, (New Orleans, U.S.A), 386-393.

Way, A. (2013). Traditional and Emerging Use-Cases for Machine Translation. *Proceedings of Translating and the Computer 35*, London, UK, 12pp.

Received May 2, 2016, accepted May 8, 2016

Baltic J. Modern Computing, Vol. 4 (2016), No. 2, pp. 152–164

Stand-off Annotation of Web Content as a Legally Safer Alternative to Crawling for Distribution

Mikel L. FORCADA, Miquel ESPLÀ-GOMIS, Juan Antonio PÉREZ-ORTIZ

Departament de Llenguatges i Sistemes Informàtics,
Universitat d'Alacant, E-03071 Alacant, Spain

{mlf,mespla,japerez}@ua.es

Abstract. Sentence-aligned web-crawled parallel text or *bitext* is frequently used to train statistical machine translation systems. To that end, web-crawled sentence-aligned bitext sets are sometimes made publicly available and distributed by translation technologies practitioners. Contrary to what may be commonly believed, distribution of web-crawled text is far from being free from legal implications, and may sometimes actually violate the usage restrictions. As the distribution and availability of sentence-aligned bitext is key to the development of statistical machine translation systems, this paper proposes an alternative: instead of copying and distributing copies of web content in the form of sentence-aligned bitext, one could distribute a legally safer *stand-off annotation* of web content, that is, files that identify where the aligned sentences are, so that end users can use this annotation to privately recrawl the bitexts. The paper describes and discusses the legal and technical aspects of this proposal, and outlines an implementation.

Keywords: bitext, parallel text, stand-off annotation, legal issues, statistical machine translation

1   The importance of sentence-aligned crawled bitext

The importance of *bitext* or *parallel text* in current translation technologies is hard to emphasize. Isabelle et al. (1993) —but also Simard et al. (1993)— are famously quoted for saying that "Existing translations contain more solutions to more translation problems than any other currently available resource", but the formulation of the concept of bitext as a translation object can be traced back to Harris (1988).

For bitexts to be used in two key translation technologies, namely *corpus-based machine translation* —particularly *statistical machine translation* (Koehn, 2009), but also *example-based machine translation* (Carl and Way, 2003)— and *computer-aided translation* (Bowker and Fisher, 2010), they have to be segmented and aligned, usually sentence by sentence. Sentence-aligned bitexts, frequently in the form of *translation memories*, are usually obtained as a by-product of computer-aided translation processes, and many of them have been made publicly available, such as DGT-MT, the translation memory of the European Commission's Directorate General for Translation (Steinberger et al., 2012); a comprehensive repository of such sentence-aligned bitexts is provided by OPUS[1] (Tiedemann, 2012).

But in view of the fact that the Internet is packed with webpages which are mutual translations, it is not uncommon for researchers and practitioners to build sentence-aligned bitext by harvesting these webpages, pairing them, sentence-aligning them, and making the resulting corpora publicly available. The most famous example would probably be the Europarl corpus (Koehn, 2005).

Contrary to what may be commonly believed, distribution of web-crawled bitext is far from being free from legal implications,[2] and may sometimes actually violate the usage restrictions of web content, as will be discussed in Section 2. As the distribution and availability of sentence-aligned bitext is key to the development of statistical machine translation systems —in particular when it comes to adapt an existing system to a specific domain (Pecina et al., 2012)—but also to save professional translation effort, Section 3 proposes an alternative: instead of copying and distributing copies of web content in the form of sentence-aligned bitext, one could distribute a legally safer *stand-off annotation* of web content, that is, files that identify where the aligned sentences are, so that end users can use software and this annotation to privately or locally recrawl the bitexts they need. Section 4 surveys related standards and technologies, and an implementation is sketched in Section 5. Concluding remarks (Section 6) end the paper.

2 Legal problems

Considering that a sentence-aligned bitext is an example of the general concept of *corpus*, and that web-crawling is an example of *compiling*, the statement by Baker et al. (2006), p. 48, is clearly pertinent, even if obvious: "Corpus compilers need to observe copyright law by ensuring that they seek permission from the relevant copyright holders to include particular texts. This can only be a difficult and time-consuming process as copyright ownership is not always clear [...]. If the corpus is likely to be made publicly available, copyright holders may require a fee for allowing their text(s) to be included".

One might think that web content is not subject to copyright, but this is seldom the case. On the one hand, some web content has explicitly stated licenses which may impact on products derived from it. For instance, Wikipedia[3] uses the Creative Commons Attribution-Sharealike license,[4] which is quite open about the reuse of content, but requires all derivatives to carry the same license. Web-based newspapers usually have more restrictive terms: for instance, the web edition of *The New York Times* uses a typical copyright notice: "You may not modify, publish, transmit, participate in the transfer or sale of, reproduce [...], create new works from, distribute, perform, display, or for

---

[1] `http://opus.lingfil.uu.se`

[2] Many parallel corpora crawled from the Internet are distributed disregarding the copyright on the original documents from which they were extracted. A clear example is the case of the Europarl corpus for which authors claim (see `http://www.statmt.org/europarl/`) that: *we are not aware of any copyright restrictions of the material.*

[3] `https://www.wikipedia.org/`

[4] `https://creativecommons.org/licenses/by-sa/3.0/`

any way exploit, any of the Content [...] in whole or in part."[5] In another example, participants in the Microblog Track of the Text Retrieval Conference (TREC) interact with a corpus of tweets stored remotely through a search API since 2013. The motivation behind this arrangement —as opposed to the one used in former editions, where the corpus could be downloaded— is to adhere to Twitter's terms of service as they "forbid redistribution of tweets, and thus it would not be permissible for an organization to host a collection of tweets for download" (Lin and Efron, 2013).

Note that usage rights management in the case of bitext corpora compiled from various sources with different licenses may be very complex, which would be particularly hard for non-experts. But what happens when web content is provided without an explicit copyright statement? One would think that it might be possible to use it freely, but this is not the case. According to customary interpretations of the Berne Convention,[6] the most important international agreement dealing with copyright joined by 170 states, copyright notices are optional, works are automatically copyrighted when they are created, and, by default, this means that acts of copying, distribution or adaptation without the author's consent are forbidden. Therefore, in most countries, copyright is automatic and "all rights reserved". The Berne Convention, as an international agreement, may not take into account the variations that copyright law may have in each country.[7] However, it authorizes countries to allow a *fair use* of copyrighted works. In line with this, the Copyright Directive of the European Union[8] states that:

> "Member States may provide for exceptions or limitations to the rights [...] in the following cases: [...] use for the sole purpose of illustration for teaching or scientific research [...] and to the extent justified by the non-commercial purpose to be achieved" (Article 5.3).

In the UK, for instance, there is a prominent *exception to copyright* dealing with text and data mining for non-commercial purposes,[9] which does not exist in other countries. Along these lines, the European Commission recently[10] outlined its vision to modernise European Union copyright rules in order to "make it easier for researchers to use text and data mining technologies to analyse large sets of data"; note, however, that corpus redistribution may still face a lot of risks and uncertainties.

All this means that, depending on the copyright terms of the source material, web-crawled bitexts may not be freely distributed. Tsiavos et al. (2014) discuss in detail the legal issues involved in the distribution of web-crawled data, and even give a number of worked examples. Two main conclusions are:

---

[5] http://www.nytimes.com/content/help/rights/terms/terms-of-service.html

[6] Berne Convention for the Protection of Literary and Artistic Works, 9 September 1886, as last revised at Paris on 24 July 1971, 1161 U.N.T.S. 30.

[7] "Copyright law is not fully harmonized at the international level and, hence, it is extremely difficult to provide a generic answer for the entirety of the situations involving more than one jurisdiction, where possible act of infringement takes place." (Arranz et al., 2013)

[8] Directive 2001/29/EC of the European Parliament and of the Council of 22 May 2001.

[9] https://www.gov.uk/guidance/exceptions-to-copyright

[10] http://europa.eu/rapid/press-release_IP-15-6261_en.htm

- In general, publish only after clearing copyright of the content with the holder (if all of the crawled content has the same public license and it allows redistribution under specific terms, one can of course avoid clearing copyright).
- Abide by a *notice and take down* procedure,[11] much in the way in which online hosts remove content following notice such as court orders or allegations that content infringes copyright.

Also, they suggest that if one cannot clear copyright, it may be safer to publish a derivative of the crawled content from which it is impossible to reconstruct the original source. In fact, when discussing *annotations* as a special case of derivative works, Tsiavos et al. (2014, p. 41) conclude that "unless [the annotations] reproduce part of the original work they do not constitute a problem". Similarly, Arranz et al. (2013) analyse the legal status of different acts involving web crawling of data and web services built around them, and state that "if what is communicated to the public is the actual data either in their original or their derivative form, then this constitutes yet another act restricted by copyright law. If, however, the end user is only the recipient of a web service that implements the web crawling and processing without any direct communication of the actual web data, then copyright law is not activated at all".

It is in this context that avoiding redistribution and moving usage rights management to the final user shows its advantages: as content is not republished but referred to, there is no need to handle copyright, and use after recrawling *chez* the end-user is more likely to be considered fair use.

3   The proposal: stand-off annotation

Following the rationale in the previous section, it is proposed that instead of publicly distributing web-crawled sentence-aligned bitexts, a *stand-off annotation* of the Internet will be distributed, an annotation detailed enough for the end user to efficiently *recrawl* locally the sentence-aligned bitext using appropriate software, on the grounds that an annotation cannot be considered a derived work but rather a description of existing content geared at a specific purpose, not too different from the concepts of *metadata* or *bibliographical reference* as used in scholarly publishing. Public distribution is avoided, and, as a result, the need to clear copyright disappears altogether for corpus compilers, and the responsibility of rights management is passed on to the end user.

Many of the usages by *end users* could actually fall into what is called *fair use*: for instance, a translator may use and modify selected segments of a web-crawled translation memory to produce the translation of a new document. The legal status of more extensive usages such as when a web-crawled sentence-aligned bitext is used to train or domain-adapt a statistical machine translation is less clear, but some machine translation systems available on the web (Google Translate[12] and Bing Translator[13]) rely in part on web-crawled content[14] and this usage, to the best of our knowledge, has not been the subject of any solid legal challenge.

---

[11] `https://en.wikipedia.org/wiki/Notice_and_take_down`

[12] `http://translate.google.com`

[13] `https://www.bing.com/translator/`

[14] `http://v.gd/tausgt` (shortened URL)

The Text Encoding Initiative[15] defines "Stand-off markup (also known as remote markup or stand-off annotation)" as "the kind of markup that resides in a location different from the location of the data being described by it. It is thus the opposite of inline markup, where data and annotations are intermingled within a single location".

The idea of stand-off annotation of corpora is not new, but to the best of our knowledge, it has not been used before to directly annotate web content *at large*, that is, *in the wild*. However, there are some examples of stand-off annotation for building bitexts from collections of documents, as it is the case of the JRC-Acquis (Steinberger et al., 2006) corpus, which is distributed as a collection of monolingual documents and a stand-off annotation file that describes the segment-aligned bitexts that can be obtained for every pair of languages with different alignment tools. In this case, this stand-off annotation is rather simple, given that the monolingual documents are preprocessed so every segment of the text is identified with a code that is later used to relate parallel segments across bitexts. This is, in fact, the usual stand-off approach to corpus annotation, where some auxiliary inline annotation is involved:

> "A middle course is for the original corpus publication to have a scheme for identifying any sub-part. Each sentence, tree, or lexical entry, could have a globally unique identifier, and each token, node or field (respectively) could have a relative offset. Annotations, including segmentations, could reference the source using this identifier scheme (a method which is known as stand-off annotation). This way, new annotations could be distributed independently of the source, and multiple independent annotations of the same source could be compared and updated without touching the source." (Bird et al., 2009, ch. 11).

We could call this *impure* stand-off, as the object being annotated has to be segmented and provided with identifiers. As this is not possible with read-only web content at large, we have to resort to *pure* stand-off annotation, as described below. The following proposals for *crawled bitext* and *crawled translation memory* are based on the concept of *stand-off annotation* of the web as it is found at the time of crawling.

3.1 Deferred bitext crawl

The core of the proposal for crawled bitext, which will be called a *deferred bitext crawl* is *a pair of uniform resource identifiers (URIs)*, one pointing at the *left document*, and another one pointing at the *right document*, such that they are selected as being mutual translations at the time of crawling. To the pair of URIs, one has to add some metadata:

- The *date and time* of annotation.
- The *languages* of the two texts, each one with an optional indicator of how confident the annotating crawler is that they are actually written in those languages.
- *Checksum information* for both the left and right documents, that will be used to ensure that the texts have not changed since they were crawled. Note that while checksum information could be weakly considered as a derivative, it does not allow the reconstruction the original content: it would have to be recrawled.

---

[15] `http://wiki.tei-c.org/index.php/Stand-off_markup`

  – Optionally, one or more indicators expressing the *confidence* with which the two
    texts are taken to be mutual translations.

This information may be used to recrawl the two sides of the bitexts and check that they
have not changed since they were crawled and classified as being a bitext. Those bitexts
not passing the test should be discarded.[16]

3.2 Deferred translation memory crawl

A product that could be derived by selecting sentence pairs from a set of *deferred
bitext crawls*, after aligning their sentences, is the *deferred sentence-aligned bitext crawl*
(also *deferred translation memory crawl* or *deferred training corpus crawl*): a set (not
necessarily ordered) of sentence pairs, each one completely independent, in which every
pair is described by:

  – The *date and time* of annotation.
  – The *languages* of the two sentences, each one with an optional confidence indicator.
  – The URI of the file from which each sentence is taken.
  – A record indicating the location of each sentence, such as the position of the first
    character of the sentence, and either the position of the last character or the length
    in characters of the sentence.
  – The checksum value (or other values that ease *integrity check*) at annotation time.
  – Optionally, one or more indicators expressing the *confidence* with which the two
    sentences are taken to be mutual translations (derived from the bitext confidences
    above, but optionally refined for this specific pair of sentences).

4 Relevant standards and technologies

This paper does not aim at proposing a final solution, but rather at trying to convince the
reader that existing technologies may make the sketch in Section 3 technically feasible
by actually advancing the main features of the solution. To that end, a survey of related
standards and technologies is provided in this section. The main technical requirement is
to have *locators* that allow us to point at specific fragments in an HTML document.[17]
Ideally, these locators should be sufficiently specific so that changes in the original
document can be detected and, in addition to this, error recovery strategies could be
implemented in order to find the segment in a different location.

4.1 Integrity checks

The W3C Web Annotation Working Group launched in 2014 with the aim of developing
a set of recommendations for web annotation, which will include specifications regarding

---

[16] "It is better to cause stand-off annotations to break on such components of the new version than
to silently allow [them] to refer to incorrect locations." (Bird et al., 2009, ch 11).

[17] All of the discussion in this paper assumes that webpage content will be in HTML, some XML-
based text format, and in some cases plain text: an extension to deal with PDF or wordprocessor
documents published in websites falls out of the scope of this paper.

robust anchoring into third-party documents. Robustness against modifications in the URL, in the content text or in the underlying structure of the HTML document is an important feature for the systems processing this kind of locators. A common solution is to extend the locator with information about the matched text along with some of the text immediately before and after it,[18] but this practice could lead to copyright infringement. A more covenient option would be in that case to rely on character positions.[19]

There is also a plethora of message-digest and checksum algorithms that may be used to detect changes in the segments pointed at by the stand-off annotation in the deferred crawls described in Section 3. In addition to the MD5[20] message digests,[21] there are alternatives such as SHA-2:[22] most have publicly available implementations.

Link death is obviously a major issue here. A number of studies have analysed the persistence of URLs over time: Gomes and Silva (2006) found that the lifetime of URLs follows a logarithmic distribution in which only a minority persists for periods longer than a few months; Lawrence et al. (2001) studied a database of computer science papers and found that around 30-40% of links were broken, but they could manually found the new location of the page (or highly related information) 80% of the times. In fact, solutions to find the new location of the content when it has been moved, have been proposed ranging from the use of *uniform resource names* (URNs)[23] to heuristic strategies for automatic fixing of dead links (Morishima et al., 2009). Park et al. (2004) found that a lexical signature consisting of several key words is usually sufficient to obtain the new location, which suggests that these key words could be incorporated into the extended locators proposed in our paper. A different, more limited[24] approach (Resnik and Smith, 2003) crawls only non-volatile resources such as the Internet Archive.[25]

4.2 Linking to a fragment of a document

In the definition of URI,[26] the only provision to refer to parts of a webpage occurs through the use of fragment identifiers using the symbol "#", as in the example: `http://server.info/folder/page.html#section2`; however, this presumes the existence of identified anchors in the HTML document. A standard that could be repurposed to

---

[18] See `https://w3c.github.io/web-annotation/model/wd/#text-quote-selector` or `https://hypothes.is/blog/fuzzy-anchoring/`.

[19] The project Emphasis by The New York Times (see `http://open.blogs.nytimes.com/2011/01/11/emphasis-update-and-source/`) uses keys made up of the first characters from the first and last words in the segment, which constitutes a more compact description and avoids the need to copy text verbatim.

[20] `https://en.wikipedia.org/wiki/MD5`

[21] `https://www.ietf.org/rfc/rfc1321.txt`

[22] `https://en.wikipedia.org/wiki/SHA-2`

[23] `https://www.w3.org/TR/uri-clarification/`

[24] Even though it is possible to use this repository for a more stable version of some contents, it is worth noting that: (a) it does not cover every website on the Internet, and (b) the websites stored in the Internet Archive are not continuously crawled, which means that some live contents may not be available until a new crawl is carried out.

[25] `https://archive.org/`

[26] RFC 3986, `https://www.ietf.org/rfc/rfc3986.txt`.

refer to specific character offsets in a webpage is RFC 5147,[27] "text/plain fragment identifiers", which however deals only with content of the *text/plain* media type, but not with *text/html* which would be the usual media type for webpage content.[28] Note that RFC 5147 already provides the means to implement *integrity checks* and explicitly supports the MD5 message digest standard.[29]

While RFC 5147 could be repurposed for general web content, it does not take into account the structure of the document; indeed, most edits to a webpage usually occur in a way that its structure is only modified locally. Using character offsets would mean that all text after each single edit could fail the integrity check and therefore be discarded: a structure-aware approach could be beneficial to avoid such massive losses of content, the closest candidates being:

- *XPointer*,[30] a system to address components of an XML document, can only be applied to valid XML documents and most webpages are not (they would have to be univocally transformed or normalized into valid XML documents, and pointing would be through the intermediate normalized document). Specific characters inside the contents of an XML element can be linked via the `substring` function.
- Cascaded style sheet (CSS) selectors,[31] used to provide a presentation for an HTML document,[32] do not require it to be a valid XML document; they can therefore operate on a wider range of webpages but they cannot address specific characters. There is some interest in extending the standard in this direction,[33] and indeed extensions to address specific letters[34] have been implemented as JavaScript libraries.
- Canonical Fragment Identifier for EPUB,[35] a method for referencing arbitrary content within electronic books in EPUB format (a format based on HTML). Its linking notation uses a combination of *child sequences*[36] (similar to those defined in XPointer with the `element` scheme) and anchor identifiers, but it is not as robust and expressive as CSS selectors or XPointer. It also allows for character offsets in the form of ranges such as 2:5.

A combination of one or more of the mentioned standards could form the basis for specifying locators that could be used to point at any character span in the web.

---

[27] `https://tools.ietf.org/rfc/rfc5147.txt`

[28] RFC 7111 (`https://tools.ietf.org/rfc/rfc7111.txt`) provides fragment identifiers for the *text/csv* media type.

[29] See also the work by Hellmann et al. (2012) for more character-level proposals.

[30] `https://www.w3.org/TR/xptr-xpointer/`

[31] `https://www.w3.org/TR/css3-selectors/`

[32] CSS selectors are also used to point at elements in the document in JavaScript.

[33] `https://css-tricks.com/a-call-for-nth-everything/`

[34] `http://letteringjs.com/`

[35] `http://www.idpf.org/epub/linking/cfi/epub-cfi.html`

[36] An example of a child sequence is 3/1 which represents the second child (counts start at zero) of an element that is the fourth child in the current context.

4.3 Leveraging TMX

A modified version of TMX, the *translation memory exchange* format[37] could be used to distribute *deferred training corpus crawls* —also called *deferred translation memory crawls*— (see section 3.2); this would allow an easy conversion into TMX —basically by retrieving the content pointed at—, ready for use as a translation memory in most computer-aided translation software; converting them to training corpora for statistical machine translation would also be quite simple and could leverage existing software to do so. The main change would affect the seg (segment) element, which would have to be substituted by a stand-off annotation of the segment, which could be called webseg, and which would contain the URL of the source document and a specification of the actual fragment inside the document; integrity check information could be either added directly to this webseg element or as a property using the standard prop element. As regards date and time, TMX already supports this information as a property of each translation unit. To avoid repeating URLs in websegs, the header could contain an element assigning an identifier to each unique source document.

4.4 An example of the TMX-inspired format

Figure 1 illustrates how the TMX format could be transformed into an XML format capable of representing *deferred sentence-aligned bitext crawls* and *deferred translation memory crawls*. This file contains a single sentence pair or *translation unit* (tu), having two *variants* (tuv), one in English and another one in Spanish (the actual texts are *About the UA* and *Sobre la UA*). A *properties* element (prop) in each *variant* contains the MD5 checksum of the text. Instead of using the standard TMX *segment* element (seg), a *web segment* element (webseg) contains a pointer to a particular segment, made up of an URL, a fragment identifier using Xpointer notation, and a character range inside the selected element (0:11 in English and 0:10 in Spanish).

5 Implementation: stand-off crawlers

Given the fact that there is a number of bilingual web crawlers able to harvest bitexts from the Internet, such as Bitextor (Esplà-Gomis and Forcada, 2010), ILSP Focused Crawler (Mastropavlos and Papavassiliou, 2011), STRAND (Resnik and Smith, 2003), BITS (Ma and Liberman, 1999), or WeBiText (Désilets et al., 2008), it seems more reasonable to consider adapting an existing parallel data crawler to produce deferred translation memories than implementing a new stand-off crawler from scratch. In general, most of these parallel data crawlers work following a similar process:

1. several documents from a given website are downloaded;
2. documents are pre-processed and their language is identified;
3. parallel documents are identified (document alignment) using heuristics;
4. optionally, parallel documents are segment-aligned.

---

[37] https://www.gala-global.org/tmx-14b

```xml
<?xml version="1.0" encoding="UTF-8"?>
<tmx version="1.4">
  <header creationtool="Deferred Corpus Creator"
      creationtoolversion="0.95"
      datatype="text/html" segtype="sentence"
      adminlang="en" srclang="en" o-tmf="web"/>
  <body>
    <tu tuid="1">
      <prop type="x-alignment_confidence">0.86</prop>
      <tuv xml:lang="en" date="20161105T153005Z">
        <prop type="x-lang_confidence">0.91</prop>
        <prop type="x-md5">
          28709ee845d8efaf62318210ecd8ca82
        </prop>
        <webseg>
          http://web.ua.es/en/about-the-ua.html#fragment(//*[@id=&
            quot;parteSuperiorPagina&quot;]/div/h1/0:11)
        </webseg>
      </tuv>
      <tuv xml:lang="es" date="20161105T153013Z">
        <prop type="x-lang_confidence">0.73</prop>
        <prop type="x-md5">
          d502972dbfc178f2c1085875890c2144
        </prop>
        <webseg>
          http://web.ua.es/va/sobre-la-ua.html#fragment(//*[@id=&
            quot;parteSuperiorPagina&quot;]/div/h1/0:10)
        </webseg>
      </tuv>
    </tu>
  </body>
</tmx>
```

Fig. 1. Example of a deferred translation memory crawl containing a single translation unit (see text for details).

Therefore, the problems faced when adapting any parallel data crawler to the purposes of our work would be similar in any of them. This section discusses how these crawlers could be adapted to produce deferred translation memories (Section 4.3).

One of the main obstacles to adapt a state-of-the-art parallel data crawler for the purpose of our work is that, in most of the cases, they do not obtain the translation memories directly from the original documents downloaded from the web: these documents are pre-processed before segment-aligning them. For example, Bitextor and ILSP Focused Crawler normalise HTML documents into XHTML by using the tool *Apache Tika*,[38] and remove boilerplates with the tool *Boilerpipe*.[39] In addition, most crawlers remove the HTML mark-up before segment alignment. This means that both the HTML structure and the content of the documents may be modified before obtaining the final segment alignment. To deal with this problem it would be necessary to annotate the text in the document with the reference of its position in the original document. This could be done by using additional HTML mark-up, which would be preserved during pre-processing.

After document alignment and HTML mark-up cleaning, every document would consist of a collection of text blocks for which their current offset is mapped to their

---

[38] http://tika.apache.org/
[39] http://code.google.com/p/boilerpipe/

position in the original document. At this point, sentence splitting is carried out, which yields several segments from a single text block for which its position in the original document is known. It will therefore be necessary to obtain the position of every segment in the original document, which should be straightforward knowing that every text block appears in a known position of the HTML tree in the original document. In this case, it is sufficient to keep track of the offset of the first and last characters of the segments obtained taking the position identifier of the original document as a reference.

By adapting existing parallel data crawlers to keep track of the processing carried out to transform the original documents to the final segment-aligned parallel corpus, a TMX-like document such as the one described in Section 4.3 could be obtained by replacing the actual sentence pairs obtained after sentence alignment by the mapping to their original locations.

6 Concluding remarks

This paper has laid the foundations and advanced a proposal for a new way to distribute web-crawled sentence-aligned bitext to avoid legal problems associated to distribution. The main idea is to distribute a stand-off annotation of the *wild* web content that makes up the aligned sentences or translation units, which is called a *deferred translation memory crawl* or *deferred training corpus crawl*. It is proposed that a modification of the existing TMX standard for translation memories is used as the basis of the new standoff format. This makes it easy to modify existing crawlers such as Bitextor and ILSP Focused Crawler to produce this kind of output. Although in this paper a tentative syntax to point at the linked segments has been outlined, it could change and evolve as specifications regarding robust anchoring to third-party documents are developed by the recently created W3C Web Annotation Working Group. If the proposal in this paper is adopted, we could be looking at massive repositories of deferred translation memories that could be legally distributed without having to manage the copyright of the original content, and which could be used by end users (professional translators, statistical machine translation practitioners) to recrawl the web and use the selected content under *fair use* provisions.

Acknowledgements

Funding from the European Union Seventh Framework Programme FP7/2007-2013 under grant agreement PIAP-GA-2012-324414 (Abu-MaTran) is acknowledged. The authors would like to thank the anonymous reviewers for their valuable suggestions.

References

Victoria Arranz, Khalid Choukri, Olivier Hamon, Núria Bel, and Prodromos Tsiavos. PANACEA project deliverable 2.4, annex 1: Issues related to data crawling and licensing. `http://cordis.europa.eu/docs/projects/cnect/4/248064/080/deliverables/001-PANACEAD24annex1.pdf`, 2013.

Paul Baker, Andrew Hardie, and Tony McEnery. *A glossary of corpus linguistics*. Edinburgh University Press, 2006.

Steven Bird, Ewan Klein, and Edward Loper. *Natural Language Processing with Python*. O'Reilly, 2009. `http://www.nltk.org/book/ch11.html`.

Lynne Bowker and Des Fisher. Computer-aided translation. *Handbook of Translation Studies*, 1: 60, 2010.

Michael Carl and Andy Way. *Recent advances in example-based machine translation*, volume 21. Springer Science & Business Media, 2003.

Alain Désilets, Benoit Farley, M Stojanovic, and G Patenaude. WeBiText: Building large heterogeneous translation memories from parallel web content. In *Proceedings of Translating and the Computer*, pages 27–28, London, UK, 2008.

Miquel Esplà-Gomis and Mikel L. Forcada. Combining content-based and URL-based heuristics to harvest aligned bitexts from multilingual sites with bitextor. *The Prague Bulletin of Mathematical Linguistics*, 93:77–86, 2010.

Daniel Gomes and Mário J. Silva. Modelling information persistence on the web. In *Proceedings of the 6th International Conference on Web Engineering*, ICWE '06, 2006.

Brian Harris. Bi-text, a new concept in translation theory. *Language Monthly*, 54:8–10, 1988.

Sebastian Hellmann, Jens Lehmann, and Sören Auer. Linked-data aware URI schemes for referencing text fragments. In *Proceedings of the 18th International Conference on Knowledge Engineering and Knowledge Management*, pages 175–184, Galway City, Ireland, 2012.

Pierre Isabelle, Marc Dymetman, George Foster, Jean-Marc Jutras, Elliott Macklovitch, François Perrault, Xiaobo Ren, and Michel Simard. Translation analysis and translation automation. In *Proceedings of the 1993 conference of the Centre for Advanced Studies on Collaborative research: distributed computing-Volume 2*, pages 1133–1147. IBM Press, 1993.

Philipp Koehn. Europarl: A Parallel Corpus for Statistical Machine Translation. In *Proceedings of the 10th Machine Translation Summit*, pages 79–86, Phuket, Thailand, 2005.

Philipp Koehn. *Statistical machine translation*. Cambridge University Press, 2009.

Steve Lawrence, David M. Pennock, Gary William Flake, Robert Krovetz, Frans M. Coetzee, Eric Glover, Finn Årup Nielsen, Andries Kruger, and C. Lee Giles. Persistence of web references in scientific research. *Computer*, 34(2):26–31, 2001.

J. Lin and M. Efron. Overview of the TREC-2013 Microblog Track. In *Proceedings of the Twenty-Second Text REtrieval Conference (TREC 2013)*, 2013.

Xiaoyi Ma and Mark Liberman. Bits: A method for bilingual text search over the web. In *Machine Translation Summit VII*, pages 538–542, Singapore, Singapore, 1999.

Nikos Mastropavlos and Vassilis Papavassiliou. Automatic acquisition of bilingual language resources. In *Proceedings of the 10th International Conference of Greek Linguistics*, 2011.

Atsuyuki Morishima, Akiyoshi Nakamizo, Toshinari Iida, Shigeo Sugimoto, and Hiroyuki Kitagawa. Bringing your dead links back to life: A comprehensive approach and lessons learned. In *Proceedings of the 20th ACM Conference on Hypertext and Hypermedia*, 2009.

Seung-Taek Park, David M. Pennock, C. Lee Giles, and Robert Krovetz. Analysis of lexical signatures for improving information persistence on the world wide web. *ACM Trans. Inf. Syst.*, 22(4):540–572, 2004.

Pavel Pecina, Antonio Toral, Vassilis Papavassiliou, Prokopis Prokopidis, Josef Van Genabith, and RIC Athena. Domain adaptation of statistical machine translation using web-crawled resources: a case study. In *Proceedings of the 16th Annual Conference of the European Association for Machine Translation*, pages 145–152, 2012.

Philip Resnik and Noah A. Smith. The Web as a parallel corpus. *Computational Linguistics*, 29 (3):349–380, 2003.

Michel Simard, George F. Foster, and François Perrault. Transsearch: A bilingual concordance tool. *Centre d'innovation en technologies de l'information, Laval, Canada*, 1993.

R. Steinberger, B. Pouliquen, A. Widiger, C. Ignat, T. Erjavec, and D. Tufiş. The JRC-Acquis: A multilingual aligned parallel corpus with 20+ languages. In *Proceedings of the 5th International Conference on Language Resources and Evaluation*, pages 2142–2147, Genoa, Italy, 2006.

Ralf Steinberger, Andreas Eisele, Szymon Klocek, Spyridon Pilos, and Patrick Schlüter. DGT-TM: A freely available translation memory in 22 languages. In *Proceedings of the 8th International Conference on Language Resources and Evaluation (LREC'2012)*, 2012.

Jörg Tiedemann. Parallel data, tools and interfaces in OPUS. In *LREC*, pages 2214–2218, 2012.

Prodromos Tsiavos, Stelios Piperidis, Maria Gavrilidou, Penny Labropoulou, and Tasos Patrikakos. Qtlaunchpad public deliverable d4.5.1: Legal framework. `http://www.qt21.eu/launchpad/system/files/deliverables/QTLP-Deliverable-4_5_1_0.pdf`, 2014.

Received May 2, 2016 , accepted May 9, 2016

Baltic J. Modern Computing, Vol. 4 (2016), No. 2, pp. 165–177

Combining Translation Memories and Syntax-Based SMT

Experiments with Real Industrial Data

Liangyou LI[1], Carla PARRA ESCARTÍN[2], Qun LIU[1]

[1] ADAPT Centre, School of Computing, Dublin City University, Ireland
[2] Hermes Traducciones, Madrid, Spain

{liangyouli,qliu}@computing.dcu.ie
carla.parra@hermestrans.com

Abstract. One major drawback of using Translation Memories (TMs) in phrase-based Machine Translation (MT) is that only continuous phrases are considered. In contrast, syntax-based MT allows phrasal discontinuity by learning translation rules containing non-terminals. In this paper, we combine a TM with syntax-based MT via sparse features. These features are extracted during decoding based on translation rules and their corresponding patterns in the TM. We have tested this approach by carrying out experiments on real English–Spanish industrial data. Our results show that these TM features significantly improve syntax-based MT. Our final system yields improvements of up to +3.1 BLEU, +1.6 METEOR, and -2.6 TER when compared with a state-of-the-art phrase-based MT system.

Keywords: machine translation, translation memory, syntax-based SMT

1 Introduction

A Translation Memory (TM) is a database which stores legacy translations. Translators use them in their work because TMs allow them to increase their productivity by retrieving past translations and help them to enhance terminology and style cohesion across projects. Given an input sentence, a TM provides the most similar source sentence in the database together with its target translation as the reference for post-editing. If the input sentence was already translated in the past, the translator does not necessarily post-edit it. In the case of similar sentences (called "fuzzy matches"), the Computer Assisted Translation tool highlights the differences between the input sentence and the one stored in the TM to enhance the post-editing task. Different coloring schemes are used to highlight changes and additions to the source text in the TM to help the translator spot quicker the post-edits needed. As TMs can help produce high quality and consistent translations for repetitive materials, they are believed to be useful for Statistical Machine Translation (SMT).

The combination of TM and SMT (henceforth referred as "TM combination") has been explored in many ways and it has shown to improve translation quality. Unlike the well-known pipeline approaches (Koehn and Senellart, 2010; Ma et al., 2011), which use a TM combination at sentence-level, run-time TM combination (namely, combining the TM and SMT during decoding) can make a better use of the matched sub-sentences (Wang et al., 2013; Li et al., 2014a). Such run-time combination has been explored on Phrase-Based (PB) MT (Koehn et al., 2003). However, PBMT systems making use of TMs only take into consideration continuous segments and thus generalizations such as the translation of the English *call. . . off* into the Spanish *cancelar* cannot be learned.

In this paper, we explore the possibility of using a run-time TM combination on syntax-based MT. Syntax-based MT learns translation rules which can be easily extrapolated to new sentences by allowing non-terminals. In our approach, for each applied translation rule during decoding, we identify a corresponding pattern in the TM and then extract sparse features which are subsequently added to our system.

In our experiments, the TM combination is done on the hierarchical phrase-based (HPB) model (Chiang, 2005) and the dependency-to-string (D2S) model (Xie et al., 2011; Li et al., 2014b). The experimental results on real English–Spanish data[3] show that syntax-based models produce significantly better translations than phrase-based models. After adding the TM features, the syntax-based models are further significantly improved.

2 TMs in SMT

Combining TMs and SMT together has been explored in different ways in recent years. He et al. (2010a) presented a recommendation system which used a Support Vector Machine (Cortes and Vapnik, 1995) binary classifier to select a translation from the outputs of a TM and an SMT system. He et al. (2010b) extended this work by re-ranking the N-best list of SMT and TM outputs. Koehn and Senellart (2010) and Ma et al. (2011) used TMs in a pipeline manner. Firstly, they identified the matched part from the best match in the TM and merged their translation with the input. Then, they forced their phrase-based SMT system to translate the unmatched part of the input sentence. One major drawback of these methods is that they do not distinguish whether a match is good or not at phrase-level.

Wang et al. (2013) proposed an improved method by using TM information on phrases during decoding. This method extracts features from the TM and then uses pre-trained generative models to estimate one or more probabilities added to phrase-based systems. However, their work requires a rather complex process to obtain training instances for these pre-trained models. Li et al. (2014a) simplified this method by extracting sparse features and directly adding them to systems. In experiments, this simplified method was comparable to the one in Wang et al. (2013). However, in both works, features are designed for phrase-based models.

---

[3] Our data belongs to a translation company and is further described in Section 5.1.

3 Syntax-Based SMT

Typically, syntax-based decoders are based on the CYK algorithm (Kasami, 1965; Younger, 1967; Cocke and Schwartz, 1970). It searches for the best derivation $d^* = r_1 r_2 \cdots r_N$ among all possible derivations D, as in Equation (1),

$$d^* = \operatorname*{argmax}_{d \in D} P(d) \tag{1}$$

where r_i are the translation rules. Translations are carried out bottom-up. For each span of an input sentence, the decoder finds rules to translate it. The translation of a large span can be obtained by combining translations from its sub-spans using the syntactic rules containing non-terminals.

In this paper, we use two syntax-based models for our experiments. One is the HPB model (Chiang, 2005) which is based on formal syntax. The other one is the D2S model (Xie et al., 2011; Li et al., 2014b) which is based on dependency structures generated by the Stanford parser[4].

3.1 Hierarchical Phrase-Based Translation

A hierarchical phrase is an extension of a phrase by allowing gaps where other hierarchical phrases are nested. The HPB model is formulated by a synchronous context free grammar (SCFG) where gaps are represented by a generic non-terminal symbol X. Rules in the HPB are in the following form:

$$X \to \langle \gamma, \alpha, \sim \rangle,$$

where γ is a string over source terminal symbols and non-terminals, α is a string over target terminal symbols and non-terminals, and $\sim$ is a one-to-one mapping between non-terminals in γ and α. An example of a rule is as follows:

$$X \to \langle \text{Bolivia holds } X_1, \text{Bolivia sostiene } X_1 \rangle,$$

where the index on each non-terminal indicates the mappings. These rules can be automatically learned from parallel corpora based on word alignments.

3.2 Dependency-to-String Translation

In the D2S model, there are two kinds of rules. One is the head rule which specifies the translation of a source word. For example:

$$\text{holds} \to \text{sostiene}$$

The other one is the head-dependent (HD) rule which consists of three parts: the HD fragment[5] s of the source side, a target string t and a one-to-one mapping ϕ from variables in s to variables in t, as in:

$$s = \text{(\underline{Bolivia}) holds } (x_1\text{:selection})$$
$$t = \text{Bolivia sostiene } x_1$$
$$\phi = \{x_1\text{:selection} \to x_1\}$$

---

[4] `http://nlp.stanford.edu/software/lex-parser.shtml`
[5] An HD fragment is composed of a head node and all of its dependents.

Algorithm 1: Procedure for extracting a translation pattern from a TM instance.

Data: A rule r for an input sentence I, a TM instance (S, T, A)
Result: A translation pattern R for r

1 let $[i, j]$ denote the span covered by r;
2 $\langle [i_k, j_k] \rangle, k = 1 \cdots n$ are n subspans covered by non-terminals in r;
3 **for** *each span* $[i_k, j_k]$ **do**
4   find a corresponding TM source span $[i_k^s, j_k^s]$, according to string edits;
5   find a TM target span $[i_k^t, j_k^t]$, according to word alignment A;
6 **end**
7 find corresponding TM source and target spans $[i^s, j^s]$ and $[i^t, j^t]$ for $[i, j]$;
8 s = words in span $[i^s, j^s]$ and replacing phrases covered by $\langle [i_k^s, j_k^s] \rangle$ with non-terminals;
9 t = words in span $[i^t, j^t]$ and replacing phrases covered by $\langle [i_k^t, j_k^t] \rangle$ with non-terminals;
10 $R = \langle s, t, a \rangle$, a indicates mappings between non-terminals in s and t;

---

where the underlined element denotes the leaf node. Variables in the Dep2Str model are constrained either by words (like x_1:selection) or Part-of-Speech tags (like x_1:NN).

4   TM Combination Method

Inspired by Li et al. (2014a), who directly add sparse features to the log-linear framework of SMT (Och and Ney, 2002) to combine a TM with the PB model, in this paper we extract sparse features for each applied rule during decoding and directly add them to our syntax-based SMT systems. These features can be jointly trained with other features to maximize translation quality measured by BLEU (Papineni et al., 2002).

Given an input sentence in our test set, our approach starts from retrieving the most similar sentence from a TM.[6] The similarity is measured by the so-called fuzzy match score. Concretely, we use the word-based string-edit distance in Equation (2) (Koehn and Senellart, 2010) to compute the fuzzy match score between the input sentence and the TM instance.

$$F = 1 - \frac{\text{edit\_distance}(input, tm\_source)}{\max(|\ input\ |, |\ tm\_source\ |)} \tag{2}$$

During the calculation of the fuzzy match score, we also obtain a sequence of operations, including insertion, match, substitution and deletion, which are useful for finding the TM correspondence of an input phrase.

4.1   Recognizing Patterns in TM

Instead of translating a unique continuous phrase, the rules in our system can contain non-terminals which cover previously translated phrases. Before extracting any features for a rule, we first identify its corresponding patterns in the TM. The identification procedure is illustrated in Algorithm 1.

---

[6] In our experiments, we use the training corpus of our SMT experiments as a TM.

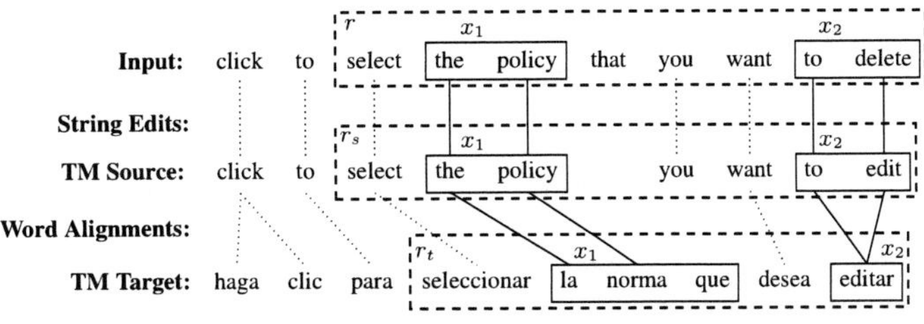

Rule: select x_1 that you want to x_2 → seleccionar x_1 que desea x_2

TM Pattern: select x_1 you want to x_2 → seleccionar x_1 desea x_2

Fig. 1. An illustration of extracting translation patterns for a rule r. Phrases in solid rectangles are covered by non-terminals (x_i). Phrases in dashed rectangles are covered by translation rules or patterns.

For an input sentence I, we first retrieve an instance $\langle S, T, A \rangle$ from the TM, where S denotes the TM source segment, T is the TM target segment, and A indicates the word alignment between S and T. During decoding, rules are applied to translate I. Each rule r covers a continuous span $[i, j]$ of I and each non-terminal in r covers a sub-span of $[i, j]$ (lines 1–2 in Algorithm 1). For the span and its sub-spans, we first find their source correspondence in S according to the string edits between I and S and then the target correspondence in T according to the word alignment A (lines 3–7). Finally, we obtain a translation pattern $R = \langle s, t, a \rangle$ by replacing phrases covered by sub-spans with non-terminals (lines 8–10). Given a translation rule, Figure 1 illustrates how to identify a corresponding pattern in the TM.

Note that special cases might exist because of various situations in string edits and word alignments. Taking Figure 1 as an example, we cannot find a correspondence in the TM source for the input word *that*. In addition, the target t in extracted patterns can be extended by unaligned words, so in such case we might have multiple targets. These cases have been taken into consideration when extracting features (cf. Section 4.2).

4.2 Extracting Features

The features we use are similar to the ones in Li et al. (2014a) but modified to handle non-terminals in rules. Let $r = \langle \gamma, \alpha \rangle$ denote a rule we are using to translate an input sentence I. A retrieved TM instance for I is $\langle S, T, A \rangle$. The rule covers an input phrase s, which corresponds to TM segments $\langle s^r, t^r = (t_1^r \cdots t_m^r) \rangle$. The following features are the same used by Li et al. (2014a):

- Feature $\mathbf{Z}_x$ ($x = 0 \cdots 10$) indicates the similarity between I and S. Each Z_x corresponds to a fuzzy match score range. For example, given a score $F(I, S) = 0.818$ which goes into the range [0.8,0.9), we obtain the feature Z_8.
- Feature $\mathbf{SEP}_x$ ($x = Y$ or N) is the indicator of whether s is a punctuation mark at the end of the input sentence I.

- Feature $\mathbf{NLN}_{xy}$ ($x = 0, 1, 2$ and $y = 0, 1, 2$ and $y < x$) models the context of s^r and s, where x denotes the number of matched neighbors (left and right words) and y denotes how many of those neighbors are aligned to target words. If s^r is unavailable, we use feature NLN_{non}.
- Feature $\mathbf{CSS}_x$ ($x = S, L, R, B$) describes the status of t^r. If t^r is unavailable, we use feature CSS_{non}. When $m = 1$ (i.e. the size of t^r is 1), $x = S$. $x = L, R, B$ means that t^r is obtained by extending unaligned words only on the left side or the right side or both sides, respectively.
- Feature $\mathbf{LTC}_x$ ($x = O, L, R, B, M$) is the indicator of whether a t_i^r is the longest or not. If t^r is unavailable, we use feature LTC_{non}. $x = O$ means t_i^r is not generated by extending unaligned words. $x = L$ (or R, B) means t_i^r is only extended on its left (or right) side (or both sides) and has the longest left (or right) side (or both sides). $x = M$ means t_i^r is extended but not the longest one.

The assumed extracted translation patterns for r are $\langle \gamma^r, \alpha^r = (\alpha_1^r \cdots \alpha_m^r) \rangle$. We modify the following features and add them to our system:

- Feature $\mathbf{SPL}_x$ measures the length of s, $x = 1 \cdots 7$ and *more*. Unlike PB models, where the phrase length is bounded, in syntax-based models we can use a rule to cover the whole input. So We use *more* to denote $\mid s \mid > 7$.
- Feature $\mathbf{SCM}_x$ ($x = L, H, M$) represents the matching status between γ and γ^r, instead of s and s^r. This notation is used because γ might contain non-terminals, which in turn means that phrases covered by these non-terminals have already been considered. If γ^r is unavailable, we use feature SCM_{non}. Otherwise, L denotes a low similarity, namely $F(\gamma, \gamma^r) < 0.5$. H indicates $F(\gamma, \gamma^r) > 0.5$, and M means $F(\gamma, \gamma^r) = 0.5$.
- Similar to the SCM_x, feature $\mathbf{TCM}_x$ ($x = L, H, M$) is the matching status between α and each α_i^r in α^r. If α^r is unavailable, we use feature TCM_{non}.
- We use the $\mathbf{CPM}_x$ feature to model the reordering information. If γ only contains terminals, the feature is CPM_{nnt}. Otherwise, if α^r is unavailable, we use feature CPM_{non}. Otherwise, α^r and α define two permutations in terms of non-terminals in γ. The two permutations are assumed to be $p = p_1 \cdots p_n$ and $p^r = p_i^r \cdots p_n^r$. We use the Spearman correlation defined in Equation (3) to score the permutations.

$$\rho = 1 - \frac{6 \sum_{i=1}^{n} (p_i - p_i^r)^2}{n(n^2 - 1)} \tag{3}$$

The range of ρ is $[-1, 1]$. We divide the score into 5 groups, each of which indicates a feature: $x = nh$ when $\rho < -0.5$, $x = nl$ when $\rho \in [-0.5, 0)$, $x = 0$ when $\rho = 0$, $x = pl$ when $\rho \in (0, 0.5)$, and $x = ph$ when $\rho \geq 0.5$.

5 Experiments

5.1 Data

With the aim of further testing whether our experiments would be useful in a real commercial setting, we run our experiments on a real industrial data set. Our data belongs to

Table 1. Statistics of English–Spanish (EN–ES) corpus.

	Training	Development	Test
#sentences	577,639	1,959	1,964
#words (EN)	7,632,983	26,451	26,134
#words (ES)	9,049,260	31,170	31,195

a translation company and consists of all segments contained in the TM of one of their clients. The TM comprises all past projects of that client and is duly maintained and curated to ensure its quality. The data belongs to a technical domain and as mentioned earlier, it is used for English→Spanish translation tasks[7].

We deleted all repeated segments from the TM as well as all segments containing HTML tags occurring within the TM segments. While repetitions were deleted to follow the best practices in running SMT experiments, the segments with HTML tags were deleted because we found out that those segments were HTML addresses that did not require a translation and would have added noise to our data. Inline tags were not treated specifically and were maintained in the data. Once our data was cleaned, we randomly split it into *training*, *development* and *test*. Table 1 summarizes the size of our data in terms of number of sentences and running words.

5.2 Settings

In our experiments, we build four baselines. The two phrase-based baselines are: **PB**, the phrase-based model in Moses with default configurations, and **PBLR**, the phrase-based model, adding three lexical reordering models (Galley and Manning, 2008) to improve its reordering ability. The two syntax-based systems are: **HPB**, the hierarchical phrase-based model in Moses with default configurations, and **D2S**, an improved dependency-to-string model which has been implemented in Moses (Li et al., 2014b).[8] We add the TM features in Li et al. (2014a) to phrase-based systems and our TM features to syntax-based systems.

Word alignment is performed by GIZA++ (Och and Ney, 2004) with the heuristic function *grow-diag-final-and*. We use SRILM (Stolcke, 2002) to train a 5-gram language model on the target side of our training corpus with modified Kneser-Ney discounting (Chen and Goodman, 1996). Batch MIRA (Cherry and Foster, 2012) is used to tune weights. BLEU (Papineni et al., 2002), METEOR (Denkowski and Lavie, 2011), and TER (Snover et al., 2006) are used for evaluation.[9]

5.3 Results and Discussion

Table 2 accounts for the results obtained for all our experiments. As may be observed, all our baselines are already pretty high and thus improvements are harder to obtain.

---

[7] Unfortunately, due to confidentiality agreements the data used in these experiments cannot be publicly released.

[8] http://computing.dcu.ie/ liangyouli/dep2str.zip

[9] https://github.com/jhclark/multeval

Table 2. Metric scores for all systems on English–Spanish. Each score is the average score over three MIRA runs (Clark et al., 2011). * means a system is better than PB at $p \leq 0.01$. $^{+}$ indicates a systems is better than PBLR at $p \leq 0.01$. **Bold** figures are significantly better than their no-TM counterparts at $p \leq 0.01$.

Systems	BLEU↑ (%)	METEOR↑ (%)	TER↓ (%)
PB	62.8	79.5	26.5
PBLR	63.5*	79.9*	26.0*
HPB	64.3^{+}	80.3^{+}	25.2^{+}
D2S	65.3^{+}	80.8^{+}	24.5^{+}
PB+TM	63.5*	79.9*	26.0*
PBLR+TM	64.2^{+}	80.3^{+}	25.5^{+}
HPB+TM	**65.9**	**81.0**	**24.3**
D2S+TM	**65.9**	**81.1**	**23.9**

This is not surprising, as we are working with an in-domain data set which is used for real translation tasks. The lexical reordering models significantly improve the PB system (+0.7 BLEU, +0.4 METEOR, and -0.5 TER). After incorporating the TM Combination approach (Li et al., 2014a), both systems (PB and PBLR) further produce significantly better translations. Both syntax-based systems (HPB and D2S) achieve significantly better results than phrase-based systems (up to +2.5 BLEU, +1.3 METEOR and -2.0 TER when comparing the PB system against the D2S system). Moreover, our TM features, when added to the HPB and D2S models, consistently improve both syntax-based baselines. In fact, these two systems (our final ones), achieve the best scores across all evaluation metrics (up to +3.1 BLEU, +1.6 METEOR, and -2.6). Example 1 shows how our D2S+TM and HPB+TM systems achieve better translations:

Example 1.

> *Source*: button which opens the password entry window .
> *Ref*: al pulsar este botón se abrirá la ventana de introducción de la contraseña .
> *TM Source*: button which opens the container settings window .
> *TM Target*: al pulsar este botón se abrirá la ventana configuración del repositorio .
> *TM Score*: 0.75
> *PBLR*: botón que abre la ventana de introducción de la contraseña .
> *HPB*: botón que abre la ventana de introducción de la contraseña .
> *D2S*: botón que abre la ventana de introducción de la contraseña .
> *PBLR+TM*: botón que abre la ventana de introducción de la contraseña .
> *HPB+TM*: al pulsar este botón se abrirá la ventana de introducción de la contraseña .
> *D2S+TM*: al pulsar este botón se abrirá la ventana de introducción de la contraseña .

When using the TM Combination, both syntax-based models achieve a BLEU score of 1, while all other systems have a BLEU score of 0.6989. It shall be noted that both translations could actually be possible, but in our data there seems to be a stylistic preference: *se abrirá*, is preferred over *que abre*, which would be a more literal but still correct translation of the English "which opens". The TM Combination method allows our systems to learn the preferred translation in this case and match the reference. We have also found cases in which an error in the syntactic analysis causes our system to

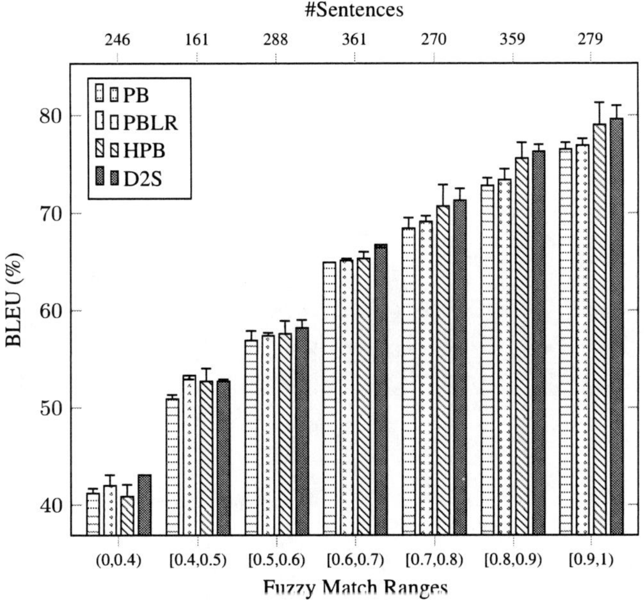

Fig. 2. BLEU scores evaluated on sentences grouped by fuzzy match scores. The symbol − on each bar indicates the BLEU scores of the systems after incorporating the TM approach.

fail (e.g. in the case of English nominal compounds), as well as cases in which our system produces a better translation than the reference.[10]

Since the fuzzy match score, as defined in Equation (2), is used to select a TM instance for an input sentence and thus is an important factor for combining the different SMT models and TM features, it is interesting to know the impact it has on the translation quality of the various systems we trained. Figure 2 shows BLEU scores of all systems evaluated on sentences grouped by fuzzy match scores. We first find that BLEU scores increase as fuzzy scores become higher. This is reasonable, since a higher fuzzy score means that we can find a similar sentence in the training data. The TM approach results in an improvement on almost all ranges. Such improvement is more consistent in the higher fuzzy ranges, namely [0.7,1). This also suggests that although TM instances with lower fuzzy scores could be useful, those with higher fuzzy scores are more reliable.

Another interesting finding is that D2S is consistently better than HPB. The main reason could be that rules in D2S are guided by linguistic annotations. In comparison with D2S, however, HPB benefits more when combined with the TM approach. In fact, when compared with their respective baselines (the same model without incorporating the TM approach), the HPB model is the one which experiences the highest improve-

---

[10] A qualitative analysis of our test set is being done to determine the real impact of our approach.

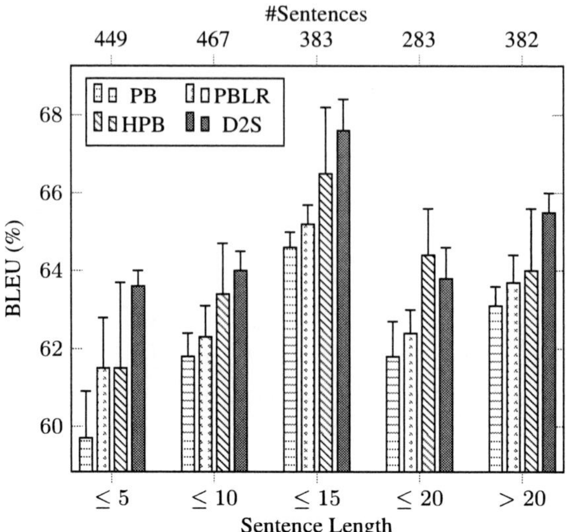

Fig. 3. BLEU scores evaluated on sentences grouped by sentence length. The symbol − on each bar indicates the BLEU scores of the systems after incorporating the TM approach.

ment (+1.6 BLEU, +0.7 METEOR, and -0.9 TER). This finding suggests that the TM approach could enhance the rule selection when linguistic annotations are unavailable, and that the TM approach achieves its greatest potential when combined with syntax-based models.

Finally, since syntax-based models learn translation rules which have a better generalization and reordering ability, we grouped sentences according to their length and evaluated our different systems by their respective sentence-length groups. The results for all systems are shown in Figure 3. As may be observed, the syntax-based systems, especially D2S, outperform the phrase-based models in all length ranges. Moreover, the TM combination consistently improves the results for all systems.

Bearing in mind that the ultimate goal would be to integrate an SMT system in a real commercial setting for MT Post-Editing tasks (MTPE), the results obtained suggest that the best option would be to use the D2S+TM system. Parra Escartín and Arcedillo (2015) investigated the productivity thresholds for MTPE tasks running an experiment with 10 professional translators in a real commercial setting. They found out that for English→Spanish MTPE tasks the productivity gain thresholds were of 45–50 BLEU and 25–30 TER. Given the results obtained by our systems, it seems that even the state-of-the-art baseline would already allow for a faster post-editing.

6   Conclusion

In this paper, we have explored how TM approaches can be used to enhance syntax-based SMT systems. To test our approach, we used real data from a translation company and trained, tuned and tested different SMT systems on such data. The results of our experiments are very promising, particularly because improvements were achieved over already high baseline systems. The combination of the TM approach with other existing SMT systems yielded better overall scores (up to +3.1 BLEU, +1.6 METEOR, and −2.6 TER when compared with a state-of-the-art phrase-based MT system) in all MT evaluation metrics and for all sentence lengths.

Another interesting finding was that better BLEU scores seem to be obtained for the highest fuzzy match bands. In future research, we plan to run experiments of our TM Combination method taking only into consideration the higher fuzzies ([0.7,1)) to test whether better results are obtained and a threshold shall be established. We would also like to test our approach on public corpora and use a different data set from the TM to train SMT systems. It would be also interesting to know how effective each sparse feature is.

Acknowledgements

This research has received funding from the People Programme (Marie Curie Actions) of the European Union's Framework Programme (FP7/2007-2013) under REA grant agreement n° 317471. The ADAPT Centre for Digital Content Technology is funded under the SFI Research Centres Programme (Grant 13/RC/2106) and is co funded under the European Regional Development Fund. We also thank the anonymous reviewers for their insightful comments and suggestions.

References

Chen, S. F., Goodman, J. (1996). An Empirical Study of Smoothing Techniques for Language Modeling. *Proceedings of the 34th Annual Meeting on Association for Computational Linguistics*, Santa Cruz, California, 310–318.

Cherry, C., Foster, G. (2012). Batch Tuning Strategies for Statistical Machine Translation. *Proceedings of the 2012 Conference of the North American Chapter of the Association for Computational Linguistics: Human Language Technologies*, Montreal, Canada, 427–436.

Chiang, D. (2005). A Hierarchical Phrase-based Model for Statistical Machine Translation. *Proceedings of the 43rd Annual Meeting on Association for Computational Linguistics*, Ann Arbor, Michigan, 263–270.

Clark, J. H., Dyer, C., Lavie, A., Smith, N. A. (2011). Better Hypothesis Testing for Statistical Machine Translation: Controlling for Optimizer Instability. *Proceedings of the 49th Annual Meeting of the Association for Computational Linguistics: Human Language Technologies: Short Papers - Volume 2*, Portland, Oregon, 176–181.

Cocke, J., Schwartz, J. T. (1970). Programming Languages and Their Compilers: Preliminary Notes. Technical report, Courant Institute of Mathematical Sciences, New York University, New York, NY.

Cortes, C., Vapnik, V. (1995). Support-Vector Networks. *Machine Learning*, 20(3):273–297.

Denkowski, M., Lavie, A. (2011). Meteor 1.3: Automatic Metric for Reliable Optimization and Evaluation of Machine Translation Systems. *Proceedings of the Sixth Workshop on Statistical Machine Translation*, Edinburgh, Scotland, 85–91.

Galley, M., Manning, C. D. (2008). A Simple and Effective Hierarchical Phrase Reordering Model. *Proceedings of the Conference on Empirical Methods in Natural Language Processing*, Honolulu, Hawaii, 848–856.

He, Y., Ma, Y., van Genabith, J., Way, A. (2010a). Bridging SMT and TM with Translation Recommendation. *Proceedings of the 48th Annual Meeting of the Association for Computational Linguistics*, Uppsala, Sweden, 622–630.

He, Y., Ma, Y., Way, A., Van Genabith, J. (2010b). Integrating N-best SMT Outputs into a TM System. *Proceedings of the 23rd International Conference on Computational Linguistics: Posters*, Beijing, China, 374–382.

Kasami, T. (1965). An Efficient Recognition and Syntax-Analysis Algorithm for Context-Free Languages. Technical report, Air Force Cambridge Research Lab, Bedford, MA.

Koehn, P., Hoang, H., Birch, A., Callison-Burch, C., Federico, M., Bertoldi, N., Cowan, B., Shen, W., Moran, C., Zens, R., Dyer, C., Bojar, O., Constantin, A., Herbst, E. (2007). Moses: Open Source Toolkit for Statistical Machine Translation. *Proceedings of the 45th Annual Meeting of the ACL on Interactive Poster and Demonstration Sessions*, Prague, Czech Republic, 177–180.

Koehn, P., Och, F. J., Marcu, D. (2003). Statistical Phrase-based Translation. *Proceedings of the 2003 Conference of the North American Chapter of the Association for Computational Linguistics on Human Language Technology - Volume 1*, Edmonton, Canada, 48–54.

Koehn, P., Senellart, J. (2010). Convergence of Translation Memory and Statistical Machine Translation. *Proceedings of AMTA Workshop on MT Research and the Translation Industry*, Denver, Colorado, USA, 21–31.

Li, L., Way, A., Liu, Q. (2014a). A Discriminative Framework of Integrating Translation Memory Features into SMT. *Proceedings of the 11th Conference of the Association for Machine Translation in the Americas, Vol. 1: MT Researchers Track*, Vancouver, BC, Canada, 249–260.

Li, L., Xie, J., Way, A., Liu, Q. (2014b). Transformation and Decomposition for Efficiently Implementing and Improving Dependency-to-String Model In Moses. *Proceedings of SSST-8, Eighth Workshop on Syntax, Semantics and Structure in Statistical Translation*.

Ma, Y., He, Y., Way, A., van Genabith, J. (2011). Consistent Translation using Discriminative Learning - A Translation Memory-Inspired Approach. *Proceedings of the 49th Annual Meeting of the Association for Computational Linguistics: Human Language Technologies*, Portland, Oregon, USA, 1239–1248.

Och, F. J., Ney, H. (2002). Discriminative Training and Maximum Entropy Models for Statistical Machine Translation. *Proceedings of the 40th Annual Meeting on Association for Computational Linguistics*, Philadelphia, Pennsylvania, 295–302.

Och, F. J., Ney, H. (2004). The Alignment Template Approach to Statistical Machine Translation. *Compututational Linguistics*, 30(4):417–449.

Papineni, K., Roukos, S., Ward, T., Zhu, W.-J. (2002). BLEU: A Method for Automatic Evaluation of Machine Translation. *Proceedings of the 40th Annual Meeting on Association for Computational Linguistics*, Philadelphia, Pennsylvania, 311–318.

Parra Escartín, C., Arcedillo, M. (2015). Living on the edge: productivity gain thresholds in machine translation evaluation metrics. *Proceedings of the Fourth Workshop on Post-editing Technology and Practice*, Miami, Florida, 46–56.

Snover, M., Dorr, B., Schwartz, R., Micciulla, L., Makhoul, J. (2006). A Study of Translation Edit Rate with Targeted Human Annotation. *Proceedings of Association for Machine Translation in the Americas*, Cambridge, Massachusetts, USA, 223–231.

Stolcke, A. (2002). SRILM-an Extensible Language Modeling Toolkit. *Proceedings of the 7th International Conference on Spoken Language Processing*, Denver, Colorado, USA, 257–286.

Wang, K., Zong, C., Su, K.-Y. (2013). Integrating Translation Memory into Phrase-Based Machine Translation during Decoding. *Proceedings of the 51st Annual Meeting of the Association for Computational Linguistics (Volume 1: Long Papers)*, Sofia, Bulgaria, 11–21.

Xie, J., Mi, H., Liu, Q. (2011). A Novel Dependency-to-string Model for Statistical Machine Translation. In *Proceedings of the Conference on Empirical Methods in Natural Language Processing*, Edinburgh, United Kingdom, 216–226.

Younger, D. H. (1967). Recognition and Parsing of Context-Free Languages in Time n^3. *Information and Control*, 10(2):189–208.

Received May 2, 2016 , accepted May 9, 2016

Baltic J. Modern Computing, Vol. 4 (2016), No. 2, pp. 178–189

The Trouble with Machine Translation Coherence

Karin SIM SMITH[§], Wilker AZIZ[†], Lucia SPECIA[§]

§Department of Computer Science, University of Sheffield, UK
†Institute for Logic, Language and Computation
University of Amsterdam, The Netherlands

{kmsimsmith1,l.specia}@sheffield.ac.uk , w.aziz@uva.nl

Abstract. This paper introduces the problem of measuring coherence in Machine Translation. Previously, local coherence has been assessed in a monolingual context using essentially coherent texts. These are then artificially shuffled to create an incoherent one. We investigate existing models for the task of measuring the coherence of machine translation output. This is a much more challenging case where coherent source documents are machine translated into a target language and the task is to distinguish them from their human translated counterparts. We benchmark state-of-the-art coherence models, and propose a new model which explores syntax following a more principled method to learn the syntactic patterns. This extension outperforms existing ones in the monolingual shuffling task on news data, and performs well in our new, more challenging task. Additionally, we show that breaches in coherence in the translation task are much more difficult to capture by any model.

Keywords: Machine Translation, Discourse, Coherence Modelling

1   Introduction

A coherent discourse is said to be one that has meaningful connections between its utterances (Jurafsky and Martin, 2009). The task of automatically evaluating text coherence has been addressed within applications such as text summarisation and ordering (Lapata, 2005; Barzilay and Lapata, 2008), where shuffled sentences or inadequate summaries can lead to less coherent documents. Coherence has then been measured with entity grids, discourse relations and syntax patterns, with experiments run on the original and the artificially modified texts to distinguish coherent from incoherent texts.

We introduce the more challenging problem of evaluating the coherence of documents generated by Machine Translation (MT) systems. This is a very different scenario. Firstly, it is more subtle as the sudden breaks in transitions or shifts of focus which result from shuffling in the traditional monolingual test scenario are absent, as sentences are translated in their original (source) order. Secondly, the machine translated output may contain other textual issues, such as ungrammatical fragments, which can affect the application of such models in various ways, making it harder to pinpoint coherence-related problems. Finally, judgements on the coherence of the translations may be dependent on the source text. Nevertheless, measuring coherence in MT is important: given the way translations are generated by standard MT systems, on a sentence-by-sentence basis, several phenomena spanning sentence boundaries can lead to incoherent document translations, such as incorrect co-referencing, inadequate discourse markers, and lack of lexical cohesion, as established by previous corpus analyses (Sim Smith et al., 2015).

We apply three existing coherence models to original, shuffled and machine translated texts in an attempt to evaluate their ability to discriminate between coherent and incoherent documents: an entity-grid model (Barzilay and Lapata, 2008), an entity graph similarity metric (Guinaudeau and Strube, 2013), and a model based on syntactic patterns (Louis and Nenkova, 2012). In addition, we propose a fully generative extension of the syntax-based coherence model. We illustrate the difference between assessing the output from MT systems and assessing the coherence of shuffled texts in a highly consistent, structured corpus.

The remainder of this paper, is organised as follows: in Section 2 we review related work on coherence and cohesion in the context of MT. Section 3 covers the background of the coherence models used in this paper. Experiments and results are discussed in Section 4.

2   Related Work

There has been recent work in the area of lexical cohesion in MT (Wong and Kit, 2012); Xiong et al., 2013a; Xiong et al., 2013b; Tiedemann, 2010; Hardmeier, 2012; Carpuat and Simard, 2012), as a sub-category of coherence, looking at the linguistic elements which hold a text together. However, there seems to be little work in the wider area of coherence as a whole. Coherence is indeed a more complex discourse element to define in the first place. While it does include cohesion, it also describes how a text becomes semantically meaningful overall, and how easy it is for the reader to follow.

Louwerse (2005) defines "cohesion as continuity in word and sentence structure, and coherence as continuity in meaning and context". While lexical cohesion can be detected and addressed to some extent, the semantics, meaning and contextual indicators necessary for coherence assessment are much more difficult to capture, even though judging coherence is an intuitive process for a human reader. Coherence is undeniably a complex cognitive process, which is however guided by elements of discourse that we believe can be modelled automatically to some extent.

Most previous computational models for assessing coherence have focused on entity transitions, syntactic patterns and discourse relations. The most popular models are detailed in Section 3. In what follows we describe these models, and our work to apply these models to MT. Lin et al. (2011) evaluate the coherence of texts from discourse role transitions in a grid-based model, on the basis that there is a preferential, canonical, ordering of discourse relations that leads to coherent texts. Burstein et al. (2010) use the entity-grid for student essay evaluation, which is a scenario closer to ours. They used a range of additional features specifically targeting grammar and style. These proved useful for discriminating good from bad quality essays, but it is unclear how much of the problem with low quality essays was due to coherence issues. Their features are not publicly available for us to assess this.

Somasundaran et al. (2014) consider how lexical chains affect discourse coherence. They use lexical chaining features such as length, density, and link strength to detect textual continuity, elaboration, lexical variety and organisation, all vital aspects of coherent texts. They claim that the interaction between lexical chains and discourse cues can also show whether cohesive devices are organised in a coherent fashion.

Recently, Li and Hovy (2014) developed a coherence model based on distributed sentence representation. They used recurrent and recursive neural networks to perform ordering and readability tasks. They leverage semantic representations to establish coherent orderings, using original texts as positive examples and shuffled versions as negative ones for optimising the neural networks.

Li et al. (2015) train a hierarchical Long-Short Term Memory (LSTM) to explore neural Natural Language Generation, and assess whether local semantic and syntactic coherence can be represented at a higher level, namely paragraphs. In their model, different LSTM layers represents word embeddings, sentences, and paragraphs. They are then able to regenerate the text to a degree that indicates neural networks are able to capture certain elements of coherence.

Lin and Li (2015) use a hierarchical recurrent neural network language model (RNNLM) to combine a word-level model with a sentence-level model for document modeling. They claim that their model captures both intra- and inter-sentential sequences. They assess their model on an MT reranking task, progressively reranking consecutive sentences. In the MT domain, Xiong et al. (2013) attempt to improve lexical coherence with a topic-based model. They extract a coherence chain for the source sentence, and project it onto the target sentence to try and make lexical choices taken during decoding more coherent. They report very marginal improvement with respect to a baseline system in terms of automatic evaluation. This could indicate that current evaluation metrics are limited in their ability to account for improvements related to discourse. Gong et al. (2015) attempt to integrate their lexical chain and topic-based metrics into traditional BLEU and METEOR scores, showing greater correlation with human judgements on MT output.

While the task of automatically evaluating text coherence has been addressed previously within applications such as multi-document text summarisation or in terms of optimal ordering within shuffled texts, our aim is to further investigate these components in an MT context without the use of a reference translation. We ultimately expect to be able to bias the translation process to ensure coherence in MT.

3   Coherence Models

Here we describe some of the most popular coherence models, all of which we reimplement and test in our experiments, as well as our improvement over a syntax-based model (Section 3.4).

3.1 Entity-grid approach

The entity-based approach (Lapata, 2005; Barzilay and Lapata, 2008), in particular the Centering Theory (Grosz et al., 1995) it is based on, derives from the idea that entities in a coherent text are distributed in a certain manner. This theory states that coherent texts are characterised by salient entities in strong grammatical roles, such as subject or object. The focus of the entity-based approach uses this knowledge, via patterns in terms of prominent syntactic constructions, to distinguish coherent from non-coherent texts. Entity grids are constructed by identifying the discourse entities in the documents under consideration and constructing a 2D grid for each document, whereby each column corresponds to the entity, i.e. noun being tracked, and each row represents a particular sentence in the document.

An **entity transition** is defined as a consecutive occurrence of an entity with a given syntactic role, namely, subject (S), object (O), or other (X). Absences of entities in sentences, or nulls, are recorded with a dash. Transitions are observed by examining the grid vertically for each entity. The assumption is that incoherent texts have more breaks in the entity transitions, and thus lower scores.

Lapata (2005) introduces a generative model of document coherence based on entity transitions. Equation 1 shows this formulation, where m is the number of entities, n is the number of sentences in a document D, and $r_{s,e}$ is the role taken by entity e in sentence s. Observe that the model makes a Markov assumption, under which an entity's role is independent of all but its h preceding roles.

$$p(D) = \frac{1}{m \cdot n} \prod_{e=1}^{m} \prod_{s=1}^{n} p(r_{s,e} | r_{(s-h),e} \cdots r_{(s-1),e}) \tag{1}$$

Our objective with this model, as with all others in this paper, is to assess whether the coherence model allows us to discriminate between Human Translation (HT) and MT.

For our experiments, a POS tagger[1] is used to identify nouns and subsequently a parser[2] is used to establish the grammatical role of each of these nouns. The original model presumes that grids of coherent texts have a few dense columns and many sparse ones, and that entities occurring in the dense columns are more often be subjects or objects. It assumes that these characteristics are less common in texts exhibiting lower coherence (Lapata, 2005). In our experiments, the MT displays no more sparse columns than the reference counterpart. It would seem that given how preeminent the focused nouns are, these are captured in the MT output. There are, however, differences in transition patterns, in that some patterns are more common in the MT than the HT, such as 'OO', or other patterns with strong object positions. This seems to indicate a more simplistic style by MT systems. Quantitative results for the experiments with the entity-grid model are given in Section 4.

---

[1] http://nlp.stanford.edu/software/tagger.shtml
[2] http://nlp.stanford.edu/software/lex-parser.shtml

3.2 Entity graph approach

Guinaudeau and Strube (2013) adapted the entity-grid into a graph format using a bipartite graph which they claim avoids the data sparsity issues encountered by Barzilay and Lapata (2008) and achieves equal performance, without training. Additionally, their representation can track any cross-sentential references, as opposed to only those present in adjacent sentences.

The graph tracks the presence of all entities and connections to the sentences they occur in, taking all nouns in the document as discourse entities, as recommended by Elsner and Charniak (2011). The coherence of a text in this model is measured by calculating the average outdegree of a projection, summing the shared edges.

The general form of the coherence score assigned to a document in this approach is shown in Equation 2. This is a centrality measure based on the average outdegree across the N sentences represented in the document graph. The outdegree of a sentence s_i, denoted $o(s_i)$, is the total weight of edges leaving that sentence, a notion of how connected (or how central) it is. This weight is the sum of the contributions of all edges connecting s_i to any $s_j \in D$.

$$s(D) = \frac{1}{N} \sum_{i=1}^{N} o(s_i) \quad = \frac{1}{N} \sum_{i=1}^{N} \sum_{j=i+1}^{N} W_{i,j} \tag{2}$$

We reimplemented the algorithm in Guinaudeau and Strube (2013) (using syntactic projection) and ran experiments with the same objective and datasets as for the grid model. Quantitative results for the experiments with the entity-graph model are given in Section 4.

We have also experimented with other languages and noted that syntactic differences do indeed change the transition parameters. This varies depending on the language pair. In particular, it has been proven that the same patterns of syntactic constructions do not hold for German, for example, where topological fields are more relevant. We therefore limit ourselves to reporting results on English.

3.3 Syntax-based model

Motivated by the strong impact syntax has in text coherence, Louis and Nenkova (2012) propose both a local and a global coherence model based on syntactic patterns. Our implementation focuses on their local coherence model. It follows the hypothesis that in a coherent text consecutive sentences will exhibit syntactic regularities, and that these regularities can be captured in terms of co-occurrence of syntactic items.

The units of syntax can be context-free grammar productions (e.g. S $\rightarrow$ NP VP) or d-sequences (a sequence of sibling constituents at depth d starting from the root, possibly annotated with the left-most child node they dominate, e.g. NP$_{NN}$ VP$_{VB}$). The model conditions each sentence on the immediately preceding sentence, both seen as sequences of syntactic patterns. Each sentence is assumed to be generated one pattern at a time and patterns are assumed independent of each other.

The parameters of the model are "unigram" and "bigram" patterns over a vocabulary of syntactic items (i.e. productions or d-sequences) which are directly observed from training data by relative frequency counting.

$$p(D) = \prod_{(u_1^m, v_1^n) \in D} \prod_{j=1}^{n} \frac{1}{m} \sum_{i=1}^{m} \frac{c(u_i, v_j) + \alpha}{c(u_i) + \alpha|V|} \tag{3}$$

The coherence of a document under the model is given by Equation 3, where (u_1^m, v_1^n) represents adjacent sentences, and $c(\cdot)$ is a function that counts how often a pattern (or a pair of patterns) was observed in the training data. To account for unseen syntactic patterns at test time, their model is smoothed by a constant α (and $|V|$ is the size of the vocabulary of syntactic tokens).

In our experiments, we derived the syntactic items in the form of the d-sequence, defined as the leaves of the parse tree at a given depth (in our experiments of depth 2, 3, 4), and annotated with the left-most leaf. The choice of d-sequences results in what we believe to be an informative representation. Further experiments could use grammatical productions as an alternative.

3.4 Syntax-based model with IBM 1

The syntax model by Louis and Nenkova (2012) does not model latent alignments. This is possible under the assumption that all available alignment configurations have been directly observed in the training data. It is worth highlighting that in reality the training data is incomplete in the sense that it lacks alignment information. We introduce alignments between syntactic patterns in adjacent sentences as a latent variable. Our model does that based on the IBM model 1 (Brown et al., 1993), where the current sentence is generated by the preceding one, one pattern at a time, with a uniform prior over alignment configurations. The latent alignment variable allows us to model the fact that some patterns are more likely to trigger certain subsequent patterns.

In IBM model 1, a latent alignment function $a : j \mapsto i$ maps patterns in v_1^n (current sentence) to patterns in u_0^m (preceding sentence), where u_0 is a special NULL symbol which models insertion. The score of a document is given by Equation 4.

$$P(D) = \prod_{(u_1^m, v_1^n) \in D} p(v_1 \ldots v_n, a_1 \ldots a_n | u_0 \ldots u_m) \tag{4}$$

Here n is the current sentence and m the preceding sentence. As the alignment is hidden, we marginalise over all possible configurations, which is tractable due to an independence assumption (that items align independently of each other). Equation 5 shows this tractable marginalisation.

$$p(D) = \prod_{(u_1^m, v_1^n) \in D} \prod_{j=1}^{n} \sum_{i=0}^{m} p(v_j | u_i) \tag{5}$$

We resort to Expectation Maximisation (EM) to estimate the parameters in Equation 5 (Brown et al., 1993): due to the convexity of IBM model 1, EM is guaranteed to converge to a global optimum. Moreover, as we observe more data this model converges to better parameters.

A similar solution was proposed in a different context by Soricut and Marcu, (2006) in their work on word co-occurrences.

Table 1: Number of documents and sentences in the training (Gigaword) and test (WMT14) sets.

Corpus	Portion	Documents	Sentences
Gigaword	12/2010	41,564	774,965
WMT14	de-en	164	3,003
WMT14	fr-en	176	3,003
WMT14	ru-en	175	3,003

To avoid assigning 0 probability to documents containing unseen patterns, we modify the training procedure to treat all the singletons as pertaining to an unknown category (UNK), thus reserving probability mass for future unseen items.[3] In addition to this special UNK item, we also include NULL alignments, which together with UNK will smooth the bigram counts.

4 Experiments and Results

4.1 Datasets

To estimate the parameters of the entity-grid and syntax-based models (e.g. distribution over entity role transitions and syntactic patterns), we use the most recent portion of English LDC Gigaword corpus, excluding 2 sections.[4] Table 1 displays information about the size of these datasets.

To test our models on the translation task, we use WMT14 test data as corpus (Bojar et al., 2014), considering submissions from all participating MT systems (including statistical, rule-based, hybrid) in the translation shared task for three language pairs, namely, 13 German-English (de-en) systems, 9 French-English (fr-en) systems, and 13 Russian-English (ru-en) systems.

We assume that the HT (reference) is a coherent text, and that the MT output may or may not be coherent. While the former is a fair assumption, we do acknowledge that many outputs from MT systems may be coherent. However, we are not aware of any datasets with translated data which have been annotated for coherence. This is a challenging task in itself, as judging coherence is a complex and subjective task which requires, at the very least, well trained annotators. Our hypothesis is that a good coherence model should be able to score human translations as having higher coherence than their counterpart machine translations in most cases.

For the shuffling task we also use the MT data, taking the HT documents as the coherent texts and shuffled versions of them to create incoherent ones.

4.2 Metrics

We evaluated the results according to a number of metrics, defined as follows: m is a model, $d \in D$ a document, r the reference or original (non-shuffled) version and $s \in S$

---

[3] The hypothesis, backed by the Zipf's law, is that unseen items are singletons that we have not yet observed, and that singletons we did observe would remain so if we had observed some more data.

[4] https://catalog.ldc.upenn.edu/LDC2003T05

shuffled or MT output. Then let $\text{win}_m(d_r, d_s)$ return 1 if model m scores reference document d_r higher than a shuffled or MT document d_s, and 0 otherwise. We can define tie and lose analogously. Finally, $\text{first}_m(d_r)$ returns 1 if the reference ranks first, and $\text{solo}_m(d_r)$ returns 1 if the reference occupies a position alone in the ranking. Our various model evaluation methods are defined as follows:

ref$_>$ how often a model ranks reference documents higher than any of their shuffled or MT counterparts: $\frac{1}{|D||S|} \sum_d \sum_s \text{win}_m(d_r, d_s)$

ref$_\geq$ how often a model ranks the reference no worse than any of their shuffled or MT counterparts: $\frac{1}{|D||S|} \sum_d \sum_s \text{win}_m(d_r, d_s) + \text{tie}_m(d_r, d_s)$

ref$_{1*}$ how often the reference is ranked strictly higher than every other system: $\frac{1}{|D|} \sum_d \text{first}_m(d_r) \times \text{solo}_m(d_r)$

4.3 Results on shuffling task

To test our hypothesis that patterns of syntactic items between adjacent sentences can be better modelled through a latent alignment, we conducted the traditional shuffling experiment with our reference text and a randomly shuffled version of it. The aim was to check whether our formulation for the syntax model, based on IBM model 1, outperforms the original syntax model. Thus we are comparing grammatically correct and coherent sentences instead of MT output.

From our results (Table 3), it is clear that our adaptation (henceforth IBM1) improves over the original syntax model (LN) by a large margin. In fact, in most cases it also outperforms the entity grid. Noteworthy is the fact that the $\text{ref}_>$ metric discriminates how often a model ranks the unshuffled documents strictly higher than any other version, not just equal to them, as the $\text{ref}_\geq$ does. We experimented at varying depths, displayed as d in our results, but display only the best performing ones.

The difference between our experiment and those reported elsewhere (Barzilay and Lapata, 2008; Louis and Nenkova, 2012) is that the experiments elsewhere have been on a specific corpus widely used for coherence prediction, the Earthquakes and Accidents corpus[5]. The scores we report are therefore not as high. By way of comparison, we also include results on the aforementioned corpus (Table 2). Here the $\text{ref}_\geq$ metric results for our reimplementation of the syntax model are close those of the original local model with d-sequences (Louis and Nenkova, 2012).

Results for previous grid experiments were obtained using supervised training where the parameters are trained on this same Earthquakes and Accidents corpus, then tested on a heldout section of the same dataset. We adopted a more automated approach, training on more general data. This does, however, affect the results, particularly given the consistent nature of the Earthquakes and Accidents corpus.

4.4 Results on translation task

This evaluation is conducted under the assumption that the reference documents are coherent. An obvious benefit of such a strategy is that we can assess models automatically

---

[5] http://people.csail.mit.edu/regina/coherence/CLsubmission/

Table 2: Model comparisons for shuffling experiment on Earthquakes and Accidents corpus, ref_{1*} is "accuracy" used in previous work with this corpus.

Earthquakes	ref_{1*}	$\text{ref}_{\geq}$
IBM1-d2	80.88	80.88
IBM1-d3	77.10	77.10
GRID	66.21	66.21
GRAPH	60.53	60.58
LN-d2	57.62	71.73
LN-d3	57.00	67.69

Accidents	ref_{1*}	$\text{ref}_{\geq}$
GRAPH	86.51	86.51
IBM1-d3	72.61	72.61
IBM1-d2	67.32	67.37
GRID	50.25	50.25
LN-d4	46.58	55.89
LN-d2	38.82	57.15

Table 3: Model comparisons for shuffling experiment

fr-en	ref_{1*}	$\text{ref}_{\geq}$
IBM1-d3	82.95	85.23
GRID	75.00	77.84
IBM1-d4	71.59	73.86
GRAPH	50.00	53.98
LN-d3	46.59	59.66
LN-d4	41.48	54.55

de-en	ref_{1*}	$\text{ref}_{\geq}$
GRID	79.27	80.49
IBM1-d3	76.83	76.83
IBM1-d2	71.34	71.34
GRAPH	62.80	65.24
LN-d4	53.66	62.20
LN-d2	47.56	59.15

ru-en	ref_{1*}	$\text{ref}_{\geq}$
IBM1-d3	79.43	80.00
GRID	74.86	76.00
IBM1-d2	74.86	75.43
GRAPH	50.29	54.29
LN-d4	46.29	57.71
LN-d3	45.14	57.14

and objectively without the need for any particular type of annotation (e.g. reference translations). To provide a concise summary of our findings, we aggregate the results for all MT systems in this section.

Table 4 shows the performance of our models according to different evaluation methods (scores are percentages), ranked by the first method.

Table 4: Model comparisons for translation task.

fr-en	$\text{ref}_{>}$	$\text{ref}_{\geq}$	ref_{1*}
IBM1-d4	58.24	58.66	20.45
GRID	55.54	56.68	22.16
IBM1-d3	54.19	54.62	17.61
LN-d4	45.17	55.82	14.77
GRAPH	41.62	45.60	11.93
LN-d3	41.26	59.23	15.34

de-en	$\text{ref}_{>}$	$\text{ref}_{\geq}$	ref_{1*}
GRAPH	67.03	68.62	28.66
IBM1-d2	53.52	53.56	12.20
IBM1-d3	53.05	53.05	17.68
LN-d3	43.67	60.55	8.54
LN-d4	43.34	53.38	10.37
GRID	37.71	37.71	6.10

ru-en	$\text{ref}_{>}$	$\text{ref}_{\geq}$	ref_{1*}
GRAPH	60.84	63.21	20.57
IBM1-d3	58.02	58.02	10.86
IBM1-d2	57.41	57.54	13.14
LN-d3	48.62	63.47	9.14
LN-d4	47.21	58.42	8.57
GRID	31.38	31.38	5.14

Our results show that all the models tested are more limited in their ability to assess coherence in an MT context, as the task is more difficult than that of distinguishing shuffled from original texts. The models can score machine translated texts as well as reference translations, and in some cases, even better than reference translations.

Our extension of the syntax-based model – IBM1 – consistently outperforms LN (Louis Nenkova) according to all metrics. That is because IBM1 learns a distribution over hidden alignments between syntactic items. These alignments can be seen as more plausible explanations for certain syntactic patterns. Moreover, in experiments using held out data (from WMT13), we noticed that increasing the amount of training data helps IBM1, which is guaranteed to move towards better parameters.

Overall, for a given language pair, we found that the best coherence model was able to score the human translations higher than any particular MT system for more than 58% of the documents. The best score was 67%, which is a good basis to make future improvements on.

Some models are clearly more heavily affected by the use of methods that disregard ties. The LN model typically clusters the reference together with MT systems. The other models, IBM1 and GRAPH, are less affected by differences in evaluation methods. While the figures change across methods, the trend in the ranking of models is maintained.

In general, IBM1 and GRAPH are the strongest in terms of scores, with GRID performing poorly (except for the fr-en language pair). Overall GRAPH performs better than GRID, perhaps because it offers a broader view of entity-based coherence, in that it captures links between all entities in all sentences in the text, including links over non-adjacent sentences, and as such is not as dependent on consecutive transitions. If ties are not considered, GRAPH features as the best model for two out of the three language pairs, with IBM1 performing similarly well.

Interestingly, there is a difference between language pairs. It is worth emphasising that among our three language pairs, fr-en is arguably the one with the highest MT quality. Low translation quality may have affected the performance of the models differently, as they rely on linguistic information to different extents. GRID, which performed the best for fr-en, relies heavily on the correct identification of nouns and their syntactic roles in sentences. Therefore, for the other languages, an excessive number of ungrammatical translations – and unreliable syntactic roles as a consequence – may have affected the model more significantly. Moreover, the fr-en language pair is closer than the other two, and therefore more likely to be similar syntactically in the output, which could improve performance of the GRID model. If the MT output remained similar syntactically to the source language, then GRID would not perform as well for other language pairs (it is known that the syntactic assumptions which hold for English do not do so for German). Although this potentially affects GRAPH too, it does not depend on entity transitions but models connections among all sentences in a document. Moreover, a closer inspection of the data showed that the quality of the fr-en reference translation was not as good as the de-en reference translation. Coupled with better MT output for the fr-en language pair, this would make it a harder task for the models to differentiate between HT and MT.

While GRID does well in the shuffling experiment, it does not do so well with the MT output. Clearly, shuffling and reordering is a different task entirely, as illustrated by the difference in the scores between Table 3 and Table 4. By comparison, the ability of GRAPH (as the other entity-based method) to distinguish between HT and MT output is presumably due to it not relying on the transitions between sentences, unlike GRID.

5 Conclusions and Future Work

Work on measuring text coherence has thus far been commonly limited to somewhat artificial scenarios such as sentence shuffling or insertion tasks. These operations naturally tend to break the overall logic of the text. In this paper we have investigated local coherence models for a very different scenario, where texts are automatically translated from a given language by systems of various overall levels of quality. Coherence in this scenario is much more nuanced, as elements of coherence are often present in the translations to some degree, and their absence may be connected to various types of translation errors at different linguistic levels. There are undeniably grammatical issues, but arguably a proportion of these do indirectly affect coherence.

For a given language pair, we found that the best coherence model was able to score the human translations higher than any particular MT system for more than 67.03% of the documents. Our IBM1 model performs strongly, detecting MT output from HT 58.24% of the time, which is a strong result considering that it is based on syntax alone. This model did well in the standard shuffling experiment.

We believe that the source language of the training data is crucially important in this MT domain, as noted by others (Cartoni et al., 2011), as is whether the text is original or translated (Lembersky et al., 2012). We plan to investigate filtering input data and to further expand our coherence models to integrate discourse relations and distributed representations. In addition, by way of a supplementary test to determine that our models are indeed measuring coherence not simply the differences between the MT and HT, we intend to test them on an artificial corpus containing injected coherence errors (Sim Smith et al., 2015).

References

Regina Barzilay and Mirella Lapata. (2008). *Modeling local coherence: An entity-based approach*. Comput. Linguist., 34(1):1-34, March.

Ondrej Bojar, Christian Buck, Christian Federmann, Barry Haddow, Philipp Koehn, Johannes Leveling, Christof Monz, Pavel Pecina, Matt Post, Herve Saint-Amand, Radu Soricut, Lucia Specia, and Ales Tamchyna. (2014). *Findings of the 2014 workshop on statistical machine translation*. In Proceedings of WMT, pages 12-58, Baltimore, Maryland.

Peter F. Brown, Vincent J. Della Pietra, Stephen A. Della Pietra, and Robert L. Mercer. 1993. *The mathematics of statistical machine translation: parameter estimation*. Computational Linguistics, 19(2):263-311, June.

Jill Burstein, Joel R. Tetreault, and Slava Andreyev. 2010. *Using entity-based features to model coherence in student essays*. In HLT-NAACL, pages 681-684.

Marine Carpuat and Michel Simard. 2012. *The trouble with smt consistency*. In Proceedings of WMT, pages 442-449, Montreal, Canada.

Bruno Cartoni, Sandrine Zufferey, Thomas Meyer, and Andrei Popescu-Belis. 2011. *How Comparable Are Parallel Corpora? Measuring the Distribution of General Vocabulary and Connectives*, Proceedings of the 4th Workshop on Building and Using Comparable Corpora, pages 78–86, Portland, Oregon, USA, Association for Computational Linguistics.

Micha Elsner and Eugene Charniak. 2011. *Extending the Entity Grid with Entity-Specific Features*. Proceedings of ACL, pages 125-129, Portland, Oregon, USA, Association for Computational Linguistics.

Zhengxian Gong and Min Zhang and Guodong Zhou. 2015. *Document-Level Machine Translation Evaluation with Gist Consistency and Text Cohesion*. Proceedings of the Second Workshop on Discourse in Machine Translation, pages 52-58, September, Lisbon, Portugal, Association for Computational Linguistics.

Barbara J. Grosz, Scott Weinstein, and Aravind K. Joshi. 1995. *Centering: A framework for modeling the local coherence of discourse*. Computational Linguistics, 21:203-225.

Camille Guinaudeau and Michael Strube. 2013. *Graph-based local coherence modeling*. In Proceedings of ACL, pages 93103.

Christian Hardmeier. 2012. *Discourse in statistical machine translation*. Discours 11-2012, (11).

Daniel Jurafsky and James H. Martin. 2009. *Speech and Language Processing*. Prentice Hall, 2 edition.

Mirella Lapata. 2005. *Automatic evaluation of text coherence: models and representations*. In Proceedings of IJCAI, pages 1085-1090.

Gennadi Lembersky, Noam Ordan, and Shuly Wintner. 2012. *Language models for machine translation: Original vs. translated texts*. Comput. Linguist., 38(4):799-825, December.

Jiwei Li and Eduard H. Hovy. 2014. *A model of coherence based on distributed sentence representation*. In Proceedings of the 2014 Conference on Empirical Methods in Natural Language Processing (EMNLP), pages 2039-2048. Association for Computational Linguistics.

Jiwei Li, Thang Luong, and Dan Jurafsky. 2015. *A hierarchical neural autoencoder for paragraphs and documents*. In Proceedings of ACL, pages 1106-1115, Beijing, China, July. Association for Computational Linguistics.

Liu Shujie Yang Muyun Li Mu Zhou Ming Lin, Rui and Sheng Li. 2015. *Hierarchical recurrent neural network for document modeling*. In Proceedings of EMNLP, page 899-907, Lisbon, Portugal, September. Association for Computational Linguistics.

Ziheng Lin, Hwee Tou Ng, and Min-Yen Kan. 2011. *Automatically evaluating text coherence using discourse relations*. In Proceedings of ACL, pages 997-1006.

Annie Louis and Ani Nenkova. 2012. *A coherence model based on syntactic patterns*. In Proceedings of EMNLP-CoNLL, pages 1157-1168, Jeju Island, Korea.

Max M. Louwerse and Arthur C. Graesser, 2005. *Coherence in Discourse*, pages 216-218. Encyclopedia of linguistics.

Karin Sim Smith, Wilker Aziz, and Lucia Specia. 2015. *A proposal for a coherence corpus in machine translation*. In Proceedings of the Second Workshop on Discourse in Machine Translation, pages 52-58, Lisbon, Portugal, September. Association for Computational Linguistics.

Swapna Somasundaran, Jill Burstein, and Martin Chodorow. 2014. *Lexical chaining for measuring discourse coherence quality in test-taker essays*. In Proceedings of COLING.

Radu Soricut and Daniel Marcu. 2006. *Discourse generation using utility-trained coherence models*. In Proceedings of the COLING/ACL, pages 803-810, Sydney, Australia.

Jorg Tiedemann. 2010. *Context adaptation in statistical machine translation using models with exponentially decaying cache*. In Proceedings of the 2010 Workshop on Domain Adaptation for Natural Language Processing, pages 8-15, Uppsala, Sweden.

Billy Tak-Ming Wong and Chunyu Kit. 2012. *Extending machine translation evaluation metrics with lexical cohesion to document level*. In Proceedings of EMNLP-CoNLL, pages 1060-1068.

Deyi Xiong and Min Zhang. 2013. *A topic-based coherence model for statistical machine translation*. In Proceedings of AAAI, pages 977-983.

Deyi Xiong, Guosheng Ben, Min Zhang, Yajuan Lv, and Qun Liu. 2013a. *Modeling lexical cohesion for document-level machine translation*. In Proceedings of IJCAI.

Deyi Xiong, Yang Ding, Min Zhang, and Chew Lim Tan. 2013b. *Lexical chain based cohesion models for document-level statistical machine translation*. In Proceedings of EMNLP, pages 1563-1573.

Received May 2, 2016 , accepted May 10. 2016

Baltic J. Modern Computing, Vol. 4 (2016), No. 2, pp. 190–202

Pivoting Methods and Data for
Czech-Vietnamese Translation via English

Duc Tam HOANG, Ondřej BOJAR

Charles University in Prague, Faculty of Mathematics and Physics,
Institute of Formal and Applied Linguistics

hoangdt@comp.nus.edu.sg, bojar@ufal.mff.cuni.cz

Abstract. The statistical approach to machine translation (MT) relies heavily on large parallel corpora. For many language pairs, this can be a significant obstacle. A promising alternative is pivoting, i.e. making use of a third language to support the translation. There are a number of pivoting methods, but unfortunately, they were not evaluated in comparable settings. We focus on one particular language pair, Czech↔Vietnamese translation, with English as the pivoting language, and provide a comparison of several pivoting methods and the baseline (direct translation). Besides the experiments and analysis, another contribution is the datasets that we have collected and prepared for the three languages.

Keywords: Statistical Machine Translation, Czech-Vietnamese, parallel corpus, pivoting methods, phrase table triangulation, system cascades

1   Introduction

Large parallel corpora are of utmost importance for statistical machine translation (SMT) for producing reliable translations. Unfortunately, for most pairs of living languages, the amount of available parallel data is not sufficient. "Pivoting" methods make use of a third language ("pivot language") to support the translation.

Over past years, a number of pivoting methods have been proposed. Most of the works were conducted using *multi-parallel corpora* such as Europarl (Koehn, 2005), where the same text is available in more than two languages. In a realistic condition, the two corpora, source-pivot corpus and pivot-target corpus, are *independent*, i.e. coming from different sources. We expect that some of the approaches are more beneficial in only one of the two conditions and for sure, some approaches utilizing multilingual corpora are not applicable for independent corpora at all (Kumar et al., 2007; Chen et al., 2008).

In this work, we carry out experiments to directly compare several methods of pivoting. We select Czech and Vietnamese, a relatively unexplored language pair, for the experiments. English is chosen for the role of pivot language because it offers the largest parallel corpora with both Czech and Vietnamese.

This paper has two main contributions. (1) The paper evaluates a wide range of pivoting methods in a directly comparable setting and under the more realistic condition where the parallel corpora are independent (as opposed to multi-parallel). (2) It is the first study which focuses on machine translation between Czech and Vietnamese. It describes and publishes the corpora that we have collected and processed.

The remainder of this paper is organized as follows. Section 2 discusses related work of pivoting methods. Section 3 describes the dataset that we collected, prepared and released. Section 4 presents experimental set up, results and discussions. Finally, Section 5 concludes the paper.

2   Pivoting Methods

Pivoting is formulated as the translating task from a source language to a target language through one or more pivot languages. An important, yet mostly overlooked aspect in pivoting is the relation between the source-pivot and pivot-target corpora. For example, Chen et al. (2008) reduce the size of the phrase table by filtering out phrase pairs if they are not linked by at least one common pivot phrase. Kumar et al. (2007) combine word alignments using multiple pivot languages to correct the alignment errors trained on the source-target parallel data. Both methods (implicitly) rely on the fact that the corpora contain the same sentences available in multiple languages. While this is a reasonable assumption for a *multi-parallel corpus*, the methods are not applicable for *independent parallel corpora*.

In our study, we compare pivoting methods which can be applied under the perhaps more realistic condition that the source-pivot and pivot-target corpora are independent (Tiedemann, 2012a; Tiedemann and Nakov, 2013). This section discusses such methods and highlights their difference and potential. Each method has a number of configuration options which significantly affect the translation quality, we explore them empirically in Section 4 below.

2.1 Synthetic Corpus/Phrase Table

The synthetic corpus method (Gispert and Mariño, 2006; Galuščáková and Bojar, 2012) and the phrase table (PT) translation method (called synthetic phrase table) (Wu and Wang, 2007) aim to generate training data from MT output. Specifically, an MT system, which translates pivot language into the source or target language, is employed to translate a corpus or a phrase table of the other language pair. The result is a source→target corpus or phrase table with one side "synthetic", i.e. containing MT translated data. The synthetic corpus or phrase table is then used to build the source→target MT system.

Using MT translated data is generally seen as a bad thing. The model can easily reproduce errors introduced by the underlying MT system. In practice, however, machine-generated translations need not be always harmful, especially when they compensate for the lack of direct bilingual training data. For example, Gispert and Mariño (2006) report impressive English↔Catalan translation results by translating the English-Spanish corpus using a Spanish→Catalan MT system. The results are on par with the translation quality of English↔Spanish translation. Similarly, Galuščáková and Bojar (2012) observe that pivoting through Czech was better than direct translation from English to Slovak, due to a large difference in training data size.

Between the two methods, the task of translating a phrase table poses different challenges compared to the task of translating a corpus. Phrasal input is generally much shorter than a sentence and a lot of contextual information is lost (even considering the limited scope of existing language models).

2.2   Phrase Table Triangulation

The phrase table triangulation method (Cohn and Lapata, 2007; Zhu et al., 2014), sometimes called simply triangulation, generates an artificial source-target phrase table by directly joining two phrase tables (source-pivot and pivot-target) on common pivot phrases.

Once the tables are combined, approaches to triangulating the two phrase tables diverge in how they set the scores for the phrases. There are two options for estimating the necessary feature scores of the new phrase table: multiplying the original posterior probabilities or manipulating the original co-occurrence counts of phrases.

The first option views the triangulation as a generative probabilistic process on two sets of phrase pairs, s-t and p-t. Assuming the independent relations between three languages, the conditional distribution $p(s|t)$ is estimated over source-target phrase pair s-t by marginalising out the pivot phrase p:

$$\begin{aligned} p(s|t) &= \sum_p p(s|p,t) \times p(p|t) \\ &\approx \sum_p p(s|p) \times p(p|t) \end{aligned} \tag{1}$$

Afterwards, the feature values of identical phrases pairs are combined in the final phrase table. Either the scores are summed up or maximized (i.e. taking the higher of the score values).

The second option estimates the co-occurrence count of the source and target phrases $c(s,t)$ from the co-occurrence counts $c(s,p)$ and $c(p,t)$ of the component phrase pairs. Afterwards, the feature scores are estimated by the standard phrase extraction (Koehn, 2010).

$$c(s,t) = \sum_p f(c(s,p), c(p,t)) \tag{2}$$

In Equation 2, function f is the desired approximation function. Zhu et al. (2014) proposed four functions f: minimum, maximum, arithmetic mean and geometric mean.

Phrase table triangulation methods have received much attention, yet they have not been tested with two disjoint and independent corpora.

2.3 System Cascades

A widely popular method, system cascades (Utiyama and Isahara, 2007), simply uses two black-box machine translation systems in a sequence. The first system translates the input from the source language into the pivot language. The second system picks up the pivot hypothesis and translates it into the target language.

Formally, the problem of finding the best sentence $\hat{e}$ for a foreign input sentence f is defined as maximizing the translation score from source sentence f to a pivot sentence p, then from p to target sentence e:

$$\hat{e} \approx \underset{e, p_i}{\arg\max}\, p_{smt}(p_i|f) \times p_{smt}(e|p_i) \tag{3}$$

where p_i is a pivot hypothesis of the first MT system and serves as the input of the second system.

Because investigating all possible pivot sentences p is too expensive, p is chosen from the list of n-best translations of the source sentence. Sometimes, the first system is not capable of providing a list of possible translations and pivot hypotheses are limited to $n = 1$, taking the top candidate only.

2.4 Phrase Table Interpolation for System Combination

Each of the pivoting methods described above leads to a separate MT system. This opens a possibility of combining these systems, hoping that the strengths of one method would offset the weaknesses of other methods. We choose to combine multiple systems by linearly interpolating translation models. This method, called "phrase table interpolation", is defined as follows:

$$p(e|f; \lambda) = \sum_{i=1}^{n} \lambda_i p_i(e|f) \tag{4}$$

where λ_i is the interpolation weight of translation model i and satisfies the condition $\sum_i \lambda_i = 1$.

We note that the system cascades method does not have a single phrase table. It directly uses the two SMT systems, rather than building a new SMT system. It thus does not lend itself to this combination method. We circumvent the problem by creating a synthetic phrase table from the development and test sets, each translated with the cascades method. We pair the translated text with the original text to create a small synthetic corpus. A phrase table is then extracted from the synthetic corpus and used in the combination.

3   Dataset Created and Released

Czech and Vietnamese are the national languages of the Czech Republic and Vietnam, respectively. Furthermore, the two languages are not under-resourced on their own, but the amount of bilingual corpora between them is very limited despite the large Vietnamese community living in the Czech Republic. So far, no effort has been put into developing an MT tool specifically for this language pair.

We wish to investigate the potential of pivoting methods for translating between Czech and Vietnamese. After carefully examining the potential of all possible pivot languages, we decide to select English as the sole pivot language. It is the only language that provides sufficient resources to act as a bridge between Vietnamese and Czech.

We created and released two sets of multilingual datasets: a set of test data and a set of parallel corpora.

3.1   WMT Test Data

Our test set was derived from the WMT 2013 shared task,[1] which consists of 3000 aligned sentences from newspapers. We opted for the 2013 set, because more recent WMT test sets were no longer multi-parallel across all the languages. The WMT 2013 test set spanned across six languages (Czech, English, German, French, Spanish and Russian) and we extended it to include Vietnamese.

Table 1. Statistics of test data

	# sentences	# words
Czech	3,000	48,472
English	3,000	56,089
Vietnamese	3,000	75,804

Our contribution was created by human translators working in two stages. The first stage delivered a Vietnamese translation from the English side of the WMT 2013 test set, sometimes by post-editing machine-translated text. The second stage was a careful check to arrive at fluent Vietnamese text. Finally, we prepared a multi-lingual test set for Czech, English and Vietnamese. Table 1 gives the statistics of the test set.

3.2   Training Data

The training data is composed of parallel corpora among the source, target and pivot languages. For Czech-English language pair, we used CzEng 1.0, a Czech-English parallel corpus (Bojar et al., 2012) to train the translation model. For Czech-Vietnamese and English-Vietnamese, we collected available bitexts from the Internet as there were no ready-made corpora sufficient to train the translation models.

---

[1] http://www.statmt.org/wmt13

Table 2. Statistics of Czech-Vietnamese training data

	Original		Cleaned	
	Czech	Vietnamese	Czech	Vietnamese
# sentences	1,337,199	1,337,199	1,091,058	1,091,058
# words	9,128,897	12,073,975	6,718,184	7,646,701
# unique words	224,416	68,237	195,446	59,737

Table 3. Statistics of English-Vietnamese training data

	Original		Cleaned	
	English	Vietnamese	English	Vietnamese
# sentences	2,035,624	2,035,624	1,113,177	1,113,177
# words	16,638,364	17,565,580	8,518,711	8,140,876
# unique words	91,905	78,333	69,513	58,286

We collected data from two main sources: OPUS[2] and TED talks.[3] OPUS is a growing multilingual corpus of translated open source documents. It covers over 90 languages and includes data from several domains (Tiedemann, 2012b). The majority of Vietnamese-English and Vietnamese-Czech bitexts in OPUS were subtitles from motion pictures. As such, these bitexts were not always close translations; due to various constraints of the domain, the texts were often just paraphrases. The later source contained selected TED talks which were provided in English and equipped with transcripts in Czech and/or Vietnamese. There were 1198 talks for which English and Vietnamese transcripts are available. There were 784 TED talks for which Czech and Vietnamese transcripts are available.

Our preliminary analysis indicated that the collected datasets were noisy to the extent that the noise would harm the performance of SMT approaches. Hence, we opted for a semi-automatic cleanup of the corpora (both Czech-Vietnamese and English-Vietnamese). We improved the corpus quality by two steps: normalizing and filtering. The normalizing step cleaned up the corpora based on some typical formatting patterns in subtitles and transcripts (e.g. we tried to rejoin sentences spanning over multiple subtitles). The filtering step relied on the filtering tool used in the development of the CzEng corpus (Bojar et al., 2012). We trained the tool on a set of 1,000 sentence pairs which had been selected randomly from the corpus and manually annotated. Overall, the normalization and filtering reduced the size of the Czech-Vietnamese corpus by about 32.25% and the size of the English-Vietnamese corpus by about 51.29% (the number of words). The statistics of the training data is shown in Table 2 and 3. Our analysis showed that the cleaning phrase helped in improving the performance of the translation model trained on the collected datasets.

---

[2] http://opus.lingfil.uu.se
[3] https://www.ted.com/talks

4 Experiments

We empirically evaluate the pivoting methods in the context of Czech↔Vietnamese translation. We also carry out a brief evaluation on the quality of Czech↔English and English↔Vietnamese translations. This provides an insight into the corpus quality, which affects the final performance of pivoting methods.

4.1 Setup

The experiments are carried out using using Moses framework (Koehn et al., 2007). Instead of Moses standard EMS, we use Eman (Bojar and Tamchyna, 2013) to manage the large number of experiments.

We use the standard phrase-based SMT approach which follows the log-linear model. The model features include the translation model, language model, distance-based reordering, word penalty and phrase penalty (no lexicalized reordering model). The translation models are trained on the parallel data that we have prepared (see Section 3). Word alignments are created automatically on the bitexts using Giza++ (Och and Ney, 2003), followed by the standard phrase extraction (Koehn et al., 2003). Three language models are trained using the KenLM language modeling toolkit (Heafield, 2011) with the order of 5.

For the tuning and final evaluation, we split the prepared Czech-English-Vietnamese WMT 2013 set into two parts: the first 1500 sentences as the development set and the remaining 1500 sentences as the test set. The log-linear model is optimized by tuning on the development data with minimum error rate training (MERT, Och (2003)) as the tuning method and BLEU as the tuning metric (Papineni et al., 2002).

The pivoting methods are implemented and processed using the available data that we have. The experimental results are evaluated using BLEU (as implemented in Moses scorer; single-reference, lowercased, and in the tokenization used by the MT system). We also carry out manual evaluation for the final results.

4.2 Baseline Systems

We first build the SMT system by training on the direct parallel data for all 6 translation directions among Czech, English and Vietnamese. Of the 6 component systems, we use the SMT systems trained on the direct Czech↔Vietnamese parallel data as the baseline system.

Table 4 shows the experimental results of six component systems on the test set. We can see that the Czech→Vietnamese and Vietnamese→Czech baseline systems attain very low results (10.59 and 7.62 BLEU points). This is not surprising. Despite the preparation step, the Czech↔Vietnamese training data is still noisy. The essence of transcribed bitexts is paraphrasing, which may be correct in a particular context but incorrect in general. Furthermore, the properties of the examined languages (Czech inflective with very rich morphology, Vietnamese analytic with rather fixed word order) render the Czech-Vietnamese translation as a difficult problem.

Our analysis shows that the component systems for English↔Vietnamese translation perform relatively well. This is attributed by the similarity between English and

Table 4. Performance of baseline systems by direct translation

Direction	Label	BLEU
Czech→English	cs→en	23.23
English→Czech	en→cs	15.26
Vietnamese→English	vi→en	33.88
English→Vietnamese	en→vi	34.45
Czech→Vietnamese	cs→vi	**10.59**
Vietnamese→Czech	vi→cs	**7.62**

Vietnamese, notably the small number of inflectional morphemes. With the collected dataset, we attain competitive results compared to current English↔Vietnamese MT translation.

4.3 Results of Pivoting Methods

4.3.1 Phrase Table Translation We choose to conduct the phrase table translation method, which is similar to the *synthetic corpus* method. To create synthetic Czech↔Vietnamese PTs, there are two options:

1. Translating the English side of English↔Vietnamese phrase tables into Czech using the English→Czech component MT system.
2. Translating the English side of Czech↔English phrase tables into Vietnamese using the English→Vietnamese component MT system.

After translation, the probabilities and lexical weights are kept from the original phrase tables.

Table 5. Performance of synthetic phrase table method

Option	vi→cs	cs→vi
Translating English↔Vietnamese phrase table	7.34	9.67
Translating Czech↔English phrase table	8.40	12.09
Direct Translation (Baseline)	7.62	10.59

Table 5 shows the performance of the two options. We see that translating the large CzEng 1.0 phrase table by the small systems achieves better results than the other way around, regardless of the translation direction. We note that not only the CzEng 1.0 PT has a better coverage, but also the English→Vietnamese system delivers translations of a relatively good quality. The English→Czech system faces the problem of incorrect word forms even though the morphemes are correct. We also note that the PT translation method which involves translating Czech↔English phrase table attains better results than the baseline systems. This shows the potential of pivoting methods over the direct translation.

4.3.2 Phrase Table Triangulation We followed two specific options to conduct phrase table triangulation. Each option in turn offers a number of ways to merge the feature values of identical pivoted phrase pairs.

1. Pivoting posterior probabilities, merging by the summation or maximization function
2. Pivoting the co-occurrence counts, approximating by the minimum, maximum, arithmetic mean or geometric mean function

For each of the translation directions, these two options result in six phrase tables which have the same phrase pairs but different feature values. Table 6 shows the performance of all the setups.

Table 6. Comparison between the six options of PT triangulation method

Option	Function	vi→cs	cs→vi
1	summation	**7.44**	**10.28**
1	maximization	7.21	9.64
2	minimum	7.24	9.86
2	maximum	6.38	7.64
2	arithmetic mean	6.25	6.95
2	geometric mean	7.05	9.24
Direct Translation (Baseline)		7.62	10.59

First, we can see that both options of the triangulation method receive lower BLEU scores, compared to the phrase table translation method. The result is rather interesting because the triangulation method has an appealing description. It is generally considered a good system, sometimes outperforming direct translation. The primary reason for the failure here is the high level of noise created by triangulation. The method doubles the amount of noise in both phrase tables, thus decreasing the overall performance. Moreover, as our corpora are independent, the overlapping part is small. This results in a low coverage of phrases.

Second, re-estimating co-occurrence counts appears to be less effective than combining the probabilities directly. The primary reason is the difference between two phrase tables. The Czech-English phrase table is much larger than the English-Vietnamese phrase table. As the co-occurrence counts are biased either the large PT or the small PT, thus minimizing the difference between valid and noise phrase pairs. Hence, the noisy pairs acquire probabilities as high as the valid pairs. When the co-occurrence counts are

Table 7. Performance of system cascades method

n	1	2	5	10	20	30	50	75	100
cs→vi	9.05	9.19	9.33	9.50	9.70	9.70	9.80	**9.82**	9.82
vi→cs	13.35	13.51	13.65	13.71	13.77	**13.83**	13.73	13.75	13.79

biased towards the large PT (i.e. the maximum and arithmetic mean functions), the high number of common phrases worsens the probabilities.

Another observation shows that computation of the new probability favours summation over maximization. It is reasonable that the final probability of a source- target pairs should be computed over all middle-phrases rather than just one phrase. One unit (word or phrase) may have more than one translation in other language.

4.3.3 System Cascades For system cascades, we use the component systems to translate each step of the process. There are two directions of translation, which lead to two different settings for the system cascades method.

For Vietnamese→Czech system cascades method, we first use the Vietnamese→English component MT system to translate the input from Vietnamese into English. We then use the English→Czech component MT system to translate the English sentence into Czech.

For Czech→Vietnamese system cascades method, we first use the Czech→English component MT system to translate the input from Czech into English. We then use the English→Vietnamese component MT system to translate the English sentence into Vietnamese.

In our experiments, we select n from $\{1, 2, 5, 10, 20, 30, 50, 75, 100\}$ to verify the effectiveness of using n-best translations instead of just selecting the top hypothesis. The list of n-best translations allows the second system to compensate for errors of the first system's single-best output, thus producing a better translation.

Table 7 confirms our claim that the n-best list of hypotheses helps system cascades. Furthermore, the system cascades method achieves higher results than the baseline system and other pivoting methods. The promising performance of system cascades comes from the fact that the method uses complete translations. During the translation process, pivoting sentences are broken into phrases separately for each of the two phrase tables. Only a small portion of phrases remains intact during the process. In most of the cases, the segmentation into phrases is different for the pivot-target translation and for the source-pivot translation.

4.3.4 Combination through Phrase Table Interpolation We adopt the uniform weights to perform phrase table interpolation, which has shown to be robust (Cohn and Lapata, 2007). We adapt all four features of the standard Moses SMT translation model: the phrase translation probabilities and the lexical weights.

Table 8. Automatic evaluation of Czech↔Vietnamese translation

Method	PT Size	vi→cs	cs→vi
Direct Translation	8.70M	7.62	10.59
PT Translation	53.21M	8.40	12.09
PT Triangulation	61.50M	7.44	9.86
System Cascades	0.08M	9.82	**13.83**
Combination (PT Interpolation)	95.00M	**10.12**	**13.80**

Table 8 summarizes our experimental results using automatic scoring. It includes the results of the individual systems and the combined system, which is built based on the interpolated phrase table.

We further conduct manual evaluation over the final results of Czech→Vietnamese translation. We perform relative ranking among 5 systems, the established practice of WMT. To interpret this 5-way ranking, we adopt the technique used by WMT until 2013 (before TrueSkill): we extract the 10 pairwise comparisons from each ranking. For a given system, we report the proportion of pairs in which the system was ranked equally or higher than its competitor (out of all pairs where the system was evaluated), see the column "≥ Others" in Table 9. Additionally, we report a simpler interpretation of the 5-way ranking following Bojar et al. (2011). Each 5-way ranking is called a "block" and we report how often each system was among the winners in this block. Since we are comparing 5 systems, all our blocks include all systems, so "≥ All in block" simply means the rate of wins.

Table 9. Manual evaluation of Czech→Vietnamese translation

Method	≥ Others	≥ All in Block
Direct Translation	0.76	0.56
PT Translation	0.71	0.48
PT Triangulation	0.77	0.56
System Cascades	**0.86**	**0.56**
Combination (PT Interpolation)	**0.85**	**0.60**

Tables 8 and 9 provide the same picture: the system combination improves a little over the system cascades method.

We note that the performance of a specific method heavily depends on languages, domains and corpora in question. For example, system cascades achieved the best results with our datasets and the performance of phrase table translation is better when translating the larger (Czech-English) phrase table with the smaller (English-Vietnamese) MT system than the other way around, regardless of the final translation direction (Czech↔Vietnamese) using the translated phrase table.

5   Conclusion

We carried our a set of experiments with baseline direct translation and three types
of pivoting methods, optionally concluded by a last step that combines the different
approaches to a single system, improving over each of the individual components. Our
comparative study suggests that in absence of a multi-parallel corpus, simple cascading
of systems outperforms methods manipulating the phrase table.

To support further experiments in Czech↔Vietnamese machine translation, we as-
sembled and described two training corpora and created one test set. The corpora are
available in the Lindat repository:

- http://hdl.handle.net/11234/1-1594 (WMT13 Vietnamese Test Set)
- http://hdl.handle.net/11234/1-1595 (CsEnVi Pairwise Parallel Corpus)

Acknowledgement

This work has received funding from the European Union's Horizon 2020 research and
innovation programme under grant agreement no. 645452 (QT21).

This work has been using language resources developed, stored and distributed by
the LINDAT/CLARIN project of the Ministry of Education, Youth and Sports of the
Czech Republic (project LM2010013).

References

Bojar, Ondřej and Aleš Tamchyna. 2013. The design of Eman, an experiment manager. *The
Prague Bulletin of Mathematical Linguistics*, 99:39–56.

Bojar, Ondřej, Miloš Ercegovčević, Martin Popel, and Omar Zaidan. 2011. A Grain of Salt for
the WMT Manual Evaluation. In *Proceedings of the Sixth Workshop on Statistical Machine
Translation*, pages 1–11, Edinburgh, Scotland, July. Association for Computational Linguistics.

Bojar, Ondřej, Zdeněk Žabokrtský, Ondřej Dušek, Petra Galuščáková, Martin Majliš, David
Mareček, Jiří Maršík, Michal Novák, Martin Popel, and Aleš Tamchyna. 2012. The joy
of parallelism with CzEng 1.0. In *Proceedings of the 2012 International Conference on
Language Resources and Evaluation*.

Chen, Yu, Andreas Eisele, and Martin Kay. 2008. Improving statistical machine translation
efficiency by triangulation. In *Proceedings of the International Conference on Language
Resources and Evaluation*.

Cohn, Trevor and Mirella Lapata. 2007. Machine translation by triangulation: Making effective
use of multi-parallel corpora. In *Proceedings of the 45th Annual Meeting of the Association
for Computational Linguistics*.

Galuščáková, Petra and Ondřej Bojar. 2012. Improving SMT by Using Parallel Data of a Closely
Related Language. In *Proceedings of the Fifth International Conference Baltic Human Language Technologies*, volume 247 of *Frontiers in AI and Applications*, pages 58–65, Amsterdam, Netherlands. IOS Press.

Gispert, Adrià De and José B. Mariño. 2006. Catalan-english statistical machine translation
without parallel corpus: Bridging through spanish. In *Proceedings of 5th International Conference on Language Resources and Evaluation*, pages 65–68.

Heafield, Kenneth. 2011. KenLM: faster and smaller language model queries. In *Proceedings of the 2011 Sixth Workshop on Statistical Machine Translation*.

Koehn, Philipp, Franz Josef Och, and Daniel Marcu. 2003. Statistical phrase-based translation. In *Proceedings of the 2003 Conference of the North American Chapter of the Association for Computational Linguistics - Human Language Technologies*.

Koehn, Philipp, Hieu Hoang, Alexandra Birch, Chris Callison-Burch, Marcello Federico, Nicola Bertoldi, Brooke Cowan, Wade Shen, Christine Moran, Richard Zens, Chris Dyer, Ondřej Bojar, Alexandra Constantin, and Evan Herbst. 2007. Moses: open source toolkit for statistical machine translation. In *Proceedings of the 45th Annual Meeting of the Association for Computational Linguistics*.

Koehn, Philipp. 2005. Europarl: A parallel corpus for statistical machine translation. In *MT Summit*, volume 5, pages 79–86.

Koehn, Philipp. 2010. *Statistical Machine Translation*. Cambridge University Press.

Kumar, Shankar, Franz Josef Och, and Wolfgang Macherey. 2007. Improving word alignment with bridge languages. In *Proceedings of the 2007 Joint Conference on Empirical Methods in Natural Language Processing and Computational Natural Language Learning*.

Och, Franz Josef and Hermann Ney. 2003. A systematic comparison of various statistical alignment models. *Computational Linguistics*, 29(1):19–51.

Och, Franz Josef. 2003. Minimum error rate training in statistical machine translation. In *Proceedings of the 41st Annual Meeting on Association for Computational Linguistics*.

Papineni, Kishore, Salim Roukos, Todd Ward, and Wei-Jing Zhu. 2002. BLEU: a method for automatic evaluation of machine translation. In *Proceedings of the 40th Annual Meeting on Association for Computational Linguistics*.

Tiedemann, Jörg and Preslav Nakov. 2013. Analyzing the use of character-level translation with sparse and noisy datasets. In *Proceedings of the International Conference Recent Advances in Natural Language Processing RANLP 2013*, pages 676–684, Hissar, Bulgaria, September. INCOMA Ltd. Shoumen, BULGARIA.

Tiedemann, Jörg. 2012a. Character-based pivot translation for under-resourced languages and domains. In *Proceedings of the 13th Conference of the European Chapter of the Association for Computational Linguistics*, pages 141–151, Avignon, France, April. Association for Computational Linguistics.

Tiedemann, Jorg. 2012b. Parallel data, tools and interfaces in OPUS. In *Proceedings of the Eight International Conference on Language Resources and Evaluation*.

Utiyama, Masao and Hitoshi Isahara. 2007. A comparison of pivot methods for phrase-based statistical machine translation. In *Proceedings of the 2007 Conference of the North American Chapter of the Association for Computational Linguistics Human Language Technologies*.

Wu, Hua and Haifeng Wang. 2007. Pivot language approach for phrase-based statistical machine translation. In *Proceedings of the 45th Annual Meeting of the Association for Computational Linguistics*.

Zhu, Xiaoning, Zhongjun He, Hua Wu, Conghui Zhu, Haifeng Wang, and Tiejun Zhao. 2014. Improving pivot-based statistical machine translation by pivoting the co-occurrence count of phrase pairs. In *Proceedings of the 2014 Conference on Empirical Methods in Natural Language Processing*.

Received May 3, 2016 , accepted May 10, 2016

Baltic J. Modern Computing, Vol. 4 (2016), No. 2, 203-217

Detecting Grammatical Errors in Machine Translation Output Using Dependency Parsing and Treebank Querying

Arda TEZCAN, Véronique HOSTE, Lieve MACKEN

Department of Translation, Interpreting and Communication,
Ghent University, Groot-Brittanniëlaan 45, 9000 Ghent, Belgium

{arda.tezcan, veronique.hoste, lieve.macken}@ugent.be

Abstract. Despite the recent advances in the field of machine translation (MT), MT systems cannot guarantee that the sentences they produce will be fluent and coherent in both syntax and semantics. Detecting and highlighting errors in machine-translated sentences can help post-editors to focus on the erroneous fragments that need to be corrected. This paper presents two methods for detecting grammatical errors in Dutch machine-translated text, using dependency parsing and treebank querying. We test our approach on the output of a statistical and a rule-based MT system for English-Dutch and evaluate the performance on sentence and word-level. The results show that our method can be used to detect grammatical errors with high accuracy on sentence-level in both types of MT output.

Keywords: Machine Translation, Quality Estimation, Dependency Parsing, Treebanks

1. Introduction

Despite the continuous progress that has been made over the last decades, Machine Translation (MT) systems are far from perfect. Moreover, MT quality not only varies between different domains or language pairs but also from sentence to sentence. Even though it has been shown that using MT leads to productivity gains in computer-assisted translation (CAT) workflows (Guerberof, 2009; Depraetere et al., 2014), to produce high-quality translations, humans still need to intervene in the translation process and do this usually by post-editing (correcting) the MT output. Post-editing MT output requires post-editors to detect translation errors prior to correcting them. Hence, automatic quality estimation (QE) systems not only aim to estimate the post-editing effort at segment level to filter low quality translations (Specia et al, 2009), but also to detect the location and the nature of errors at word level (Ueffing and Ney, 2007; Bach et al., 2011).

MT errors can be analysed as adequacy and fluency errors. While adequacy is concerned with how much of the source content and meaning is also expressed in the target text, fluency is concerned with to what extent the translation is well formed and adheres to the norms of the target language. The distinction between adequacy and fluency has been used in different translation error taxonomies (Lommel et al., 2014; Daems, Macken and Vandepitte, 2014). Besides the difficulties of transferring source content and meaning to a target sentence, the task of producing grammatically correct sentences remains to be challenging for MT systems, independent of the domain of text to be translated and the type of MT system (Costa et al., 2015; Daems et al., 2015). This motivates us to examine the use of dependency structures, which represent the abstract grammatical relations that hold between constituents, for detecting grammatical errors in machine-translated text.

A dependency tree is a rooted, directed acyclic graph, which represents all words in a sentence as nodes and grammatical relations between the words as edges. A labelled dependency tree, additionally, incorporates the nature of the grammatical relationships between the words as annotations of relation names on the edges of the tree. Dependency trees are interesting for the QE task due to the fact that the dependents may span discontinuous parts of the input sentence and are suited for representing languages with word order variations and discontinuous constituencies such as Dutch.

In this paper, we present two new approaches for QE on sub-segment level, and more specifically for detecting grammatical errors in Dutch MT output. In the first approach, we use the partial dependency parses as an indicator of problematic text fragments when no parse covers the complete input. In the second approach, we query the sub-trees of the dependency tree of an MT sentence against a treebank of correct Dutch sentences by using dependency relation and syntactic category information on phrase and lexical level. The number of matching constructions is then considered to be an indicator of possible translation errors for a given sub-tree. In addition to using these two approaches separately, we combine them together and evaluate the three approaches on the output of an English-to-Dutch statistical and rule-based MT system. We evaluate the performance on sentence and word-level by comparing the detected errors to manually annotated errors.

The remainder of this work is as follows: In Section 2, we describe related research. In Section 3, our approach is outlined in detail and in Section 4, we describe the data sets we used. In Section 5, we give the results of our experiments. Finally, in Section 6, we conclude by discussing the results and future work.

2. Related work

QE is the task of providing a quality indicator for machine-translated text without relying on reference translations (Gandrabur and Foster, 2003). Most work on QE has focused on segment level, which aims to provide a binary or continuous quality score for the whole machine-translated sentence that reflects the post-editing time or the number of edits that are required to correct the MT output (Blatz et al., 2004; Specia et al., 2009; Hardmeier et al., 2011). QE on word or sub-segment level, on the other hand, has received less attention.

Estimating the quality of MT output on word or sub-segment level has a number of advantages compared to sentence-level QE. First of all, word-level QE systems can highlight problematic text fragments in machine-translated text to guide the post-editors. Furthermore, since the overall quality of an MT system depends on the individual errors it makes, word-level QE systems can easily be extended to estimate segment-level quality (de Souza et al., 2014; Tezcan et al., 2015). Word-level QE systems can additionally be used for improving MT quality by providing valuable information about the location, the frequency and the type of errors MT systems make (Popovic and Ney, 2011) or by combining correct text fragments from different MT systems (Ueffing and Ney, 2007).

In one of the early works on word-level QE, Blatz et al. (2004) used a collection of features to build a binary classifier that provides confidence scores for each word in machine-translated text. Besides using features that capture the relationships between source and target words, such as the word posterior probabilities and semantic similarities, they used additional target-language features that were based on basic syntax checking and word frequency. A recent work on word-level QE is QuEst++ (Specia et al., 2015), which is an open-source toolkit for QE on word, sentence and document level. QuEst++ consists of two main modules: a feature extraction and a Machine Learning (ML) module. For word-level QE, besides using features that explore the word alignments and POS-similarities between source and target texts, QuEst++ uses target-language features that are derived from n-gram language models. As n-gram language models rely primarily on local context, they can capture short-distance dependencies (e.g. article-noun agreements), but they fail to capture long-distance dependencies such as non-adjacent subject-verb agreements. The idea of using dependency structures in QE is not new. Bach et al. (2011) compared the dependency relations of Arabic source sentences and English MT translations and incorporated child-father and children correspondences as features in their ML system. They used source and target dependency structure features together with source-side and alignment content features to train a classifier for predicting word-level quality. Hardmeier et al. (2011) used tree kernels over constituency and dependency parses of MT input and output in conjunction with Support Vector Machine (SVM) classification for QE.

A number of studies focused on detecting grammatical errors. Stymne and Ahrenberg (2010) used a mainly rule-based Swedish grammar checker not only to assess the grammaticality of their English-Swedish SMT system, but also for post-processing the MT output by applying the grammar checker suggestions. Ma and McKeown (2011), on the other hand, used feature-based lexicalized tree adjoining grammars (FB-LTAG) to detect and filter ungrammatical translations generated by their MT system. A Tree Adjoining Grammar (TAG) consists of a number of elementary trees, which can be combined with substitution and adjunction operations and while the derivation trees in TAG resemble dependency structures, the derived trees are phrase-structure trees (Joshi and Rambow, 2013).

The approaches we propose differ from previous work in several ways. First of all, we use only dependency tree information of the target language to detect grammatical errors in the MT output and by doing so we make a clear distinction on the type of MT errors we target. Second, in this exploratory study, we do not consider the QE task as a ML problem. Instead we try to gain insights in the strengths and weaknesses of the information the dependency structures provide for the QE task on sub-segment level, so that we can incorporate informative features in a ML system in the future. From this perspective, this method shows similarities to the GrETEL tool described by Augustinus et al. (2012), which allows users to query Dutch strings against a treebank and search for similar syntactic constructions. This application uses XPath[1] for treebank querying and

---

[1] http://www.w3.org/TR/xpath

can extract sub-trees from full parse trees to allow partial matching. And finally, we evaluate the error detection system against a corpus of MT errors (containing fine-grained manual error annotations), which allows us to focus on grammatical errors only. The evaluation method we use therefore does not involve post-editing speed or number of edits that post-editors make as quality indicators, both of which can be subject to noise due to the changes made in the MT output that are not related to errors.

3. Detecting grammatical errors in machine-translated text

The two error detection approaches that we propose make use of the Alpino parser (van Noord, 2006), a wide-coverage Head-driven Phrase Structure Grammar (HPSG) for Dutch. Alpino constructs for each input sentence a parse forest containing all possible parses. If Alpino is unable to build a parse covering the complete input, the best sequence of non-overlapping parses (each spanning a maximal portion of the input) from this forest is selected (van Noord, 2001). In the first approach, this best sequence of non-overlapping partial parses is used for error. In the second approach, the sub-trees of the final parse tree are extracted and queried against a treebank that contains dependency parses of domain-specific correct Dutch sentences.

3.1. Partial parses

Under the assumption that the parser is accurate enough (Van Noord (2006) reports F-scores of 88.5 or higher, evaluated on different test sets), the fact that Alpino cannot generate a parse for the complete sentence might be an indication of grammatical errors. In the first approach, we simply consider the boundaries of the partial parses as an indicator of errors in the MT output and mark the first n words to the left and right of the parse boundaries as errors. This approach uses Alpino-specific output and can only be adapted to other parsers if they output partial parsing information. While choosing different n values do not have an impact on the error detection performance on sentence-level, it has an impact on the word-level evaluation, as the higher n values means a higher number of words being annotated in the MT output. We discuss the impact of choosing different n values on error detection performance in Section 5. Figure 1 shows (a) an English sentence and (b) the Alpino parse of the corresponding MT output in Dutch, in which the boundaries of the partial parses are indicated by means of square brackets. With n set to 1, the words in bold are considered as erroneous words.

(a)   Unfortunately, these women rarely have the financial means to pay for it.
*(b) **[Helaas]** [,] **[deze** vrouwen hebben zelden de financiële middelen om te*
***betalen]** [voor] [het] [.]*

Figure 1: (a) An English sentence, (b) Alpino parse of the corresponding MT output in Dutch. Square brackets indicate the non-overlapping partial parses and the erroneous words are highlighted in bold (with $n = 1$). Correct Dutch sentence: "Helaas hebben deze vrouwen zelden de financiële middelen om ervoor te betalen".

3.2. Treebank querying

The Alpino parser constructs a single XML tree and provides categorical information at the level of syntactic constituency and dependency information containing the semantic relations between constituents (Schuurman, 2003). The Alpino XML additionally contains detailed Part-of-Speech (POS) information at the lexical level using the CGN/D-COI tagset (Van Eynde, 2005). An example dependency tree obtained from Alpino is shown in Figure 2 and the Alpino XML for the highlighted sub-tree in Figure 3, which ignores some attributes for expository purposes.

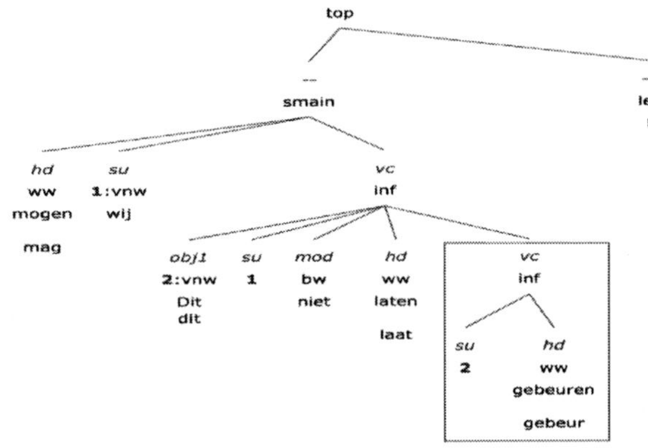

Figure 2. The Alpino dependency tree for the sentence "Dit mogen wij niet laten gebeuren! (En: *We cannot let this happen!)*"

```
<node begin="0" cat="inf" end="6" rel="vc">
    <node begin="0" end="1" index="2" rel="su"/>
    <node begin="5" end="6" lemma="gebeuren" postag="WW(inf,vrij,zonder)" rel="hd"
            word="gebeuren"/>
</node>
```

Figure 3. The Alpino-XML structure for the sub-tree highlighted in Figure 2

Some of the important attributes in the Alpino-XML are *cat* (syntactic category), *rel* (grammatical function), *postag* (part-of-speech tag), *word, lemma, index, begin* (starting position) and *end* (end position). The *index* attribute is used to encode control relations by means of co-indexing. The *postag* attribute in the Alpino-XML additionally provides sub-features for a given lexical item. For example, in Figure 3, the *postag* for the word "gebeuren (*happen*)" is given as "*WW(inf,vrij,zonder)*", which categorizes the word as a verb (*WW*) and more specifically as an infinitive (*inf*), position as free (*vrij*) and inflection as none (*zonder*). To detect errors in the MT output, we collect different sub-trees of depth 1 for a given parse tree and query these against the treebank to search for similar constructions. The sub-trees do not contain any explicit information about the surface forms of words and consist of the following types of information:

- the *rel, begin* and *end* attributes for each node

- the *postag* attribute for terminal nodes and *cat* attribute for non-terminal nodes, when available[2]

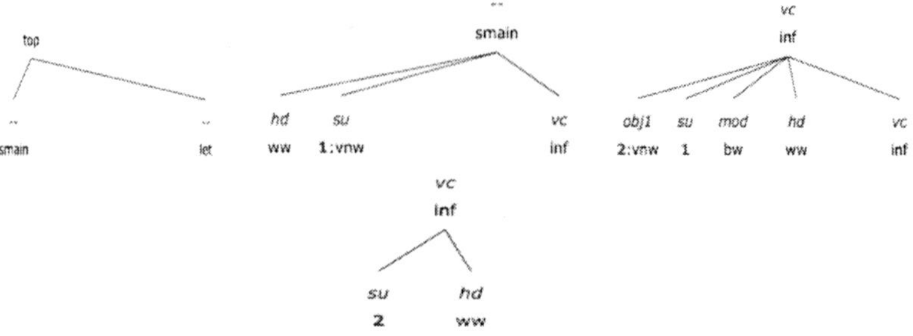

Figure 4. The collected sub-trees from the full parse tree of Figure 2.

(a)

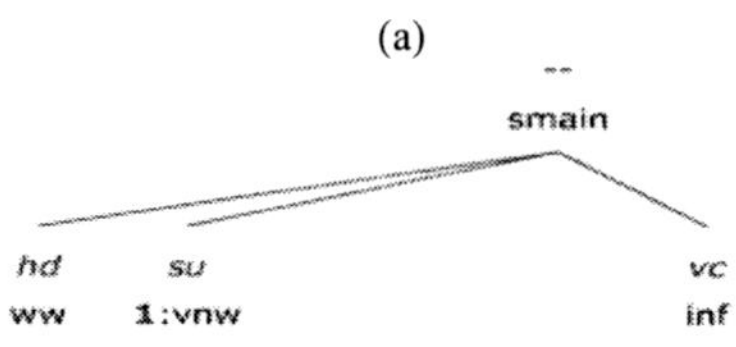

(b)

```
//node[@rel="--" and @cat="smain" and node[@postag="WW(pv,tgw,mv)" and @rel="hd" and
node[@postag="VNW(pers,pron,nomin,vol,1,mv)" and @rel="su" and node[@rel="vc" and @cat="inf"]
```

(c)

```
//node[@rel="--" and @cat="smain" and node[@postag="WW(pv,tgw,mv)" and @rel="hd" and @begin >
../../node[@rel="--" and @cat="smain"]/@begin and @end =
../node[@postag="VNW(pers,pron,nomin,vol,1,mv)" and @rel="su"]/@begin] and
node[@postag="VNW(pers,pron,nomin,vol,1,mv)" and @rel="su" and @begin =
../node[@postag="WW(pv,tgw,mv)" and @rel="hd"]/@end and @end < ../../node[@rel="--" and
@cat="smain"]/@end] and node[@rel="vc" and @cat="inf" and @begin = ../../node[@rel="--" and
@cat="smain"]/@begin and @end = ../../node[@rel="--" and @cat="smain"]/@end]]
```

Figure 5. An example sub-tree (a) and the corresponding XPath query without (b) and with (c) word order constraints indicated by *@begin* and *@end* arguments

Next, for each collected sub-tree a query in XPath is generated. The XPath[3] standard implements a query language for XML documents, which can be used for searching and extracting information from treebanks, using applications like BaseX. The generated XPath query for each node is additionally enriched with starting and end positions to respect the exact word order observed in a given MT output, using the begin and end attributes of the XML. This extension is done to be able to query the treebank not only

---

[2] Nodes consisting of control relations do not explicitly contain *postag* or *cat* attributes
[3] http://basex.org

for similar constructions with respect to the dependency relation, syntactic category and POS, but also for the order of the constituents. Figure 5 shows (a) the second sub-tree in Figure 4, the corresponding basic XPath query (b) and the extended XPath query that respects the word order of the given structure (c).

Once the XPath queries are generated for each sub-tree, they are used to query the treebank to search for similar constructions and mark errors using BaseX. The motivation for treebank querying is that if a given sub-tree, which consists of dependency relation, syntactic category, POS and word order information, has occurred in large corpus of dependency trees less than a certain threshold value T, the sub-tree is grammatically incorrect. In that case we mark all words of the sub-tree as erroneous. We discuss the impact of choosing different T values on error detection performance in Section 5. This method is applicable to other parsers (such as the Stanford Parser (De Marneffe et al., 2006)) provided that the output can be converted to the Alpino XML structure or a similar XML structure.

4. Data sets

We use two types of data sets: one data set to evaluate the error detection systems and one data set to construct the treebank. We use the SCATE taxonomy and corpus of MT errors (Tezcan et al., in press) to evaluate the performance of the different error detection approaches. The SCATE error taxonomy is a hierarchical taxonomy, which distinguishes between adequacy and fluency error annotations: errors that can be detected on the target sentence alone (on monolingual level) are considered as fluency errors, whereas errors that can only be detected by looking at both source and target sentences are considered as accuracy errors. Based on the hierarchical structure, both accuracy and fluency errors are categorized further. The fluency errors, being the focus of this study, are further divided into *grammar, lexicon, orthography, multiple errors* and *other fluency errors*. While the first three sub-categories are based on common linguistic notions, *multiple errors* correspond to a combination of fluency errors that are difficult to identify separately, e.g. a word order error combined with wrong word forms or wrong lexical choices. *Other fluency errors* refer to errors that do not belong to any other fluency error categories. Multiple annotations on the same text span are possible.

The SCATE corpus of MT errors is a collection of sentences from the Dutch Parallel Corpus (Macken et al., 2011) consisting of 698 source sentences in English and the MT output for each source segment in Dutch, obtained from two types of MT architectures, namely a Statistical Machine Translation (SMT) System (Google Translate[4]) and a Rule-Based Machine Translation (RBMT) System (Systran[5]). The sentences in this corpus belong to three text types: external communication, non-fictional literature and journalistic texts. Table 1 gives an overview of the number of segments containing errors and the number of error annotations for each data set in the SCATE corpus of MT errors. Based on the definitions of the SCATE fluency error categories, we used all sentences (698) in the SCATE corpus of MT errors but kept only the *grammar* and *multiple error* annotations to assess the performance of the proposed approaches on detecting grammatical errors.

---

[4] http://translate.google.com
[5] SYSTRAN Enterprise Edition, version 7.5

Table 1. Number of segments containing errors (#segments) and the number of error annotations (#annotations) in the SCATE corpus of MT errors, per error category, per data set. The same information is additionally provided for the merged annotation set of *grammar* and *multiple errors*.

	SMT		RBMT	
	#segments	#annotations	#segments	#annotations
Fluency errors (total)	**536**	**1524**	**563**	**1806**
Grammar errors	435	936	421	855
Orthography errors	192	243	223	284
Lexicon errors	176	232	329	527
Multiple errors	106	112	123	140
Other fluency errors	1	1	0	0
Grammar + Multiple Errors	**463**	**1048**	**451**	**995**

To build the treebank, we used 160,201 Dutch sentences from the Dutch Parallel Corpus. These sentences were collected from the same three text types that are used in the SCATE corpus of MT errors but do not include the sentences that are subject to evaluation. All sentences were automatically parsed with the Alpino parser. An XML database was created from this collection of parse trees using BaseX, in which the XML attributes are indexed. BaseX was also used to make XPath queries against this database of parse trees to mark errors.

5. Experiments and results

Using the error detection approaches described in Section 3, we built three different MT error detection systems: a system which uses the partial parses obtained from the Alpino parser (P), a system which uses the matches obtained from the treebank for each sub-tree being queried against (X) and a system which combines the output from the first two systems ($P+X$). We evaluate the output of these three systems both on sentence and word level. The sentence-level evaluation is used to assess whether the QE systems can detect sentences containing errors, whereas the word-level evaluation is used to assess whether the systems can locate the errors in the sentence.

5.1. Sentence-level evaluation: Grammar Errors

As the sub-tree extraction method we propose in Section 3.2 does not impose any constraints on the maximum number of child nodes a sub-tree can contain, the X system

Table 2. Number and the percentage of sub-trees in the treebank, with a specific number of child nodes.

	N=1	N=2	N=3	N=4	N=5	N=6	N>=7
Number of subtrees	287	156426	847204	452830	145873	49287	18981
Percentage of subtrees	0%	9%	51%	27%	9%	3%	1%

is subject to data sparsity especially if the queried sub-trees contain a high number of child nodes. This problem is clearly visible in the distribution of sub-trees with different number of child nodes (N) over all the trees in the treebank, in Table 2.

As it can be seen from Table 2, 96% of all the sub-trees that occur in the treebank contain five of less child nodes. We can therefore expect the X system to erroneously flag errors in sub-trees consisting of a higher number of child nodes even though they do not contain grammatical errors, but due to the fact that such sub-trees never occur in the treebank. The first evaluation we make therefore aims to measure the error detection performance of different versions of the X system that query only the sub-trees that consist of equal or less child nodes than the given threshold *MAXN*. The precision, recall and F1 scores for each X system are provided in Figure 6, for the SMT and the RBMT output.

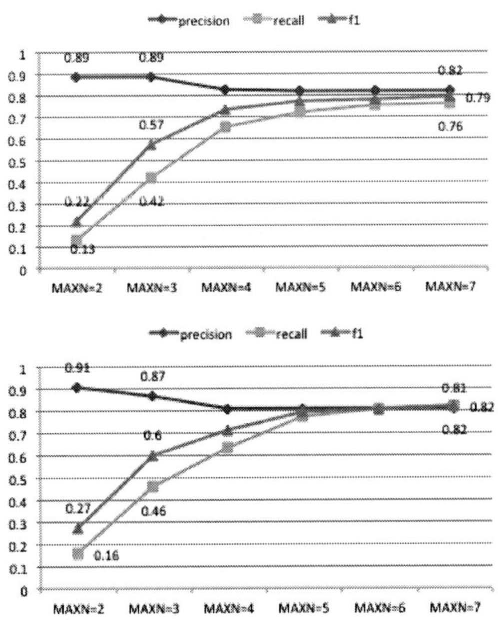

Figure 6. Sentence-level evaluation of the different versions of the system X, with respect to MAXN on the SMT (above) and the RBMT (below) output: Precision, Recall and F1 scores for detecting grammar errors

As MAXN values can be combined with different threshold values T, various versions of the X system can be built. To have a better understanding of the impact of different T values on the error detection performance, we choose an X system with high precision (MAXN=3) on both types of MT output and refer to this as the X system in the remainder of this study. A simple analysis of the annotations obtained by this system shows us that 10% and 11% of the annotations (SMT and RBMT respectively) marked non-adjacent words and these annotations were able to capture agreement errors such as the determiner-noun agreement problems as in "onze medisch project *(EN: our medical project)*", which should be rephrased as "ons medisch project".

Next, we evaluate the performance of the three types of error detection systems (*P*, *X* and *P+X*) on detecting grammatical errors at the sentence level, and compare the results for the SMT and the RBMT output in Figures 7 and 8. For the *X* system, we include the results obtained from the different versions, using different *T* values as threshold.

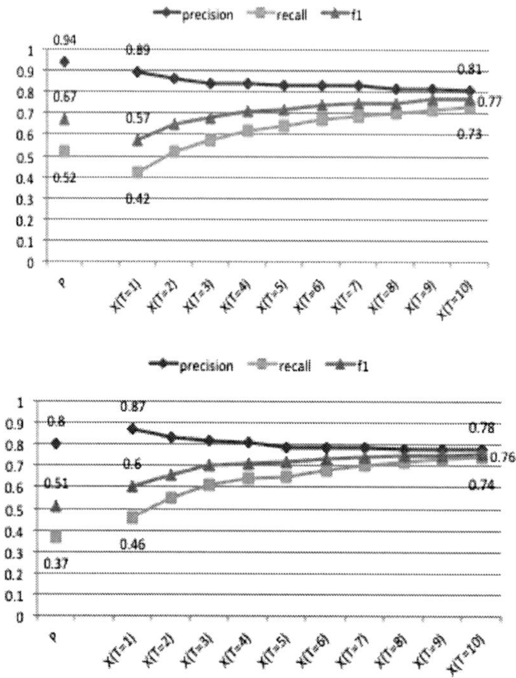

Figure 7. Sentence-level evaluation of the two systems *P* and *X* on SMT (above) and RBMT (below) output: Precision, Recall and F1 scores for error detection performance on grammar errors

We can make a number of observations from Figure 7. First of all, the *P* system performs better overall on detecting grammatical errors in the SMT output compared to the RBMT output. While the *X(T=1)* system shows a higher precision for the SMT system, it shows higher recall for the RBMT system. When we evaluate the *X* system using increasing *T* values, we see a similar trend for both types of MT output, namely minor losses in precision and major gains on recall, which leads to increased F1 scores. However, with increasing *T* values, the system potentially annotates more words per sentence, which should be taken into account for error detection on word-level. We discuss the impact of high *T* values on the performance of word-level error detection in Section 5.2.

If we compare Figures 7 and 8, we can see that the third error detection system (*P+X*) has a higher recall for both types of MT output and for all values of *T* (for the *X* system), which is an indication that the two types of error detection systems detect different grammar errors. In Figure 8, we see that for both types of MT output, the increasing *T* values brings minor losses on precision and major gains on recall, similar to our observations from Figure 7. A final comparison on sentence level performance can be made with a trivial baseline system, which would mark all sentences (698) as erroneous. Based on the data statistics provided in Table 1, this baseline would score 0,66 and 0,63 on precision with respect to the evaluations made on the SMT and the RBMT output and score 1 on recall for both systems, yielding F1 scores of 79,5 on the SMT output and 77 on the RBMT output. Even though these results would be comparable to the F1 scores we observe in Figures 7 and 8, the strength of the error detection systems being evaluated in this study is the high precision scores they achieve.

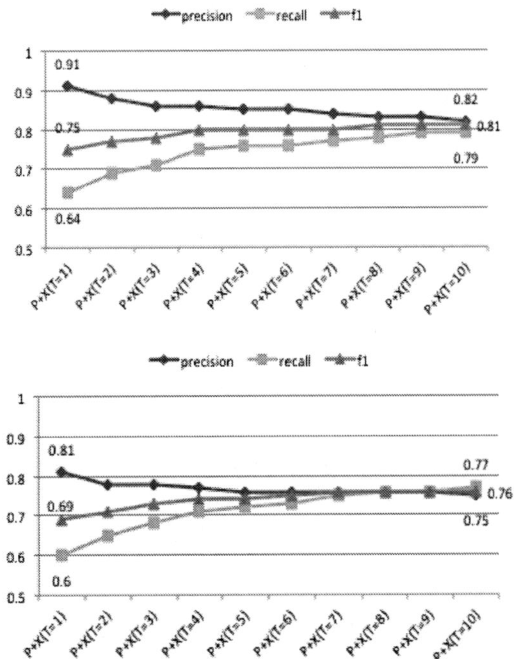

Figure 8. Sentence-level evaluation of the system $P+X$ on SMT (above) and RBMT (below) output: Precision, Recall and F1 scores for error detection performance on grammar errors

5.2. Word-level evaluation

We additionally evaluate the two error detection systems P and X on word level. In this evaluation, each word is considered either erroneous or not and this binary distinction is used to evaluate the error detection performances of the two systems. Since choosing different values of n has an impact on the number of errors being marked by the P system, in this evaluation, we include different versions of this system, which are based on different n values. The evaluation results for detecting errors on word-level are provided in Figure 9, per system.

In Figure 9, we see relatively low precision, recall and F1 scores for all systems. Even though it is difficult to compare, given that we only target grammar errors in this study, similar F1 results have been observed in the WMT 2015 word-level QE task (Bojar et al., 2015) ranging between 16 and 43. It seems that even though these systems perform well on sentence-level error detection, they are not able to locate the errors within the MT output with high accuracy. So, word-level QE seems to be a more challenging task. One reason for the poorer performance of these systems on word-level error detection can be due to the parsing issues that surface in other parts of the MT output and not on the sub-trees which contain the erroneous words themselves.

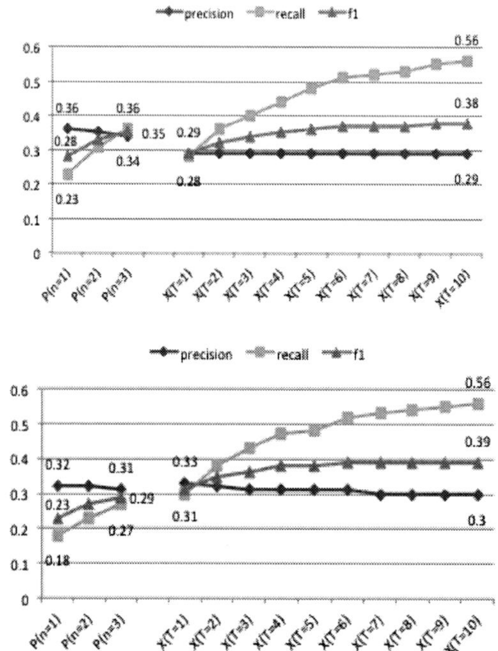

Figure 9. Word-level evaluation of the two systems *P* and *X* on SMT (left) and RBMT (right) output: Performance with respect to precision, recall and F1 scores for locating grammar errors, per system.

Table 3. The average ratio of the number of errors marked erroneous by the error detection systems to the number of words marked in the reference error annotations, per error detection system, per MT type. This comparison is made on the sentences for which there is at least one word being marked as an error both by the error detection systems and in the reference error annotation set.

	P(n= 1)	P(n= 2)	P(n= 3)	X(T= 1)	X(T= 2)	X(T= 3)	X(T= 4)	X(T= 5)	X(T= 6)	X(T= 7)	X(T= 8)	X(T= 9)	X(T= 10)
SMT	0,94	1,28	1,58	1,66	1,7	1,73	1,77	1,86	1,88	1,94	1,96	1,97	2
RBMT	0,86	1,14	1,37	1,38	1,57	1,65	1,73	1,76	1,82	1,88	1,89	1,9	1,91

Figure 9 additionally shows us that the *P* system performs better on SMT output (for all performance measures and for all values of *n*). We can also see that the performance of both systems improves, with respect to recall and F1 measures, with increasing *n* and *T* values. However, this increase affects the number of words being marked as error as well as the precision and recall scores. In Table 3, we compare the number of words marked as erroneous between the output of the two error detection systems, *P* and *X*, and the reference error annotations in the evaluation set.

From Table 3, we can see that except for the *P(n=1)* system, all versions of both error detection systems mark more words on average than the number of words being annotated as errors in the reference error annotation set. The optimal values of *n* and *T* would therefore depend on the goal of such an error detection system. If the systems are used for highlighting errors in the MT output, higher values of *n* and *T* can highlight too many words. On the other hand, if the goal is to extract features for predicting post-editing speed, lower values of these parameters could restrict the amount of useful information. Depending on the scenario and the optimal values of *n* and *T*, these two approaches can be combined (as *P+X*) in many different ways.

6. Conclusion and future work

We proposed two approaches that use dependency structures for detecting grammatical errors in Dutch MT output. One approach uses the partial parses generated by the Alpino parser, while the second approach uses simple corpus statistics of sub-trees occurring in a treebank. We evaluated the error detection performance of systems based on these two approaches at sentence and word level on SMT and RBMT output and showed that such systems can effectively be used to detect grammatical errors for both types of MT architectures. A third system, which combines the two approaches together, yields especially high precision scores on sentence-level error detection.

While the partial parses generated by the Alpino parser can be considered as information that is language and system-specific, querying sub-trees of automatically generated parse trees against a treebank is a language-independent approach. Moreover, by building the treebank from automatically parsed sentences, we show that this approach does not require manual corrections on parse trees in order to be effective and can be used with larger automatically generated treebanks in combination with queries of sub-trees containing a higher number of nodes in the future. The treebank querying approach currently marks all words spanned under a sub-tree, when an error is detected. This often marks too many words as erroneous. We would like to adapt this method to detect specific grammar errors, such as article-noun or adjective-noun agreements, which can locate the erroneous words alone, without spanning the complete sub-trees in which they appear.

Having shown that the proposed methods provide valuable information about grammatical errors in MT output, we would like to analyse the correlation between the output of these error detection systems with post-editing effort, with respect to post-editing speed and the number of edits that are involved in the post-editing task. Besides being used as standalone tools, these error detection systems can provide useful features for building ML systems. We would also like to use the proposed approaches to generate features of an ML system for QE on sub-segment level. The extracted features can be combined with other fluency features, such as the features obtained from n-gram language models that can model local context and adequacy features that capture meaning-transfer errors. ML systems can additionally be used to optimize the n parameter for the P system and T and $MAXN$ parameters for the X system.

Acknowledgements

This research has been carried out in the framework of the SCATE project funded by the Flemish government agency IWT.

References

Augustinus, L., Vandeghinste, V., Van Eynde, F. (2012). Example-Based Treebank Querying. In: *Proceedings of the 8th International Conference on Language Resources and Evaluation*, Istanbul, Turkey, 3161–3167.

Bach, N., Huang, F., Al-Onaizan, Y. (2011). Goodness: A method for measuring machine translation confidence. In: *Proceedings of the 49th Annual Meeting of the Association for Computational Linguistics: Human Language Technologies,* Association for Computational Linguistics, Portland, Oregon, USA, 211–219.

Blatz, J., Fitzgerald, E., Foster, G., Gandrabur, S., Goutte, C., Kulesza, A., Sanchis, A., Ueffing, N. (2004). Confidence estimation for machine translation. In: *Proceedings of the 20th international conference on Computational Linguistics*, Association for Computational Linguistics, Geneva, Switzerland, 315.

Bojar, O., Buck, C., Federmann, C., Haddow, B., Koehn, P., Leveling, J., Monz, C., Pecina, P., Post, M., Saint-Amand, H., Soricut, R. (2014). Findings of the 2014 workshop on statistical machine translation. In: Proceedings of the Ninth Workshop on Statistical Machine Translation Association for Computational Linguistics, Baltimore, MD, USA, 12–58.

Costa, Â., Ling, W., Luís, T., Correia, R., Coheur, L. (2015). A linguistically motivated taxonomy for Machine Translation error analysis. In: Machine Translation, 29(2), 127-161.

Daems, J., Macken, L., Vandepitte, S. (2013). Quality as the sum of its parts: A two-step approach for the identification of translation problems and translation quality assessment for HT and MT+ PE. In: Proceedings of MT Summit XIV Workshop on Post-Editing Technology and Practice, 63–71.

Daems, J., Vandepitte, S., Hartsuiker, R., Macken, L. (2015). The impact of machine translation error types on post-editing effort indicators. In: 4th Workshop on Post-Editing Technology and Practice, Association for Machine Translation in the Americas, Miami, Florida, USA, 31–45.

De Marneffe, M. C., MacCartney, B., Manning, C. D. (2006). Generating typed dependency parses from phrase structure parses. In: Proceedings of the 5th International Conference on Language Resources and Evaluation, Genoa, Italy, 449–454.

de Souza, J. G., Politecnica de Valencia, U., Buck, C., Turchi, M., Negri, M. (2014). FBK-UPV-UEdin participation in the WMT14 Quality Estimation shared-task. In: Proceedings of the Ninth Workshop on Statistical Machine Translation, Baltimore, USA, 322–328.

Depraetere, I., De Sutter, N., Tezcan, A. (2014). Post-edited quality, post-editing behaviour and human evaluation: a case study. In: Post-editing of machine translation: processes and applications, 78–108.

Guerberof, A. (2009). Productivity and quality in MT post-editing. In: MT Summit XII-Workshop: Beyond Translation Memories: New Tools for Translators MT, Ottawa, Ontario, Canada, 8.

Hardmeier, C. (2011). Improving machine translation quality prediction with syntactic tree kernels. In: Proceedings of the 15th conference of the European Association for Machine Translation, Leuven, Belgium, 233–240.

Joshi, A., Rambow, O. (2003). A formalism for dependency grammar based on tree adjoining grammar. In: Proceedings of the Conference on Meaning-Text Theory, Paris, France, 207–216.

Lommel, A., Uszkoreit, H. Burchardt, A. (2014). Multidimensional Quality Metrics (MQM): A Framework for Declaring and Describing Translation Quality Metrics. In: Revista tradumàtica: traducció i tecnologies de la informació i la comunicació, (12), 455–463.

Ma, W. Y., McKeown, K. (2011). System Combination for Machine Translation Based on Text-to-Text Generation. In: Proceedings of Machine Translation Summit XIII, Xiamen, China, 546–553.

Macken, L., De Clercq, O. Paulussen, H. (2011). Dutch parallel corpus: a balanced copyright-cleared parallel corpus. In: Meta: Translators' Journal, 56(2), 374-390.

Popović, M., Ney, H. (2011). Towards automatic error analysis of machine translation output. In: Computational Linguistics, 37(4), 657-688.

Schuurman, I., Schouppe, M., Hoekstra, H., Van der Wouden, T. (2003). CGN, an annotated corpus of spoken Dutch. In: Proceedings of 4th International Workshop on Language Resources and Evaluation, Lisbon, Portugal, 340-347.

Gandrabur, S., and Foster, G. (2003). Confidence estimation for text prediction. In: Proceedings of the Conference on Natural Language Learning, Edmonton, Canada, 95–102.

Specia, L., Turchi, M., Cancedda, N., Dymetman, M., Cristianini, N. (2009). Estimating the sentence-level quality of machine translation systems. In: Proceedings of the 13th Conference of the European Association for Machine Translation, Barcelona, Spain, 28-37.

Specia, L., Paetzold, G., Scarton, C. (2015). Multi-level Translation Quality Prediction with QuEst++. In: 53rd Annual Meeting of the Association for Computational Linguistics and Seventh International Joint Conference on Natural Language Processing of the Asian Federation of Natural Language Processing: System Demonstrations, Beijing, China, 115-120.

Stymne, S., Ahrenberg, L. (2010). Using a Grammar Checker for Evaluation and Postprocessing of Statistical Machine Translation. In: Proceedings of the Seventh International Conference on Language Resources and Evaluation, Valetta, Malta, 2175–2181.

Tezcan, A., Hoste, V., Macken. L. (in press). SCATE Taxonomy and Corpus of Machine Translation Errors. In: Trends in e-tools and resources for translators and interpreters. Leiden: Brill Academic Publishers.

Tezcan, A., Hoste, V., Desmet, B., Macken, L. (2015). UGENT-LT3 SCATE system for machine translation quality estimation. In: Proceedings of the Tenth Workshop on Statistical Machine Translation, Lisboa, Portugal, 353–360.

Ueffing, N., Ney, H. (2007). Word-level confidence estimation for machine translation. In: Computational Linguistics, 33(1), 9–40.

Van Eynde, F. (2005). Part Of Speech Tagging En Lemmatisering Van Het D-Coi Corpus. Intermediate, project-internal version, available at http://odur.let.rug.nl/vannoord/Lassy/POS_manual.pdf

van Noord, G. (2006). At last parsing is now operational. In: TALN06. Verbum Ex Machina. Actes de la 13e conference sur le traitement automatique des langues naturelles, Leuven, Belgium, 20–42.

van Noord, G. (2001). Robust parsing of word graphs. In: Robustness in Language and Speech Technology, Springer Netherlands, 205–238.

Received May 1, 2016, accepted May 11, 2016

Baltic J. Modern Computing, Vol. 4 (2016), No. 2, pp. 218–229

Potential and Limits of Using Post-edits as Reference Translations for MT Evaluation

Maja POPOVIĆ[1], Mihael ARČAN[2], Arle LOMMEL[3]

[1] Humboldt University of Berlin
[2] Insight Centre for Data Analytics, NUI Galway, Ireland
[3] Common Sense Advisory (CSA Research)

`maja.popovic@hu-berlin.de, mihael.arcan@insight-centre.org,`
`arle.lommel@gmail.com`

Abstract. This work investigates the potential use of post-edited machine translation (MT) outputs as reference translations for automatic machine translation evaluation, focusing mainly on the following important question: *Is it necessary to take into account the machine translation system and the source language from which the given post-edits are generated?*
In order to explore this, we investigated the use of post-edits originating from different machine translation systems (two statistical systems and two rule-based systems), as well as the use of post-edits originating from two different source languages (English and German). The obtained results shown that for comparison of different systems using automatic evaluation metrics, a good option is to use a post-edit originating from a high-quality (possibly distinct) system. A better option is to use it together with other references and post-edits, however post-edits originating from poor translation systems should be avoided. For tuning or development of a particular system, post-edited output of this same system seems to be the best reference translation.

Keywords: machine translation evaluation, reference translations, post-edited translations

1 Introduction

The evaluation of the machine translation (MT) output is an important and difficult task. The fastest way is to use an automatic evaluation metric, which compares the obtained output with a human translation of the same source text and calculates a numerical score related to their similarity. Despite all disadvantages and criticisms, such metrics are still irreplaceable for many tasks (such as rapid development of a new system, tuning of a statistical MT system, etc.) and are considered as at least baseline metrics for MT quality evaluation. All these metrics (n-gram based such as BLEU [Papineni et al., 2002] and METEOR [Banerjee and Lavie, 2005], edit-distance based such as TER [Snover et al., 2006], etc.) are reference-based, i.e. a human reference translation is needed as a gold standard. Since there is usually not only one single best translation of a text, the best way of evaluating an MT output would be to compare it with many references

– nevertheless, creating each reference translation is a time consuming and expensive process. Therefore, automatic MT evaluation is usually carried out using only a single reference.

On the other hand, MT has considerably improved in the recent years so that the use of MT outputs as a starting point for human translation has become a common practice. Therefore, ever-increasing amounts of post-edited machine translation outputs (PEs) are being collected. These represent very valuable data and are being used for a number of applications, such as automatic quality prediction, adaptation, etc. Among other things, post-edits are more similar to MT outputs than "independent" references, thus being potentially more useful for automatic evaluation and/or tuning. However, their use as reference translations has been scarcely investigated so far.

This work explores two scenarios: comparing four distinct MT systems using PEs originating from these systems, as well as comparing translations from two different source languages using PEs originating from these source languages. In addition, the effects of using multiple references are reported in terms of variations and standard deviations of automatic scores for different number of references.

1.1 Related work

Post-edited translations have been used for many applications, such as automatic prediction of translation quality [Specia, 2011], analysing various aspects of post-editing effort [Tatsumi and Roturier, 2010, Blain et al., 2011], human and automatic analysis of performed edit operations [Koponen, 2012, Wisniewski et al., 2013], as well as improving translation and language model of an SMT system by learning from post-edits [Bertoldi et al., 2013, Denkowski et al., 2014, Mathur et al., 2014]. The cache-based approach, introduced in [Bertoldi et al., 2013], makes it possible to periodically add knowledge from PEs into an SMT system in real-time, without the need to stop it. The main idea behind the cache-based models is to mix a large global (static) model with a small local (dynamic) model estimated from recent items observed in the history of the input stream. In [Wisniewski et al., 2013], the PEs are used as references for automatic estimation of performed edit operations, namely substitutions, deletions, insertions and shifts. [Denkowski et al., 2014] report the improvements of the BLEU scores calculated on independent references as well as on PEs in order to emphasise the suitability of their methods for the post-editing task.

A number of publications deals with the usage of multiple references for automatic MT evaluation. Using pseudo-references, i.e. raw translation outputs from different MT systems has been investigated in [Albrecht and Hwa, 2007, Albrecht and Hwa, 2008] and it is shown that, even though these are not correct human translations, it is beneficiary to add pseudo-references instead of using one single reference. Adding automatically generated paraphrases together to a set of standard human references for tuning has been investigated in [Madnani et al., 2008], and it is shown that the paraphrases are improving automatic scores BLEU and TER when the number of multiple human references is less than four. Recently, multiple references have been explored in [Qin and Specia, 2015] in terms of using recurring information in these references in order to generate better version of BLEU and NIST [Doddington, 2002] metrics by better n-gram weighting.

To the best of our knowledge, no systematic investigation regarding the use of post-edited translation outputs as reference translations has been carried out yet.

2 Research questions

Although the PEs are intuitively better suitable for MT evaluation than standard human references because they are closer to the MT output structure, there are several important questions which have to be taken into account:

1. Should the PE originate from the very same MT system, or is it acceptable to use any PE?
2. Is the source language of any importance?
3. Does the system type (statistical or rule-based) have any impact?

In order to systematically explore the potential and limits of post-edits and answer these questions, following scenarios are investigated:

- using PEs produced by four distinct MT systems;
- using PEs generated from two different source languages;

The PEs are used for system comparison in order to explore variations and possible bias of the obtained automatic scores. Apart from the use of each post-edit separately, the effects of combining them in the form of multiple references has been investigated. In addition, the effect of the source language has also been explored in terms of tuning an SMT system. The details about the experiments and the obtained results are described in the next two sections.

3 Experiments

3.1 Data sets

For investigation of effects described in the previous section, two suitable data sets containing different language pairs, target languages and domains were available:

1. TARAXÜ texts [Avramidis et al., 2014] containing German-to-English, German-to-Spanish and English-to-German raw translations and PEs of WMT news texts generated by two SMT (phrase-based and hierarchical) and two RBMT systems;
2. OPENSUBTITLES texts from the PE^{2}rr corpus [Popović and Arčan, 2016] containing Serbian and Slovenian subtitle raw translations and PEs generated by phrase-based SMT systems from English and from German.

Both data sets contain single standard reference translations, as well as sentence-level human rankings.

For the TARAXÜ WMT texts, post-editing and ranking were performed by professional translators, and for the PE^{2}rr OPENSUBTITLES texts by researchers familiar with machine and human translation highly fluent both in source and in target languages. Details about the texts can be seen in Table 1.[4]

---

[4] Although the texts are already publicly available, they are also available in the exact form used in this work at `https://github.com/m-popovic/multiple-edits-refs`.

Table 1: Data statistics

domain	language pair	# source sentences	avg. target sent. length	# of PE
WMT	de-en	240	22.9	4
(TARAXÜ)	de-es	40	26.8	4
	en-de	272	21.9	4
	es-de	101	23.2	4
OPEN	en-sr	440	8.3	2
SUBTITLES	de-sr	440	8.1	2
(PE^{2}rr)	en-sl	440	8.7	2
	de-sl	440	8.5	2

It should be noted that, although there are more (larger) publicly available data sets containing post-edited MT outputs, none of these sets contains post-edits originating from different translation systems or from different source languages, which are requested to answer the questions posed in Section 2.

3.2   Evaluation methods

For all experiments, BLEU scores [Papineni et al., 2002] and character n-gram F scores, i.e. CHRF3 scores [Popović, 2015], calculated using different PEs are reported. BLEU is used as a well-known and widely used metric, and CHRF3 as a simple tokenisation-independent metric, which has shown very good correlations with human judgements on the WMT-2015 shared metric task [Stanojević et al., 2015], both on the system level as well as on the segment level, especially for morphologically rich(er) languages.

For both scores, Pearson's system-level correlation coefficient r is reported for each PE. For CHRF3, segment-level Kendall's τ correlation coefficient is presented as well. For both correlation coefficients, the ties in human rankings were excluded from calculation. In all tables, post-edited MT outputs are marked with ^{pe}.

Initially, for each of the two data sets the scores were calculated separately for each target language. Nevertheless, since no differences related to the target language were observed, the results were merged.

4   Results

4.1   Post-edits from (four) different translation systems

In order to investigate PEs originating from different MT systems, the TARAXÜ corpus was used, where each source sentence was translated by four MT systems. Although there is certain overlap, i.e. some of the source sentences are human translations of other source sentences, the majority of them are unique. BLEU and CHRF3 scores are calculated separately using each of PEs as reference, as well as for combinations of multiple PEs. The scores, together with system-level and segment-level correlation coefficients, are presented in Table 2.

Table 2: BLEU (left) and CHRF3 (right) scores calculated on PEs originating from four distinct MT systems (two SMT and two RBMT) and on an independent reference translation; the scores are strongly biased towards the particular system and slightly biased towards the system type; the best option is to use PE of a high performance system or multiple references without PEs of poor quality systems.

BLEU scores # reference(s)	translation output s1	s2	RB1	RB2	corr. sys
1 $s1^{pe}$	**41.0**	25.8	22.5	20.0	-.40
$s2^{pe}$	27.8	**35.4**	21.2	19.7	-.99
$RB1^{pe}$	22.4	19.4	**46.6**	25.9	.75
$RB2^{pe}$	21.7	19.4	28.8	**41.3**	.77
reference	12.7	11.4	12.0	10.6	-.15
2 two SMT^{pe}	43.4	38.0	27.0	24.7	-.97
two $RBMT^{pe}$	27.0	23.6	48.7	43.5	**.99**
3 no $s1^{pe}$	34.8	38.1	49.5	44.4	.93
no $s2^{pe}$	43.8	31.1	49.5	44.5	**.98**
no $RB1^{pe}$	44.3	38.9	35.6	43.9	.20
no $RB2^{pe}$	44.4	38.8	48.9	32.2	.19
4 all^{pe}	44.9	39.4	50.0	45.1	.92
5 all^{pe}+ref	46.5	40.8	51.6	45.8	.88
human ranks	57.6	47.6	69.3	67.4	

CHRF3 scores # reference(s)	translation output s1	s2	RB1	RB2	corr. sys	seg
1 $s1^{pe}$	**67.9**	55.8	55.7	54.4	-.24	.03
$s2^{pe}$	58.1	**63.5**	54.6	53.8	-.98	.12
$RB1^{pe}$	54.0	50.7	**72.3**	58.6	.83	.29
$RB2^{pe}$	53.3	50.6	59.4	**69.5**	.80	.24
reference	43.4	41.4	44.0	43.6	.93	.13
2 two SMT^{pe}	68.6	64.2	58.1	57.0	-.71	.30
two $RBMT^{pe}$	56.6	53.4	72.8	70.2	**.96**	**.34**
3 no $s1^{pe}$	60.9	64.3	73.0	70.4	.78	**.38**
no $s2^{pe}$	68.6	58.0	73.0	70.4	**.95**	.30
no $RB1^{pe}$	68.8	64.4	62.5	70.2	.10	.14
no $RB2^{pe}$	68.9	64.5	72.9	61.4	.26	.20
4 all^{pe}	69.0	64.7	73.2	70.6	**.97**	.30
5 all^{pe}+ref	69.1	64.8	73.2	70.6	**.97**	.30
human ranks	32.0	22.0	54.8	46.5		

The following can be observed:

- each system gets the highest score when its own PE is used as a reference (bold); system level correlations are very low if the worse ranked system's PEs are used — in such scenario, worst systems obtain the highest automatic scores;
- the scores for both of SMT systems are higher if the two SMTPEs are used; analogously applies for the RBMT systems;
- the best options in terms of correlations are
  - using PE of the best ranked system;
  - not using PE of the worst ranked system;
  - using all PEs (and reference).

Table 3 presents edit distances between PEs as well as between PEs and the reference, and it can be seen that the differences are not negligible, which explains the strong bias towards the particular system. It can also be seen that the post-edits of the same system types are slightly closer ($\sim$35%) than those of the two different system types

Table 3: Edit distances between PEs originating from four distinct systems and reference; the PEs of the same system types are slightly closer than those of the two different system types; the reference is significantly different from all PEs.

edit distance	$s1^{pe}$	$s2^{pe}$	$RB1^{pe}$	$RB2^{pe}$	ref
$s1^{pe}$	/	34.3	41.0	42.9	70.0
$s2^{pe}$	34.2	/	41.9	42.4	70.1
$RB1^{pe}$	40.5	41.5	/	35.4	70.9
$RB2^{pe}$	41.7	41.3	34.7	/	69.6
ref	69.0	69.2	70.6	70.5	/

($\sim$42%), as well as that there is a large distance ($\sim$70%) between the reference and each of the PEs.

An example of German-to-English translation outputs, PEs and the corresponding reference is presented in Table 4.

Table 4: Example of post-edited German-to-English MT outputs originating from four distinct translation systems.

system	translation output	PE
s1	There are also a few cars off the road.	There are also a few cars off the road.
s2	Few cars are off the road.	A few cars are also off the road.
RB1	Also a few Pkws lie in the street ditch.	Also, a few cars are lying on the side of the street.
RB2	Also a few car lies in the ditch.	A few cars are also lying in the ditch.
	reference:	Also several cars ended up in a ditch.

4.2 Post-edits from (two) different source languages

For exploring influence of the source language, the OPENSUBTITLES texts were used, where each of the parallel German and English source sentences was translated by a corresponding phrase-based SMT system. The effects of the source language on the automatic scores are shown in Table 5. Since there are only two systems to compare, system-level Pearson's correlation coefficient can be either 1 or -1.

It can be noted that:

- the source language strongly influences the results: for each translation output, the automatic scores are always higher when its own PE is used;

Table 5: BLEU (left) and CHRF3 (right) scores calculated on SMTPEs originating from two different source languages and on an independent reference translation; the results are strongly biased towards the source language; the best option is to use PE of a high performance system or multiple references without PEs of poor systems.

BLEU scores reference(s)	translation output en→x	de→x	corr. sys
1 en→x^{pe}	**47.7**	23.9	1
de→x^{pe}	24.4	**45.5**	-1
reference	24.8	17.2	1
2 en→x^{pe}+ref	51.3	28.2	1
de→x^{pe}+ref	35.9	47.9	-1
both^{pe}	50.4	48.0	1
3 both^{pe}+ref	53.0	49.2	1
human ranks	38.6	21.1	

CHRF3 scores reference(s)	translation output en→x	de→x	corr. sys	seg
1 en→x^{pe}	**64.7**	44.6	1	.42
de→x^{pe}	45.8	**62.6**	-1	.13
reference	47.8	39.4	1	.44
2 en→x^{pe}+ref	65.6	47.8	1	.42
de→x^{pe}+ref	54.6	63.4	-1	.28
both^{pe}	66.5	63.8	1	.48
3 both^{pe}+ref	67.2	64.3	1	**.50**
human ranks	38.6	21.1		

- using PE of the better ranked system yields good correlation, whereas using PE from the worse system claims that this system is better;
- the scores obtained by the independent reference are more similar to those obtained by the PE generated from English.

Furthermore, Table 6 shows that edit distances between PEs are rather large, about 45%. Similar edit distance can be seen between the independent reference and the PE originating from English, whereas for the PE originating from German it is much larger – over 55%. At this point, it is important to note that the original source language of all used texts is English – the German source text as well as the Serbian and Slovenian references are human translations of the English original. Therefore, the fact that the PE originating from German source is an "outlier" confirms the previous findings about the importance of the original source language, e.g. [Kurokawa et al., 2009, Lembersky et al., 2013], namely that (i) a translated text has different characteristics than the same text written directly in the given language, as well as that (ii) the direction of human translation has impact on MT, so that it is better to train MT system in the corresponding direction, i.e. using original texts as the source language and human translations as the target language.

4.3   Multiple reference effects

Apart from the main questions posed in Section 2, an additional question has been raised during the realisation of the described experiments – what are the actual effects of the use of multiple references vs. the use of a single reference?

The advantage of multiple references is surely well known as mentioned in Section 1.1, however our question is – what is exactly happening with the automatic scores? In order to answer it, we explored the variations in automatic scores when different

Table 6: Edit distances between post-edits originating from two different source languages and an independent reference translation.

edit distance	en-x^{pe}	de-x^{pe}	reference
en$\rightarrow$x^{pe}	0	44.6	44.7
de$\rightarrow$x^{pe}	45.7	0	56.4
reference	45.2	55.6	0

numbers of multiple references are used. For this experiment, apart from the two data sets described in previous sections, an additional small data set[5] was explored as well. This data set consists of only 20 English source sentences from technical domain, however each source sentence corresponds to 12 different human translations into German, i.e. 12 multiple references. Each source sentence has been automatically translated by four distinct translation systems, two statistical and two rule-based (albeit not the same as those used for experiments in Section 4.1), but no post-editing has been performed.

For each of the three data sets, average BLEU and CHRF3 values and their standard deviations (σ) for different numbers of available reference translations are calculated and results are presented in Table 7. It can be seen that:

- average values are logarithmically increasing with increasing number of multiple references;
- standard deviations are
  - dropping with increasing number of multiple references
  - close to zero only for more than 10 references
  - smaller for the MT systems of lower performance

These tendencies can be equally observed for all data sets, no matter how many PEs (more similar to MT outputs) and how many independent references (less similar to MT outputs) are used.

4.4 Tuning

A preliminary experiment regarding tuning on PEs originating from different source languages has been carried out using the OPENSUBTITLES data set: (i) the translation system was tuned with MERT [Och, 2003] on BLEU using (i) the independent reference (standard method), (ii) using the PE originating from the corresponding language and (iii) using the PE originating from the other language.

The results for another test set (not the one used for tuning) containing 2000 sentences[6] are presented in Table 8 showing that tuning on the post-edit from the corresponding source language produces best BLEU and METEOR scores.

This confirms the effect of the source language bias and indicates a potential of using PEs of a MT system for tuning and development of this system.

---

[5] also available at `https://github.com/m-popovic/multiple-edits-refs`
[6] also available at the aforementioned repository

Table 7: Effects of the number of multiple references: average BLEU and CHRF3 scores with standard deviations for different number of (independent) references ranging from 1 to 12. The results are obtained on the texts used in previous sections (a), (b) as well as on a small text with a large number (12) of independent reference translations (c).

(a) PEs of four different systems + one reference

	number of references	SMT1		SMT2		RBMT1		RBMT2	
		avg.	σ	avg.	σ	avg.	σ	avg.	σ
BLEU	1	25.1	9.3	22.3	8.0	26.2	11.5	23.5	10.2
	2	35.0	7.0	30.8	5.9	37.3	9.5	33.3	8.3
	3	40.3	5.3	35.4	4.4	43.6	7.6	38.8	6.7
	4	43.9	3.4	38.5	2.8	48.2	5.2	42.8	4.6
	all (5)	46.5	/	40.8	/	51.6	/	45.8	/
CHRF3	1	55.3	7.9	52.4	7.2	57.2	9.1	56.0	8.4
	2	62.0	5.7	58.4	5.0	64.6	7.0	62.9	6.2
	3	65.1	4.5	61.3	3.8	68.3	5.7	66.2	5.0
	4	67.4	2.9	63.3	2.6	71.0	4.2	68.7	3.5
	all (5)	69.1	/	64.8	/	73.2	/	70.6	/

(b) PEs of two source languages + one reference

	number of references	en→x		de→x	
		avg.	σ	avg.	σ
BLEU	1	32.3	10.9	28.9	12.1
	2	45.9	7.0	41.4	9.3
	all (3)	53.0	/	49.2	/
CHRF3	1	52.8	8.5	48.9	9.9
	2	62.2	5.4	58.3	7.4
	all (3)	67.2	/	64.3	/

(c) twelve references

	number of references	sys1		sys2		sys3		sys4	
		avg.	σ	avg.	σ	avg.	σ	avg.	σ
BLEU	1	32.1	8.4	29.4	9.7	23.2	6.5	13.3	5.0
	2	41.6	6.0	39.2	9.2	29.2	4.2	17.7	2.9
	10	61.2	1.7	62.4	2.0	40.5	0.6	26.0	0.6
	11	62.0	1.2	63.3	1.3	40.8	0.4	26.3	0.4
	all (12)	62.8	/	64.0	/	41.1	/	26.6	/
CHRF3	1	63.6	7.8	61.5	8.6	56.0	5.6	54.2	5.7
	2	71.1	5.1	69.3	6.8	62.0	3.3	60.0	3.7
	10	80.5	0.5	81.3	1.1	68.6	0.3	67.1	0.3
	11	80.7	0.3	81.7	0.6	68.8	0.2	67.3	0.2
	all (12)	81.0	/	82.0	/	69.0	/	67.5	/

Table 8: Effects of source language on tuning of an SMT system: MERT tuning on BLEU using independent reference, post-edit from the corresponding source language and post-edit from another source language. The best BLEU and METEOR scores are obtained when the corresponding source language post-edit is used.

translating	tuned on	BLEU	METEOR	translating	tuned on	BLEU	METEOR
en→sr	ref	20.1	39.2	en→sl	ref	26.0	45.2
	en→sr^{pe}	**21.6**	**39.9**		**en→sl^{pe}**	**26.5**	**45.3**
	de→sr^{pe}	20.8	39.8		de→sl^{pe}	25.5	44.4
de→sr	ref	17.2	35.4	de→sl	ref	18.1	36.6
	en→sr^{pe}	16.8	35.5		en→sl^{pe}	18.4	36.7
	de→sr^{pe}	**18.0**	**35.5**		**de→sl^{pe}**	**18.8**	**37.1**

5 Discussion

Knowing how difficult the generation of (even a single) references/PEs is, the following findings from the results described in Section 4 can be summarised:

- for comparison of different systems, using single PE of a high quality translation output yields reliable automatic scores; the scores are even more reliable if the PE is generated by an external system – otherwise, the ranking would be still correct but the scores will be biased to this particular system;
- using multiple PEs (and references) is generally beneficial – however, it is better to have fewer PEs of high quality translation outputs than more PEs of low quality translation outputs;
- evaluation of low quality translation outputs is less prone to variability and is generally more reliable, except if (one of) the used reference(s) is its own PE; on the other hand, high quality translation outputs can easily be underestimated if using a single reference/PE;
- for tuning and development of a particular system, the PE from this very system should be used.

6 Summary and outlook

This work has examined the potential and limits of the use of post-edited MT outputs as reference translations for automatic MT evaluation. The experiments have shown that the post-edited translation outputs are definitely useful as reference translations, but it should be kept in mind that the obtained automatic evaluation scores are strongly biased towards the actual system by which the used PE is generated, as well as towards the source language from which the used PE originates. The best option for comparison of different systems using a single PE is to use PE of a high quality translation output which is, if possible, generated by an independent system.

Multiple references are in principle beneficial, although PEs generated from low quality translation outputs should be avoided. Further investigation concerning both quality and quantity of multiple references should be carried out.

For tuning an SMT system, the best option is to use a PE generated by this same system. Nevertheless, it should be noted that this was a preliminary experiment, so that further confirmation of reported findings on more data and language pairs is necessary.

Acknowledgments

This publication has emanated from research supported by the TRAMOOC project (Translation for Massive Open Online Courses), partially funded by the European Commission under H2020-ICT-2014/H2020-ICT-2014-1 under Grant Agreement Number 644333, and by a research grant from Science Foundation Ireland (SFI) under Grant Number SFI/12/RC/2289 (Insight)

References

Joshua S. Albrecht, Rebecca Hwa (2007). Regression for Sentence-level MT Evaluation with Pseudo-references. In *Proceedings of the 45rd Annual Meeting of the Association for Computational Linguistics (ACL-07)*, pages 296–303, Prague, Czech Republic, July.

Joshua S. Albrecht and Rebecca Hwa. 2008. The Role of Pseudo-references in MT evaluation. In *Proceedings of the 3rd Workshop on Statistical Machine Translation (WMT-08)*, pages 187–190, Columbus, Ohio, June.

Eleftherios Avramidis, Aljoscha Burchardt, Sabine Hunsicker, Maja Popović, Cindy Tscherwinka, David Vilar Torres, and Hans Uszkoreit. 2014. The taraXÜ Corpus of Human-Annotated Machine Translations. In *Proceedings of the 9th International Conference on Language Resources and Evaluation (LREC-14)*, pages 2679–2682, Reykjavik, Iceland, May.

Satanjeev Banerjee and Alon Lavie. 2005. METEOR: An Automatic Metric for MT Evaluation with Improved Correlation with Human Judgements. In *Proceedings of the ACL-05 Workshop on Intrinsic and Extrinsic Evaluation Measures for MT and/or Summarization*, pages 65–72, Ann Arbor, MI, June.

Nicola Bertoldi, Mauro Cettolo, and Marcello Federico. 2013. Cache-based Online Adaptation for Machine Translation Enhanced Computer Assisted Translation. In *Proceedings of MT Summit XIV*, Nice, France.

Frédéric Blain, Jean Senellart, Holger Schwenk, Mirko Plitt, and Johann Roturier. 2011. Qualitative Analysis of Post-Editing for High Quality Machine Translation. In *Proceedings of Machine Translation Summit XIII*, Xiamen, China, September.

Michael Denkowski, Chris Dyer, and Alon Lavie. 2014. Learning from Post-Editing: Online Model Adaptation for Statistical Machine Translation. In *Proceedings of the 14th Conference of the European Chapter of the Association for Computational Linguistics (EACL-14)*, pages 395–404, Gothenburg, Sweden, April.

George Doddington. 2002. Automatic Evaluation of Machine Tanslation Quality using n-gram Co-occurrence Statistics. In *Proceedings of the ARPA Workshop on Human Language Technology*, pages 128–132, San Diego, CA, March.

Maarit Koponen. 2012. Comparing human perceptions of post-editing effort with post-editing operations. In *Proceedings of the 7th Workshop on Statistical Machine Translation (WMT-12)*, pages 181–190, Montréal, Canada, June.

David Kurokawa, Cyril Goutte, and Pierre Isabelle. 2009. Automatic Detection of Translated Text and its Impact on Machine Translation. In *Proceedings of MT Summit XII*, pages 81–88, Ottawa, Canada, August.

Gennadi Lembersky, Noam Ordan, and Shuly Wintner. 2013. Improving Statistical Machine Translation by Adapting Translation Models to Translationese. *Computational Linguistics*, 39(4):999–1024, December.

Nitin Madnani, Philip Resnik, Bonnie J. Dorr, and Richard Schwartz. 2008. Are multiple reference translations necessary? Investigating the value of paraphrased reference translations in parameter optimization. In *Proceedings of the 8th Conference of the Association for Machine Translation in the Americas (AMTA-08)*, Waikiki, Hawaii, October.

Prashant Mathur, Mauro Cettolo, Marcello Federico, and José Guillerme Carmago de Souza. 2014. Online Multi-User Adaptive Statistical Machine Translation. In *Proceedings of the 11th Conference of the Association for Machine Translation of the Americas (AMTA-14)*, pages 152–165, Vancouver, Canada, October.

Franz Josef Och. 2003. Minimum Error Rate Training in Statistical Machine Translation. In *Proceedings of the 41th Annual Meeting of the Association for Computational Linguistics (ACL 03)*, pages 160–167, Sapporo, Japan, July.

Kishore Papineni, Salim Roukos, Todd Ward, Wei-Jing Zhu (2002). BLEU: a Method for Automatic Evaluation of Machine Translation. In *Proceedings of the 40th Annual Meeting of the Association for Computational Linguistics (ACL-02)*, pages 311–318, Philadelphia, PA, July.

Maja Popović. 2015. chrF: Character n-gram F-score for Automatic MT Evaluation. In *Proceedings of the 10th Workshop on Statistical Machine Translation (WMT-15)*, pages 392–395, Lisbon, Portugal, September.

Maja Popović, Mihael Arčan. 2016. PE2rr corpus: Manual Error Annotation of Automatically Pre-annotated MT Post-edits. In *Proceedings of the 10th International Conference on Language Resources and Evaluation (LREC-16)*, Portorož, Slovenia, May.

Ying Qin and Lucia Specia. 2015. Truly Exploring Multiple References for Machine Translation Evaluation. In *Proceedings of the 18th Annual Conference of the European Association for Machine Translation (EAMT-15)*, pages 113–120, Antalya, Turkey, May.

Matthew Snover, Bonnie Dorr, Richard Schwartz, Linnea Micciulla, and John Makhoul. 2006. A Study of Translation Error Rate with Targeted Human Annotation. In *Proceedings of the 7th Conference of the Association for Machine Translation in the Americas (AMTA-06)*, pages 223–231, Boston, MA, August.

Lucia Specia. 2011. Exploiting Objective Annotations for Measuring Translation Post-editing Effort. In *Proceedings of the 15th Annual Conference of the European Association for Machine Translation (EAMT-11)*, pages 73–80, Leuven, Belgium, May.

Miloš Stanojević, Amir Kamran, Philipp Koehn, and Ondřej Bojar. 2015. Results of the WMT15 Metrics Shared Task. In *Proceedings of the 10th Workshop on Statistical Machine Translation (WMT-15)*, pages 256–273, Lisbon, Portugal, September.

Midori Tatsumi and Johann Roturier. 2010. Source Text Characteristics and Technical and Temporal Post-editing Effort: What is their Relationship? In *Proceedings of the Second Joint EM+/CGNL Worskhop Bringing MT to the user (JEC-10)*, pages 43–51, Denver, Colorado, November.

Guillaume Wisniewski, Anil Kumar Singh, Natalia Segal, and François Yvon. 2013. Design and Analysis of a Large Corpus of Post-edited Translations: Quality Estimation, Failure Analysis and the Variability of Post-edition. In *Proceedings of MT Summit XIV*, pages 117–124, Nice, France, September.

Received May 2, 2016 , accepted May11, 2016

Baltic J. Modern Computing, Vol. 4 (2016), No. 2, pp. 230–242

Can Text Simplification
Help Machine Translation?

Sanja ŠTAJNER[1] and Maja POPOVIĆ[2]

[1] Data and Web Science Group, University of Mannheim, Germany
[2] Humboldt University of Berlin, Germany

sanja@informatik.uni-mannheim.de, maja.popovic@hu-berlin.de

Abstract. This article explores the use of text simplification as a pre-processing step for statistical machine translation of grammatically complex under-resourced languages. Our experiments on English-to-Serbian translation show that this approach can improve grammaticality (fluency) of the translation output and reduce technical post-editing effort (number of post-edit operations). Furthermore, the use of more aggressive text simplification methods (which do not only simplify the given sentence but also discard irrelevant information thus producing syntactically very simple sentences) also improves meaning preservation (adequacy) of the translation output.

1   Introduction

Machine translation for under-resourced languages is facing a number of problems. First, there is not enough parallel data to build robust statistical machine translation (SMT) systems. Second, most of these languages (including Serbian) have a very rich morphology and suffer from data sparsity when it comes to less frequently used cases, tenses, etc. Third, there is a number of syntactic differences which are difficult to capture. For English-to-Serbian SMT, a number of language related problems has been identified so far (Popović and Arčan, 2015). Most of them are related to syntactic differences, e.g. missing verb parts due to distinct structure of certain verb tenses, incorrect prepositions, or incorrect translations of English sequences of nouns.

In this paper, we explore whether it is possible to improve the performance of the machine translation for under-resourced languages by introducing a pre-processing step in which source sentences are first simplified by an automatic text simplification (ATS) system. We focus on English-to-Serbian MT and apply two state-of-the-art ATS systems as a pre-processing step for simplifying the original English sentence before feeding it into a phrase-based SMT system.

We exploit two different types of ATS systems, a more conservative one (which, while simplifying the input sentence lexically and syntactically, retain all the information contained in the original sentence), and the more aggressive one (which, while simplifying the input sentence lexically and syntactically, also tries to reduce the amount of information by discarding irrelevant information and high-level details). In this way, we address two different usage scenarios in MT: (1) when it is important to maintain all the information contained in the source text (e.g. translations of whole texts or documents); and (2) when it is enough to get a gist of the source text (e.g. skimming through news articles and looking for the most important news).

The results of the human evaluation of the news articles translated using the two above-mentioned approaches, in terms of grammaticality (fluency) and meaning preservation (accuracy) of the output, and the analysis of the post-editing effort (number of post-edit operations) shows that both approaches improve the MT output.

The remainder of the article is structured as follows. Section 2 briefly reports on the existing approaches to automatic text simplification and motivates our choice of ATS systems. Section 3 describes the chosen ATS systems in more details, presents the datasets and the SMT system used in experiments and describes the evaluation procedure. Section 4 presents and discusses the results of our experiments, while Section 5 summarises the main findings and presents ideas for future research.

2   Related Work

Automatic text simplification (ATS) systems aim to transform original texts into their lexically and syntactically simpler variants. In theory, they could also simplify texts on the discourse level, but most of the systems still operate only on the sentence level.

The motivation for building the first ATS systems was to improve the performance of machine translation systems and other text processing tasks, e.g. parsing, information retrieval, and summarisation (Chandrasekar et al., 1996). It was argued that simplified sentences (which have simpler sentential structures and reduced ambiguity) could lead to improvements in the quality of machine translation (Chandrasekar, 1994).

Since then, a great number of ATS systems has been proposed not only for English, but also for other languages, e.g. Basque (Aranzabe et al., 2013), Portuguese (Specia, 2010), Spanish (Saggion et al., 2015), French (Brauwers et al., 2014), and Italian (Barlacchi and Tonelli, 2013).

For English, the state-of-the-art ATS systems range from those performing only lexical (Glavaš and Štajner, 2015) or only syntactic (Siddharthan, 2011) simplification, to those combining lexical and syntactic simplification (Angrosh and Siddharthan, 2014). Recently, several ATS systems have been proposed which do not only simplify given text/sentences but also reduce the amount of information contained by removing high-level details, such as appositions, adverbial phrases, or purely descriptive sentences ((Glavaš and Štajner, 2013), (Siddharthan et al., 2014), (Narayan and Gardent, 2014)).

However, in these twenty years, the motivation for building ATS systems has shifted from improving text processing systems to making texts more accessible to wider audiences (e.g. children, non-native speakers, people with low literacy levels, and people with various language or learning disabilities). Therefore, ATS systems have only been evaluated for the quality of the generated output, its readability levels, and usefulness in making texts more accessible to target populations (reducing reading speed and improving comprehension). To the best of our knowledge, there has been no evaluation of the state-of-the-art ATS systems in terms of how much (if at all) they can help improve MT systems (which was, as previously mentioned, their first intended goal and main motivation).

3   Experiments

In this study, we use two state-of-the-art ATS systems:

1. **TS-A**: A combination of lexical TS system (Glavaš and Štajner, 2015) with the EventSimplify (Glavaš and Štajner, 2013) which performs syntactic simplification with a significant content reduction. This is the most "aggressive" system of all above-mentioned systems which perform content reduction (Section 2), i.e. it is the system which performs the highest level of content reduction and achieves the most readable (simplest) output (due to a high number of sentence splitting operations).
2. **TS-C**: The lexico-syntactic TS system proposed by Angrosh and Siddhathan (2014) which belong to the "conservative" ATS systems which do not perform any content reduction and thus, completely preserve the original meaning of the sentence;

We used 100 news articles from the EMM NewsBrief[3] for which the output of the EventSimplify (Glavaš and Štajner, 2013) ATS system was freely available.[4] We further focused on the output of the event-wise simplification scheme (which achieved the highest readability of all four provided schemes) and applied the lexical simplification system (Glavaš and Štajner, 2015) on top of it in order to obtained a full simplification system which encompasses lexical simplification, syntactic simplification and content reduction (TS-A). Next, we applied the TS-C system on all those 100 original articles.

3.1   Text Simplification Systems

The examples presented in Table 1 illustrate the potential of the two ATS systems used (*TS-C* and *TS-A*) and differences among them. In general, the TS-A performs more sentence splitting than the TS-C (see examples 2, 3, and 4 in Table 1, with the extreme case of producing four simplified sentences instead of one original sentence in the fourth example). The TS-A system also removes some details (e.g. *"several minutes later"* in the third example, or *"in Port St. John"* in the second example), or entire subordinate clauses (e.g. *"a steep fall from.."* in the first example).

The main focus of both ATS systems is on structural simplification, although there are occasional cases of lexical simplification as well (e.g. *"arrived"* $\rightarrow$ *"came"* in the second example, or *"recieved"* $\rightarrow$ *"got"* and *"refuge"* $\rightarrow$ *"shelter"* in the fourth example).

It is interesting to note that both systems (though TS-A more frequently) also simplify the tense of the verbs, as in the following examples: *"before* **turning** *the gun* $\rightarrow$ *"After that, ...* **turned** *the gun* (ex. 2), *"Deputies arrived... to hear ..."* $\rightarrow$ *"Deputies came ... Deputies* **heard**...*"* (ex. 3), and **"had received"** $\rightarrow$ **"got"** (ex. 4). Furthermore, the AT-C system consistently changes constructions of the type **"<clause>, X said."** into **"X said that <clause>"** (as illustrated in the second example in Table 1).

---

[3] http://emm.newsbrief.eu/NewsBrief/clusteredition/en/latest.html
[4] http://takelab.fer.hr/data/evsimplify/

Table 1. Examples of sentence simplification performed by the two ATS systems (TS-C and TS-A). Differences to the original sentences are shown in bold.

Ex.	Version	Sentence
1	Original	Vladimir Putin's United Russia party won less than 50% of Sunday's vote, a steep fall from its earlier two-thirds majority, according to preliminary results.
	TS-C	Vladimir Putin's United Russia party won less than 50% Sunday's vote, **according to preliminary results. This is a steep fall from its earlier two-thirds majority.**
	TS-A	Putin's United Russia party won less than 50%.
2	Original	A Florida mother shot her four children early Tuesday morning before turning the gun on herself at her home in Port St. John, police said.
	TS-C	**Police said that a** Florida mother shot her four children early Tuesday morning before turning the gun on herself at her home in Port St. John
	TS-A	A Florida mother shot her four children early Tuesday morning. **After that, a Florida mother turned** the gun on herself at her home.
3	Original	Deputies arrived at the house several minutes later to hear more shots fired.
	TS-C	Deputies **came** at the house several minutes later to hear more shots fired.
	TS-A	Deputies **came** to the house. **Deputies heard** more shots.
4	Original	The Chinese Embassy said it had received a report that a dozen Chinese fishing boats had taken refuge in a lagoon of Huangyan Island to escape foul weather when the Philippine gunboat blocked the lagoon entrance and sent 12 Philippine soldiers to harass the Chinese fishermen.
	TS-C	The Chinese Embassy said it **also got** a report that a dozen Chinese fishing boats had taken refuge in a lagoon of Huangyan Island to escape foul weather. **Then the Philippine gunboat sent 12 Philippine soldiers to harass the Chinese fishermen. At that time, the gunboat blocked the lagoon entrance.**
	TS-A	The Chinese Embassy had received a report. A dozen Chinese fishing **ships** had taken **shelter** in a lagoon of Huangyan Island. The Philippine gunboat blocked the lagoon entrance. **The Philippine gunboat** sent 12 Philippine soldiers to harass the Chinese fishermen.

As ATS systems do not always produce perfectly grammatical output and lexical simplification sometimes lead to changed meaning (Angrosh and Siddharthan, 2014; Glavaš and Štajner, 2015), we manually inspected a randomly selected subset of 65 original sentences and their automatically simplified sentences produced by both systems (TS-A and TS-C).[5] In those cases where the meaning or grammaticality was incorrect, we performed a minimal post-editing (PE) necessary to restore the original meaning and grammaticality of the sentence. As the goal of this PE is not to make any further simplifications and the mistakes were easy to notice, this type of PE was very fast (11.3 seconds per sentence for TS-A and 15.2 seconds per sentence for TS-C) and did not even require a native speaker or trained annotator, but only someone with the proficiency level of English. For illustration, several sentences are given in Table 2.

Table 2. Examples of post-editing performed on the automatically simplified sentences generated by the TS-C and TS-A systems. Differences between the automatically simplified sentences and their PE versions are shown in bold.

Ex.	Version	Sentence
1	Original	Ex-Soviet leader Mikhail Gorbachev says Russian authorities must annul the parliamentary vote results and hold a new election.
	TS-C (no PE)	Ex-Soviet leader Mikhail Gorbachev says. Russian authorities must annul the parliamentary vote results. These authorities hold a new election.
	TS-C (PE)	Ex-Soviet leader Mikhail Gorbachev says **that** Russian authorities must annul the parliamentary vote results. These authorities **must** hold a new election.
2	Original	A 21-year-old man was arrested on April 30, on suspicion of murder and was released on bail until May 29 pending further enquiries.
	TS-C (no PE)	A 21-year-old man was arrested on April 30, on suspicion of murder. This man was **followed** until May 29 pending further enquiries.
	TS-C (PE)	A 21-year-old man was arrested on April 30, on suspicion of murder. This man was **released** until May 29 pending further enquiries.
	TS-A (no PE)	A 21-year-old man was arrested on April 30 on suspicion. A 21-year-old man was released on **jail** until May 29.
	TS-A (PE)	A 21-year-old man was arrested on April 30 on suspicion of murder. A 21-year-old man was released on **bail** until May 29.

---

[5] This subset of sentences was later used for MT experiments and human evaluation and post-editing.

3.2 Statistical Machine Translation System

For the machine translation from English to Serbian, we used the ASISTENT system.[6] It is a freely available SMT system, based on the widely used phrase-based SMT framework (Koehn et al., 2003) and it supports translations from English to Slovene, Croatian and Serbian and vice versa. Additionally, translations between those three Slavic languages are also possible.

The system was trained using the Moses toolkit (Koehn et al., 2007). The word alignments were built with GIZA++ (Och and Ney, 2003), and the 5-gram language model was built using the SRILM toolkit (Stolcke, 2002) The training dataset originates from the OPUS website[7] (Tiedemann, 2012) where three domains were available for the Serbian-English language pair: the enhanced version of the SEtimes corpus[8] (Tyers and Alperen, 2010) containing "news and views from South-East Europe", OpenSubtitles[9], and the KDE localisation documents and manuals, i.e. technical domain. Approximately 20.7M sentences, in total, were used for training (20.5M subtitles, 200,000 news, 30,000 technical), and 2,000 sentences were used for tuning (retaining the same proportions of the sentences from the three corpora as in the training dataset).

The English-to-Serbian part of the ASISTENT system (Arčan et al., 2016) was tested on 2,000 sentences from the three corpora used for training and tuning (the 2,000 sentences which were not used for training and tuning) and achieved a 38.88 BLEU score (Papineni et al., 2002), a 31.18 METEOR score (Denkowski and Lavie, 2014), and a 61.62 chrF3 score (Popović, 2015).

3.3 Evaluation Procedure

From the initial set of 100 news articles, we randomly selected 65 original sentences and evaluated all translation outputs (from original sentences, and TS-A and TS-C systems, which led to a total of 195 target sentences) with respect to the following aspects:

1. adequacy, i.e. meaning preservation
2. fluency, i.e. grammaticality
3. technical post-editing effort, i.e. amount of necessary edit operations

Each of the tasks has been carried out separately, i.e. the evaluation of adequacy and fluency were carried out in two separate passes, and post-editing was carried out in the third pass.

For adequacy, a quality score from 1 to 5 was assigned to each segment according to the following guidelines:

- 1 = very bad (regardless of a potentially good grammaticality)
- 2 = difficult to understand and different from the source meaning
- 3 = the main idea is preserved but some parts are unclear/different from the source
- 4 = understandable with minor ambiguities/differences

---

[6] http://server1.nlp.insight-centre.org/asistent/

[7] http://opus.lingfil.uu.se/

[8] http://nlp.ffzg.hr/resources/corpora/setimes/

[9] http://www.opensubtitles.org/

- 5 = perfectly understandable (regardless of a potentially poor grammar)

For fluency scores, the following guidelines were used:

- 1 = very bad (regardless of a potentially good meaning preservation)
- 2 = many grammatical errors
- 3 = a number of grammatical errors but mostly minor ones
- 4 = almost correct (a small number of minor errors)
- 5 = perfectly grammatical (regardless of possible loss/change of meaning)

The post-editing effort was analysed in the following way:

- Each translated segment was post-edited by looking into the corresponding source segment, i.e. using English originals for translations of originals, using the corresponding simplified English sentences for translations of simplified segments.
- The raw edit counts and edit rates (raw counts normalised with the segment length) were calculated using Hjerson (Popović, 2011) for:
  - five classes of edits/errors
  - all edit operations

Reference translations were not available.

4   Results and Discussion

The average adequacy and fluency scores, and the percentages of sentences with each of the scores are presented in Table 3. It can be noted that the use of TS-C does not improve the overall adequacy, but it might improve fluency, whereas the use of TS-A improves MT in both aspects.

Table 3. Average scores for adequacy and fluency (first row) and percentage of sentences for each of the five scores (1–5).

Score	Adequacy			Fluency		
	Orig	TS-C	TS-A	Original	TS-C	TS-A
Average	3.17	3.02	3.63	2.91	3.13	3.45
1	15.2	13.0	6.5	4.3	2.3	2.3
2	10.9	17.4	8.7	23.9	17.4	11.4
3	32.6	32.6	30.4	47.8	45.6	31.8
4	23.9	28.3	23.9	23.9	34.8	47.7
5	17.4	8.7	30.4	0	0	6.8

A closer look into the distribution of the sentence scores indicates that the use of the TS-C system in MT decreases the number of sentences with very bad accuracy score, but it also decreases the number of sentences with perfect adequacy scores. The TS-A system, however, significantly increases the number of sentences with perfect adequacy scores, at the same time decreasing the number of sentences with low adequacy scores.

As for the fluency, both TS systems significantly increase the number of sentences with high fluency scores (score 4, and in the case of TS-A, score 5 as well) while at the same time they decrease the number of sentences with low fluency scores. It should be noted that the fluency is generally problematic for the SMT system – none of the original English sentences has been translated into a perfectly grammatical sentence, and the use of TS-C does not succeed in improving this either. However, the use of the TS-A system leads to a 6.8% of sentences being translated into perfectly grammatical sentences.

Table 4. Percentage of changes in adequacy and fluency scores.

(a) Adequacy

Original	TS-C					TS-A				
	1	2	3	4	5	1	2	3	4	5
1	10.9	**2.2**	**2.2**	**0**	**0**	4.3	2.2	2.2	**4.3**	**2.2**
2	0	4.3	**4.3**	**2.2**	**0**	0	2.2	**6.5**	0	**2.2**
3	2.2	8.7	15.2	**6.5**	**0**	2.2	2.2	15.2	**2.2**	**10.9**
4	0	0	4.3	17.4	**2.2**	0	0	4.3	13.0	**6.5**
5	0	2.2	6.5	2.2	6.5	0	2.2	2.2	4.3	8.7

(b) Fluency

Original	TS-C					TS-A				
	1	2	3	4	5	1	2	3	4	5
1	2.2	**2.2**	**0**	**0**	**0**	0	**4.3**	**0**	**0**	**0**
2	0	4.3	**17.4**	**2.2**	**0**	0	2.2	**8.7**	**13.0**	**0**
3	0	8.7	21.8	**17.4**	**0**	2.2	2.2	17.4	**19.6**	**6.5**
4	0	2.2	6.5	15.2	**0**	0	2.2	4.3	13.0	**4.4**
5	0	0	0	0	0	0	0	0	0	0

Table 4 presents the results of further analysis, showing the percentage of each particular change in adequacy and fluency scores for each of the TS systems. The desired changes (from lower to higher score) are presented in bold.

For the TS-C system, it is confirmed that a number of sentences with a bad adequacy score is improved, and on the other hand, a number of sentences with a good adequacy score is deteriorated. The majority of sentences does not change. As for the fluency, the main improvement comes from improving poor sentences into medium ones and medium sentences into almost good ones. The majority of sentences does not change.

For the TS-A system, the main changes in adequacy originate from improving sentences with very bad adequacy scores even up to perfect, and from the improvement of sentences with a medium adequacy score into perfect. The main contribution for fluency, using the TS-A system, comes from improving medium sentences into almost perfect, and from improving poor ones into medium and almost good.

For illustration, Table 5 contains several examples of original sentences, their automatically simplified sentences by both systems and the fluency and adequacy scores for the produced translations into Serbian. The first example shows how a strong reordering of clauses within a sentence (without any sentence splitting) can improve both fluency and adequacy of the translation output. The second example demonstrates how even one lexical change (replacement of a phrasal verb with a more frequently used non-phrasal verb) can also improve the fluency and adequacy of the translation. The third example shows how much sentence splitting and its combination with lexical simplification can improve the translation in the case of a long source sentence. In the penultimate example, we again see how much sentence splitting in a combination with tense simplification and discarding details can improve translation, leading to a perfect fluency and adequacy. The last example demonstrates how retaining only the most important information can improve the fluency of the translation output.

4.1 Post-Editing Effort

Results for the post-editing effort are shown in Table 6. The overall raw count of edit operations decreases for both TS systems albeit significantly more for the TS-A, which is expected since the sentences are shorter. Edit rates also decrease for both TS systems, but more for the TS-C due to the reduced sentence lengths of the TS-A system.

Furthermore, the TS-A reduces raw counts for each of the five error classes, whereas the improvement with the TS-C comes mainly from the reduction of reordering errors. This is still an important improvement since it has been shown that the reordering edit operations strongly correlate with the cognitive post-editing effort (Popović et al, 2014).

Table 7 shows the percentage of improved, deteriorated and unchanged sentences for both TS systems with regard to all evaluation aspects, i.e. adequacy, fluency, edit rate, and raw count of edit operations.

For about one half of the sentences (54.3% for the TS-C and 43.5% for the TS-A) the adequacy scores do not change. Among those sentences which do change the adequacy score, in the case of the TS-C, more sentences deteriorate their score than improve it (26.1% as opposed to 19.6%), while in the case of the TS-A, in contrast, more sentences improve their adequacy instead of deteriorating it (39.1% as opposed to 17.4%).

The number of sentences that improve their fluency is higher than the number of sentences that deteriorate it for both TS systems, and it is particularly pronounced for TS-A.

Edit rates are improved significantly with using the TS-C (47.8%) and for the majority of sentences (54.3%) using the TS-A. Raw counts of edit operations are improved for more than one half of the sentences by the TS-C (60.9%) and for more than 82% of the sentences by the TS-A.

Table 5. Examples of the adequacy and fluency scores received for the translation of original sentence and two automatically simplified sentences (using the TS-C and TS-A systems), for the cases where TS led to improvements in the output. Differences between the original sentences and their automatically simplified versions are shown in bold.

Ex.	Version	A	F	Sentence
1	Original	2	3	"As we emerge from a decade of conflict abroad and economic crisis at home, it's time to renew America," Obama said, speaking against a backdrop of armored vehicles and a U.S. flag.
	TS-C	4	4	**Speaking against a backdrop of armored vehicles and a U.S. flag, Obama said it's time to renew America as we emerge from a decade of conflict abroad and economic crisis at home.**
2	Original	3	2	Several Israeli security delegations have visited Egypt during the past two months to **decide on** a new embassy location.
	TS-C	4	4	Several Israeli security delegations have visited Egypt during the past two months to **choose** a new embassy location.
3	Original	1	2	The Chinese Embassy said it had received a report that a dozen Chinese fishing boats had taken refuge in a lagoon of Huangyan Island to escape foul weather when the Philippine gunboat blocked the lagoon entrance and sent 12 Philippine soldiers to harass the Chinese fishermen.
	TS-C	2	3	The Chinese Embassy said it **also got** a report that a dozen Chinese fishing boats had taken refuge in a lagoon of Huangyan Island to escape foul weather. Then the Philippine gunboat **sent 12 Philippine soldiers to harass the Chinese fishermen. At that time, the gunboat blocked the lagoon entrance.**
	TS-A	3	3	The Chinese Embassy had received a report. **A** dozen Chinese fishing **ships** had taken **shelter** in a lagoon of Huangyan Island. The Philippine gunboat blocked the lagoon entrance. **The Philippine gunboat** sent 12 Philippine soldiers to harass the Chinese fishermen.
4	Original	4	3	A Florida mother shot her four children early Tuesday morning before turning the gun on herself at her home in Port St. John, police said.
	TS-A	5	5	A Florida mother shot her four children early Tuesday morning. **After that, a Florida mother turned** the gun on herself at her home.
5	Original	4	3	Vladimir Putin's United Russia party won less than 50% of Sunday's vote, a steep fall from its earlier two-thirds majority, according to preliminary results.
	TS-A	4	4	Putin's United Russia party won less than 50%.

Table 6. Raw counts and edit rates (%) normalised with the segment length.

Edit	Raw counts			Edit rates (%)		
Operations	Orig.	TS-C	TS-A	Orig.	TS-C	TS-A
Σ errors	565	542	321	46.2	43.0	45.0
Morphology	209	210	132	17.2	16.9	18.6
Order	100	66	43	8.2	5.3	6.1
Omission	76	80	38	5.8	5.9	5.0
Addition	21	26	10	1.7	2.1	1.4
Mistranslation	159	160	98	13.1	12.8	13.8

Table 7. Percentage of sentences with better/worse/same sentences with respect to adequacy (A), fluency (F), edit rate (ER) and raw edit counts (REC).

%	TS-C				TS-A			
	A	F	ER	REC	M(A)	G(F)	ER	REC
better	19.6	39.1	60.9	47.8	39.1	52.1	54.3	82.6
worse	26.1	17.4	34.8	39.1	17.4	15.2	45.6	8.7
same	54.3	43.5	4.3	13.0	43.5	32.6	0	8.7

5 Summary and Outlook

In this article, we investigated whether the state-of-the-art automatic text simplification systems (ATS) can improve English-to-Serbian machine translation (MT) if used as a pre-processing step to simplify source sentences before translating them with the SMT system. We tested this hypothesis by using two ATS systems, a more "conservative" one (TS-C) which only performs lexical and syntactic simplifications, and a more "aggressive" one (TS-A) which performs more lexical and syntactic changes but also performs a significant content reduction thus leading to a loss of some information details.

All the presented results indicate that the use of the TS-C can improve the fluency of the MT output and reduce technical and cognitive post-editing effort through reduction of reordering errors. The use of the TS-A introduces even more improvements for adequacy, fluency and all types of edit operations, but at the cost of losing some details in the information. This approach, however, could be very useful for tasks where the main meaning of the text is crucial and the loss of some details is affordable.

In addition, our results show that the use of a TS system as a pre-processing step in a MT pipeline is only useful for a subset of sentences, whereas the rest of the sentences either deteriorates or remains unchanged. Therefore a method for filtering sentences into two or three classes (TS improves/TS worsens or TS improves/TS does not influence/TS worsens) would be very useful and should be investigated in the future work.

In future research, we will also include more language pairs and domains.

Acknowledgements

We would like to thank Mihael Arčan for the help with the English-to-Serbian SMT system, and to Goran Glavaš, Advaith Siddharthan and Mandya Angrosh for the help with the automatic text simplification systems.

References

Mandya Angrosh and Advaith Siddharthan. 2014. Hybrid text simplification using synchronous dependency grammars with hand-written and automatically harvested rules. In *Proceedings of the 14th Conference of the European Chapter of the Association for Computational Linguistics (EACL)*, Gothenburg, Sweden, pages 722–731.

María Jesús Aranzabe, Arantza Díaz de Ilarraza, and Itziar Gonzalez-Dios. 2013. Transforming Complex Sentences using Dependency Trees for Automatic Text Simplification in Basque. *Procesamiento del Lenguaje Natural*, Volume 50, pages 61–68.

Mihael Arčan, Maja Popović and Paul Buitelaar. Asistent – a machine translation system for Slovene, Serbian and Croatian. In *Proceedings of the 10th Conference on Language Technologies and Digital Humanities*, Ljubljana, Slovenia.

Gianni Barlacchi and Sara Tonelli. 2013. ERNESTA: A Sentence Simplification Tool for Children's Stories in Italian. In *Computational Linguistics and Intelligent Text Processing*, pages 476–489.

Laetitia Brouwers, Delphine Bernhard, Anne-Laure Ligozat and Thomas François. 2014. Syntactic Sentence Simplification for French. In *Proceedings of the EACL Workshop on Predicting and Improving Text Readability for Target Reader Populations (PITR)*, Gothenburg, Sweden, pp. 47–56.

Raman Chandrasekar. 1994. Hybrid Approach to Machine Translation using Man Machine Communication. *PhD Thesis*. Tata Institute of Fundamental Research, University of Bombay, Bombay, India.

Raman Chandrasekar, Christine Doran and Bangalore Srinivas. 1996. Motivations and Methods for Text Simplification. In *Proceedings of the Sixteenth International Conference on Computational Linguistics (COLING)*, pages 1041–1044.

Michael Denkowski and Alon Lavie. 2014. Meteor Universal: Language Specific Translation Evaluation for Any Target Language. In *Proceedings of the EACL 2014 Workshop on Statistical Machine Translation*, pages 376–380.

Goran Glavaš and Sanja Štajner. 2013. Event-Centered Simplification of News Stories. In *Proceedings of the Student Workshop held in conjunction with RANLP Conference*, Hissar, Bulgaria, pages 71–78.

Goran Glavaš and Sanja Štajner. 2015. Simplifying Lexical Simplification: Do We Need Simplified Corpora? In *Proceedings of the 53rd Annual Meeting of the Association for Computational Linguistics and the 7th International Joint Conference on Natural Language Processing (Volume 2: Short Papers)*, pages 63–68.

Philipp Koehn and Franz Josef Och and Daniel Marcu 2003. Statistical phrase-based translation. in *Proceedings of the Conference of the North American Chapter of the Association for Computational Linguistics on Human Language Technology - Volume 1*, pages 48–54.

Philipp Koehn, Hieu Hoang, Alexandra Birch, Chris Callison-Burch, Marcello Federico, Nicola Bertoldi, Brooke Cowan, Wade Shen, Christine Moran, Richard Zens, Chris Dyer, Ondřej Bojar, Alexandra Constantin, Evan Herbst. 2007. Moses: Open source toolkit for statistical machine translation. In *Proceedings of the 45th Annual Meeting of the ACL on Interactive Poster and Demonstration Sessions*, Stroudsburg, PA, USA.

Shashi Narayan and Claire Gardent. 2014. Hybrid Simplification using Deep Semantics and Machine Translation. In *Proceedings of the 52nd Annual Meeting of the Association for Computational Linguistics (ACL)*, pages 435–445.

Franz Josef Och and Hermann Ney. 2003. A Systematic Comparison of Various Statistical Alignment Models. *Computational Linguistics*, 29(1):19–51.

Kishore Papineni, Salim Roukos, Todd Ward and Wei-Jing Zhu. 2002. BLEU: a Method for Automatic Evaluation of Machine Translation. In *Proceedings of the 40th Annual Meeting of the Association for Computational Linguistics (ACL)*, pages 311–318.

Maja Popović. 2011. Hjerson: An Open Source Tool for Automatic Error Classificatio n of Machine Translation Output. *The Prague Bulletin of Mathematical Linguistics*, pages 59–68, Prague, Czech Republic, October.

Maja Popović, Arle Lommel, Aljoscha Burchardt, Eleftherios Avramidis, Hans Uszkoreit. 2014. Relations between different types of post-editing operations, cognitive effort and temporal effort. In *Proceedings of the 17th Annual Conference of the European Association for Machine Translation (EAMT 14)*, pages 191–198, Dubrovnik, Croatia.

Maja Popović. 2015. chrF: character n-gram F-score for automatic MT evaluation. In *Proceedings of the 10th Workshop on Statistical Machine Translation*, pages 392–395.

Maja Popović, Mihael Arčan. 2015. Identifying main obstacles for statistical machine translation of morphologically rich South Slavic languages. In *Proceedings of the 18th Annual Conference of the European Association for Machine Translation (EAMT-15)*, pages 97–104, Antalya, Turkey.

Horacio Saggion, Sanja Štajner, Stefan Bott, Luz Rello, Simon Mille and Biljana Drndarević. 2015. Making It Simplext: Implementation and Evaluation of a Text Simplification System for Spanish. *ACM Transactions on Accessible Computing*, Volume 6, Chapter 14.

Advaith Siddharthan. 2011. Text Simplification using Typed Dependencies: A Comparison of the Robustness of Different Generation Strategies. In *Proceedings of the 13th European Workshop on Natural Language Generation (ENLG)*, pages 2–11.

Angrosh Mandya, Tadashi Nomoto and Advaith Siddharthan. 2014. Lexico-syntactic text simplification and compression with typed dependencies. In*Proceedings of the 25th International Conference on Computational Linguistics (COLING)*, Dublin, Ireland, pages 1996–2006.

Lucia Specia. 2010. Translating from complex to simplified sentences. In*Proceedings of the 9th international conference on Computational Processing of the Portuguese Language*, pages 30–39.

Andreas Stolcke. 2002. SRILM – an extensible language modeling toolkit. volume 2, pages 901–904, Denver, CO, September.

Jörg Tiedemann. 2012. Parallel data, tools and interfaces in OPUS. In *Proceedings of the 8th International Conference on Language Resources and Evaluation (LREC)*, pages 2214–2218.

Francis M. Tyers and Murat Alperen. 2010. South-East European Times: A parallel corpus of the Balkan languages. In *Proceedings of the LREC Workshop on Exploitation of Multilingual Resources and Tools for Central and (South-) Eastern European Languages*, pages 49–53, Valetta, Malta.

Received May 2, 2016 , accepted May 12, 2016

Baltic J. Modern Computing, Vol. 4 (2016), No. 2, pp. 243–255

A Portable Method for Parallel and Comparable Document Alignment

Thierry ETCHEGOYHEN, Andoni AZPEITIA

Vicomtech-IK4, Donostia / San Sebastián, Gipuzkoa, Spain

{tetchegoyhen, aazpeitia}@vicomtech.org

Abstract. We present a document alignment method based on expanded lexical translation sets and document-level Jaccard similarity. We compare our approach to state-of-the-art methods on a variety of alignment tasks, showing that it outperforms alternative methods in most scenarios for both parallel and comparable corpora. The proposed method is highly portable, requiring only minimal seed information and no task-specific training, thus providing the means for an efficient exploitation of multilingual documents.

Keywords: Document alignment, Comparable corpora, Parallel corpora

1 Introduction

Multilingual document alignment is an important step in the creation of the parallel resources that are necessary for data-driven approaches to translation such as statistical machine translation (Brown et al. 1990). This part of the overall bitext creation process faces a variety of alignment scenarios. The input might for instance take the form of unordered collections of parallel documents in several languages, from which an alignment needs to be computed to pair those documents that are translations of each other. A second major scenario relates to the exploitation of comparable corpora, where large collections of multilingual documents need to be paired prior to mining parallel or similar sentences. With comparable corpora seen as a reservoir of training material for machine translation (Muntaneu and Marcu 2005), a particular effort needs to be placed on the development of efficient methods for comparable document alignment.

A single method that works efficiently for both parallel and comparable corpora would offer a flexible solution to the general issue of document alignment and reduce adaptation efforts from one alignment scenario to another. In this work, we present such a method, termed DOCAL, which explores the use of minimal information to enhance portability by relying only on automatically extracted lexical translations, expanded token sets and the Jaccard coefficient for the computation of document-level similarity. Components of the approach have been previously explored and used to evaluate document similarity, and we demonstrate the potential of their conjoined use for document alignment on a variety of alignment tasks and corpora. We compare our approach to state-of-the-art methods for each alignment scenario, showing that DOCAL outperforms alternative methods in the majority of cases.

The paper is organised as follows. Section 2 presents related work in mulitlingual document alignment; Section 3 describes the DOCAL approach; in Section 4 we present controlled experiments with both parallel and comparable documents for various language pairs and domains; finally, Section 5 summarises the results and offers concluding remarks.

2 Multilingual document alignment

The alignment of multilingual documents has been performed with a variety of techniques, depending on their degree of parallelism and comparability.

For strictly parallel document alignment, simple approaches based on file name matching can be the most efficient methods, as they do not rely on any analysis of the content of documents. Unfortunately, this approach relies on uniform and consistent file naming conventions across languages, an assumption which is often defeated in practice, even in professional repositories (Tiedemann 2011). Thus, when filename-based alignment is part of a document alignment pipeline, it is often combined with content-based alignment methods (Chen et al. 2004). The usefulness of document metadata was explored in depth by Resnik and Smith (2003), who exploit URL properties and structural tags to gather bilingual corpora from HTML pages on the Web. This approach too has the advantage of not requiring the examination of textual content to retrieve parallel documents, although it is tied to the assumed structural properties of the documents. Another approach based on document properties instead of content is Chen and Nie (2000), who developed the PTMINER system, a cross-language information retrieval system that exploits URL properties as well, along with document size and language identifiers.

Enright and Konrad (2007) describe a simple and fast method for parallel document alignment based on hapax legomena, i.e. aligning documents by counting the number of unique words that appear in both documents. Patry and Langlais (2005) train an Ada-Boost classifier that includes several features such as length, entities, and punctuation, achieving high results on their controlled experiments. Patry and Langlais (2011) describe their PARADOCS system in detail, which includes the following components: an information retrieval module based on hapaxes and numerical entities; a classifier that includes three features based on edit-distance between document representations, number of entities, and optimal edit-distance over the document collection; and a third filtering component with the ability to remove alignment duplicates, i.e. to remove all document pairs where alignments have been established between a given target document and more than one source document.

Chen et al. (2004) developed the Parallel Text Identification system, which includes a filename-based module and a semantic similarity component based on a vector space model with frequency-weighted term vectors. The BITS system is another alternative proposed by Ma and Liberman (1999) for bilingual text mining on the Web, measuring content similarity by counting the ratio of token translation pairs over the total number of tokens in the source document, where translation pairs are determined within fixed windows of text.

Several approaches have targeted comparable documents specifically. Muntaneu and Marcu (2005), for instance, proposed a binary classification approach to comparable sentence alignment, using date-aligned documents as input. Fung and Cheung (2004) present the first exploration of very non-parallel corpora, using a document similarity measure based on bilingual lexical matching defined over mutual information scores on word pairs. Uszkoreit et al. (2010) describe a large-scale parallel document mining method that involves translating all source documents into English then using n-gram matching through multiple scoring steps. Ion et al. (2011) describe the EMACC system, which uses an expectation-maximization algorithm to align textual units. Their approach is similar in spirit to the modelling computed at word level by IBM models and they use automatically created bilingual lexicons to apply the EM algorithm on document units. They report state-of-the-art results on a range of alignment scenarios that cover 6 language pairs and varied degrees of comparability between documents.

Li and Gaussier (2013) describe a comparability assessment method that measures the overall proportion of words for which a translation can be found in a comparable corpus using bilingual dictionaries. Their core methodology underlies the CCNUNLP system, which is amongst the approaches evaluated in Section 4. Besides EMACC and CCNUNLP, two other systems are part of the further described controlled experiments. LINA, described in Morin et al. (2015), is based on the hapax method of Enright and Konrad, extended with two strategies: they first use pigeon hole reasoning, where alignments mapping multiple sources to the same target are removed and only the pairs with the highest number of shared words are kept; cross-lingual information specific to Wikipedia is then exploited, breaking remaining alignment ties using the ordering provided by document pairs in a third language. The AUT system, described in Zafarian et al. (2015), employs four main components: a vectorisation module that maps documents to a common feature space, a topic model, a module for named entity detection, and a word feature mapping module based on machine translation.

The Jaccard coefficient (Jaccard 1901), which is a core component of the approach we present, is one of the standard similarity metrics used for text comparison and information retrieval (Manning and Schütze 1999), although cosine-based methods with weighted term vectors are often preferred to determine text similarity. Prochasson and Fung (2011), for instance, use the Jaccard coefficient to evaluate word association for rare word extraction from comparable corpora. Paramita et al. (2013) describe a comparable document similarity measure based on the Jaccard index computed over sentence pairs in the documents, filtering first sentences with large proportions of entities and numbers, and compute document similarity scores as the average of the sentence-based Jaccard similarity scores. In the next section, we describe an approach centred on this coefficient over expanded lexical sets.

3   DOCAL

DOCAL is a simple method to measure multilingual document similarity which aims for portability and ease of deployment. The core of the approach relies on expanded lexical translation sets, defined at the document level, and the Jaccard coefficient computed on those sets. In other words, we extract token sets from each pair of documents, create two corresponding sets with the lexical translations of the tokens, augment the original sets through two operations of set expansion described below, and compute the ratio of intersection over union on the original token sets and their corresponding translation sets.

More specifically, let d_i and d_j be two tokenised documents in languages l_1 and l_2, respectively, S_i the set of tokens in d_i, S_j the set of tokens in d_j, T_{ij} the set of expanded lexical translations into l_2 for all tokens in S_i, and T_{ji} the set of expanded lexical translations into l_1 for all tokens in S_j. From these elements, the similarity score is computed as in Equation 1:

$$sim_{docal} = \frac{\frac{|T_{ij} \cap S_j|}{|T_{ij} \cup S_j|} + \frac{|T_{ji} \cap S_i|}{|T_{ji} \cup S_i|}}{2} \tag{1}$$

That is, the score is defined as the average of the Jaccard similarity coefficients computed in both translation directions.

Lexical translations are extracted from seed parallel corpora, with translation probabilities computed according to the IBM models (Brown et al. 1993).[1] For each token, the k-best translation options are selected among the alternatives ranked according to their lexical translation probability. The actual probability values are not used beyond the provided ranking, i.e. all selected translations are equally considered in the computation of similarity. The main reason for this is the fact that, in most cases, the lexical translations are extracted from a different domain than the one at hand, and lexical distributions are likely to be different. We thus opted for simple set membership for all selected translation variants and used a default value for k.[2]

The Jaccard coefficient presents properties that are of interest for document alignment. As it results in a real value between 0 and 1, it allows for a bounded comparison of similarities within the document space. More importantly, when compared to a related measure such as the Dice index, the Jaccard coefficient penalizes more those sets with a small number of shared entries; this property is useful to penalize documents where the common terms are mostly functional words, for instance. As compared to cosine similarity, it provides for lesser tolerance over sets with large member disparity.

We now describe in turn the aforementioned set expansion operations and available optimisations of the core method. It is worth noting that no particular filtering is per-

---

[1] We used GIZA++ (Och and Ney 2003) to extract lexical translation tables. Although lexical translation modelling is sometimes based only on IBM model 1 in related work on comparable corpora, it is standard practice in statistical machine translation to use more sophisticated IBM models, usually up to model 4. We followed the latter approach, as the same tables can thus be used as components for both comparable corpora exploitation and SMT system development. We measured the impact of using one approach or the other on identical test sets and did not find any significant difference on document alignment results.

[2] We used 5 as a default for all language pairs, as a compromise between larger sets with less reliable translation candidates and smaller sets which may miss translation alternatives in comparable corpora. Note that optimal values for k could be empirically determined on domain-specific development sets for each language pair; such document-level tuning sets are however not usually available.

formed on the token sets, leaving punctuation marks alongside functional and content words, thus reducing document pre-processing to the minimal operation of tokenisation.

Out-of-vocabulary expansion. As we cannot guarantee that seed translations will cover the domain at hand satisfactorily, it is necessary to expand the translation sets with tokens that may be indicators of similarity although absent from translation tables. Since we do not lowercase the tokenised text,[3] case information is available throughout the text and all capitalised tokens are added to the sets if they are not found in the translation tables.[4] This simple operation, which we perform at set creation time, provides coverage for named entities, which can be viewed as important indicators of content similarity given their low relative frequency. The same process applies to numbers as well, which can also be strong indicators of similarity, in particular when they denote dates.

The effectiveness of this procedure varies between corpora, as it depends on both the amounts of entities in a given domain and the ability of the core method to discriminate between different documents without the inclusion of said entities. Thus, on the EITB test sets described in Section 4.3, its impact was not measurable, whereas on the French-English test sets of the Wikipedia task described in Section 4.2, it provided gains of over 30 points on all three metrics. We include this procedure in all experiments described in the remainder of the paper, as it would be unlikely to cause underperformance in any case.

Common prefix expansion. A common issue in statistical translation is morphological variation, with surface variants of a given lemma usually considered as independent unrelated units. This generates well-known data sparseness issues, which can be minimised through morphosyntactic analysis and lemmatisation. For under-resourced languages however, the resources for these processes might not be readily available or accurate enough, and a common approach relies on simple stemming through the use of manually created lists of endings. Surface forms are thus matched against possible endings and stemmed forms derived accordingly. For languages with rich inflectional morphology, however, these lists can contain hundreds of forms and their use is error prone, as several morphological phenomena need to be taken into account for a proper decomposition of endings and roots. Additionally, matching each surface form against large lists of endings is computationally costly.

To avoid both issues, we include a set expansion strategy that relies on longest common prefixes (LCP), which we compute over the minimal sets of elements that may have a common stem, defined to be the following two set differences: $T'_{ij} = T_{ij} - S_j$ and $T'_{ji} = T_{ji} - S_i$. Then for each element in T'_{ij} (respectively T'_{ji}) and each element in S_j (respectively S_i), if a common prefix is found with a minimal length of n characters,

---

[3] In all the results we present, the texts are not truecased either, to maintain the number of operations and required models to a minimum. Truecasing would provide a better treatment of sentence initial words but it remains to be tested whether this process would have a significant impact on document-level sets.

[4] Checking for their presence in lexical translation tables allows one to distinguish between out-of-vocabulary tokens and entities with an existing translation, e.g. *Germany* translated into Spanish *Alemania*.

the prefix is added to both translation sets.[5] This approach reduces the problem to prefix comparison over the minimal necessary set of elements, as it exploits the nature of the alignment problem instead of generating stemmed candidates against large lists of endings.[6]

As is the case for the inclusion of surface-defined entities, the impact of LCP is expected to vary between corpora, for similar reasons. For all experiments reported in Section 4, the contribution of this operation was marginal at best and the reported results were obtained with a variant of DOCAL that does not include LCP. We nonetheless describe it here as an additional option with the potential to improve document alignment in other use cases.[7]

Document candidates. In some document alignment scenarios, a target-to-source alignment process based on the Cartesian product of the document sets might be the optimal approach, as the alignment space is guaranteed to be searched exhaustively. Since this approach has quadratic complexity, it is however computationally prohibitive if the volumes of documents reach a certain amount. Experiments with DOCAL indicate limits of practicality being reached with over 260 million possible pairings on a single server with 64 Gigas of RAM and 16 cores.

For scenarios where the volume of documents renders an exhaustive comparison unsustainable, a standard cross-linguistic information retrieval (CLIR) approach is adopted. Target documents are first indexed using the Lucene search engine[8] and retrieved by building a query over the expanded translation sets created from each source document.

On the Spanish-English pair of the Europarl Version 7 corpus,[9] which contains 9.433 Spanish documents and 9.673 English documents, DOCAL performs alignment over the 91.235.976 possible pairings of the Cartesian product in 223 minutes and 13 seconds; the CLIR strategy over the same corpus executes the alignment process over 943.300 pairs in 33 minutes and 45 seconds, with an additional 1 minute and 5 seconds for indexing.

The two approaches are used in the experiments described in Section 4, with CLIR being used for the large volumes of documents in the Wikipedia task, and the Cartesian product being employed with the other datasets, where documents number in the thousands of documents at most.

Alignment filtering. As the alignment process is executed from source to target documents, a given target document can be taken as the best alignment for more than one source document. This results in correct alignments that end up hidden, often with

---

[5] Throughout the experiments we describe, n was set to 3, arbitrarily assumed to be the minimal length of a stem.

[6] To further improve the efficiency of the system, we use an implementation based on hash maps with minimal-length prefixes as keys and two sets as values for the original and translated tokens that have a given prefix in common. LCP is then computed on these reduced sets of elements.

[7] Experiments on internally available sets of parallel technical manuals showed improvements including LCP over the base version of DOCAL.

[8] https://lucene.apache.org.

[9] Available at http://www.statmt.org/europarl/.

scores that are marginally lower than the top alignment scores assigned by the similarity metric. A simple solution to this issue consists in removing all alignments between a source document d_i and a target d_j if the latter is aligned to a different source document with a better similarity score.[10]

This process often produces large improvements, as it allows previously hidden good alignments to surface. On most of the experiments described in Section 4, the strategy led to significant improvement, with over 10 points gains in some scenarios. We include this alignment filtering as a default, although we will present some of the results with and without it to illustrate the gains obtained with this strategy.

4   Controlled experiments

To compare our approach with competing methods for document alignment, we evaluated system performance in three different scenarios that cover different language pairs, domains and degrees of comparability. We first performed document alignment on the EUROPARL corpus as a testbench for accuracy on parallel document alignment. We then applied DOCAL alignment to the WIKIPEDIA test sets selected for the 2015 BUCC shared task on similar document alignment, to measure the approach against recent results obtained by competing systems. Finally, we performed document alignment for a difficult language pair that includes one under-resourced language, namely Basque, using the EITB corpus of strongly comparable documents in the news domain. We describe the experimental setup and results for each scenario in turn.

In all experiments, DOCAL was tested with identical settings; as no training phase is necessary in the approach, those settings reduced to fixing the number of k-best lexical translations to 5. Unless otherwise specified, the lexical translation tables were created with GIZA++ on the JRC-Acquis Communautaire corpus.[11]

For the experiments on comparable corpora in Sections 4.2 and 4.3, we report results obtained with two different usages of the method: DOCAL.A refers to the core of the system, i.e. the basic translation sets augmented with capitalised tokens and numbers; DOCAL.B refers to the same system as DOCAL.A but augmented with the best alignment optimisation strategy described in Section 3.

4.1   EUROPARL

The Europarl corpus (Koehn 2005) is one of the main bitexts available, created from professional translations of parliamentary proceedings and covering the official EU languages. It is thus an appropriate resource to test parallel document alignment methods.

---

[10] Morin et al. (2015) refer to their similar removal of multiple source alignments as the *pigeonhole* method, following common terminology. To distinguish our version of the process from theirs, for presentation reasons we use the phrase *best alignment optimisation*.

[11] We used the latest available version of the corpus, as of November 2015, in the OPUS repository: http://opus.lingfil.uu.se/JRC-Acquis.php.

As various results have been reported on different versions of the corpus over the years, we applied DOCAL on two versions of the corpus, nameley versions 2 and 5.[12]

As a baseline, we implemented the previously described approach in Enright and Kondrak (2007), where hapaxes are defined over words with a minimal length of 4 characters. For the Spanish-English pair, the results match the accuracy reported in their paper, and the two methods gave highly accurate alignments: both methods fail on the one empty document in the corpus, while they differ on the one document with mixed language content, which only DOCAL aligns correctly. For later releases of the corpus however, results with the hapax method dropped sharply, either because of the larger sets of documents considered or because of the larger amount of documents with minimal textual content that can be found in the later releases (amounting to just one sentence in some cases). In contrast, results obtained with DOCAL were markedly better, although with a significant drop in F1 measure as well. The drops were similar across the three language pairs that we tested, as shown in Table 1. To investigate the specific impact of documents with minimal content, we prepared a variant of version 5 where all documents containing only one line of text were filtered.[13]. The results on this variant improved to higher scores, closer to those observed for version 2, with DOCAL providing markedly better results. The comparatively lower scores obtained on version 5 across the board do however show that the EUROPARL corpus can be useful to measure approaches to parallel document alignment, contrary to the conclusion reached by Enright and Kondrak (2007), which was based on version 2 of the corpus.

Table 1. Best F1 measures on Europarl

SYSTEM	CORPUS	ES-EN	FR-EN	NL-EN
HAPAX	EUPV2	99.6	99.6	99.6
DOCAL	EUPV2	**99.9**	**99.9**	**99.9**
HAPAX	EUPV5	54.2	54.5	50.3
DOCAL	EUPV5	**83.7**	**82.6**	**83.7**
HAPAX	EUPV5.2	72.9	72.5	67.2
DOCAL	EUPV5.2	**95.8**	**94.9**	**95.7**

Patry and Langlais (2011) applied their PARADOCS system on version 5 of the corpus, although the results they report render a direct comparison difficult: they use various corpus slices based on document length, a setup which we did not reproduce here,[14] and report percentage gains over the hapax-based method, and not absolute measures.

---

[12] We used the versions available as of February 2016 at the address: http://www.statmt.org/europarl/. We refer to version 2 as EUPV2 and to version 5 as EUPV5.

[13] We refer to this variant as EUPV5.2 in the table.

[14] They also indicate that the first sentences of each document were removed, which would directly eliminate the previously mentioned one-liner documents that are part of the version 5 we used.

They indicate F1 results of 95 and 93 for French-English and Dutch-English, respectively, for documents of at most 100 sentences. With all due caveats given experimental protocol differences, the DOCAL approach gave similar or better results on these pairs, as we reached 94.9 and 95.7 for these two language pairs on the full-length documents.

4.2 WIKIPEDIA

The 2015 Shared Task on Document Similarity, organised within the 8th workshop on Building and Using Comparable Corpora,[15] is the first task to provide a common testbench for the computation of similarity over a large collection of multilingual documents (Sharoff et al. 2015). The dataset is composed of static Wikipedia articles in three language pairs: English-French, English-Chinese and English-German. The articles were selected based on Wikipedia interlanguage links, provided the links were bidirectional and the documents matched size similarity criteria; the test sets were composed of articles with the interlanguage links removed. The task was to provide up to 5 target documents for each document in the test set, ranked according to the similarity scores assigned by the aligners to the document pairs.

Three measures were computed to assert the quality of the alignments, following standard TREC evaluation procedures:[16] SUCCESS@1 indicates the proportion of source articles for which the correct target article has been ranked in the top position; SUCCESS@5 measures the proportion of source articles for which the correct target has been ranked within the top 5 positions; finally, the MRR metric indicates the mean reciprocal range, i.e. the average over the 1/N scores assigned to correct target articles ranked at position N. For practical document alignment, the SUCCESS@1 results can be seen as the most significant, as these are the alignments that would be retained in actual usage of the systems.

Three systems participated in the task, all previously described in Section 2: LINA, whose results are reported with pigeon hole reasoning (referred to as LINA.P) and with alignment ties broken using the links from a third language (referred to as LINA.CL); the CCNUNLP system based on the approach in Li and Gaussier (2013); and the AUT system, described in Zafarian et al. (2015). The results for the AUT system having been reported as affected by a data processing bug, with all metric results close to zero, we do not include them in the tables below.

Results for the French-English and German-English pair are reported in Table 2. For the first pair, DOCAL performed markedly better than the alternative approaches, with an increase of almost 20 points on the SUCCESS@1 measure over the best reported system. It also obtained the best results on all other metrics in its variant where only the best alignments are retained. The base version of DOCAL also performs better on the SUCCESS@1 metric, although by a smaller margin.

As shown in Table 3, DOCAL performed markedly better for German-English as well, with gains of around 20 points on all three metrics over the best scoring version of LINA.[17]

---

[15] See: https://comparable.limsi.fr/bucc2015/.

[16] Text Retrieval Conference, see http://trec.nist.gov/.

[17] Results from the LINA system were the only ones available for this language pair.

Table 2. Results on the French-English Wikipedia task

SYSTEM	SUCCESS@1	SUCCESS@5	MRR
LINA.P	0.300	0.374	0.329
LINA.CL	0.577	0.606	0.590
CCNUNLP	0.607	0.764	0.669
DOCAL.A	0.636	0.693	0.659
DOCAL.B	**0.795**	**0.795**	**0.795**

Table 3. Results on the German-English Wikipedia task

SYSTEM	SUCCESS@1	SUCCESS@5	MRR
LINA.P	0.249	0.355	0.290
LINA.CL	0.607	0.639	0.622
DOCAL.A	0.649	0.621	0.688
DOCAL.B	**0.819**	**0.819**	**0.819**

Finally, results for the Chinese-English pair are shown in Table 4. For this language pair, the translation tables used by DOCAL were trained on 2 million parallel sentences extracted from the MULTIUN corpus, a collection of translated United Nations documents;[18] Chinese word segmentation was done with the Stanford segmenter (Tseng et al. 2005).[19] This is the only alignment scenario where one of the evaluated systems performs better than DOCAL among the selected tasks, with a marked difference for the SUCCESS@5 metric, a lower though significant difference for MRR, but a negligible difference of 0.014 points for the most important SUCCESS@1 metric. As the CCNUNLP system also relies on bilingual lexical information, it would be interesting to assess the difference in coverage and precision between the tables employed by each system; we did not however have the relevant information to perform this comparison. In further work, we will explore the impact of larger lexical translation tables for this language pair, as we only used a portion of the available training data for the experiment reported here.

Table 4. Results on the Chinese-English Wikipedia task

SYSTEM	SUCCESS@1	SUCCESS@5	MRR
CCNUNLP	**0.710**	**0.861**	**0.769**
DOCAL.A	0.576	0.601	0.576
DOCAL.B	0.696	0.696	0.696

---

[18] Available at: http://opus.lingfil.uu.se/MultiUN.php.

[19] http://nlp.stanford.edu/softhetware/segmenter.shtml

4.3 EITB

The final experiments were performed on the EITB corpus, a collection of strongly comparable documents in the news domain produced by the Basque public broadcaster Euskal Irrati Telebista.[20]

We manually aligned 299 documents in both languages as test set and applied DO-CAL along with the EMACC expectation maximisation tool directly, i.e. on the cartesian product of documents; EMACC was set with default values. The lexical translation tables were created with GIZA++ using a parallel corpus of 645,223 aligned sentences extracted from the IVAP corpus, a collection of professional translations of public administration texts released by the Instituto Vasco de Administración Pública. Table 5 presents the results.

Table 5. Results on the Basque-Spanish EITB task

SYSTEM	PRECISION	RECALL	F1
EMACC	90.7	84.6	87.5
DOCAL.A	90.0	**90.0**	90.0
DOCAL.B	**91.1**	89.3	**90.2**

Although EMACC is a state-of-the-art aligner for comparable documents which obtained competitive results on this test set, the simpler DOCAL method reached better marks in terms of precision, recall and F1 measure. It also performed better in terms of execution time, as the complete alignments were computed in 1.568 seconds, as opposed to the 7 minutes and 9.693 seconds needed by EMACC, on the same environment with 48G of RAM and 16 cores. For a rather difficult language pair, we consider these results to be quite satisfactory.

5 Conclusions

We presented a simple approach to document alignment based on lexical translation sets derived from automatically created bilingual tables, simple set expansion procedures, and the Jaccard similarity coefficient.

To test the merits of this approach, we performed a series of controlled experiments on a varied set of corpora, with results that matched or outperformed those obtained with currently available methods. The comparison was performed over corpora exhibiting varying degrees of comparability, from fully parallel documents of the Europarl corpus to large document sets of comparable Wikipedia data. The experiments covered six different language pairs that included Germanic, Romance, Asian and under-resourced

---

[20] See Etchegoyhen et al. (2016) for a detailed description of this corpus, which will be made available in the META-SHARE repository (http://www.meta-share.eu/) as the *Basque_Spanish_EITB_comparable_corpus*, under the CC - BY - NC - SA licence for academic users and the MS - C - NO RED - FF licence for commercial users.

languages, thus indicating the strong potential of the proposed method to handle language and domain variation.

The DOCAL approach requires no specific adaptation process, nor rich feature sets, to improve over state-of-the-art results. Additionally, it can be successfully applied as is to parallel or comparable corpora without task-specific training phases. It is thus a highly portable and easy to deploy method, which proved effective for the alignment of parallel and comparable multilingual documents.

In future work, we will explore potential improvements for the proposed approach, with further evaluations of the impact of lexical translation coverage and precision.

Acknowledgements

This work was partially supported by the Basque Government under project TRADIN and the Spanish Ministerio de Economa y Competividad under project ADAPTA. We wish to thank the anonymous reviewers for their insightful comments.

References

Brown, P. F., Cocke, J., Pietra, S. A. D., Pietra, V. J. D., Jelinek, F., Lafferty, J. D., Mercer, R. L., and Roossin, P. S. (1990). A statistical approach to machine translation. *Computational linguistics*, 16(2):79–85.

Brown, P. F., Pietra, V. J. D., Pietra, S. A. D., and Mercer, R. L. (1993). The mathematics of statistical machine translation: Parameter estimation. *Computational linguistics*, 19(2):263–311.

Chen, J., Chau, R., and Yeh, C.-H. (2004). Discovering parallel text from the World Wide Web. In *Proceedings of the second workshop on Australasian information security, Data Mining and Web Intelligence, and Software Internationalisation-Volume 32*, pages 157–161. Australian Computer Society, Inc.

Chen, J. and Nie, J.-Y. (2000). Parallel web text mining for cross-language IR. In *Content-Based Multimedia Information Access - Volume 1*, RIAO '00, pages 62–77, Paris, France, France. Centre des hautes études internationales d'informatique documentaire.

Enright, J. and Kondrak, G. (2007). A fast method for parallel document identification. In *Human Language Technologies 2007: The Conference of the North American Chapter of the Association for Computational Linguistics; Companion Volume, Short Papers*, pages 29–32. Association for Computational Linguistics.

Etchegoyhen, T., Azpeitia, A., and Perez, N. (2016). Exploiting a large strongly comparable corpus. To appear in *Proceedings of the 10th edition of the Language Resources and Evaluation Conference*.

Fung, P. and Cheung, P. (2004). Mining very non-parallel corpora: Parallel sentence and lexicon extraction via bootstrapping and E.M.. In *Proceedings of Empirical Methods in Natural Language Processing*, pages 57–63.

Ion, R., Ceauşu, A., and Irimia, E. (2011). An expectation maximization algorithm for textual unit alignment. In *Proceedings of the 4th Workshop on Building and Using Comparable Corpora: Comparable Corpora and the Web*, pages 128–135. Association for Computational Linguistics.

Jaccard, P. (1901). Distribution de la flore alpine dans le bassin des Dranses et dans quelques régions voisines. *Bulletin de la Société Vaudoise des Sciences Naturelles*, 37:241 – 272.

Koehn, P. (2005). Europarl: A Parallel Corpus for Statistical Machine Translation. In *Proceedings of the 10th Machine Translation Summit*, pages 79–86.

Li, B. and Gaussier, E. (2013). Exploiting comparable corpora for lexicon extraction: Measuring and improving corpus quality. In *Building and Using Comparable Corpora*, pages 131–149. Springer.

Ma, X. and Liberman, M. (1999). Bits: A method for bilingual text search over the web. In *Machine Translation Summit VII*, pages 538–542.

Manning, C. D. and Schütze, H. (1999). *Foundations of statistical natural language processing*, volume 999. MIT Press.

Morin, E., Hazem, A., Boudin, F., and Clouet, E. L. (2015). Lina: Identifying comparable documents from Wikipedia. In *Eighth Workshop on Building and Using Comparable Corpora*.

Munteanu, D. S. and Marcu, D. (2005). Improving machine translation performance by exploiting non-parallel corpora. *Computational Linguistics*, 31(4):477–504.

Och, F. J. and Ney, H. (2003). A systematic comparison of various statistical alignment models. *Computational linguistics*, 29(1):19–51.

Paramita, M. L., Guthrie, D., Kanoulas, E., Gaizauskas, R., Clough, P., and Sanderson, M. (2013). Methods for collection and evaluation of comparable documents. In *Building and Using Comparable Corpora*, pages 93–112. Springer.

Patry, A. and Langlais, P. (2005). Automatic identification of parallel documents with light or without linguistic resources. In *Proceedings of the 18th Canadian Society Conference on Advances in Artificial Intelligence*, AI'05, pages 354–365, Berlin, Heidelberg. Springer-Verlag.

Patry, A. and Langlais, P. (2011). Identifying parallel documents from a large bilingual collection of texts: Application to parallel article extraction in wikipedia. In *Proceedings of the 4th Workshop on Building and Using Comparable Corpora: Comparable Corpora and the Web*, pages 87–95. Association for Computational Linguistics.

Prochasson, E. and Fung, P. (2011). Rare word translation extraction from aligned comparable documents. In *Proceedings of the 49th Annual Meeting of the Association for Computational Linguistics: Human Language Technologies-Volume 1*, pages 1327–1335. Association for Computational Linguistics.

Resnik, P. and Smith, N. A. (2003). The web as a parallel corpus. *Computational Linguistics*, 29(3):349–380.

Sharoff, S., Zweigenbaum, P., and Rapp, R. (2015). BUCC shared task: Cross-language document similarity. *Proceedings of the 8th Workshop on Building and Using Comparable Corpora*, pages 74–78.

Tiedemann, J. (2011). *Bitext alignment*. Synthesis Lectures on Human Language Technologies. Morgan & Claypool Publishers.

Tseng, H., Chang, P., Andrew, G., Jurafsky, D. and Manning, C. (2005). A conditional random field word segmenter. In *Proceedings of the Fourth SIGHAN Workshop on Chinese Language Processing*.

Uszkoreit, J., Ponte, J. M., Popat, A. C. and Dubiner, M. (2010). Large scale parallel document mining for machine translation. In *Proceedings of the 23rd International Conference on Computational Linguistics*.

Zafarian, A., Aghasadeghi, A., Azadi, F., Ghiasifard, S., Alipanahloo, Z., Bakhshaei, S., and Ziabary, S. M. M. (2015). AUT Document alignment framework for BUCC workshop shared task. *ACL-IJCNLP 2015*, page 79.

Received May 2, 2016 , accepted May 13, 2016

Baltic J. Modern Computing, Vol. 4 (2016), No. 2, pp. 256–268

Semantic Textual Similarity in Quality Estimation

Hanna BÉCHARA[1], Carla PARRA ESCARTÍN[2], Constantin ORĂSAN[1],
Lucia SPECIA[3]

[1] University of Wolverhampton, Wolverhampton, UK
[2] Hermes Traducciones, Madrid, Spain
[3] University of Sheffield, Sheffield, UK

Hanna.Bechara@wlv.ac.uk, carla.parra@hermestrans.com,
C.Orasan@wlv.ac.uk, l.specia@sheffield.ac.uk

Abstract. Quality Estimation (QE) predicts the quality of machine translation output without the need for a reference translation. This quality can be defined differently based on the task at hand. In an attempt to focus further on the adequacy and informativeness of translations, we integrate features of semantic similarity into QuEst, a framework for QE feature extraction. By using methods previously employed in Semantic Textual Similarity (STS) tasks, we use semantically similar sentences and their quality scores as features to estimate the quality of machine translated sentences. Preliminary experiments show that finding semantically similar sentences for some datasets is difficult and time-consuming. Therefore, we opt to start from the assumption that we already have access to semantically similar sentences. Our results show that this method can improve the prediction of machine translation quality for semantically similar sentences.

Keywords: Quality Estimation, Semantic Textual Similarity, Machine Translation

1 Introduction

Machine Translation Quality Estimation (MTQE) has been gaining increasing interest in Machine Translation (MT) output assessment, as it can be used to measure different aspects of correctness. Furthermore, Quality Estimation (QE) tools forego the need for a reference translation and instead predict the quality of the output based on the source.

In this paper, we address the use of semantic correctness in QE by integrating STS measures into the process, without relying on a reference translation. We propose a set of features that compares MT output to a semantically similar sentence, that has already been assessed, using monolingual STS tools to measure the semantic proximity of the sentence in relation to the second sentence.

The rest of this paper is organised as follows: Section 2 features the state of the art in QE and the context for our research. Section 3 introduces our approach to integrating semantic information into QE. Section 4 details our experimental set-up, including the tools we use for our experiments. Section 5 explains our experiments, details our new STS features and summarises the results we observe when adding these features to QuEst. Finally, Section 6 presents our concluding remarks and plans for future work.

2   Previous Work

Early work in QE built on the concept of confidence estimation used in speech recognition (Gandrabur and Foster, 2003, Blatz et al., 2004). These systems usually relied on system-dependent features, and focused on measuring how confident a given system is rather than how correct the translation is.

Later experiments in QE used only system-independent features based on the source sentence and target translation (Specia et al., 2009b). They trained a Support Vector Machine (SVM) regression model based on 74 shallow features, and reported significant gains in accuracy over MT evaluation metrics. At first, these approaches to QE focused mainly on shallow features based on the source and target sentences. Such features include n-gram counts, the average length of tokens, punctuation statistics and sentence length among other features. Later systems incorporate linguistic features such as part of speech tags, syntactic information and word alignment information (Specia et al., 2010).

In the context of QE, the term "quality" itself is flexible and can change to reflect specific applications, from quality assurance, gisting and estimating post-editing (PE) effort to ranking translations. Specia et al. (2009a) define quality in terms of PE efficiency, using QE to filter out sentences that would require too much time to post-edit. Similarly, He et al. (2010) use QE techniques to predict human PE effort and recommend MT outputs to Translation Memory (TM) users based on estimated PE effort. In contrast, Specia et al., 2010 use QE to rank translations from different systems and highlight inadequate segments for post-editing.

Since 2012, QE has been the focus of a shared task at the annual Workshop for Statistical Machine Translation (WMT) (Callison-Burch et al., 2012). This task has provided a common ground for the comparison and evaluation of different QE systems and data at the word, sentence and document level (Bojar et al., 2015).

There have been a few attempts to integrate semantic similarity into the MT evaluation (Lo and Wu, 2011, Castillo and Estrella, 2012). The results reported are generally positive, showing that semantic information is not only useful, but often necessary, in order to assess the quality of machine translation output.

Specia et al. (2011) bring semantic information into the realm of QE in order to address the problem of meaning preservation. The authors focus on what they term "adequacy indicators" and human annotations for adequacy. The results they report show improvement with respect to a majority class baseline. Rubino et al. (2013) also address MT adequacy using topic models for QE. By including topic model features that focus on content words in sentences, their system outperforms state-of-the-art approaches specifically with datasets annotated for adequacy. Biçici (2013) introduce the use of referential translation machines (RTM) for QE. RTM is a computational model for judging monolingual and bilingual similarity that achieves state-of-the-art results. The authors report top performance in both sentence level and word-level tasks of WMT

2013. Camargo de Souza et al. (2014) propose a set of features that explore word alignment information in order to address semantic relations between sentences. Their results show that POS indicator features improve over the baseline at the shared task for QE at the workshop for machine translation. Kaljahi et al. (2014) employ syntactic and semantic information in quality estimation and are able to improve over the baseline when combining these features with the surface features of the baseline. Our work builds on previous work, focusing on the necessity of semantic information for MT adequacy. As far as we are aware, our work is the first to explore quality scores from semantically similar sentences as surrogate to the quality of the current sentence.

3   Our Approach

In this paper, we propose integrating semantic similarity into the quality estimation task. As STS relies on monolingual data, we employ the use of a second sentence that bears some semantic resemblance to the sentence we wish to evaluate.

Our approach is illustrated in Figure 1, where sentences A and B are two semantically similar sentences with a similarity score R. Our task is to assess the quality of sentence A with the help of sentence B which has already undergone machine translation evaluation, either through post-editing or by human evaluation (e.g. assessed on a scale from 1–5). As both sentences, A and B are semantically similar, our hypothesis is that their translations are also semantically similar and thus we can use the reference of sentence B to estimate the quality of sentence A.

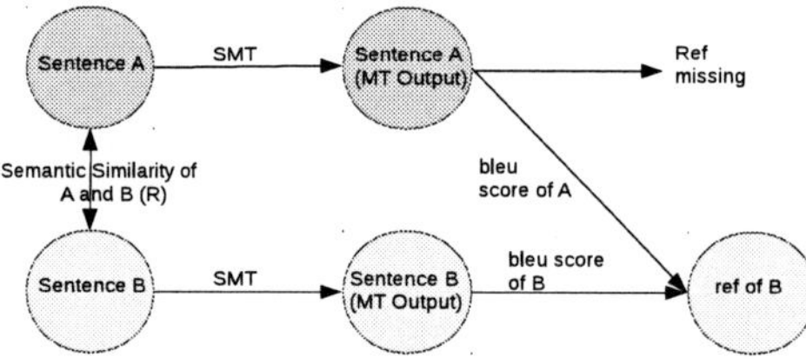

Fig. 1. Predicting the Quality of MT Output using a Semantically Similar Sentence B

For each sentence A, for which we wish to estimate MT quality, we retrieve a semantically similar sentence B which has been machine translated and has a reference translation or a quality assessment value. We then extract the following three scores (that we use as STS features):

Semantic Textual Similarity (STS) score: R represents the STS between the source sentence pairs (sentence A and sentence B). This is a continuous score ranging from 0 to 5. We calculate this score using the MiniExperts system designed for SemEval2015 (cf. Section 4.2) in all but one of our experiments, where we already have human annotations about STS. This experiment, the oracle experiment represents scores we could achieve if our STS was perfect.

Quality Score for Sentence B: We calculate the quality of the MT output of Sentence B. This is either a S-BLEU score based on a reference translation, or a manual score provided by a human evaluator.

S-BLEU Score for Sentence A: We have no human evaluation or reference translation for Sentence A, but we can calculate a quality score using Sentence B as a reference. We use sentence-level BLEU (S-BLEU) (Lin and Och, 2004). S-BLEU is designed to work at the sentence level and will still positively score segments that do not have a high order n-gram match.

4 Experimental Setting

In this section, we start with a brief introduction to the QuEst framework, followed by a description of the settings for the experiments described in this paper.

4.1 The QuEst Framework

QuEst (Specia et al., 2013) is an open source framework for MTQE.[4] In addition to a feature extraction framework, QuEst also provides the machine learning algorithms necessary to build the prediction models. QuEst gives access to a large variety of features, each relevant to different tasks and definitions of quality.

As QuEst is a state-of-the-art tool for MTQE and is used as a baseline in recent QE tasks, such as previous workshops for machine translation (Callison-Burch et al., 2012, Bojar et al., 2013, Bojar et al., 2014 and Bojar et al., 2015), we use its 17 features as a baseline to allow for comparison of our work to a state-of-the-art system.

The baseline features are system independent and include shallow surface features such as the number of punctuation marks, the average length of words and the number of words. Furthermore, these features include n-gram frequencies and language model probabilities. A full list of the baseline features can be found in Table 1.

4.2 MiniExpert's STS Tool

In our experiments, we use the MiniExpert's submission to Semeval2015's Task 2a (Béchara et al., 2015). The source code is easy to use and available on GitHub.[5] The system uses a SVM regression model to predict the STS scores between two English

---

[4] https://github.com/lspecia/quest

[5] https://github.com/rohitguptacs/wlvsimilarity

Table 1. Full List of QuEst's Baseline Features

ID	Description
1	number of tokens in the source sentence
2	number of tokens in the target sentence
3	average source token length
4	LM probability of source sentence
5	LM probability of the target sentence
6	average number of occurrences of the target word within the target sentence
7	average number of translations per source word in the sentence (as given by IBM 1 table thresholded so that prob(t|s) > 0.2)
8	average number of translations per source word in the sentence weighted by the inverse frequency of each word in the source corpus
9	percentage of unigrams in quartile 1 of frequency (lower frequency words) in a corpus of the source language
10	percentage of unigrams in quartile 4 of frequency (higher frequency words) in a corpus of the source language
11	percentage of bigrams in quartile 1 of frequency of source words in a corpus of the source language
12	percentage of bigrams in quartile 4 of frequency of source words in a corpus of the source language
13	percentage of trigrams in quartile 1 of frequency of source words in a corpus of the source language
14	percentage of trigrams in quartile 4 of frequency of source words in a corpus of the source language
15	percentage of unigrams in the source sentence seen in a corpus
16	number of punctuation marks in source sentence
17	number of punctuation marks in target sentence

sentences. The authors train their system on a variety of linguistically motivated features inspired by deep semantics with distributional Similarity Measures, Conceptual Similarity Measures, Semantic Similarity Measures and Corpus Pattern Analysis.

The system performs well and obtained a mean 0.7216 Pearson correlation in the shared task, ranking 33 out of 74 systems.

We train the STS tool on the SICK dataset Marelli et al., 2014, a dataset specifically designed for semantic similarity and used in previous SemEval tasks, augmented with training data from previous SemEval tasks (SemEval2014 and SemEval2015).

4.3 Statistical Machine Translation System

All of our experiments require MT output to run MTQE tasks. To that end, we use the state-of-the-art phrase based Statistical Machine Translation (SMT) system Moses (Koehn et al., 2007). We build 5-gram language models with Kneser-Ney smoothing trained with SRILM, (Stolcke, 2002), and run the GIZA++ implementation of IBM word alignment model 4 (Och and Ney, 2003), with refinement and phrase-extraction heuristics as described in Koehn et al. (2003). We use Minimum Error Rate Training (MERT) (Och, 2003) for tuning.

In order to keep our experiments consistent, we use the same SMT system for all datasets. We focus on English into French translations and we use the Europarl corpus (Koehn, 2005) for training. We train on 500,000 unique English–French sentences and then tune our system (using MERT) on 1,000 different unique sentences also from the Europarl corpus. We also train a French–English system to retrieve the backtranslations used in some of our experiments.

5   Experiments

As mentioned earlier, all our datasets focus on MTQE for English→French MT output. In all our experiments we have a set of machine translated sentences A for which we need a QE and a set of sentences B, semantically similar to the set of sentences A and for which we have some type of evaluation score available.

In early experiments, we attempted to use freely available datasets used in previous workshops on machine translation (WMT2012 and WMT2013) for the translation task and within the news domain (Bojar et al., 2013). The WMT datasets have two main advantages: first, they allow us to compare our system with previous systems for QE and render our experiments replicable. Second, they have manual evaluations that are available with the machine translations. Each sentence in the WMT dataset comes with a score between 1 and 5, provided by human annotators. However, this method proved to be too time-consuming, as it often required scoring thousands of sentences before finding two that were similar.

The first obstacle we faced in testing our approach with these datasets was the collection of similar sentences against which to compare and evaluate. We automatically searched large parallel corpora for sentences that yielded high similarity scores. These corpora included the Europarl corpus (Koehn, 2005), the Acquis Communautaire (Steinberger et al., 2006) and previous WMT data (from 2012 and 2013).

Furthermore, the STS system we use (see Section 4.2) returned many false-positives. Some sentences which appeared similar to the STS system were actually too different to be usable. This led to noisy data and unusable results. The scarcity of semantically similar sentences and the computational cost of finding these sentences, lead us to look into alternate datasets, preferably those with semantic similarity built into the corpus: the DGT-TM and the SICK dataset.

All our experiments have the same set-up. In all cases, we used 500 randomly selected sentences for testing, and the remaining sentences in the respective data-set for training QuEst. We automatically search large parallel corpora for sentences that yield high similarity scores using the STS system described in section 4.2.

We attempt to predict the quality scores of the individual sentences, using the STS features described above, added to QuEst's 17 baseline features. We compare our results to both the QuEst baseline (cf. Section 4.1). and the majority class baseline[6]. We also test our STS-related features separately, without the baseline features, and compare them to the system with the combined system (STS+baseline).

We use the Mean Absolute Error (MAE) to evaluate the prediction rate of our systems. MAE measures the average magnitude of the errors on the test set, without considering their direction. Therefore, it is ideal for measuring the accuracy for continuous variables. MAE is calculated as per Equation 1.

$$MAE = \frac{1}{n} \sum |x_i - y|$$

(1)

---

[6] The Mean Absolute Error calculated using the mean rating in the training set as a projected score for every sentence in the test set.

where n is the number of instances in the test set, x_i is the score predicted by the system, and y is the observed score. In our experiments, we use S-BLEU scores as the observed score.

5.1 DGT-TM

We use the 2014 release of the Directorate General for Translation – Translation Memory (DGT-TM) to test our system. The DGT-TM is a corpus of aligned sentences in 22 different languages created from the European Union's legislative documents (Steinberger et al., 2006). We randomly extract 500 unique sentences (B), then search the rest of the TM for the 5 most semantically similar sentences (A) for each of these 500 sentences (STS score $>$ 3). This results in 2,500 sentences A (500x5) and their semantically similar sentence pairs B. We make sure to avoid any overlap in sentence A so that while semantically similar sentence B might recur, sentence A will remain unique. we assign an STS score to the resulting dataset using the system described in Section 4.2. We then translate these sentence pairs using the translation model described in Section 4.3 and use S-BLEU to assign evaluation scores for the MT outputs of Sentence A and B.

Of these 2,500 sentence pairs and their MT outputs, we use 2,000 sentence pairs to train an SVM regression model on Quest's baseline features using using sentence A and its MT output as the source and target sentence. We further use sentence B's S-BLEU score and its STS score with sentence A. We use the remaining 500 sentences to test our system. Table 2 shows a sample sentence (Sentence B) from the DGT-TM along its semantically similar retrieved match (Sentence A) and the machine translation output for each sentence. The MiniExpert's STS system gave the original English sentence pair a STS score of 4.46, indicating that only minor details differ.

Table 2. DGT-TM Sample Sentence

	Sentence A
Source	In order to ensure that the measures provided for in this Regulation are effective , it should enter into force *on the day of its publication*
MT	afin de garantir que les mesures prévues dans ce règlement sont efficaces , il devrait entrer en vigueur *sur le jour de sa publication* ,
	Sentence B
Source	In order to ensure that the measures provided for in this Regulation are effective , this Regulation should enter into force *immediately* ,
MT	afin de garantir que les mesures prévues dans ce règlement sont efficaces , ce règlement doit entrer en vigueur *immédiatement* ,
STS	4.46

Results: Our results are summarised in Table 3, which shows that the MAE for the combined features (QuEst + STS features) is considerably lower than that of QuEst on its own. This means that the additional use of STS features can improve QuEst's predictive power. Even the 3 STS features on their own outperformed QuEst's baseline features. These results show that our method can prove useful in a context where semantically similar sentences are accessible.

Table 3. Predicting the S-BLEU scores for DGT-TM - Mean Absolute Error

	MAE
QuEst Baseline (17 Features)	0.120
STS (3 Features)	0.108
Combined (20 Features)	0.090

5.2 SICK Dataset

In order to further test the suitability of our approach for semantically similar sentences, we use the SICK dataset for further experiments. SICK (Sentences Involving Compositional Knowledge) is a dataset specifically designed for compositional distributional semantics. It includes a large number of English sentence pairs that are rich in lexical, syntactic and semantic phenomena. The SICK dataset is generated from existing datasets based on images and video descriptions, and each sentence pair is annotated for relatedness (similarity) and entailment by means of crowd-sourcing techniques (Marelli et al., 2014). This means that we did not need to use the STS tool to annotate the sentences. The similarity score is a score between 1 and 5, further described in Table 4. As these scores are obtained by averaging several separate annotations by distinct evaluators, they are continuous, rather than discrete. As SICK already provides us with sentence pairs of variable similarity, it cuts out the need to search extensively for similar sentences. Furthermore, the crowd-sourced similarity scores act as a gold standard that eliminates the uncertainty introduced by the automatic STS tool. This dataset lacks a reliable reference translation to compare against, however.

Table 4. STS scale used by SemEval

0	The two sentences are on different topics
1	The two sentences are not equivalent, but are on the same topic
2	The two sentences are not equivalent, but share some details
3	The two sentences are roughly equivalent, but some important information differs/is missing
4	The two sentences are mostly equivalent, but some unimportant detail differs/missing
5	The two sentences are completely equivalent, as they mean the same thing

We extract 5,000 sentence pairs to use in our experiments and translate them into French using the MT system described in Section 4.3. The resulting dataset consists of 5,000 semantically similar sentence pairs and their French machine translations. Of this set, 4,500 are used to train an SVM regression model in the same manner as described in Section 5.1. The remaining 500 sentences are used for testing.

As the SICK dataset is monolingual and therefore lacking in a reference translation, we opted to use a back-translation (into English) as a reference instead of a French translation for these results. A back-translation is a translation of a translated text back into the original language. Back-translations are usually used to compare translations with the original text for quality and accuracy, and can help to evaluate equivalence of meaning between the source and target texts. In machine translation contexts, they can be used to create a pseudo-source that can be compared against the original source. He et al. (2010) used this back-translation as a feature in QE with some success. They compared the back-translation to the original source using fuzzy match scoring and used the result to estimate the quality of the translation. The intuition here is that the closer the back translation is to the original source, the better the translation is in the first place.

Following this idea, we use the S-BLEU scores of the back-translations as stand-ins for the MT quality scores. We use the MT system described in Section 3.3 for the back-translations.

Table 5 shows a sample sentence from the resulting dataset, including the original English sentence pairs and each sentence's MT output. The crowd-sourced STS score for this sentence pair is 4, indicating that only minor details differ.

Table 5. SICK Sample Sentence

	Sentence A
Source	Several children are *lying* down and are raising their knees
MT	Plusieurs enfants sont couchés et élèvent leurs genoux
	Sentence B
Source	Several children are *sitting* down and have their knees raised
MT	Plusieurs enfants sont assis et ont soulevé leurs genoux
STS	4

Results: Results on the SICK datasets are summarised in Table 6. The lowest error rate (MAE) is observed for the system that combined our STS-based features with QuEst's baseline features (Combined (20 Features)) just as in the DGT-TM experiments. We observe that even the STS features on their own outperformed QuEst in this environment.

Table 6. Predicting the S-BLEU scores for SICK - Mean Absolute Error

	MAE
QuEst Baseline (17 Features)	0.200
STS (3 Features)	0.189
Combined (20 Features)	0.177

The cherry-picked examples in Table 7 are from the SICK dataset, and show that a high STS score between the source sentences can contribute to a high prediction accuracy. In both examples, the predicted score for Sentence A is close to the actual observed score.

Table 7. SICK Sample Prediction

	Sentence A	Sentence B
Source	Dirt bikers are riding on a trail	Two people are riding motorbikes
MT	Dirt Bikers roulent sur une piste	Deux personnes font du vélo motos
S-BLEU:	0.55 (Predicted) 0.6 (Actual)	0.84
STS	3.6	
Source	A man is leaning against a pole and is surrounded	A man is leaning against a pole and is surrounded by people
MT	Un homme est appuyée contre un poteau et est entouré par des gens	Un homme est appuyée contre un poteau et est entouré
S-BLEU:	0.91 (Predicted) 1 (Actual)	0.91
STS	4.2	

Furthermore, when we filtered the test set for the SICK experiments for sentences with high similarity (4+), we observed an even higher drop in MAE, as demonstrated in Table 8. This suggests that our experiments perform especially well if we select for sentences with high similarity.

Table 8. Predicting the S-BLEU scores for SICK sentences with high similarity - Mean Absolute Error

	MAE
QuEst Baseline (17 Features)	0.20
Combined (20 Features)	0.15

6   Conclusion and Future Work

In this paper we presented 3 semantically motivated features that augment QuEst's baseline features. We tested our approach on three different datasets and the results are encouraging, showing that these features can improve over the baseline when a sufficiently similar sentence against which to compare is available.

Several factors can be enhanced to further improve our system. To start with, the use of S-BLEU to evaluate our system is not ideal. Criticisms of BLEU and n-gram matching metrics in general are addressed by Callison-Burch et al. (2008), who show that BLEU fails to correlate to (and even contradicts) human judgement. More importantly, BLEU itself does not measure meaning preservation. Therefore, to evaluate our system more thoroughly, we would need to compare it to human judgements. In order to address the criticisms of both BLEU and the back-translations, we are currently collecting manual evaluations of the French SICK MT output sentences. Before a full manual evaluation is performed, we cannot conclusively state that our results on the SICK dataset are valid in a real world setting.

Another case worth addressing further is that where the retrieved matches are so similar to the original, that they could be acting as a pseudo-reference. While the examples show that this is not always the case, this phenomenon bears further investigation in future research.

The MiniExpert's tool which we use to determine the STS scores for the DGT–TM is trained on very different data (the SICK corpus and SemEval data), which may affect its accuracy. This may explain why it did not work as well as expected given its reported performance. However, the lack of readily available semantically annotated data to train on limits us in this regard. Furthermore, our features rely on the existence of semantically similar sentences against which we can compare our translations. These sentences are not always readily available and, as explained earlier in Section 5, searching large corpora for similar sentences can be computationally costly and time-consuming.

In spite of these short-comings, this approach can be quite useful in settings where we wish to predict the quality of sentences within a very specific domain. One potential such scenario, would be post-editing tasks in which professional translators are asked to post-edit MT output of specialized texts. As translators use Translation Memories (TMs) to ensure the quality of their work, such TMs could be used to obtain semantically similar sentences to the ones in the MTPE task and compute with our approach a QE score. The results we obtained in the case of SICK are encouraging in this respect and in future work we plan to investigate this further.

Acknowledgements

This work is supported by the People Programme (Marie Curie Actions) of the European Union's Framework Programme (FP7/2007-2013) under REA grant agreement n° 317471.

References

Béchara, H., Costa, H., Taslimipoor, S., Gupta, R., Orasan, C., Corpas Pastor, G., and Mitkov, R. (2015). MiniExperts: An SVM approach for Measuring Semantic Textual Similarity. In 9th *Int. Workshop on Semantic Evaluation*, SemEval'15, pages 96–101, Denver, Colorado. ACL.

Biçici, Ergun (2013). Referential translation machines for quality estimation. In *Proceedings of the Eighth Workshop on Statistical Machine Translation*, pages 343–351, Sofia, Bulgaria.

Blatz, J., Fitzgerald, E., Foster, G., Gandrabur, S., Goutte, C., Kulesza, C., Sanchis, A., and Ueffing, N. (2004). Confidence estimation for machine translation. In *Proceedings of the 20th International Conference on Computational Linguistics (CoLing-2004)*, pages 315–321.

Bojar, O., Buck, C., Callison-Burch, C., Federmann, C., Haddow, B., Koehn, P., Monz, C., Post, M., Soricut, R., and Specia, L. (2013). Findings of the 2013 Workshop on Statistical Machine Translation. In *Proceedings of the Eighth Workshop on Statistical Machine Translation*, pages 1–44, Sofia, Bulgaria. Association for Computational Linguistics.

Bojar, Ondrej and Buck, Christian and Federmann, Christian and Haddow, Barry and Koehn, Philipp and Leveling, Johannes and Monz, Christof and Pecina, Pavel and Post, Matt and Saint-Amand, Herve and Soricut, Radu and Specia, Lucia and Tamchyna, Aleš (2014). Findings of the 2014 Workshop on Statistical Machine Translation. In *Proceedings of the Ninth Workshop on Statistical Machine Translation*, pages 12–58, Sofia, Bulgaria. Association for Computational Linguistics.

Bojar, O. and Chatterjee, R. and Federmann, C. and Haddow, B. and Huck, M. and Hokamp, C. and Koehn, P. and Logacheva, V. and Monz, C. and Negri, M. and others 2015 Findings of the 2015 Workshop on Statistical Machine Translation

Callison-Burch, C., Fordyce, C., Koehn, P., Monz, C., and Schroeder, J. (2008). Further Meta-Evaluation of Machine Translation. In *Proceedings of the Third Workshop on Statistical Machine Translation (WMT)*, pages 70–106.

Callison-Burch, C., Koehn, P., Monz, C., Post, M., Soricut, R., and Specia, L., editors (2012). *Proceedings of the Seventh Workshop on Statistical Machine Translation*. Association for Computational Linguistics, Montréal, Canada.

Castillo, J. and Estrella, P. (2012). Semantic textual similarity for mt evaluation. In *Proceedings of the Seventh Workshop on Statistical Machine Translation*, WMT '12, pages 52–58, Stroudsburg, PA, USA. Association for Computational Linguistics.

Gandrabur, S. and Foster, G. (2003). Confidence estimation for translation prediction. In *Proceedings of the Seventh Conference on Natural Language Learning at HLT-NAACL 2003 - Volume 4*, CONLL '03, pages 95–102, Stroudsburg, PA, USA. Association for Computational Linguistics.

He, Y., Ma, Y., van Genabith, J., and Way, A. (2010). Bridging SMT and TM with Translation Recommendation. In *Proceedings of the 28th Annual Meeting of the Association for Computational Linguistics*, pages 622–630.

Kaljahi, R. and Foster, J. and Roturier, J. (2014). Syntax and Semantics in Quality Estimation of Machine Translation, In *Syntax, Semantics and Structure in Statistical Translation*, pages 67.

Koehn, P. (2005). Europarl: A parallel corpus for statistical machine translation. In *MT summit*, volume 5, pages 79–86.

Koehn, P., Hoang, H., Birch, A., Callison-Burch, C., Federico, M., Bertoldi, N., Cowan, B., Shen, W., Moran, C., Zens, R., Dyer, C., Bojar, O., Constantin, A., and Herbst, E. (2007). Moses: Open Source Toolkit for Statistical Machine Translation. In *Proceedings of the Association for Computational Linguistics (ACL)*, pages 177–180.

Koehn, P., Och, F., and Marcu, D. (2003). Statistical Phrase-Based Translation. In *Proceedings of the Human Language Technology Conference and the North American Chapter of the Association for Computational Linguistics (HLT/NAACL)*, pages 48–54.

Lin, C.-Y. and Och, F. J. (2004). Automatic evaluation of machine translation quality using longest common subsequence and skip-bigram statistics. In *Proceedings of the 42Nd Annual Meeting on Association for Computational Linguistics*, ACL '04, Stroudsburg, PA, USA. Association for Computational Linguistics.

Lo, C.-k. and Wu, D. (2011). Meant: An inexpensive, high-accuracy, semi-automatic metric for evaluating translation utility via semantic frames. In *Proceedings of the 49th Annual Meeting of the Association for Computational Linguistics: Human Language Technologies-Volume 1*, pages 220–229. Association for Computational Linguistics.

Marelli, M., Menini, S., Baroni, M., Bentivogli, L., Bernardi, R., and Zamparelli, R. (2014b). A sick cure for the evaluation of compositional distributional semantic models. In *LREC'14*, Reykjavik, Iceland.

Och, F. (2003). Minimum Error Rate Training in Statistical Machine Translation. In *Proceedings of the Association for Computational Linguistics (ACL)*, pages 160–167.

Och, F. and Ney, H. (2003). A Systematic Comparison of Various Statistical Alignment Models. In *Proceedings of the Association for Computer Linguistics (ACL)*, pages 29(1):19–51.

Rubino, Raphael and Souza, José Guilherme Camargo and Foster, Jennifer and Specia, Lucia. Topic Models for Translation Quality Estimation for Gisting Purposes. In Machine Translation Summit XIV, pages 295–302.

, Camargo de Souza, José Guilherme and González-Rubio, Jesús and Buck, Christian and Turchi, Marco and Negri, Matteo. FBK-UPV-UEdin participation in the WMT14 Quality Estimation shared-task. In Proceedings of the Ninth Workshop on Statistical Machine Translation, pages 322–328.

Specia, L., Raj, D., and Turchi, M. (2010). Machine Translation Evaluation versus Quality Estimation. In *Machine Translation Volume 24, Issue 1*, pages 39–50.

Lucia Specia and Najeh Hajlaoui and Catalina Hallett and Wilker Aziz. Predicting Machine Translation Adequacy. In Machine Translation Summit XIII, pages 513–520.

Specia, L., Shah, K., De Souza, J. G. C., and Cohn, T. (2013). QuEst - A translation quality estimation framework. In *Proceedings of the Association for Computational Linguistics (ACL), Demonstrations*.

Specia, L., Turchi, M., Cancedda, N., Dymetman, M., and Cristianini, N. (2009a). Estimating the Sentence-Level Quality of Machine Translation Systems. In *13th Annual Meeting of the European Association for Machine Translation (EAMT-2009)*, pages 28–35.

Specia, L., Turchi, M., Wang, Z., Shawe-Taylor, J., and Saunders, C. (2009b). Improving the confidence of machine translation quality estimates.

Steinberger, R., Pouliquen, B., Widiger, A., Ignat, C., Erjavec, T., and Tufis, D. (2006). The JRC-Acquis: A multilingual aligned parallel corpus with 20+ languages. In *Proceedings of the 5th International Conference on Language Resources and Evaluation (LREC–2006*, pages 2142–2147.

Stolcke, A. (2002). SRILM - an Extensible Language Modeling Toolkit. In *Proceedings of the International Conference on Spoken Language Processing (ICSLP)*, pages 901–904.

Received May3, 2016 , accepted May 13, 2016

Baltic J. Modern Computing, Vol. 4 (2016), No. 2, pp. 269–281

Climbing Mount BLEU: The Strange World of Reachable High-BLEU Translations

Aaron SMITH[1,2], Christian HARDMEIER[1], Jörg TIEDEMANN[3]

[1] Uppsala University
[2] Convertus AB, Uppsala, Sweden
[3] University of Helsinki

aaron.smith@convertus.se, christian.hardmeier@lingfil.uu.se,
jorg.tiedemann@helsinki.fi

Abstract. We present a method for finding oracle BLEU translations in phrase-based statistical machine translation using exact document-level scores. Experiments are presented where the BLEU score of a candidate translation is directly optimised in order to examine the properties of reachable translations with very high BLEU scores. This is achieved by running the document-level decoder Docent in BLEU-decoding mode, where proposed changes to the translation of a document are only accepted if they increase BLEU. The results confirm that the reference translation cannot in most cases be reached by the decoder, which is limited by the set of phrases in the phrase table, and demonstrate that high-BLEU translations are often of poor quality.

Keywords: Statistical machine translation, oracle decoding, BLEU, Docent

1 Introduction

This paper presents a method for finding oracle translations in phrase-based (PB) statistical machine translation (SMT) using exact document-level BLEU scores. The method, which we call BLEU decoding, is implemented in the document-level machine translation decoder Docent. BLEU decoding is a stochastic hill climbing algorithm: changes are proposed by the decoder to an initial translation and only accepted if they increase BLEU.

Analysing the translations obtained in this way we corroborate previous research on the problem of reference reachability: perfect BLEU scores, corresponding to the decoder finding the reference translation exactly, are rarely possible; meanwhile we add to the extensive literature on problems and biases with the BLEU metric itself, showing for the first time clear examples of sentences from documents with high BLEU scores with obvious poor translation quality.

The paper is structured in the following manner: Section 2 describes the BLEU metric, Section 3 presents the Docent decoder and BLEU decoding, Section 4 details experiments carried out with BLEU decoding and presents their results, while Section 5 comprises a discussion.

2 BLEU

The BLEU score, introduced by Papineni et al. (2002), is a metric for evaluating the quality of a candidate translation by comparing it to one or more reference translations. For $1 \leq n \leq N$, where normally $N = 4$, each n-gram in each candidate sentence is checked against all of the references in order to calculate precision. To count towards precision, the candidate n-gram need only appear in one of the references; this helps to account for possible variations in style and word choice. However, the same n-gram appearing more than once in the candidate is only counted multiple times if it also appears multiple times in a single reference. BLEU is then based on the geometric average of these so-called modified n-gram precisions p_n.

As multiple references are employed in calculating BLEU, it is difficult to take recall into account, which could lead to short sentences scoring unfairly highly. To prevent this from occurring, a brevity penalty is introduced, lowering the BLEU score for cases where the length of the candidate translation c is less than the length of the reference translation r. The equation for BLEU is as follows:

$$\text{BLEU} = \min\left(\exp\left(1 - r/c\right), 1\right) \cdot \exp\left(\sum_{n=1}^{N} \frac{\log p_n}{N}\right) \tag{1}$$

Obvious problems with BLEU are that it gives all words equal weighting and harshly punishes synonyms and elaborations, as well as words such as 'thus' or 'however' spliced occasionally into a text (see Callison-Burch et al. (2006) for a full discussion of these shortcomings). Chiang et al. (2008) meanwhile describe several situations where they are able to obtain highly dubious improvements in BLEU. They point out, for example, that if translating multiple genres at the same time, one can generate longer sentences within a specific genre where the translation quality is known to be higher, and shorter sentences in other more difficult genres. This will generate higher overall BLEU scores due to the fact that the brevity penalty works on whole documents rather than sentence-by-sentence, but the final translation quality would clearly have been higher if combined systems had been used, each optimised for a particular genre.

Despite these and other issues, however, BLEU has been shown to correlate extremely well with human judgement of translation quality in many cases (Agarwal and Lavie, 2008; Farrús et al., 2012). There have been a lot of recent efforts to develop more sophisticated metrics that counteract some of BLEU's weaknesses (Macháček and Bojar, 2013), but for the time being it remains ubiquitous in SMT. For this reason, the computation of oracle BLEU hypotheses is an active field (Wisniewski et al., 2010; Sokolov et al., 2012). Oracle BLEU hypotheses are those in the search space of a PBSMT decoder with the highest BLEU scores. Ultimately we want our translation systems to find these hypotheses on unseen data; calculating them when a reference is available can help identify deficiencies in current systems and facilitate the development of new techniques. BLEU oracles are also useful during feature-weight tuning, though it has been pointed out that relying too heavily on BLEU here can lead to poor results (Liang et al., 2006; Chiang, 2012).

3 Docent

Docent is a decoder for phrase-based SMT (Hardmeier et al., 2013). In Docent's search algorithm, feature models have access to a complete translation of a whole document at all stages of the search process. The algorithm is a stochastic variant of standard hill climbing: at each step, the decoder generates a successor of the current translation by randomly applying one of a set of state-changing operations at a random location in the document, and accepts the new translation only if it has a better score than the previous translation. Implemented operations include changing the translation of a phrase, changing the word order by swapping the positions of two phrases or moving a sequence of phrases, and resegmenting phrases.

The original motivation behind Docent was to facilitate the development of models with cross-sentence dependencies. A classic problem is that of pronominal anaphora resolution: identifying the antecedents of pronouns in order, for example, to correctly translate from English into languages that have grammatical gender for inanimate nouns. This type of problem is very difficult to solve in standard SMT decoders, which have hard-wired assumptions of sentence independence.

The standard tool-kit of sentence-level models, such as the phrase table, n-gram language models and distortion cost are implemented in Docent, along with document-level models including a length parity model, a semantic language model and several readability models. The initial translation can be created either by generating a random segmentation and taking random translations from the phrase table in monotonic order, or by a run from Moses.

Docent is not designed to perform better than Moses when only sentence-level features are used; its advantage lies in the ability to use features that disable recombination. Information about Docent's performance can be found in Hardmeier et al. (2012).

3.1 BLEU decoding

BLEU decoding is the name we have given to a particular mode of decoding in Docent whereby proposed changes to the translation are only accepted by the decoder if they result in an increase in the BLEU score. A new feature model, `BleuModel`, was implemented in Docent. Before decoding begins, `BleuModel` processes and stores the lengths of the reference translations, as well as the lengths of individual sentences within those translations and n-gram counts for $1 \leq n \leq 4$. Once an initial candidate translation for each document has been created, `BleuModel` calculates the BLEU score. The clipped counts for each sentence, required to calculate BLEU, are recorded along with the length of the candidate translation. In this way the counts for a particular sentence need only be updated when Docent proposes a change to that sentence; this makes `BleuModel` a particularly efficient feature model.

In the following section experiments are carried out in *pure* BLEU-decoding mode in Docent, that is to say the weights of all standard feature functions are set to zero, and only changes to the translation that increase BLEU are accepted. The aim is to examine the properties of translations with very high BLEU scores that are reachable by the decoder.

4   Experiments

A German-English Moses translation model was trained on just over 1.5 million sentences from Europarl v7. The test data was a set of 3052 sentences from the newstest2013 data, divided into 52 separate documents. Two types of experiments were carried out, firstly with the candidate translation initialised by running Moses (with a 5-gram language model trained with KenLM on 2.2 million Europarl sentences and feature weights tuned using MERT on a development set of 2525 sentences from the newstest2009 data), and secondly by random initialisation (i.e. random segmentation and random phrase translation). Docent was then run in BLEU-decoding mode: only changes to the translation that increased BLEU were accepted. Model and BLEU scores were monitored at exponentially increasing intervals, after iterations $2^8, 2^9, ..., 2^{25}$. The motivation for this sampling is that many more proposed changes to the translation are accepted in the beginning: as decoding progresses and the translation improves, there are simply more iterations between each interesting event.

4.1   Moses-based initial translation

Fig. 1 shows how BLEU scores evolve across the 52 test documents during decoding from initial translations produced by Moses. The initial BLEU scores after Moses de-

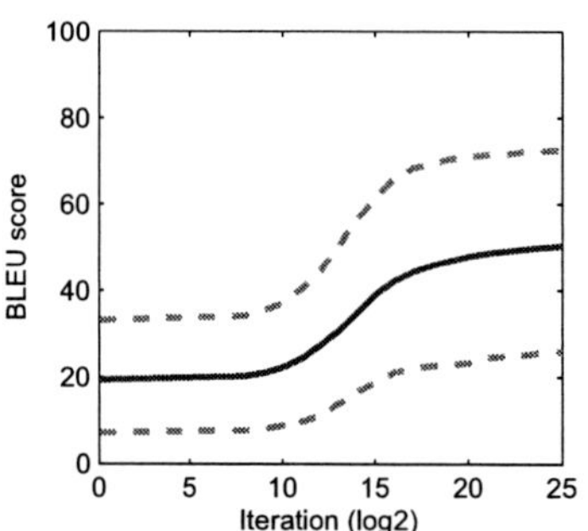

Fig. 1. Progression of the minimum, mean, and maximum BLEU scores across 52 test documents during BLEU decoding from an initial configuration based on a Moses run.

coding ranged from 7.2 to 33.1, with a mean of 19.3; after subsequently running Docent in BLEU-decoding mode, the mean had increased to 50.4, with a range from 25.9 to 72.5. A substantial and consistent increase in BLEU, as expected, is thus observed.

Given the huge increase in mean BLEU score from 19.3 to 50.4, conventional wisdom would say that the quality of the translations after BLEU decoding should be much higher. However, looking at our BLEU-decoded documents it quickly became clear that this was not the case: many of the translations appeared to have deteriorated in quality. To confirm this, we evaluated the first 100 sentences from the test data, randomising the order in which the two competing translations were presented so that it was not possible to know which translation was which, and judged which of the two was of better translation quality. We found that the Moses translation was judged to be superior in 59 cases, the BLEU-decoded translation in 23, and in 18 cases the two translations were judged to be of equal quality.

This is a striking result that deserves restating: despite an increase in mean BLEU score from 19.3 to 50.4, the translations are worse in 59 out of 100 sentences studied. Moreover, it is fair to say that sentences that got worse often got a lot worse, whereas sentences that improved generally did so only marginally. Although we have only studied 100 sentences systematically, it is clear to us that this pattern holds over the whole test set, and even in other experiments with different data sets and language pairs. Let us take a look at some demonstrative examples to understand how this can happen:

(Example 1)

SRC: *in diesem sinne untergraben diese maßnahmen teilweise das demokratische system der usa .*

REF: *in this sense , the measures will partially undermine the american democratic system .*

MOS: *in this sense , undermine these measures in the **democratic system** of the united states .*

BLEU: *the **democratic system** ‖ in this sense , the measures ‖ partially undermine the american .*

The fragments in bold show n-grams for $n \geq 2$ where the Moses and BLEU translations match the reference. The pipe symbol ‖ is used to separate contiguous non-overlapping n-gram matches. We see here by comparing to the reference (REF) that the Moses translation (MOS) is quite poor, with *these measures* appearing as the object, rather than subject, of the verb *undermines*. With some effort, however, the true sense of the phrase can be understood from this translation. This is not the case, however, with the BLEU-optimised translation, which is completely unintelligible. The problem is that BLEU decoding has worked hard to increase the number of n-gram matches, leading to the phrase *partially undermine the american*, which unbeknown to BLEU needs to be followed by *democratic system* to retain the meaning of the original sentence. The Moses translation meanwhile includes *the democratic system of the united states*, a perfectly acceptable equivalent to *the american democratic system*, but one that BLEU decoding does not like.

BLEU decoding produces an even more nonsensical translation in the following example:

> **(Example 2)**
>
> **SRC:** *am wichtigsten ist es aber , mit seinem arzt zu sprechen , um zu bestimmen , ob er durchgeführt werden sollte oder nicht .*
>
> **REF:** *but the important thing is to have a discussion with your doctor to determine whether or not to take it .*
>
> **MOS:** *the most* **important thing is** *, however , with his* **doctor to** *speak , in order* **to determine whether** *it should be carried out* **or not** *.*
>
> **BLEU:** ***the important thing is to have a*** *doctor performed but , with* ***to take it .*** *talking* **to determine whether or not to** *s*

Again we see that while the original Moses translation, although far from perfect, has some merit, the BLEU-decoded version is junk. It is telling that there are no 4-gram matches at all in the Moses translation, while the long matching fragments in the BLEU translation ensure that there are as many as eight such matches. The BLEU translation also has a higher unigram precision; indeed, for all $1 \leq n \leq 4$, the number of matching n-grams is much higher in the BLEU translation than the Moses translation.

In a third example BLEU decoding does in fact produce an intelligible translation:

> **(Example 3)**
>
> **SRC:** *es ist auch ein risikofaktor für mehrere andere krebsarten .*
>
> **REF:** *it is also a risk factor for a number of others .*
>
> **MOS:** *there* **is also a risk factor for a number of** *other types of cancer .*
>
> **BLEU:** ***it is also a risk factor for a number of others .*** *cancers*

In this example the Moses translation is actually very good; a more literal translation of the source sentence than the reference, which lacks a direct translation of *krebsarten* (*cancers* or *types of cancer*). After BLEU decoding the sentence has been transformed: it now matches the whole of the reference, but with the word *cancers* added after the full-stop. It is straightforward to see why the BLEU translation leads to a higher BLEU score: the extra couple of tokens at the end of the matching fragment increase the precision for all n-grams. It is in many ways the reference itself here which is the problem: BLEU decoding has been tricked into trying to mimic a less-literal reference translation rather than stick with a perfectly valid translation from the standard log-linear model. Despite being intelligible and matching the reference, it is highly doubtable that there is any benefit to a system finding this translation over the Moses translation.

4.2   Model scores during BLEU decoding

In the standard setting for statistical machine translation, we decode to maximise the combined scores of a set of features, then use BLEU as an independent evaluation metric. In pure BLEU-decoding mode we are able to turn the tables somewhat, and look at what happens to the model score as decoding proceeds. Of course, BLEU has been shown to correlate better with translation quality than model score, but we would still expect the two to correspond to some extent: this is why we normally build our systems around this set of features. With this in mind, Fig. 2 shows how the model score, for a standard set of features with MERT-tuned weights, varies as BLEU increases.

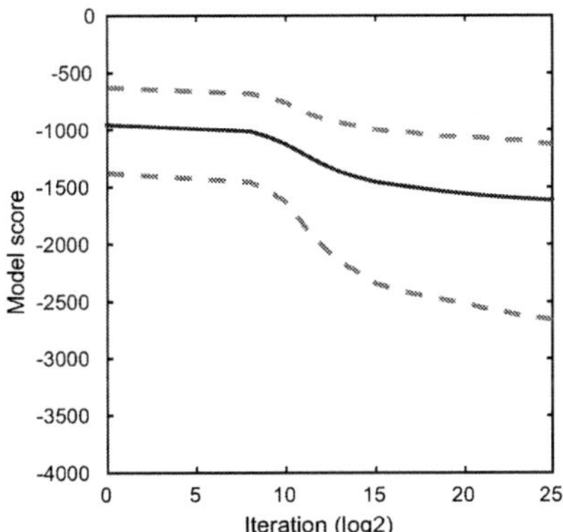

Fig. 2. Progression of the minimum, mean, and maximum model scores across 52 test documents during BLEU decoding from an initial configuration based on a Moses run

We observe that the model scores decrease as decoding progresses and BLEU increases; Docent in BLEU-decoding mode is able to find translations with high BLEU scores that score poorly on the traditional set of PBSMT features. The Moses-based initialisation procedure works of course to maximise the model score, so it would be unrealistic to expect it to increase much more during BLEU decoding, unless we had reason to believe that there was significant search error in the Moses decoding process. The fact that the model score drops in this way however adds weight to the point made earlier by the example sentences, that we have high BLEU scores but many poor quality sentences. These results suggest that by letting BLEU run wild, we move far away from the part of the search space containing good translations.

4.3 Random initial translation

Fig. 3 shows how the BLEU scores evolve among the 52 test documents during decoding from an random initial translation. We again observe a large increase in BLEU scores; on this occasion the mean BLEU score at the beginning of the decoding process was 3.6 (with range 0.0 to 6.6); after running Docent in BLEU-decoding mode it had increased to 50.2 (with range 24.9 to 71.5). The figure for the mean at the end of decoding is very similar to that of 50.4 obtained when decoding from Moses-based initial translations, suggesting that the initial translation does not have a great effect on the final result.

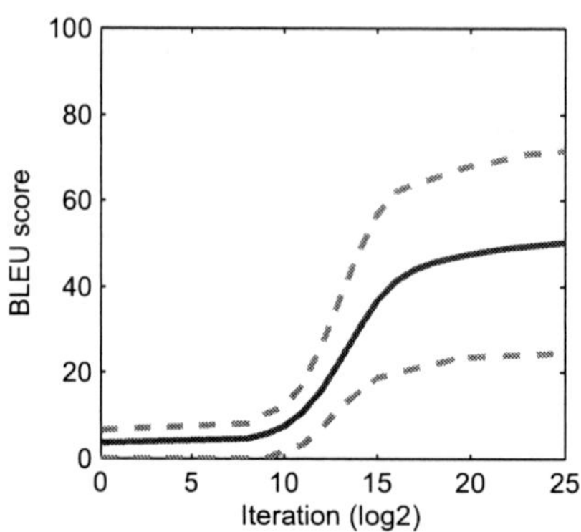

Fig. 3. Progression of the minimum, mean, and maximum BLEU scores across 52 test documents during BLEU decoding from a random initial configuration.

We can now go back to an example sentence from the previous experiment and add two new translations: the random initial translation (RAND) and the revised version of this after BLEU decoding (BLEU2):

(Example 2)

SRC: *am wichtigsten ist es aber , mit seinem arzt zu sprechen , um zu bestimmen , ob er durchgeführt werden sollte oder nicht .*

REF: *but the important thing is to have a discussion with your doctor to determine whether or not to take it .*

MOS: *the most **important thing is** , however , with his **doctor to** speak , in order **to determine whether** it should be carried out **or not** .*

BLEU: *the important thing is to have a doctor performed but , with to take it . talking to determine whether or not to s*

RAND: *most important of all has it , which from his own medical with talking about with a view to set , **whether or not** report implement to be **or not** ‖ **it** .*

BLEU2: *talking **but the important thing is to** its **to have a** ‖ **doctor to determine whether or not to take it** . or report implement to*

While BLEU and BLEU2 are not identical, they are strikingly similar in that they share many phrases and contiguous sets of words, as well as the property that they make very little sense. This suggests that the type of translation in which BLEU decoding results is independent of the initial translation; the initial translations – MOS and RAND – of BLEU and BLEU2 are clearly very different from each other. It is also interesting to compare BLEU2 with its antecedent RAND. While neither of these translations can be said to convey much of the sense of the original German sentence, it could perhaps be argued that BLEU2 is slightly more sensical than RAND. Perhaps the chunks that match the reference do actually help to bring through some trace of meaning. One way to compare the random initial translation to the BLEU-decoded version is to look again at the model scores.

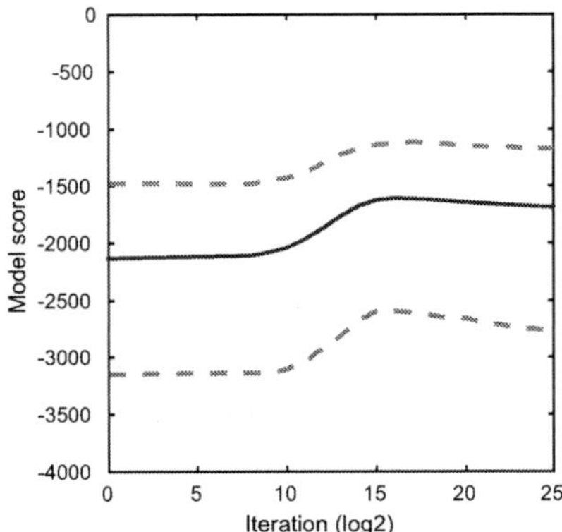

Fig. 4. Progression of the minimum, mean, and maximum model scores across 52 test documents during BLEU decoding from a random initial configuration.

Fig. 4 shows a slight increase in model scores at the beginning of decoding, followed by a gradual decline, but with final values still above the initial translation. We can therefore draw the conclusion that BLEU decoding from a random initial translation does result in translations that are slightly better, in some meaningful sense, than the initial translation. It is however clear by looking at the example sentences that the improvement in quality is nowhere near that which would be normally be expected given the jump in mean BLEU score from 3.6 to 50.2.

4.4   BLEU decoding towards reachable translations

We saw in the previous sections that the mean BLEU score after 2^{25} iterations of BLEU decoding was 50.4 when the initial translation came from Moses, and 50.2 when the initial translation was randomly chosen. While these are undoubtedly high BLEU values, they are still a long way from 100, which would represent the decoder finding the reference translation exactly. It is natural to wonder why this is the case; what is stopping the BLEU score getting much higher. BLEU decoding bears some resemblance to the technique of forced decoding, where the training data is decoded in such a way that guarantees the reference be found, in order to re-calculate phrase translation probabilities. Wuebker et al. (2010) reported being able to match the reference 95% percent of the time, while Foster and Kuhn (2012) report slightly lower performance. Note however that in these cases it is the same training data used for the original phrase extraction that is force-decoded, unlike in our case where BLEU decoding is carried out on a separate test/development data.

There are two obvious candidates to explain the failure of BLEU decoding to find the reference exactly. One is the availability of the right phrases in the phrase table. Reference reachability has long been known to be a problem in PBSMT (Liang et al., 2006). This is also the problem in forced decoding, where despite the fact that the phrases are extracted from the same data being decoded, it is not always possible to force-decode every sentence (Foster and Kuhn, 2012). Another possibility might be that the decoder's hill-climbing algorithm tends to get stuck in local maxima. The fact that the initial configuration apparently plays no role speaks against this hypothesis, but not definitively. Another test that can be carried out is to give the decoder a pseudo-reference translation, that is not really a true reference at all, but simply another random translation generated by Docent. As Docent generates this translation from phrases in the phrase table, it is guaranteed that the reference is theoretically reachable by the decoder.

The experimental set-up was similar to that described in Section 4, the only difference being the switch from the genuine reference translation to a simulated reference generated randomly by Docent. The 52 test documents were decoded from random initial translations.

The average BLEU score before decoding was 6.8, with range from 4.2 to 12.9; after 2^{25} iterations it was 98.4, with range 96.8 to 99.6 (Fig. 5). The contrast between Fig. 5

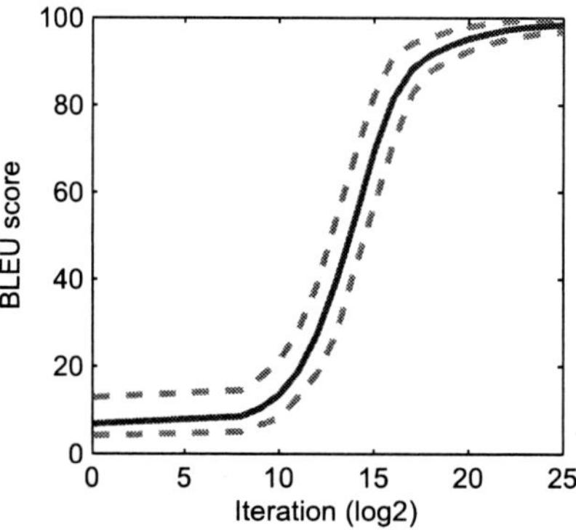

Fig. 5. Progression of the minimum, mean, and maximum BLEU scores across 52 test documents during BLEU decoding towards a reachable configuration.

and Fig. 3 is striking. These results confirm that, when the necessary phrases are in the phrase table, the decoder in BLEU-decoding mode is able to get extremely close to the reference translation. Note that the monotonic way in which random initial translations are generated in Docent makes it somewhat easier for the decoder to find the reference translations than in a real-world case where extensive reordering is necessary. We also tested however decoding from a random initial translation towards a Moses translation as the pseudo-reference, where more reordering is likely to be necessary, and again found BLEU scores in the high 90s.

This suggests that the lower BLEU scores for decoding towards genuine reference translation are as high, or almost as high, as they can possibly get, on this data given the phrases in the phrase table. BLEU scores near to 100 are simply impossible on this data set given a genuine reference translation and the phrases available to the decoder. The poor quality translations demonstrated by the examples in the previous section are therefore probably as good as it gets in terms of BLEU score: there are no translations that the decoder can conceivably reach with significantly higher BLEU scores.

5   Discussion

This paper presented BLEU decoding, a method for finding oracle BLEU translations using exact document-level scores for a phrase-based SMT decoder. Previous attempts to find oracle translations, for use in feature-weight tuning for example, have relied on sentence-level approximations to BLEU. As other authors have shown, however, optimising BLEU at the sentence-level and document-level are not always equivalent (Chiang et al., 2008).

By performing experiments with BLEU decoding, we explored the view from the top of Mount BLEU, examining in detail high-BLEU regions of the search space. While it might be assumed that translations in this region would be of high quality, results presented here show this not to be the case if the reference translation is not reachable by the decoder. Despite an increase in mean BLEU score from 19.3 to 50.4 across 52 documents from newstest2013 translated in BLEU-decoding mode from an initial translation generated by Moses, there was a clear drop in translation quality (59 out of 100 sentences were judged to be worse, and only 23 judged better). We observed long n-gram matches interleaved with strings of nonsense, leaving many sentences unintelligible. This makes sense given how BLEU works, favouring long n-gram matches and saying nothing about parts that do not match. An even larger increase in mean BLEU score, from 3.6 to 50.2, was observed when decoding from a random initial translation, but results were similar in terms of translation quality.

What do these results say about BLEU as an evaluation metric? Initial impressions might suggest that the evidence presented here is damning for BLEU: it has been clearly shown that it can be 'cheated': very bad translations can get high BLEU scores. This is not the first time problems with BLEU have been highlighted (Callison-Burch et al., 2006; Chiang et al., 2008), and research into better metrics is a very active field (Macháček and Bojar, 2013). However, it must be remembered that the experiments presented here used BLEU in a very different fashion from that for which it was designed. Papineni et al. (2002) demonstrated clearly that when translation quality is manipulated as the independent variable in experiments, there is a strong correlation with BLEU as the dependent variable. This does not imply, and indeed the opposite has been shown in this paper, that manipulating BLEU as an independent variable will necessarily result in high quality translations.

Another way of saying this is as follows: if translations are produced independently of BLEU, then BLEU is often a good metric to distinguish their quality; however this does not imply that actively looking for translations with high BLEU score will result in high quality. There is clearly a high-BLEU area of the search space with low quality translations. This problem has previously been encountered by researchers working on feature-weight tuning (Liang et al., 2006; Chiang, 2012). Searching for weights that produce high BLEU scores on development data is a central part of many standard tuning algorithms such as MERT (Och, 2003), PRO (Hopkins and May, 2011) and MIRA (Watanabe et al., 2007). In reality feature models are selected in such a way that ending up in this strange region of the search space is unlikely, but if we blindly optimise feature weights using BLEU, we could run the risk of moving dangerously close.

Despite these problems, BLEU decoding may still have the potential to be applied during tuning to improve translation quality. We have seen that in its pure form, BLEU decoding leads us far from the area of the search space containing good translations, and optimising our models towards finding these regions is unlikely to be a good idea. However, by combining BLEU decoding with other regular SMT features, we may be able to keep the decoder in higher-quality areas of the search space, using the BLEU feature model to find the best translations within this constrained region. The principle behind BLEU decoding can also be implemented for other translation metrics, either to include as additional features in the tuning process, or in order to stress test the metric itself.

References

A. Agarwal and A. Lavie. 2008. METEOR, M-BLEU and M-TER: Evaluation Metrics for High-Correlation with Human Rankings of Machine Translation Output. In *Proceedings of the Third Workshop on Statistical Machine Translation*, pages 115–118.

C. Callison-Burch, M. Osborne, and P. Koehn. 2006. Re-evaluating the Role of BLEU in Machine Translation Research. In *11th Conference of the European Chapter of the Association for Computational Linguistics*, pages 249–256.

D. Chiang, S. DeNeefe, Y. S. Chan, and H. T. Ng. 2008. Decomposability of Translation Metrics for Improved Evaluation and Efficient Algorithms. In *Proceedings of the 2008 Conference on Empirical Methods in Natural Language Processing*, pages 610–619.

D. Chiang. 2012. Hope and Fear for Discriminative Training of Statistical Translation Models. *Journal of Machine Learning Research*, 13:1159–1187.

M. Farrús, M. R. Costa-jussà, and M. Popović. 2012. Study and Correlation Analysis of Linguistic, Perceptual and Automatic Machine Translation Evaluations. *Journal of the American Society for Information Science and Technology*, 63(1):174–184.

G. Foster and R. Kuhn. 2012. Forced Decoding for Phrase Extraction. Technical Report, Université de Montreal.

C. Hardmeier, J. Nivre, and J. Tiedemann. 2012. Document-Wide Decoding for Phrase-Based Statistical Machine Translation. In *Proceedings of the 2012 Joint Conference on Empirical Methods in Natural Language Processing and Computational Natural Language Learning*, pages 1179–1190.

C. Hardmeier, S. Stymne, J. Tiedemann, and J. Nivre. 2013. Docent: A Document-Level Decoder for Phrase-Based Statistical Machine Translation. In *Proceedings of the 51st Annual Meeting of the Association for Computational Linguistics: System Demonstrations*, pages 193–198.

M. Hopkins and J. May. 2011. Tuning as Ranking. In *Proceedings of the 2011 Conference on Empirical Methods in Natural Language Processing*, pages 1352–1362.

P. Liang, A. Bouchard-Côté, D. Klein, and B. Taskar. 2006. An End-to-End Discriminative Approach to Machine Translation. In *Proceedings of the 44th Annual Meeting of the Association for Computational Linguistics*.

M. Macháček and O. Bojar. 2013. Results of the WMT13 Metrics Shared Task. In *Proceedings of the Eighth Workshop on Statistical Machine Translation*, pages 45–51.

F. J. Och. 2003. Minimum Error Rate Training in Statistical Machine Translation. In *Proceedings of the 41st Annual Meeting on Association for Computational Linguistics - Volume 1*, pages 160–167.

K. Papineni, S. Roukos, T. Ward, and W. J. Zhu. 2002. BLEU: a Method for Automatic Evaluation of Machine Translation. In *Proceeding of the 40th Annual Meeting of the Association for Computationial Linguistics*, pages 311–318.

A. Sokolov, G. Wisniewski, and F. Yvon. 2012. Computing Lattice BLEU Oracle Scores for Machine Translation. In *Proceedings of the 13th Conference of the European Chapter of the Association for Computational Linguistics*, pages 120–129.

T. Watanabe, J. Suzuki, H. Tsukada, and H. Isozaki. 2007. Online Large-Margin Training for Statistical Machine Translation. In *Proceedings of the 2007 Joint Conference on Empirical Methods in Natural Language Processing and Computational Natural Language Learning*, pages 764–773.

G. Wisniewski, A. Allauzen, and F. Yvon. 2010. Assessing Phrase-Based Translation Models with Oracle Decoding. In *Proceedings of the 2010 Conference on Empirical Methods in Natural Language Processing*, pages 933–943.

J. Wuebker, A. Mauser, and H. Ney. 2010. Training Phrase Translation Models with Leaving-One-Out. In *Proceeding of the 48th Annual Meeting of the Association for Computational Linguistics*, pages 475–484.

Received May8, 2016 , accepted May 15, 2016

Baltic J. Modern Computing, Vol. 4 (2016), No. 2, pp. 282–291

Interactive-Predictive Translation based on Multiple Word-Segments

Miguel DOMINGO, Álvaro PERIS, Francisco CASACUBERTA

Pattern Recognition and Human Language Technology Research Center
Camino de Vera s/n, 46022 Valencia, Spain

midobal@prhlt.upv.es, lvapeab@prhlt.upv.es, fcn@prhlt.upv.es

Abstract. Current machine translation systems require human revision to produce high-quality translations. This is achieved through a post-editing process or by means of an interactive human–computer collaboration. Most protocols belonging to the last scenario follow a left-to-right strategy, where the prefix of the translation is iteratively increased by successive validations and corrections made by the user. In this work, we propose a new interactive protocol which allows the user to validate all correct word sequences in the translation generated by the system, breaking the left-to-right barrier. We evaluated our proposal through simulated experiments, obtaining large reductions of the human effort.

Keywords: machine translation, computer-assisted translation, interactive-predictive machine translation

1 Introduction

Machine Translation (MT) technology is still far from producing perfect translations (Dale, 2016). Therefore, translation errors must be corrected by a human in a later post-editing stage.

The Interactive-Predictive Machine Translation (IMT) field arose as an alternative to classic post-editing systems, aiming to reduce human post-editing effort and increase efficiency. This paradigm strives for combining the knowledge of a human translator and the efficiency of an MT system. Notable contributions to IMT technology were carried out around the *TransType* (Foster et al., 1997; Langlais and Lapalme, 2002), *TransType2* (Barrachina et al., 2009; Casacuberta et al., 2009); and *CasMaCat* (Martínez-Gómez et al., 2012; Alabau et al., 2013; González-Rubio et al., 2013; Sanchis-Trilles et al., 2014) projects, among others (Koehn, 2009; Huang et al., 2012; Cai et al., 2013; Green et al., 2014; Torregrosa et al., 2014; Azadi and Khadivi, 2015; Marie and Max, 2015).

Especially interesting is the so-called prefix-based IMT (Barrachina et al., 2009). In this approach, the user corrected the first wrong word (from left-to-right) of the translation suggested by the system. Then, the system proposed an alternative hypothesis, compatible with the user feedback. A cumbersome phenomenon noticed in this protocol happened when the non-validated part of the sentence contained correct words. If such words were modified by the system in following predictions, the user had to edit words that were correct in previous iterations. Therefore, the effort made by the user was increased and the system had an annoying behavior.

To overcome this weakness, we propose a new IMT approach which allows the user to select, at each interaction, all correctly translated word segments. Hence, correct parts of the current translation are kept in successive hypothesis produced during the human–machine interaction, reducing the number of corrections required and avoiding the aforementioned issue. This approach relies on the idea from González-Rubio et al. (2016) of breaking down the prefix constraint.

The proposed protocol shares some similarities with Marie and Max (2015) in that we select word segments from a translation hypothesis. However, on the one hand, our protocol contains more types of user interactions such as word corrections and word deletions (see Section 2); and, on the other hand, we have different goals in mind: Marie and Max (2015) aim at increasing translation quality with the help of a human user, and we aim at reducing the human effort of generating a translation in an IMT framework.

The rest of this paper is structured as follows: Section 2 describes our segment-based IMT approach. After that, in Section 3, we report the experiments conducted in order to assess our proposal and the results of those experiments. Finally, conclusions of the work are drawn in Section 4.

2   Segment-Based Search

The goal of the IMT protocol developed in this work is to offer more freedom to the human agent, empowering the selection of the correct segments of a translation hypothesis. To achieve this, we allow the user to select, remove, or replace parts of a translation suggestion. The system then reacts to this human feedback, producing a new compatible hypothesis. Fig. 1 shows an example of an IMT session using the proposed segment-based approach.

2.1   Statistical Framework

Barrachina et al. (2009) proposed an statistical framework for the prefix-based IMT approach, where human and computer iteratively collaborated for translating a source sentence $\mathbf{x}$. In this framework, at the beginning of the process, the system proposes a translation hypothesis $\mathbf{y}$. Then, the user searches, from left-to-right, the first wrong word in $\mathbf{y}$ and corrects it. With this action, the user defines a valid translation prefix $\hat{\mathbf{p}}$. At the next iteration, the system generates a suffix $\tilde{\mathbf{s}}$ that completes $\hat{\mathbf{p}}$ in order to (hopefully) obtain a better translation of $\mathbf{x} : \mathbf{y}' = \hat{\mathbf{p}}\tilde{\mathbf{s}}$. This process is repeated until the user accepts the complete suggestion of the system. At each iteration, $\tilde{\mathbf{s}}$ is obtained as the most probable of all possible suffixes $\mathbf{s}$, given the prefix $\hat{\mathbf{p}}$ and the source sentence $\mathbf{x}$:

$$\tilde{\mathbf{s}} = \arg\max_{\mathbf{s}} Pr(\mathbf{s} \mid \mathbf{x}, \hat{\mathbf{p}}) \tag{1}$$

source (x): Et la question n ' a pas encore été évaluée chez les patients atteints de cancer gastrique

target translation (ŷ): And the issue has not been evaluated in gastric cancer patients

IT-0	T	And the issue has not yet been investigated among patients with gastric cancer
IT-1	U	And the issue has not been **evaluated** among patients with gastric cancer
	T	And the issue has not been evaluated not in gastric cancer patients with
IT-2	U	And the issue has not been evaluated in gastric cancer patients #
	T	And the issue has not been evaluated in gastric cancer patients
END	U	And the issue has not been evaluated in gastric cancer patients

Fig. 1: Segment-based IMT session to translate a French sentence into English. At the initial iteration (*IT-0*), the system suggests an initial translation. Then, at iteration 1, the user selects those segments to keep ("*And the issue has not*", "*been*" and "*gastric cancer*"); deletes a word ("*yet*"); and substitutes "*investigated*" by "*evaluated*", which is added to the segment. With this information, the system suggests a new hypothesis. Similarly, at iteration 2, the user selects new valid segments ("*in*" and "*patients*"), deletes words that are in the middle of two segments ("*not*"), and inputs an *end of sentence* mark (illustrated as "*#*"). The session ends when the user accepts the last translation suggested by the system.

This equation can be straightforwardly rewritten as:

$$\tilde{\mathbf{s}} = \arg\max_{\mathbf{s}} Pr(\hat{\mathbf{p}}, \mathbf{s} \mid \mathbf{x}) \qquad (2)$$

Therefore, at each iteration, the process consists of a regular search in the space of the translations but constrained by the prefix $\hat{\mathbf{p}}$.

The protocol proposed in our work follows this iterative procedure but, at each iteration, the user is free to validate all correct subsequences of words (segments) from $\mathbf{y}$. The user has also the possibility of deleting all words located between two segments (merging both segments into one), and either correcting a wrong word (as in the prefix-based approach) or inserting a new word between two segments.

Let $\mathbf{f} = \hat{\mathbf{f}}_1, \ldots, \hat{\mathbf{f}}_N$ be a feedback signal, where $\hat{\mathbf{f}}_1, \ldots, \hat{\mathbf{f}}_N$ is the sequence of N segments validated by the user in an interaction (including a one-word segment with the new word). The goal is to generate a sequence $\mathbf{h} = \tilde{\mathbf{h}}_1, \ldots, \tilde{\mathbf{h}}_N$ of new translation segments (an $\tilde{\mathbf{h}}_i$ for each pair of validated segments $\hat{\mathbf{f}}_i$, $\hat{\mathbf{f}}_{i+1}$; being $1 \leq i < N$) to obtain a (hopefully) better translation of $\mathbf{x}$: $\mathbf{y}' = \hat{\mathbf{f}}_1, \tilde{\mathbf{h}}_1, \ldots, \hat{\mathbf{f}}_N, \tilde{\mathbf{h}}_N$. In our statistical framework, the best translation segments are obtained as:

$$\tilde{\mathbf{h}}_1, \ldots, \tilde{\mathbf{h}}_N = \arg\max_{\mathbf{h}_1, \ldots, \mathbf{h}_N} Pr(\mathbf{h}_1, \ldots, \mathbf{h}_N \mid \mathbf{x}, \hat{\mathbf{f}}_1, \ldots, \hat{\mathbf{f}}_N) \qquad (3)$$

which can be rewritten as:

$$\tilde{\mathbf{h}}_1, \ldots, \tilde{\mathbf{h}}_N = \arg\max_{\mathbf{h}_1, \ldots, \mathbf{h}_N} Pr(\hat{\mathbf{f}}_1, \mathbf{h}_1, \ldots, \hat{\mathbf{f}}_N, \mathbf{h}_N \mid \mathbf{x}) \qquad (4)$$

This last equation is very similar to the classical prefix-based IMT equation (Eq. (1)), with the main difference being that the search process in Eq. (1) is limited to the space of suffixes constrained by $\hat{\mathbf{p}}$, while the search in Eq. (4) is in the space of possible substrings of the translations of $\mathbf{x}$, constrained by the sequence of segments $\hat{\mathbf{f}}_1, \ldots, \hat{\mathbf{f}}_N$.

3 Experiments

3.1 Corpora

We tested our proposal in four tasks from different domains: the **EMEA** corpus[1] (Tiedemann, 2009), formed by documents from the *European Medical Agency*; the **EU** corpus (Barrachina et al., 2009), extracted from the *Bulletin of the European Union*; the **TED** corpus[2] (Federico et al., 2011), a collection of recordings of public speeches covering a variety of topics; and the **Xerox** corpus (Barrachina et al., 2009), extracted from *Xerox* printer manuals. To the best of our knowledge, excluding EMEA, all corpora have been used in previous IMT works (Tomás and Casacuberta, 2006; Barrachina et al., 2009; González-Rubio et al., 2013). The partition sets used in this work are the same than those used in the aforementioned works.

All datasets have been tokenized by means of the standard tool provided with the `Moses` toolkit (Koehn et al., 2007)—exempting Chinese sentences, which were split into words using the Standford word segmenter (Tseng et al., 2005). Sentences have been kept truecased, except for the Zh–En language pair, since Chinese has no case information. Table 1 shows the corpora main features.

Table 1: Corpora statistics. K denotes *thousands* and M *millions*. $|S|$ stands for *number of sentences*, $|W|$ for *number of words* and $|V|$ for *size of the vocabulary*.

		EMEA (Fr/En)	EU (Es/En)	TED (Zh/En)	Xerox (Es/En)
Train	$|S|$	1.1M	214K	106.9K	55.6K
	$|W|$	14.3M/17.0M	6M/5.4M	1.9M/2.1M	750K/665K
	$|V|$	71K/80K	84K/70K	55K/41.7K	16.8K/14K
Dev.	$|S|$	500	400	934	1012
	$|W|$	12K/10K	12K/10K	21.5K/20.1K	16K/14.4K
	$|V|$	2.9K/2.7K	3K/2.7K	3.8K/3.2K	1.8K/1.6K
Test	$|S|$	1K	800	1.6K	1.1K
	$|W|$	27K/21K	23K/20K	33.2K/31.9K	10.1K/8.4K
	$|V|$	4.5K/4.5K	4.7K/4.2K	4.5K/3.7K	2K/1.9K

3.2 Metrics

The quality of our interactive protocol is assessed according to the following metrics:

Word Stroke Ratio (WSR) (Tomás and Casacuberta, 2006): Measures the number of words edited by the user, normalized by the number of words in the final translation. In this work, we assume that the edition of a word is considered to have a constant cost (one word stroke) independently of its length.

---

[1] http://www.statmt.org/wmt14/medical-task/
[2] https://wit3.fbk.eu/mt.php?release=2012-03-test

Mouse Action Ratio (MAR) (Barrachina et al., 2009): Measures the number of mouse actions made by the user, normalized by the number of characters in the final translation. In classic IMT, the user makes a mouse action each time she needs to edit a word (to position the prompt), and one more per sentence to validate the translation. In the protocol proposed in this work, in addition to those mouse actions, the user makes two actions each time she validates a segment (clicking at the beginning and at the end of the segment), and two more each time she deletes some words located between segments[3] (same procedure as selecting segments but using the right button of the mouse).

Conceptually, WSR accounts for the physical effort of typing corrections, while MAR accounts for the cognitive effort of the supervision process (Macklovitch et al., 2005).

Additionally, to evaluate the quality of the initial translations, we have used the following well-known metric:

BiLingual Evaluation Understudy (BLEU) (Papineni et al., 2002): computes the geometric average of the modified n-gram precision, multiplied by a factor that penalizes short sentences.

3.3   Implementation

Our implementation of the segment-based IMT protocol is based on the `Moses` toolkit (Koehn et al., 2007). We profit from the feature that allows to bring external knowledge to the decoder by means of an *XML Markup* language (see Fig. 2 for an example), for validating the translation of parts of a sentence without changing the models. The decoder has an XML markup scheme that allows us to plug in the translation of parts of a sentence without changing the models. More precisely, we use the *exclusive* mode, which only takes into account the given translation for a part of a sentence—ignoring any phrases from the phrase table that overlaps with that span. With this, we can constrain the search process to follow Eq. (4).

<x translation = "And the issue has not been evaluated"> Et la question n ' a pas encore été évaluée </x><wall/> chez les patients atteints de <x translation = "gastric cancer"> cancer gastrique </x><wall/>

Fig. 2: Example of a sentence in XML markup language (corresponding to the sentence of the first iteration of Fig. 1), specifying the desired translation for some parts of the sentence: *Et la question n ' a pas encore été évaluée* must be translated as *And the issue has not been evaluated*, and *cancer gastrique* must be translated as *gastric cancer*. The tag <*wall/*> indicates to the decoder that those segments should not be reordered.

We implemented a prototype that manages the interaction between a human agent and the MT system. This is an iterative process in which the prototype, by means of the

---

[3] One mouse action is enough for selecting or deleting a one-word segment (in which case, the user would simply click on the word).

XML markup language, takes into account the feedback provided by the user, obtains a translation with `Moses`, and suggests the new hypothesis. All this takes place at the end of each iteration, with an average response time of 90 ms[4] per iteration. According to Nielsen (1993), this time is below *"the limit for having the user feel that the system is reacting instantaneously"*.

At each one of these iterations, the user has three different ways of interacting with the system (see Section 2). Such interactions affect differently in the generation of the new XML markup sentence:

Segment selection: for each segment selected by the user, we align the words of that segment with their correspondent source words (phrase alignments), and generate an XML tag to plug in that segment (the desired translation) to those source words.

Word deletion: in the same fashion as with segments, for each word to delete, we align that word with its correspondent source words and generate a new XML tag, indicating that we want to obtain an empty translation.

Word correction: each time the user corrects a word or inserts a new one, we align the new word with its correspondent source words using a hidden markov alignment model (Vogel et al., 1996).

All the MT systems used in this work were trained with the standard configuration of `Moses`, with the weights of the log-linear model being optimized by means of the Minimum Error Rate Training (MERT) procedure (Och, 2003). Lastly, a 5-gram word-based language model was estimated on the target side of the parallel corpora, using the improved KneserNey smoothing (Chen and Goodman, 1996), by means of the SRILM toolkit (Stolcke, 2002).

For the implementation of the classic prefix-based IMT systems, we made the word graph exploration and the best suffix generation for a given prefix following the procedure described by Barrachina et al. (2009): We generated a word graph for each sentence to translate. After that, treating the word graph as a weighted finite-state automaton, we parsed the prefix over it, from the initial state to any other intermediate state, to find the best path that accounts for the prefix. Finally, we obtained the corresponding translation for the best path from the intermediate state to the finale state. Therefore, our implementation of prefix-based IMT is consistent with Barrachina et al. (2009), considering that we generate word graphs with the current SMT state-of-the-art `Moses` toolkit.

3.4 Evaluation on a Simulated Environment

Since the evaluation with human agents is too slow and expensive to be applied frequently during system development, we carried out an automatic evaluation with simulated users. For this evaluation, we considered the references in the corpora as the translations the user desires. Furthermore, without loss of generality and for the sake of simplicity, we assumed that the user always corrected the left-most wrong word.

At each iteration of the IMT session, we selected those segments that were common with the reference. After that, following a left-to-right order, we compared each word of

---

[4] Tested on a machine with an Intel i5 CPU at 3.1 GHz.

the current translation with those of the reference. When we found a different word in translation and reference, if that reference word was the first one of the next selected segment, we deleted all the words between those two segments; otherwise, we input that word (merging all previous segments into one). Once translation and reference were the same, we moved on to the next sentence.

3.5 Results

Table 2 shows the user-effort results of our segment-based protocol against the prefix-based approach. Prefix-based results were obtained following the work of Barrachina et al. (2009) and are similar to those reported on the literature (Tomás and Casacuberta, 2006; Barrachina et al., 2009; González-Rubio et al., 2013). The quality of the initial translation is also displayed as an indicative of the difficulty of each task. Our proposal clearly improves prefix-based IMT in terms of user physical effort of typing corrections. The WSR is always reduced, yielding diminishes up to 29 points.

Table 2: Results of our segment-based IMT proposal, in comparison with the prefix-based approach. The quality of the initial translation is shown as an indicative of the difficulty of each task. All values are reported as percentages.

Corpus	Language	BLEU	Prefix-Based		Segment-Based	
			WSR	MAR	WSR	MAR
EMEA	Fr–En	31.3	57.8	12.4	34.4	18.8
	En–Fr	30.2	58.4	12.5	40.4	16.3
EU	Es–En	48.2	45.6	10.2	28.3	15.0
	En–Es	48.7	44.6	9.7	29.8	13.5
TED	Zh–En	11.7	83.1	22.4	54.1	28.3
	En–Zh	8.7	86.3	55.7	59.2	72.4
Xerox	Es–En	54.5	35.8	10.5	23.2	16.9
	En–Es	62.2	28.3	7.9	22.1	12.5

This reduction of typing effort comes with an increase in the number of mouse actions (from 4 up to 6.5 points of MAR), which is always smaller than the effort reduction. An exception to this comes with the En–Zh language pair since, due to Chinese nature, words have fewer number of characters, which penalizes MAR metric. This penalization results in a greater increase in MAR, although this increase is still smaller than the effort reduction. Moreover, as mentioned before, WSR and MAR account for different phenomena and thus have different cost from a human point of view (Macklovitch et al., 2005). Therefore, the physical effort is substantially decreased, while the cognitive one is slightly increased. Nonetheless, we need to test these considerations with real human users before reaching to categorical conclusions.

4 Conclusions

In this work, we have proposed a new IMT approach that overcomes the classic prefix-based IMT limitation of only correcting the prefix. Our proposal allows the user to select all correct word segments each time the system proposes a new translation. The system leverages this additional knowledge for offering more enlightened hypothesis. Hence, the human typing effort should be reduced.

We tested the proposal in a simulated environment, which confirmed that our approach effectively reduces the physical effort required, at the expense of a slight increase in the cognitive effort. As future work, we should test the improvements of our proposal with real users in order to obtain actual measures of the effort reduction.

Acknowledgments

The research leading to these results has received funding from the Ministerio de Economía y Sostenibilidad (MINECO) under project SmartWays (grant agreement RTC-2014-1466-4), and Generalitat Valenciana under project ALMAMATER (grant agreement PROMETEOII/2014/030).

References

Alabau, Vicent, Ragnar Bonk, Christian Buck, Michael Carl, Francisco Casacuberta, Mercedes García-Martínez, Jesús González-Rubio, Philipp Koehn, Luis A. Leiva, Bartolomé Mesa-Lao, Daniel Ortiz-Martínez, Hervé Saint-Amand, Germán Sanchis-Trilles, and Chara Tsoukala (2013). "CASMACAT: An Open Source Workbench for Advanced Computer Aided Translation". In: *The Prague Bulletin of Mathematical Linguistics* 100, pp. 101–112.

Azadi, Fatemeh and Shahram Khadivi (2015). "Improved Search Strategy for Interactive Machine Translation in Computer-Asisted Translation". In: *Proceedings of Machine Translation Summit XV*, pp. 319–332.

Barrachina, Sergio, Oliver Bender, Francisco Casacuberta, Jorge Civera, Elsa Cubel, Shahram Khadivi, Antonio Lagarda, Hermann Ney, Jesús Tomás, Enrique Vidal, and Juan-Miguel Vilar (2009). "Statistical Approaches to Computer-Assisted Translation". In: *Computational Linguistics* 35, pp. 3–28.

Cai, Dongfeng, Hua Zhang, and Na Ye (2013). "Improvements in Statistical Phrase-Based Interactive Machine Translation". In: *Proceedings of the International Conference on Asian Language Processing*, pp. 91–94.

Casacuberta, Francisco, Jorge Civera, Elsa Cubel, Antonio L. Lagarda, Guy Lapalme, Elliott Macklovitch, and Enrique Vidal (2009). "Human Interaction for High-quality Machine Translation". In: *Communications of the Association for Computing Machinery* 52.10, pp. 135–138.

Chen, Stanley F. and Joshua Goodman (1996). "An Empirical Study of Smoothing Techniques for Language Modeling". In: *Proceedings of the Annual Meeting on Association for Computational Linguistics*, pp. 310–318.

Dale, Robert (2016). "How to make money in the translation business". In: *Natural Language Engineering* 22.2, pp. 321–325.

Federico, Marcello, Luisa Bentivogli, Michael Paul, and Sebastian Stüker (2011). "Overview of the IWSLT 2011 evaluation campaign". In: *International Workshop on Spoken Language Translation*, pp. 11–27.

Foster, George, Pierre Isabelle, and Pierre Plamondon (1997). "Target-Text Mediated Interactive Machine Translation". In: *Machine Translation* 12, pp. 175–194.

González-Rubio, Jesús, Daniel Ortiz-Martínez, José-Miguel Benedí, and Francisco Casacuberta (2013). "Interactive Machine Translation using Hierarchical Translation Models". In: *Proceedings of the Conference on Empirical Methods in Natural Language Processing*, pp. 244–254.

González-Rubio, Jesús, José-Miguel Benedí, and Francisco Casacuberta (2016). "Beyond Prefix-Based Interactive Translation Prediction". Unpublished results.

Green, Spence, Jason Chuang, Jeffrey Heer, and Christopher D. Manning (2014). "Predictive Translation Memory: A Mixed-Initiative System for Human Language Translation". In: *Proceedings of the Annual Association for Computing Machinery Symposium on User Interface Software and Technology*, pp. 177–187.

Huang, Chung-chi, Ping-che Yang, Keh-jiann Chen, and Jason S. Chang (2012). "TransAhead: A Computer-Assisted Translation and Writing Tool". In: *Proceedings of the Conference of the North American Chapter of the Association for Computational Linguistics*, pp. 352–356.

Koehn, Philipp (2009). "A Web-Based Interactive Computer Aided Translation Tool". In: *Proceedings of the International Joint Conference on Natural Language Processing*, pp. 17–20.

Koehn, Philipp, Hieu Hoang, Alexandra Birch, Chris Callison-Burch, Marcello Federico, Nicola Bertoldi, Brooke Cowan, Wade Shen, Christine Moran, Richard Zens, Chris Dyer, Ondřej Bojar, Alexandra Constantin, and Evan Herbst (2007). "Moses: Open Source Toolkit for Statistical Machine Translation". In: *Proceedings of the Annual Meeting of the Association for Computational Linguistics*, pp. 177–180.

Langlais, Philippe and Guy Lapalme (2002). "TransType: Development-Evaluation Cycles to Boost Translator's Productivity". In: *Machine Translation* 17.2, pp. 77–98.

Macklovitch, Elliot, Nam-Trung Nguyen, and Roberto Silva (2005). *User evaluation report*. Tech. rep. Transtype2 (ISR-2001-32091).

Marie, Benjamin and Aurélien Max (2015). "Touch-Based Pre-Post-Editing of Machine Translation Output". In: *Proceedings of the Conference on Empirical Methods in Natural Language Processing*, pp. 1040–1045.

Martínez-Gómez, Pascual, Germán Sanchis-Trilles, and Francisco Casacuberta (2012). "Online Adaptation Strategies for Statistical Machine Translation in Post-Editing Scenarios". In: *Pattern Recognition* 45.9, pp. 3193–3203.

Nielsen, Jakob (1993). *Usability Engineering*. Morgan Kaufmann Publishers Inc. ISBN: 0125184050.

Och, Franz Josef (2003). "Minimum Error Rate Training in Statistical Machine Translation". In: *Proceedings of the Annual Meeting of the Association for Computational Linguistics*, pp. 160–167.

Papineni, Kishore, Salim Roukos, Todd Ward, and Wei-Jing Zhu (2002). "BLEU: a Method for Automatic Evaluation of Machine Translation". In: *Proceedings of the Annual Meeting of the Association for Computational Linguistics*, pp. 311–318.

Sanchis-Trilles, Germán, Vicent Alabau, Christian Buck, Michael Carl, Francisco Casacuberta, Mercedes García-Martínez, Ulrich Germann, Jesús González-Rubio, Robin Hill, Philipp Koehn, Luis A. Leiva, Bartolomé Mesa-Lao, Daniel Ortiz-Martínez, Hervé Saint-Amand, Chara Tsoukala, and Enrique Vidal (2014). "Interactive Translation Prediction vs. Conventional Post-editing in Practice: A Study with the CasMaCat Workbench". In: *Machine Translation* 28.3–4, pp. 217–235.

Stolcke, Andreas (2002). "SRILM - An extensible language modeling toolkit". In: *Proceedings of the International Conference on Spoken Language Processing*, pp. 257–286.

Tiedemann, Jörg (2009). "News from OPUS - A Collection of Multilingual Parallel Corpora with Tools and Interfaces". In: *Recent Advances in Natural Language Processing*. Vol. V, pp. 237–248.

Tomás, Jesús and Francisco Casacuberta (2006). "Statistical Phrase-Based Models for Interactive Computer-Assisted Translation". In: *Proceedings of the International Conference on Computational Linguistics/Association for Computational Linguistics*, pp. 835–841.

Torregrosa, Daniel, Mikel L. Forcada, and Juan Antonio Pérez-Ortiz (2014). "An Open-Source Web-Based Tool for Resource-Agnostic Interactive Translation Prediction". In: *Prague Bulletin of Mathematical Linguistics* 102, pp. 69–80.

Tseng, Huihsin, Pichuan Chang, Galen Andrew, Daniel Jurafsky, and Christopher Manning (2005). "A Conditional Random Field Word Segmenter". In: *Proceedings of the Special Interest Group of the Association for Computational Linguistics Workshop on Chinese Language Processing*, pp. 168–171.

Vogel, Stephan, Hermann Ney, and Christoph Tillmann (1996). "HMM-based Word Alignment in Statistical Translation". In: *Proceedings of the Conference on Computational Linguistics*. Vol. 2, pp. 836–841.

Received April 29, 2016 , accepted May 15, 2016

EAMT 2016, Vol. 4 (2020), No. 2, pp. 292–304

A Contextual Language Model to Improve Machine Translation of Pronouns by Re-ranking Translation Hypotheses

Ngoc-Quang LUONG, Andrei POPESCU-BELIS

Idiap Research Institute, CH-1920 Martigny, Switzerland

{ngoc-quang.luong, andrei.popescu-belis}@idiap.ch

Abstract. This paper addresses the translation divergencies of pronouns from English to French, specifically *it* and *they*, which have several gendered and non-gendered possible translations into French. Instead of using anaphora resolution, which is error-prone, we build a target language model that estimates the probabilities of a tuple of consecutive nouns followed by a pronoun. We bring evidence for the linguistic validity of the model, showing that the probability of observing a pronoun with a given gender and number increases with the proportion of nouns with the same gender and number preceding it. We use this French language model to re-rank the translation hypotheses generated by a phrase-based statistical machine translation system. While none of the pronoun-focused translation systems at the DiscoMT 2015 shared task improved over the baseline, our proposal achieves a modest but statistically significant improvement over it.

Keywords: statistical machine translation, pronoun translation, context modeling

1   Introduction

Pronoun systems do not strictly map across languages, and therefore translation divergencies of pronouns must often be addressed in machine translation (MT). For instance, depending on its function (referential or pleonastic) and on its actual referent, an occurrence of the English *it* could be translated into French by *il, elle, ce/c'* or *cela*, to mention only the most frequent possibilities.

While designers of MT systems have tried to address the problem since the early years of MT, it is only in recent years that specific strategies for translating pronouns have been proposed and evaluated (see Hardmeier, 2014, Section 2.3.1). However, in the culmination of these recent efforts at the DiscoMT 2015 shared task on pronoun-focused translation (Hardmeier et al., 2015), none of the submitted systems was able to beat a well-trained phrase-based statistical MT baseline. A large proportion of previous studies have attempted to convey information from anaphora resolution systems, albeit imperfect, to statistical MT ones (Hardmeier and Federico, 2010; Le Nagard and Koehn, 2010), or have advocated distinguishing first the functions of pronouns (Guillou, 2016).

In this paper, we present a simple yet effective approach to improve the translation of neuter English pronouns *it* and *they* into French, which outperforms the DiscoMT 2015 baseline by about 5% (relative improvement on an automatic metric). The method stems from the observation that the antecedent of a pronoun is likely to be one of the noun phrases preceding it closely; therefore, if a majority of these nouns exhibit the same gender and number, it is more likely that the correct French pronoun agrees in gender and number with them. This does not require any hypothesis on which of the nouns is the antecedent.

In what follows, we explain how to represent these intuitions in a formal probabilistic model that is instantiated from French data (Section 3), and we report on empirical observations supporting the validity of our idea (Section 4). Then, we show how our *pronominal language model (PLM)* is used to re-rank the hypotheses generated by a phrase-based statistical MT system (Section 5) and we analyze its results with respect to a baseline (Section 6). But first, we present the state of the art in pronoun translation and compare briefly our proposal with it.

2 State of the art

Using rule-based or statistical methods for anaphora resolution, several studies have attempted to improve pronoun translation by integrating anaphora resolution with statistical MT, as reviewed by Hardmeier (2014, Section 2.3.1). Le Nagard and Koehn (2010) trained an English-French translation model on an annotated corpus in which each occurrence of English pronouns *it* and *they* was annotated with the gender of its antecedent in the target side, but this solution could not outperform a baseline that was not aware of coreference links.

Integrating anaphora resolution with English-Czech statistical MT, Guillou (2012) studied the role of imperfect coreference and alignment results. Hardmeier and Federico (2010) integrated a word dependency model into an SMT decoder as an additional feature function, which keeps track of pairs of source words acting as antecedent and anaphor in a coreference link. This model helped to improve slightly the English-German SMT performance (F-score customized for pronouns) on the WMT News Commentary 2008 and 2009 test sets.

Following a similar strategy, Luong et al. (2015) linearly combined the score obtained from a coreference resolution system with the score from the search graph of the Moses decoder, to determine whether an English-French SMT pronoun translation should be post-edited into the opposite gender (e.g. *il → elle*). Their system performed best among six participants on the pronoun-focused shared task at the 2015 DiscoMT workshop (Hardmeier et al., 2015), but still remained below the SMT baseline.

A considerable set of coreference features, used in a deep neural network architecture, was presented by Hardmeier (2014, Chapters 7–9), who observed significant improvements on TED talks and News Commentaries. Alternatively, to avoid extracting features from an anaphora resolution system, Callin et al. (2015) developed a classifier based on a feed-forward neural network, which considered mainly the preceding nouns, determiners and their part-of-speech as features. Their predictor worked particularly well (over 80% of F-score) on *ce* and *ils* pronouns, and reached an overall macro F-score of 55.3% for all classes at DiscoMT 2015 pronoun prediction task, which aimed at restoring hidden pronouns from a given translation of a source text. However, at this task, none of the participants could outperform a statistical baseline using a powerful language model (Hardmeier et al., 2015). Therefore, the goal of this paper – although in the framework of pronoun-focused translation – is to extend such a language model with anaphora-inspired information, and to demonstrate improvement over a purely n-gram-based baseline.

3   Construction of a pronoun-aware language model

3.1   Overall idea of the model

The key intuition behind our proposal is that additional, probabilistic constrains on target pronouns can be obtained by examining the gender and number of the nouns preceding them, without any attempt to perform anaphora resolution, which is error-prone. For instance, considering the EN/FR translation divergency "*it* → *il/elle/...*", the higher the number of French masculine nouns preceding the pronoun, the higher the probability that the correct translation is *il* (masculine).

Of course, such an intuition, if used unconditionally, might be even more error-prone than post-editing based on anaphora resolution. Therefore, to make it operational, we propose two key solutions:

1. We estimate from parallel data the probabilistic connection between the target-side distribution of gender and number features among the nouns preceding a pronoun and the actual translation of this pronoun into French (focusing on translations of *it* and *they* which exhibit strong EN/FR divergencies).
2. We use the above information in a probabilistic way by re-ranking the translation hypotheses made by a standard phrase-based SMT system, so that this information comes into play only when the constraints from the baseline system cannot discriminate significantly before several translation options for a pronoun.

The two solutions above are implemented as a pronoun-aware language model (PLM), which is trained as explained in the next subsection, and is then used for re-ranking translation hypotheses as explained in Section 5.

3.2   Learning the PLM

The data used for training the PLM is the target side (French) of the WIT[3] parallel corpus (Cettolo et al., 2012) distributed by the IWSLT workshops. This corpus is made of transcripts of TED talks, i.e. lectures that typically last 18 minutes, on various topics from science and the humanities with high relevance to society. The TED talks are given in English, then transcribed and translated by volunteers and TED editors. The French side contains 179,404 sentences, with a total of 3,880,369 words. We will later use the parallel version, with the same number of sentence pairs, to train our baseline SMT system in Section 5 below.

To obtain the morphological tag of each word, specifically the gender and number of every noun and pronoun, we employ a French part-of-speech (POS) tagger, Morfette (Chrupala et al., 2008).

We process the data sequentially, word by word, from the beginning to the end. We keep track of the gender and number of the N most recent nouns and pronouns in a list, which is initialized as empty and is then updated when a new noun or pronoun is encountered. In these experiments, we set $N = 5$, i.e. we will examine up to four nouns or pronouns before a pronoun. This value is based on the intuition that the antecedent seldom occurs too far before the anaphor. When a French pronoun is encountered, the sequence formed by the gender/number features of the N previous nouns or pronouns, acquired from the above list, and the pronoun itself is appended to a data file which will be used to train the PLM. If the lexical item can have multiple lexical functions, including pronoun – e.g. *le* or *la* can be object pronouns or determiners – then their POS assigned by Morfette is used to filter out the non-pronoun occurrences. We only process the French pronouns that are potential translations of the English *it* and *they*, namely the following list: *il, ils, elle, elles, le, la, lui, l', on, ce, ça, c', ç, ceci, celà, celui, celui-ci, celui-là, celle, celle-ci, celle-là, ceux, ceux-ci, ceux-là, celles, celles-ci, celles-là.*

In the next step, we apply the SRILM language modeling toolkit (Stolcke, 2002), with modified Kneser-Ney smoothing, to build a 5-gram language model over the training dataset collected above, which includes 179,058 of the aforementioned sequences. The sequences are given to SRILM as separate "sentences", i.e. two consecutive sequences are never joined and are considered independently of each other. The pronouns are always ending a sequence in the training data, but not necessarily in the n-grams generated by SRILM (exemplified in Figure 1), which include n-grams that do not end with a pronoun (e.g. the fifth and the sixth ones in the figure). These will be needed for back-off search and are kept in the model used below.

-2.324736	masc.sing.	masc.plur.	*elle*		
-1.543632	fem.sing.	fem.plur.	fem.sing.	*elle*	
-0.890777	masc.sing.	masc.sing.	masc.sing.	masc.sing.	*il*
-1.001423	masc.sing.	masc.plur.	masc.plur.	masc.plur.	*ils*
-1.459787	masc.plur.	masc.plur.	masc.plur.		
-1.398654	masc.sing.	masc.plur.	masc.sing.	masc.sing.	

Fig. 1. Examples of PLM n-grams, starting with their log-probabilities, learned by SRILM.

4 Empirical validation of the PLM

We investigate in this section, using the observations collected in the PLM, the influence of the (pro)nouns preceding a pronoun on the translation of *it* or *they* into French. The goal is to test the intuition that a larger number of (pro)nouns of a given gender and number increases the probability of a translation of *it* with the same gender and number. We consider also the 'number' parameter because it is possible, under some

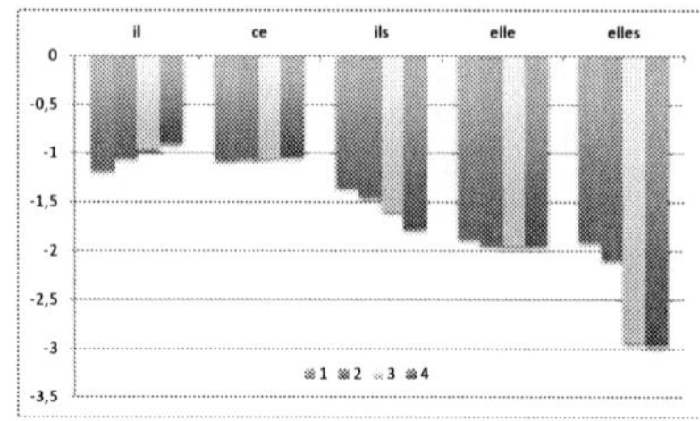

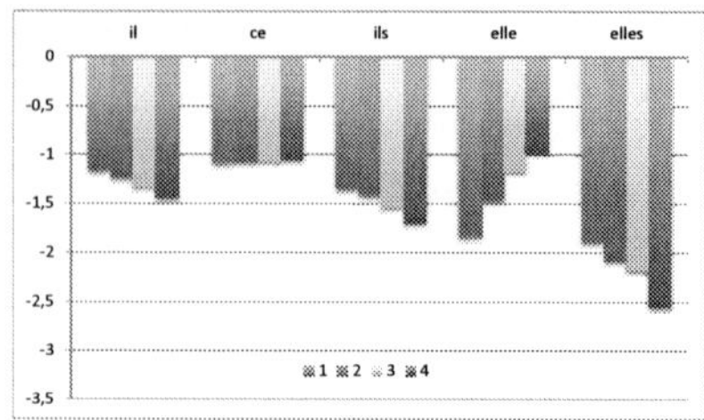

(a) masculine singular nouns   (b) feminine singular nouns

Fig. 2. Log-probabilities to observe a given pronoun depending on the number of (pro)nouns of a given gender/number preceding it, either masculine singular in (a) or feminine singular in (b). In (a), the probability of *il* increases with the number of masculine singular (pro)nouns preceding it (four bars under *il*, 1 to 4 (pro)nouns from left to right), while the probabilities of all other pronouns decrease with this number. A similar result for *elle* with respect to the other pronouns is observed in (b), depending on the number of feminine singular (pro)nouns preceding *elle*.

circumstances, that *it*, although singular, is translated into a plural (e.g. if it co-refers with a word such as *"the funeral"*, in French *"les funérailles"*), or conversely that *they* is translated into a singular (e.g. if it co-refers with a word such as *"the police"* or represents a gender-neutral singular referent).

We inspect the learned PLM and observe how the log-probability, e.g., of French masculine singular *il* varies with the number of masculine singular (pro)nouns preceding it, as represented in Figure 2(a), first four bars. To do that, we compute the average log-probability over all PLM n-grams containing exactly n time(s) (n from 1 to 4 for the bars from left to right) a masculine singular noun and finishing with *il*. The same operation can be done for other pronouns, such as *ce, ils, elle* or *elles*, as represented in the subsequent groups of bars in Figure 2(a), which all show the evolution of the probability to observe the respective pronoun after 1 or 2 or 3 or 4 masculine singular nouns (bars from left to right for each pronoun). The main result supporting our model is that this log-probability increases for *il* with the number of masculine singular (pro)nouns preceding it, and decreases for all the other pronouns, except for the neutral *ce*, for which it remains constant.

Similar observations can be made for the log-probability to observe one of the five pronouns listed above after 1 or 2 or 3 or 4 feminine singular nouns, as shown in Figure 2(b). Again, our proposal is supported by the fact that this probability increases for *elle* and decreases for all other pronouns.

For completeness, we provide in Table 1 the log-probabilities for four combinations of features ({masculine, feminine} × {singular, plural}) and the twelve most frequent French pronouns which are translations of *it* and *they*. These numbers allow a more precise view than the bar charts shown above, and confirm the variations of the probabilities observed above, as synthesized in the last columns: we indicate with ↑ a strictly increasing series of four log-probabilities, and with ↓ a decreasing one. For instance, the average log-probability of *elle* is quite low (−1.839) when it has only one feminine

Pronoun	N. of preceding nouns				Var.	Pronoun	N. of preceding nouns				Var.
	1	2	3	4			1	2	3	4	
masculine, singular						*masculine, plural*					
il	-1.166	-1.048	-0.962	**-0.891**	↑	il	-1.162	-1.196	-1.227	-1.244	↓
elle	-1.875	-1.941	-1.942	-1.943	↓	elle	-1.871	-2.046	-2.319	-2.744	↓
ils	-1.353	-1.445	-1.588	-1.768	↓	ils	-1.309	-1.135	-1.000	**-0.883**	↑
elles	-1.898	-2.081	-2.390	-2.957	↓	elles	-1.920	-2.020	-2.033	-2.197	↓
ce	-1.070	-1.056	-1.039	-1.037	↑	ce	-1.072	-1.041	-1.036	-1.044	−
c'	-1.165	-1.100	-1.066	-1.058	↑	c'	-1.183	-1.190	-1.189	-1.291	−
on	-1.376	-1.318	-1.264	-1.272	−	on	-1.411	-1.460	-1.492	-1.383	−
ça	-1.628	-1.552	-1.464	-1.462	↑	ça	-1.665	-1.657	-1.568	-1.567	−
le	-2.069	-1.970	-1.820	-1.682	↑	le	-2.038	-1.893	-1.750	-1.752	−
la	-2.681	-2.749	-2.743	-2.730	−	la	-2.604	-2.626	-2.805	-2.937	↓
lui	-2.658	-2.538	-2.311	-2.025	↑	lui	-2.663	-2.689	-2.863	-3.296	−
l'	-2.147	-2.045	-1.908	-1.753	↑	l'	-2.110	-2.083	-2.060	-2.135	−
feminine, singular						*feminine, plural*					
il	-1.161	-1.233	-1.328	-1.440	↓	il	-1.160	-1.204	-1.365	-1.441	↓
elle	-1.839	-1.465	-1.168	**-0.980**	↑	elle	-1.914	-2.101	-2.169	N.A.	−
ils	-1.347	-1.421	-1.538	-1.700	↓	ils	-1.319	-1.350	-1.550	-1.599	↓
elles	-1.887	-2.083	-2.174	-2.552	↓	elles	-1.759	-1.340	-1.059	**-0.817**	↑
ce	-1.084	-1.074	-1.065	-1.050	↑	ce	-1.078	-1.076	-1.139	-1.441	−
c'	-1.167	-1.119	-1.054	-1.036	↑	c'	-1.169	-1.228	-1.240	-1.379	↓
on	-1.409	-1.398	-1.370	-1.431	−	on	-1.395	-1.401	-1.473	-1.277	−
ça	-1.677	-1.694	-1.662	-1.746	−	ça	-1.668	-1.742	-1.916	-2.290	↓
le	-2.052	-2.175	-2.238	-2.234	−	le	-2.095	-2.172	-2.190	N.A.	−
la	-2.615	-2.402	-2.391	-2.274	↑	la	-2.759	-2.763	N.A.	N.A.	−
lui	-2.602	-2.614	-2.550	-2.480	−	lui	-2.683	-2.810	N.A.	N.A.	−
l'	-2.141	-2.098	-2.104	-1.944	−	l'	-2.210	-2.344	-2.160	N.A.	−

Table 1. The fluctuation of average log-probability of n-grams as the number of a occurrences of a specific gender/number value increases, computed over 12 frequent French pronouns. The last column (Observations) indicates the overall trend: ↑ for monotonic increase, ↓ for monotonic decrease, and − for undecided. 'N.A.' means that no instance is found.

singular (pro)noun among the four (pro)nouns preceding it, but increases to -1.465 and then -1.168 as two then three of these words are feminine singular, and finally reaches a high value of -0.980 when all of the four nouns preceding it are feminine singular.

Overall, for most third-person pronouns (*il, elle, ils, elles, le, la*) the average log-probability of the pronoun gradually increases when more and more nouns (or pronouns) of the same gender and number are found before it. By contrast, the log-probability decreases with the presence of more words of a different gender and number. For instance, for masculine plural *ils*, its log-probability drops as it is preceded by more and more masculine singular words.

However, such tendencies are not observed for the neuter indefinite pronoun *on*, the vowel-preceding object pronoun *l'*, or the indirect object pronoun *lui*, for a good reason: these pronouns can have antecedents of both genders (and sometimes, both numbers), and are expected to be independent from the investigated factor. Among the neuter impersonal pronouns (*c'* , *ce*, and *ça*), we observe that the log-probabilities of *c'* and *ce* increase with the number of masculine or feminine singular nouns, and similarly for *ça* with masculine singular nouns.

Another important observation, which holds for all four possible combinations of gender and number values, is that the log-probability of the n-gram containing four nouns of the same gender and number as the pronoun (e.g. four masculine singular nouns followed by *il*) is always higher than those containing a different pronoun (e.g. four masculine singular nouns followed by *elle* or *elles* or *ils*. In Figure 2(a)), for example, if all four preceding words are masculine singular, then the most likely pronoun is *il* (-0.891). Moreover, among the remaining pronouns, the PLM prioritizes the neuter ones (e.g. *ce*, *c'* , or *ca*) over those of the opposite gender or number. This is indeed beneficial for pronoun selection by re-ranking hypotheses from an SMT decoder, since it is preferable to reward neutral or pleonastic pronouns rather than rewarding a pronoun with a gender and number which is not shared with any of the four nouns preceding it.

5   Re-ranking translation hypotheses with the PLM

The Moses statistical MT system (Koehn et al., 2007) used in this study outputs on demand a list of N-best translation hypotheses, for every source sentence, together with their score. In production mode, only the 1-best hypothesis is output as the translation of the source. However, in this study, we will consider several translation hypotheses for the source sentences containing the pronouns *it* or *they*, and re-rank them based on additional information from the pronoun language model presented above. As a result, the 1-best hypothesis may change, and we will demonstrate in Section 6 that pronoun translation is on average improved.

For every source sentence containing at least one occurrence of *it* or *they* we re-rank the SMT hypotheses through the following steps. In the implementation, we will consider the 1000-best hypotheses for each source sentence.

1. Determine the gender and number of the four preceding nouns or pronouns, by examining the current sentence but possibly also the previous ones from the same document (TED lecture).
2. Shorten the N-best list, to avoid considering multiple translation hypotheses that have the same pronouns, as the PLM cannot change their ranking with respect to each other. Therefore, in the N-best list, we retain only the highest-ranked hypothesis among all those that have identical translated values of the source pronouns *it* and *they*. E.g., if the source sentence contains only one pronoun, we keep only the highest-ranked translation for each of the different translation possibilities that occur in the N-best list. If the source sentence contains several pronouns, we consider the tuples of translation possibilities instead of a single value. If the N-best list contains no variations in the translation of pronouns, then no re-ranking is attempted. This step thus increases the efficiency of our method, without changing its results.
3. Format the shortened list of hypotheses so that they can be scored by the PLM. We add before all the target pronouns, translations of *it* or *they* determined from the alignment provided by Moses, the gender and number features of the four preceding nouns or pronouns. We illustrate this step in Figure 3, where the four nouns

preceding the (wrong) translation of *it* are all feminine singular. Moreover, the '*'
on *il-PRN** indicates that the target pronoun *il* agrees in number with the source
one – a feature that will be used below.

4. Obtain the PLM score for each pronoun of each translation hypothesis. We invoke
   the "`ngram -debug 2`" command of the SRILM toolkit with the PLM to generate
   the scores of all possible n-grams of each hypothesis, and we select among them
   those ending by the pronoun(s) appearing in the hypothesis. As SRILM only outputs the maximal n-gram ending with each word, we only obtain one score per
   pronoun, either from a PLM 5-gram ending with a pronoun, or from a shorter one.
   The score is noted $S_{\mathrm{PLM}}(pronoun)$.

5. Compute a new score for each formatted hypothesis from the shortened list. The
   new score of each hypothesis, noted $S'(sentence)$, is the weighted sum of the score
   obtained from the Moses decoder, $S_{\mathrm{DEC}}(sentence)$ and of the PLM scores of its
   pronouns, weighted by a factor $\alpha = 5$. Moreover, we reward the PLM scores of the
   pronouns which have the same number as the source pronoun (marked with a '*'
   as shown in Fig. 3) by a factor $\beta = 5$ (these values of α and β could be optimized
   in the future on a new data set). Therefore, the new score of each hypothesis s depending on its pronouns $p \in s$ is given by:

$$S'(s) = S_{\mathrm{DEC}}(s) + \alpha * \left(\sum_{\{p \in s \mid \text{diff.nb.}\}} S_{\mathrm{PLM}}(p) + \beta * \sum_{\{p \in s \mid \text{same nb.}\}} S_{\mathrm{PLM}}(p) \right).$$

6. Finally, the hypothesis with the highest S' score is selected as the new best translation of the sentence. Moreover, its pronoun(s) are also used to update the list of
   gender/number features of (pro)nouns used for scoring subsequent pronouns with
   the PLM.

SRC−1	: The house of my mother in law was damaged by a heavy storm.
SRC	: When my wife came, *it* had lost its roof.
HYP−1	: La maison de ma belle-mère a été endommagée par une violente tempête.
HYP	: Lorsque ma femme est venue, *il-PRN** avait perdu son toit .
NP	: *fem.sing. fem.sing. fem.sing. fem.sing.*
F-HYP	: Lorsque ma femme est venue, *fem.sing. fem.sing. fem.sing. fem.sing.* *il-PRN** avait perdu son toit .

Fig. 3. Example of formatting of a translation hypothesis: we add the gender and number of the
four nouns preceding the pronoun *il*, which is tagged as PRN by Morfette (wrong translation
of the source *it* instead of *elle*). 'SRC−1' and 'HYP−1' denote the source and target sentences
before the one being processed, and 'F-HYP' denotes the formatted sentence.

6 Experiments

6.1 Settings and evaluation metrics

We trained the Moses phrase-based SMT system (Koehn et al., 2007) on the following parallel and monolingual datasets: aligned TED talks from the WIT[3] corpus (Cettolo et al., 2012), Europarl v. 7 (Koehn, 2005), News Commentary v. 9 and other news data from WMT 2007–2013 (Bojar et al., 2014). The system was tuned on a development set of 887 sentences from IWSLT 2010 provided for the shared task on pronoun translation of the DiscoMT 2015 workshop (Hardmeier et al., 2015). Our test set was also the one of the DiscoMT 2015 shared task, with 2,093 English sentences extracted from 12 recent TED talks (French gold-standard translations were made available after the task). The test set contains 809 occurrences of *it* and 307 of *they*, hence a total of 1,116 pronouns.

We compare two systems: (1) the Moses phrase-based SMT system trained as above, noted 'BL' (baseline); and (2) the system which re-ranks the N-best list generated by BL using the PLM, as described in the previous section, noted 'RR'.

Their performances are computed automatically in terms of the number of pronouns which are identical between a system and the reference translation. We use four scores noted C_1 through C_4, inspired from the metric for Accuracy of Connective Translation (Hajlaoui and Popescu-Belis, 2013). C_1 is the number of candidate pronouns which correspond identically to the ones in the reference translation, while C_2 is the number of "similar" pronouns in the reference and the candidate. "Similarity" accounts for the variants of *ce* and *ça*, with or without apostrophe, and for the two different apostrophe characters, resulting in two equivalence classes only: {*ce, c', c', c* } and {*ça, ca, ç', ç'*, *c*}. The C_3 score is the number of candidate pronouns which differ from the reference, while C_4 is the number of source pronouns left untranslated in the candidate translation. Overall, we will compare C_1 and $C_1 + C_2$ between the BL and RR systems, as well as accuracy, namely $C_1 + C_2$ divided by the total number of pronouns (1,116).

These scores rely only on the comparison of the system's pronouns (candidates) with the ones in the reference translation. Although such a metric is only an imperfect reflection of translation correctness, it is likely that increasing the first two scores (C_1 and C_2) indicates an improved quality. In theory, the target pronoun does not need to be identical to the reference one to be correct: it must only point to the same antecedent. Therefore, some variation would be acceptable to a human evaluator, but not to our metrics, which yield lower scores.

6.2 Results

The upper part of Table 2 displays the scores of the BL and RR systems in terms of pronoun metrics. The results demonstrate that RR outperforms BL on both exact translations (C_1) or acceptable translations ($C_1 + C_2$), with improvements of 21 and, respectively, 22 occurrences. Besides, although RR generates more translations that are different from the reference than BL (C_3 of 560 vs. 551), this is balanced by the fact that RR leaves fewer untranslated source pronouns (C_4 of 61 vs. 92). The accuracy of RR is 2% (absolute) or 5% (relative) higher than that of BL.

In addition, to understand more deeply about the method's performance, we also compute $C_1..C_4$ scores of all submitted systems at DiscoMT 2015 pronoun-focused translation task (Hardmeier et al., 2015) and show in the lower part of Table 2. Compared with these systems, RR is still the best-performing one, whose accuracy is 2.07% (absolute) higher than that of the best system of DiscoMT 2015 (BASELINE).

System	C1	C2	C3	C4	C1+C2	Accuracy
BL	395	78	551	92	473	.424
RR	416	79	560	61	495	**.444**
Comparison to DiscoMT 2015 submitted systems						
BASELINE	400	66	522	128	466	.417
UU-TIEDEMANN	388	69	491	168	457	.409
IDIAP	392	70	516	138	462	.414
UU-HARDMEIER	362	80	573	101	442	.396
AUTO-POSTEDIT	297	102	620	97	399	.358
ITS2	9	10	1056	41	19	.017

Table 2. Performances of BL, RR and all submitted systems at DiscoMT 2015 pronoun-focused shared task in terms of $C_1..C_4$ scores and accuracy ($(C_1 + C_2)/Total$). RR outperforms the remaining systems on both C_1 and $C_1 + C_2$ scores.

As for BLEU scores, which measure the overall quality and are not expected to be sensitive enough to the improvement of a small proportion of words, the baseline system reaches 37.80 BLEU points, while the re-ranked translations reach a marginally higher value of 37.96. These numbers show that the improvement of pronoun translation by re-ranking is not done at the expense of the overall quality, and might even be marginally beneficial to it.

To verify the significance of the improvement on pronouns, we perform a McNemar test comparing the scores of BL and RR for each pronoun, either in terms of identity to the reference (criterion C_1) or of similarity to the reference (criterion $C_1 + C_2$). The p-values of the two comparisons are respectively 0.0294 and 0.0218, showing that RR is significantly better than BL with 95% confidence. Given that at the DiscoMT 2015 shared task none of the systems was able to outperform the baseline (which was the same as the BL system presented here), we believe that this is a promising result that improves over the state of the art.

To understand in more detail the effect of our method on specific pronouns, we analyze per pronoun type the cases where the translations proposed by RR differ from those of BL. An 'improvement' means that the translation of RR is in the C_1 or C_2 case (i.e. identical or similar to the reference) and that of BL is not, while a 'degradation' means the contrary. Overall, there are 92 pronouns (out of 1,116) changed between BL and RR, amounting to 57 improvements and 35 degradations.

Table 3 shows that most modifications are made on the third person singular subject pronouns: 23 on *il* and 24 on *elle*. Among them, the improvements brought by RR surpass the degradations: +5 on *il* and +8 on *elle*. Similarly, third person plural subject pronouns are improved (+2 in both cases), although they are less affected (14 changes on *ils* and 4 on *elles*). RR produces quite often the neuter pronouns *c'* (7 times), *ça* (12 times) and *ce* (2 times), which is likely due to their rather high PLM score, regardless of the preceding gender and number features. However, only the occurrences of *c'* are clearly improved (+5). In contrast, the object pronouns are practically untouched by RR (only +1 on *le*), which is related to the rather weak influence observed in the PLM of the preceding gender and number on object pronouns.

Pronoun	Improved	Degraded	Δ
il	14	9	5
elle	16	8	8
ils	8	6	2
elles	3	1	2
ce	1	1	0
c'	6	1	5
on	2	2	0

Pronoun	Improved	Degraded	Δ
ça	6	6	0
le	1	0	1
la	0	0	0
lui	0	0	0
l'	0	0	0
y	0	1	-1
Total	57	35	22

Table 3. Performance of the re-ranking system (RR) on specific pronoun translations, in terms of improved vs. degraded pronouns with respect to the baseline (BL). The difference for each pronoun type, noted Δ, is always positive, except for the single occurrence of 'y'.

We illustrate a contribution of RR vs. BL in Figure 4. BL wrongly translates *it* into *il* in the 1-best hypothesis, and the translation into *elle* appears in the hypotheses ranked lower. However, this pronoun is preceded by a majority of feminine singular nouns in the French translation of BL (namely *commission, urgence*, and *contre-révolution*, while only *sabotage* is masculine). The PLM log-probability of the 5-gram formed by *elle* and the gender/number of the four preceding nouns is higher than that of the same n-gram ending with *il*: -1.0185 vs. -1.1871. As a result, RR succeeds in promoting the translation with *elle* as the new 1-best translation.

SRC−1	: in 1917 , the russian communists founded the emergency commission for combating counter-revolution and sabotage .
SRC	: it was led by felix dzerzhinsky .
HYP−1	: en 1917 , les communistes russes ont créé la commission d' urgence pour combattre la contre-révolution et sabotage .
HYP/BL	: *il* a été entraîné par felix dzerzhinsky .
HYP/RR	: *elle* a été emmenée par felix dzerzhinsky .
REF	: *elle* était dirigée par félix dzerjinski .

Fig. 4. Example of translation improved by RR, thanks to a majority of feminine nouns.

7   Conclusion

In this paper, we presented a method to improve the machine translation of pronouns, which relies on learning a pronoun-aware language model (PLM). The PLM encodes the likelihood of generating a target pronoun given the gender and number of the nouns or pronouns preceding it. For every source sentence of the test set containing *it* or *they*, the method re-ranks the translation hypotheses produced by a phrase-based SMT baseline, combining the decoder scores and the PLM scores of the pronoun and preceding nouns or pronouns.

Our re-ranking method outperforms the DiscoMT 2015 baseline by 5% relative improvement, while none of the systems participating in that shared task could outperform it. The method performs particularly well on all third person singular subject pronouns, but also on the neuter impersonal or pleonastic pronouns, despite the fact that they are more independent from the gender and nouns of preceding words than the subject ones. In the near future, the performance of the PLM will be tested at the shared task on pronoun prediction at the First Conference on Machine Translation (WMT 2016).

We will attempt to increase the accuracy of our model by training it on more data sets, increasing the order of n-grams (N) and optimizing the α and β parameters on a development set. Besides, we will attempt to put more weight on n-grams where the preceding (pro)nouns of the same gender and number with the given pronoun are closer to it. Longer-term future work will focus on integrating the proposed PLM into the decoder's log-linear function, although extracting gender-number n-grams at decoding time is non-trivial. Furthermore, it would be interesting to model the cases when the gender and number of preceding nouns are not the same, because in these cases, we believe that using solely the PLM scores is inadequate. Using information from anaphora resolution, or at least from features that are relevant anaphora resolution, should help address these cases.

Acknowledgments

We are grateful for their support to the Swiss National Science Foundation (SNSF) under the Sinergia MODERN project (www.idiap.ch/project/modern/, grant n. 147653) and to the European Union under the Horizon 2020 SUMMA project (www.summa-project.eu, grant n. 688139).

References

Bojar, O., Buck, C., Federmann, C., Haddow, B., Koehn, P., Leveling, J., Monz, C., Pecina, P., Post, M., Saint-Amand, H., Soricut, R., Specia, L., Tamchyna, A., 2014. Findings of the 2014 Workshop on Statistical Machine Translation. In: Proceedings of the Ninth Workshop on Statistical Machine Translation. Baltimore, MD, USA, pp. 12–58.

Callin, J., Hardmeier, C., Tiedemann, J., 2015. Part-of-speech driven cross-lingual pronoun prediction with feed-forward neural networks. In: Proceedings of the Second Workshop on Discourse in Machine Translation (DiscoMT). Lisbon, Portugal, pp. 59–64.

Cettolo, M., Girardi, C., Federico, M., 2012. WIT[3]: Web inventory of transcribed and translated talks. In: Proceedings of the 16th Conference of the European Association for Machine Translation (EAMT). Trento, Italy, pp. 261–268.

Chrupala, G., Dinu, G., van Genabith, J., 2008. Learning morphology with Morfette. In: Proceedings of the 6th International Conference on Language Resources and Evaluation (LREC). Marrakech, Morocco.

Guillou, L., 2012. Improving pronoun translation for statistical machine translation. In: Proceedings of EACL 2012 Student Research Workshop (13th Conference of the European Chapter of the ACL). Avignon, France, pp. 1–10.

Guillou, L., 2016. Incorporating pronoun function into statistical machine translation. PhD thesis, University of Edinburgh, UK.

Hajlaoui, N., Popescu-Belis, A., 2013. Assessing the accuracy of discourse connective translations: Validation of an automatic metric. In: Proceedings of the 14th International Conference on Intelligent Text Processing and Computational Linguistics (CICLING). Samos, Greece.

Hardmeier, C., 2014. Discourse in statistical machine translation. PhD thesis, Uppsala University, Sweden.

Hardmeier, C., Federico, M., 2010. Modelling pronominal anaphora in statistical machine translation. In: Proceedings of International Workshop on Spoken Language Translation (IWSLT). Paris, France.

Hardmeier, C., Nakov, P., Stymne, S., Tiedemann, J., Versley, Y., Cettolo, M., 2015. Pronoun-focused MT and cross-lingual pronoun prediction: Findings of the 2015 DiscoMT shared task on pronoun translation. In: Proceedings of the Second Workshop on Discourse in Machine Translation (DiscoMT). Lisbon, Portugal, pp. 1–16.

Koehn, P., 2005. Europarl: A parallel corpus for statistical machine translation. In: Proceedings of the 10th Machine Translation Summit. Phuket, Thailand, pp. 79–86.

Koehn, P., Hoang, H., Birch, A., Callison-Burch, C., Federico, M., Bertoldi, N., Cowan, B., Shen, W., Moran, C., Zens, R., Dyer, C., Bojar, O., Constantin, A., Herbst, E., 2007. Moses: Open source toolkit for statistical machine translation. In: Proceedings of the 45th Annual Meeting of the Association for Computational Linguistics (ACL). Prague, Czech Republic, pp. 177–180.

Le Nagard, R., Koehn, P., 2010. Aiding pronoun translation with co-reference resolution. In: Proceedings of the Joint 5th Workshop on Statistical Machine Translation and Metrics (MATR). Uppsala, Sweden, pp. 258–267.

Luong, N. Q., Miculicich Werlen, L., Popescu-Belis, A., 2015. Pronoun translation and prediction with or without coreference links. In: Proceedings of the Second Workshop on Discourse in Machine Translation (DiscoMT). Lisbon, Portugal, pp. 94–100.

Stolcke, A., 2002. SRILM – an extensible language modeling toolkit. In: Proceedings of the 7th International Conference on Spoken Language Processing (ICSLP). Denver, CO, USA, pp. 901–904.

Received May 2, 2016 , accepted May 15, 2016

Baltic J. Modern Computing, Vol. 4 (2016), No. 2, pp. 305–317

Predicting and Using Implicit Discourse Elements in Chinese-English Translation

David STEELE, Lucia SPECIA

Department of Computer Science, The University of Sheffield, UK

`dbsteele1@sheffield.ac.uk, l.specia@sheffield.ac.uk`

Abstract. In machine translation (MT) implicitation can occur when elements such as discourse markers and pronouns are not expected or mandatory in the source language, but need to be realised in the target language for a coherent translation. These 'implicit' elements can be seen as both a barrier to MT and an important source of information. However, identifying where such elements are needed and producing them are non-trivial tasks. In this paper we examine the effect of implicit elements on MT and propose methods to identify and make them explicit. As a starting point, we use human translated and aligned data to decide where to insert place holders for these elements.

We then fully automate this process by devising a prediction model to decide if and where implicit elements should occur and be made explicit. Our experiments compare statistical machine translation models built with and without these explicitation processes. Models built on data marked for discourse elements show substantial improvements over the baseline.

Keywords: Chinese-English machine translation, discourse markers, empty categories, explicitation

1 Introduction

One of the main challenges in machine translation (MT) is to model the multitude of intrinsic differences that occur between the source and target languages. The problem is even more critical when considering distant language pairs such as Chinese[1] and English, which have largely developed in separation from each other and are noted to be markedly different (Wu, 2014). Chinese has a flexible grammar, relatively free word order (Gao, 2008), and is a prolific 'pro-drop' language (Huang, 1989). In addition, the application of cohesive devices (e.g. conjunctions) is one of the most prominent features that distinguishes Chinese and English (Wu, 2014). For instance, implicit links (i.e. the absence of explicit markers) are very common in Chinese and where a relation is not

---

[1] For this paper 'Chinese' is used to mean 'Mandarin Chinese'.

made explicit it can be inferred from context. However, in MT producing the correct explicit information on the target language when it is not required on the source language poses a significant barrier that often leads to poor quality automated translations.

Examples 1 and 2 (Steele and Specia, 2014) highlight this issue and show that during the translation process[2], even for relatively simple sentences, when elements are not required in the source, but need to be realised in the target then problems can and do occur.

Ex(1) 他因为病了，没来上课。
Because he was sick, he didn't come to class. (Human Translation)
He is ill, absent. (MT)

In the second clause of the Chinese sentence the pronoun 'he' (他) is inferred from the 'he' (他) in the first clause. In addition 'so/therefore' (所以), which commonly co-occurs with 'because'(因为) in the '因为... 所以...' construct, is optional (in this case) and also omitted. Consequently the translation system performs quite poorly.

Example 2 is a modified version of Example 1, with an extra 'so'(所以) and 'he' (他) manually inserted into the second clause of the Chinese sentence.

Ex(2) 他因为病了, 所以他没来上课。
Because he was sick, (so) he didn't come to class. (Human Translation)
Because he was ill, so he did not come to class. (MT)

Grammatically these extra inserted characters are not required in the Chinese , but inserting them has enabled the MT system to produce a better translation. This suggests that recovering such elements can help to produce a smoother translation, although this in turn may still need to be further refined.

In this paper, we examine some of the effects that implicit elements have on MT. We also implement methods for recovering some of the inferred information by inserting explicit place holder tokens into the source data to help inform the automatic alignment and decoding processes. We create an initial benchmark using human translations and oracle alignments (correct word alignments provided by human experts), which we then try to automate using a classifier to predict if and where to insert place holder tokens.

Our primary results show a significant improvement over the baseline models with no place holders for discourse elements (+1 in BLEU) and are close to those obtained with annotations derived from manually produced translations and alignments.

The remainder of this paper is organised as follows: In Section 2 we examine related work. Section 3 explains in detail how we built our benchmark corpus based on datasets translated and word-aligned by humans. Section 4 details our methods used for finding implicit elements and inserting place holder tokens into our data. We also discuss our initial work on building a prediction model. Our experiments, set-up and results are outlined and discussed in Section 5. Finally, Section 6 presents our conclusions and potential directions for future work.

---

[2] The 'MT' here is produced by Google Translate: https://translate.google.co.uk/

2   Related work

In this section we outline some approaches that have been used to deal with the topics of implicitation, explicitation, and empty categories in the context of MT. These are topics that have generated increasing interest for a number of languages in recent years.

In order to contend with the type of language phenomena highlighted in Examples 1 and 2, special empty category tokens have been used in the Penn Treebank (Bies et al., 1995) and its extension, the Chinese Treebank (Xue and Xia, 2000). An empty category is an element that does not have a mapping to a surface word in a parse tree. Essentially, when translating such elements into the target, where they are explicitly required, it is problematic because the implicit information has to be retained, recovered, and realised from what otherwise appears to be non-existent components in the source.

In Meyer and Webber (2013) implicitation of DMs in MT is explored through a detailed corpus analysis. The work highlights how DMs in the source text are not always translated to comparable words in the target language. Disparities in how often this phenomenon occurs in human translated texts (18%) for English, French, and German as opposed to machine translated ones (8%) are observed and the work aims to more widely capture the natural implicitation of DMs in statistical MT (SMT).

More specifically to Chinese, Chung and Gildea (2010) examine the effects that empty categories have on MT with a specific focus on dropped pronouns (little *pro*) and control constructions (big *PRO*) . The work shows that building machine translation systems with explicitly inserted empty elements, either manually or automatically, in the training data improves the overall translation quality. They use and compare three different approaches to recover empty or null elements: pattern matching; parsing; and prediction models. Of the three, the prediction model performed the best. However, they acknowledge that there is a lot of room for improvement in order to better recover empty categories.

In Yang and Xue (2010) the term 'chasing the ghost' is used to signify the hunt for empty categories. Identification of empty categories is turned into a tagging task. Essentially, each word in a sentence is given a tag indicating whether or not it follows an empty category. A maximum entropy model is employed for the prediction of the tags. No distinctions are made between the types of tags that are identified. The results show a 63% accuracy rate in recovering empty tags when an automatic parser is used as input.

Luo and Zhao (2011) also try to predict where empty categories may appear in Chinese sentences by using a statistical tree annotator supplemented with additional information. They apply the annotator to a few distinct tasks including: predicting function tags and predicting null elements. The results show favourable comparisons with previously published results using the same data. However, the results for predicting function tags and empty elements in the Chinese were obtained using human annotated data rather than automatically generated data. In addition, some of the empty categories are placed into a single position in the tree, which prevents them from being uniquely recoverable.

Instead of 'chasing the ghost' Xiang et al. (2013) outline work that 'enlists the ghost'. They use a maximum entropy model with additional syntactic features to recover empty categories and then incorporate them into a Chinese-English MT task. The results show that the recovered empty elements contribute to improvements in both word alignment tasks and the overall quality of their MT system output.

More recently, Steele and Specia (2014) discuss divergences in the usage of DMs for Chinese and English. They illustrate how DMs are vital contextual links, and through a detailed corpus analysis highlight significant divergences in their usage. The findings show how contextual omissions (implicit data) cause problems for MT systems and often lead to incoherent automatic translations.

Steele (2015), builds upon this work with a focus on word alignments for four specific elements: 'if', 'then','because','but'. Automatic alignments are used to ascertain the occurrence of implicit markers, which is found to be quite significant. Experiments show that when artificial tokens are inserted into the data, as a proxy for these markers, and the MT systems are rebuilt, there is a significant improvement over the baseline. However, to achieve the improvement the insertions of the markers were carried out using reference data.

Clearly there is some overlap between the terms 'empty categories' and 'implicit elements', but for this paper we use the latter to refer to, amongst other things, those elements with no corresponding word alignments. Our work detailed in this paper is more general as compared to previous work: is not restricted to big or little *pro* categories, and does not rely on treebank annotations, nor on parsing.

3 A benchmark corpus

Here we describe the pre-processing of a benchmark corpus using human translated and aligned data, which we then use to build and evaluate approaches to make discourse elements explicit.

3.1 The data

The data used to build our benchmark corpus came from sections of the Gale Project provided by the Linguistic Data Consortium (LDC)[3] catalogue[4]. Each section consists of manually translated sentences from news and web broadcasts and contains oracle (i.e. produced by expert linguists) word alignments, as well as additional annotations signalling items such as non translated elements and other metadata.

Our final corpus is made up of a total of 43693 usable parallel aligned sentences[5] consisting of approximately 1.23M English words and 955K Chinese words:

- GALE Chinese-English Word Alignment and Tagging – Broadcast Training Parts 1-4. Total = 19621 usable sentences.
- GALE Chinese-English Word Alignment and Tagging Training – Newswire and Web Parts 1-4. Total = 17966 usable sentences.
- GALE Chinese-English Parallel Aligned Treebank – Training. Total = 6106 usable sentences.

---

[3] https://catalog.ldc.upenn.edu/

[4] LDC2012T16, LDC2012T20, LDC2012T24, LDC2013T05, LDC2013T23, LDC2014T25, LDC2015T04, LDC2015T18, LDC2015T06

[5] Some sentences had no alignments and so were unusable and consequently removed.

3.2 Building the sentences

Example 3 shows a typical sentence in its original format. The Chinese is character segmented and the English is space delimited. The word alignments reflect the positions (indexes starting with 1) of source and target and contain additional annotations.

Ex(3)
(Sp1) 从 那 时 开 始 这 里 就 成 了 香 港 的 一 个 禁 区 。
<Sp1> Since then , this area has become a prohibited zone in Hong Kong .
19-15(FUN) 17-10(SEM) 7,8-5[DET],6(GIS) 9[COO]-(NTR) 12,13-13,14(SEM)
18-11(SEM) 14[DEP]-12(PDE) 2,5,6-2(FUN) 3,4-3(SEM) 10,11[TEN]-7[TEN],8(GIS)
15,16[MEA]-9(GIF) -4[COO](NTR) -1[MET](MTA) 1[MET]-(MTA)

The separate parts are combined to create a parallel aligned sentence for each line of our corpus. The Chinese segments were segmented into their more common forms typically found in Chinese dictionaries. For instance, '这 里', becomes '这里' ('this area' - in the case of this sentence). This step was performed using the Stanford Chinese Segmenter (Chang, et al., 2008; Chang, et al., 2009; Tseng,et al., 2005). The word alignments were then adjusted to accommodate the changes.

The final stage of the process involves removing the meta-data/additional annotations and zero indexing the word alignments (to match other common word alignment formats). Multiple alignments are split into separate alignment points and then reordered to improve readability. Example 4 is the final version of Example 3 and shows the typical format of the sentences in our corpus.

Ex(4)
从 那时 开始 这里 就 成 了 香港 的 一 个 禁区 。 ||| since then , this area has become a prohibited zone in hong kong . ||| 0-0 1-1 2-0 3-3 3-4 5-5 5-6 6-5 6-6 7-11 7-12 8-10 9-7 10-7 11-8 11-9 12-13

4 Explicitation methods

In this section we first outline the process of recovering the implicit information and inserting tokens into our corpus using a heuristic method based on word alignment information. The main goal of such a method is to produce training data for a fully automated method. We then outline our initial fully automated method to predict implicit elements in the data without resorting to word alignment information.

4.1 A heuristic method to recover implicit elements

Here we outline the method of using data from a parallel corpus to identify and target the missing elements. This method relies on word alignments (oracle or automated) to gain knowledge of where the unaligned elements occur in the corpus. This method is suitable for building training corpora, for gaining insight on where implicitation may occur in the data, and for demonstrating the potential impact of making implicit information explicit.

However, it cannot be used in practice at decoding time, as translations for the test set (and thus word alignment information) will not be available (they will need to be generated).

To mark implicit elements, we first POS tag[6] the corpus. In this process sentence a) is transformed into sentence b), for example.

a) 自然 资源 相对 缺乏，
||| natural resources are relatively scarce .
||| 0-0 1-1 2-3 3-4 4-5

b) _ 自然 #NN _ 资源 #NN _ 相对 #AD _ 缺乏 #VV _， #PU
||| natural_JJ resources_NNS are_VBP relatively_RB scarce_JJ ._.
||| 0-0 1-1 2-3 3-4 4-5

The next step retrieves the positions of all the words on the English side that have no corresponding alignment on the Chinese side. In the case of sentence a) the word 'are' with index position 2 has not been aligned to any Chinese counterpart. This element is then tagged in one of a number of ways:

i)   are_VBP[7] (both the word and its POS type)
ii)   _VBP (a more general POS category token)
iii) <are> (just the word)
iv)   <TOK> (a hold all general place holder token)

Once the element is tagged it is inserted into the Chinese segment. In order to do this, each side of the element is examined to find the nearest aligned English neighbour. The tagged element is then placed, as a token, next to the Chinese counterpart of said neighbour. If both neighbours are equally close, the left neighbour is given preference.

In this case 'resources' (position 1) and 'relatively' (position 3) are aligned to '资源' (resources) and '相对' (relatively), respectively, on the Chinese side. The token is hence inserted immediately after the alignment point for its left neighbour ('资源', resources). Everything to the right of the insertion then moves over. Sentence c) shows the final result after the insertion of the token using the markup in i):

c) 自然 资源 are_VBP 相对 缺乏，||| natural resources are relatively scarce .

A quick check, done in the same way as Examples 1 and 2 (Section 1), showed that inserting the word 'are' (with the POS tag removed) into the sentence improves the automated translation[8] (Example 5 is the original, and Example 6 is the modified sentence).

Ex(5) 自然资源相对缺乏，

---

[6] For all POS tagging tasks (Chinese and English) we use the Stanford Log-Linear Part-Of-Speech Tagger (Toutanova et al., 2003).

[7] _VBP = Verb, non-3rd person singular present.

[8] Google Translate (https://translate.google.co.uk/)

natural resources are relatively scarce . (Human Translation)
Relative lack of natural resources, (MT)

Ex(6) 自然资源 are 相对缺乏，(token replaced with the relevant word)
natural resources are relatively scarce . (Human Translation)
Natural resources are relatively scarce, (MT)

Choosing insertions Depending on test criteria there are a number of options to consider when making the insertions. Firstly, a choice has to be made as to what POS types to make insertions for (hence the POS tagging step). We can choose to make insertions for every element with no alignment or we can, for example, exclude certain elements, such as punctuation.

For this paper we chose to include a specific subset of elements based on the discussion in Section 1. Table 1 shows a representative list of the POS tagged elements, with their corresponding Penn Treebank descriptions, and POS category frequency counts, that we used in our experiments (Section 5). The first three rows relate to our primary focus on DMs and pronouns, whereas the final row includes two elements that are often linked with the pronouns (e.g. 'it's' in Ex 7, Section 5.3). The final decision on which elements to include was made based upon frequency counts.

Table 1. The words and POS elements used in our experiments (Section 5).

POS description	Word coupled with POS tag	Frequency
Coordinating conjunctions	and_CC, or_CC, but_CC	13373
Personal pronouns	it_PRP, you_PRP, they_PRP, he_PRP, she_PRP	9672
Subordinating conjunction	if_IN, because_IN	1037
Verb singular present	's_VBZ (3rd person), are_VBP (non-3rd person)	915, 1711

With different corpora and languages it may be necessary to experiment with the number and type of tags to include. Some tags may be aligned more often in one language, but less often in another. In addition, the method or software used to process the word alignments may also give different results. For our training split of the dataset, using the oracle word alignments, 'and_CC' was inserted 12350 times across 41693 sentences, whilst 'or_CC' was only inserted 554 times. Insertions were made for the POS groups in Table 1 in over 26000 of the sentences.

Thus far, the focus has been on insertions being made using oracle word alignments. However, we also experimented with automated word alignments, where we created an equivalent corpus using the same insertion rules, but with inserts made based on alignments extracted by Fast-Align (Dyer et al., 2013). Counts for insertions made on the same corpus, but using Fast-Align alignments, vary considerably. For example, 'and_CC' has 5015 insertions (previously 12350) whilst 'or_CC' has 95 (previously 554). Table 2 shows the difference in frequency of insertions made for 'and_CC', 'or_CC', and 'the_DT' using the oracle alignments and automated alignments, respectively.

Table 2. Highlighting the differences between insertions of words based on oracle and automated alignments.

Word	Oracle alignments	Automated alignments
and_CC	12350	5015
or_CC	554	95
the_DT	1160	33751

The word 'the_DT' is included in Table 2 as an additional observation (to be explored in future work) because it does not have a direct equivalent in Chinese. In the GALE corpus 'the' is often merged with the noun it is restricting or modifying. For instance, '城市' ('city') is actually aligned to 'the city'. This method is formally applied to the function words: 'the', 'a', 'an', 'this', 'that' (Li et al., 2009).

Conversely, Fast-Align makes no such distinctions. As a result, when making insertions using the oracle alignments, insertions for 'the_DT' were made 1160 times. When performing insertions on the same data, but using Fast-Align alignments, insertions for 'the_DT' were made on 33751 occasions (roughly 29 times as many). This highlights yet another difficulty for automatic word alignment tools.

4.2   A method to predict implicit elements

Section 4.1 showed that by using heuristics based on word alignments we can locate specific unaligned elements in a sentence. These methods cannot be used for unseen test data at translation time. Our ultimate aim is to use our data with insertions made using this method to train a classifier that predicts whether or not an insertion should occur after a word in a given Chinese sentence, without resorting to any information on the English side.

For our initial model we use CRFsuite (Okazaki, 2007) and our training set of 41693 sentences (annotated automatically with insertions) to build a prediction model, treating the problem as a sequence labelling task. The test set is made up of 1000 sentences (annotated in the same way for evaluation purposes) that do not appear in the training set. Individual sentences are converted into a sequence of tokens (one per line) and each is attached to its POS category and a label signalling whether it precedes an insert or not. As an example the first word from the sentence discussed in Section 4.1 would be placed into a file like so: _ 自然 #NN #NN NON .

A template file is then used to describe each word with a number of features. For our initial experiments, the following simple features for each word in the sentence were extracted:

— the preceding two individual words and the following two individual words
– a bigram including the word itself and the word immediately to the left
– a bigram including the word itself and the word immediately to the right
– POS tags for the preceding two words and the following two words
– POS bigrams for the preceding two words through to the following two words
– POS trigrams for the preceding two words (and the word itself) through to the following two words (e.g. POS[-2] | POS[-1] | POS[0] = #DT | #LB | #NN).

The performance of the model is measured using precision and recall. For our test set that contains 598 insertions, our model labelled 123 (21%) elements as 'PRE' (preceding an insert), with a precision of 84%.

As these are early tests the results are promising, but our future work will need to address two main issues: Firstly, we are currently only predicting 21% of the implicit elements and it is anticipated that experimenting with feature extraction will yield better results. Secondly, we are currently only tagging whether a word precedes an implicit element or not (i.e. no distinction between words). We are not currently recovering any other specific, fine grained information.

However, experimentation has shown that even only having a single catch all place holder token (e.g. <TOK>) inserted into the data can still positively affect the alignment and decoding processes (Table 3, Section 5).

5 Experiments with SMT

In this section we present experiments using our corpora annotated as per Section 4 to build SMT systems. The overall aim is to compare SMT systems built and tested with raw parallel data against SMT systems where the source side of the corpus is annotated with place holder information. The corpus annotations are derived from either oracle or automated word alignments. Predicted annotations (Predicted_Inserts) in the source of the test set are produced through a fully automated process, using a classifier trained on oracle alignments. This section also provides a number of examples highlighting how some translations have changed either for better or worse.

5.1 Settings and methodology

Our SMT systems are built using the corpus described in Section 3. CDEC (Dyer et al., 2010) is used for rule extraction and decoding following the hierarchical phrase-based approach (Chiang, 2007) for Chinese-English translation. We use BLEU (Papineni et al., 2002) as the metric to evaluate the systems. For consistency, default parameters are used during different builds with the only change being the source of the word alignments.

We perform the same experiments twice, with two different splits of the corpus. For each experiment, the corpus is first randomly shuffled. The development and test sets (dev and tst in the table) are then created using the first 2000 sentences (1000 for each) in the shuffled corpus, while the training set is made up of the remaining 41693 sentences. For an oracle build, all sets (dev, tst, and training) include the human created alignments, whereas for the full automated build, Fast-Alignment (FA) alignments are used. Once the alignment points are added to the sets, each individual sentence has the format shown in Example 4 (Section 3.2).

Each experiment consists of five builds:

- **Oracle**: an SMT system built using oracle alignments (no insertions).
- **Baseline_FA**: a baseline SMT system using Fast-Align (FA) (no insertions).
- **Oracle+Inserts**: an oracle SMT system with insertions made using heuristics based on oracle alignments.

- **FA+Inserts**: an automated SMT system with insertions made using heuristics based on Fast-Align alignments.
- **Predicted_Inserts**: an SMT system with insertions made by a classifier using oracle alignments for training the classifier.

Two scores are produced for each of the five builds per experiment, one for the development set and one for the test set.

5.2 Results

Table 3 shows BLEU scores for the different experiments with the two different splits of the data. In all cases our experiments have shown that having insertions has a strong positive effect on the scores.

Table 3. Examples of the benchmark, baseline, and insertion scores.

(Experiment A)		(Experiment B)	
Build Type	*BLEU*	*Build Type*	*BLEU*
Oracle (dev)	17.81	Oracle (dev)	18.54
Oracle (tst)	18.34	Oracle(B) (tst)	18.59
Baseline_FA (dev)	16.59	Baseline_FA (dev)	17.16
Baseline_FA (tst)	16.76	Baseline_FA (tst)	17.02
Oracle+Inserts (dev)	18.62	Oracle+Inserts (dev)	19.37
Oracle+Inserts (tst)	19.11	Oracle+Inserts(tst)	19.38
FA+Inserts (dev)	17.80	FA+Inserts (dev)	18.08
FA+Inserts (tst)	18.00	FA+Inserts (tst)	18.40
Predicted_Inserts (dev)	16.95	Predicted_Inserts (dev)	17.42
Predicted_Inserts (tst)	17.20	Predicted_Inserts (tst)	17.41

As expected, out of all systems, the Oracle builds perform the best. However, the builds using inserts and Fast-Align (FA+Inserts) show a compelling improvement of up to 1.38 BLEU points over the baseline (Baseline_FA) on the test sets. Similarly, the Oracle builds with inserts (Oracle+Inserts) show a convincing improvement over the plain Oracle builds. More noteworthy is the fact that modest but credible improvements of up to 0.44 are made with our fully automated builds (Predicted_Inserts) over the baseline (Baseline_FA).

5.3 Going beyond BLEU scores

BLEU by itself does not give information about what improvements have been made and why, so here we provide some examples, taken from our translations, to show the changes. Upon manual inspection of our test translations we noted that a large negative factor was the abundance of out of vocabulary (OOV) words, a possible side effect of the limited sized corpus we used.

Each of the following examples are taken from translations produced by our SMT systems built using inserts based on Fast-Align (FA+Inserts) and have four distinct parts: i) the original sentence (source and target); ii) the source with (automatic) insertions (if any) that appear in the sentence; iii) our (FA+Inserts) system translation (with inserts in the source data); iv) baseline translation (no inserts in the source data). In each case the ideal output is for item iii) to be a good coherent sentence that closely maps to the target sentence in item i) and is smoother than the baseline translation shown in item iv).

Ex(7)

  i 因为 便宜。|||because it 's cheap .
  ii 因为 it_PRP 's_VBZ 便宜。
  iii because it 's cheaper .
  iv because cheaper .

Ex(8)

  i 就说 这个 人 长得 像 猴子。|||say, this person looks like a monkey.
  ii No direct insertions made in this sentence
  iii that is to say this person looks like a monkey .
  iv that is to say , who looks like a monkey .

Ex(9)

  i 这 次 会谈 主要 讨论 三 国 在 经贸 文化 等 领域 的 合作，没有 涉及 历史 问题。|||the meeting focused on the three nations ' cooperation in economy , trade and culture , and did not touch on any history problems .
  ii 这 次 会谈 主要 讨论 三 国 在 经贸 and_CC 文化 等 领域 的 合作，and_CC 没 有 涉及 历史 问题。
  iii this meeting primarily discuss cooperation in the fields of economics and trade, culture, in the three countries , and there is no problem involved in history.
  iv talks this time will primarily discuss cooperation in areas such as economics and trade , culture , the three countries have on the issue of history .

Ex(10)[9]

  i 后来 又 说 学生 会 人 太少，没 精力。|||later he said the student association had no energy due to a shortage of hands .
  ii 后来 he_PRP 又 说 学生 会 人 太少，没 精力。
  iii later , he also said that the student association people . no , energy .
  iv later , people will also said that students 太少, i did n't energy .

Ex(11)

---

[9] The original Chinese sentence in example 8 does not contain the phrase 'shortage of hands' but rather: 人 (people) 太少 (too few)... An MT system will therefore struggle to produce the actual phrase 'shortage of hands'.

i 中朝 友谊 已经 成为 双方 共同 的 宝贵 财富。 III the friendship between china
and north korea has become a precious treasure for the two sides .
ii 中朝 and_CC 友谊 已经 成为 双方 共同 的 宝贵 财富。
iii north korea and friendship has become the peoples of both sides together .
iv the friendship between china and north korea has become a precious wealth of both
sides together .

In examples 7-10 the sentences translated using data containing inserts are generally much better than the baseline translations. Having inserts appears to affect the overall alignment and decoding process (e.g. weights), so even those sentences without inserts within the actual sentence boundary itself (example 8) often still show improvements.

Occasionally, having inserts did not help. In example 11, the baseline translation is clearly better. The insert appears to cause degradation, which could be attributed to conflict with the character pair '中朝' ('zhōng cháo'). By itself '中朝' already has the meaning 'China and North Korea', but the way it is written here is akin to 'sino-DPRK (Democratic People's Republic of Korea)'. That is, the common forms of each country (中国 - China, 北朝鲜 - North Korea) have been truncated and used in a specific (less common) way, which already carries the 'and' information within. Essentially, our insertion of 'and_CC', outside of this tight character pair, introduces extra complexity that is clearly difficult for the MT system to deal with.

6 Conclusions and future work

In this paper, we first presented an approach for locating and tagging implicit elements in a parallel aligned corpus. We applied this information to an insertion task that placed proxy tokens for implicit elements into the source data. The data was then used to train SMT systems that were stronger than our baselines.

The source data with the newly inserted elements was also used to train a binary classifier that ultimately was able to predict where implicit elements should occur on unseen data. The data was again used to train SMT systems and the results showed improvements over the baseline.

We faced a barrier with OOV words, which could perhaps be resolved by using a larger dataset. In addition, we observed a strong variance in how items such as function words are treated by oracle and automated alignments. Alignment software lacks the judgement factor of human translation and the gulf in the variance is something that needs to be addressed, or in the least, explored.

Future work will target improvements on our prediction method. We only experimented with a relatively simple set of features. We believe that improving the CRF template and using a wider array of pertinent features will significantly enhance the prediction model, particularly in terms of recall. This, in turn, should lead to further improvements in the quality of translations produced by our SMT systems.

References

Bies, A., Ferguson, M., Katz, K., and MacIntyre, R. (1995). *Bracketing Guidelines for Treebank II Style*. Penn Treebank Project.

Chang P.C., Gally, M., and Manning, C. (2008) *Optimizing Chinese Word Segmentation for Machine Translation Performance*. In ACL 2008 Third Workshop on Statistical Machine Translation.

Chang, P.C., Tseng, H., Jurafsky, D., and Manning, C.D. (2009). *Discriminative Reordering with Chinese Grammatical Relations Features*. Proc. Third Workshop on Syntax and Structure in Statistical Translation.

Chiang, D. (2007). *Hierarchical phrase-based translation*. Proc. ACL, 33(2), pp. 201‑228.

Chung, T. and Gildea, D. (2010) *Effects of Empty Categories on Machine Translation*. Proc. Conference on Empirical Methods in Natural Language processing, pp. 636-645.

Dyer, C., Lopez, A., Ganitkevitch, J., Weese, J., Ture, F., Blunsom, P., Setiawan, H., Eidelman, V., and Resnik, P. (2010). *CDEC: A decoder, Alignment, and Learning Framework for Finite-state and Context-free Translation Models*. Proc. ACL, System Demonstrations, Uppsala, Sweden, pp. 7‑12.

Dyer, C., Chahuneau, V., and Smith N.A. (2013) *A Simple, Fast and Effective Reparameterization of IBM Model 2*. Proc. NAACL, Atlanta, June 09-15.

Gao, Q. (2008). *Word Order in Mandarin: Reading and Speaking*. Proc. 20th North American Conference on Chinese Linguistics (NACCL-20) Conf., Ohio, USA.

Huang, J. (1989) *Pro-drop in Chinese a Generalized Control Approach*. In: Jaeggli, O and Safir, K. (editors) The NUll Subject Parameter, pp. 185-214.

Li, X., Ge, N., and Strassel, S. (2009) *Tagging Guidelines for Chinese-English Word Alignment - Version 1.0*. LDC

Luo, X. and Zhao, B. (2011) *A Statistical Tree Annotator and Its Applications*. Proc. 49th annual meeting ACL, pages 1230-1238, Portland, Organ, June 19-24.

Meyer T. and Webber B. (2013). *Implicitation of Discourse Connectives in (Machine) Translation*. Proc. 1st DiscoMT Workshop at ACL 2013 (51st Annual Meeting of the Association for Computational Linguistics), Sofia, Bulgaria, pp. 19-26.

Okazaki, N. (2007). *CRFsuite: a fast implementation of Conditional Random Fields (CRFs)*, http://www.chokkan.org/software/crfsuite/.

Papineni, K., Roukos, S., Ward, T., and Zhu, W. (2002). *BLEU: a Method for Automatic Evaluation of Machine Translation*. Proc. 40th ACL, Philadelphia, PA, pp. 311-318.

Steele, D. and Specia, L. (2014) *Divergences in the Usage of Discourse Markers in English and Mandarin Chinese*. In: (TSD) Lecture Notes in Computer Science, 8655:189‑200, Springer Berlin Heidelberg. pp. 189-200.

Steele, D. (2015) *Improving the Translation of Discourse Markers for Chinese into English*. Proc. Proceedings of NAACL-HLT (ACL) 2015 Student Research Workshop (SRW),Denver, Colorado, June 1st, pp. 311-318,

Toutanova, K., Klein, D., Manning, C., and Singer, Y. (2003). *Feature-Rich Part-of-Speech Tagging with a Cyclic Dependency Network*. Proc. NAACL-HLT, pp. 252-259.

Tseng, H., Chang P.C., Andrew, G., Jurafsky, D., and Manning, C. (2005) *A Conditional Random Field Word Segmenter*. In Fourth SIGHAN Workshop on Chinese Language Processing.

Wu, J. (2014) *Shifts of Cohesive Devices in English-Chinese Translation*. Proc. Theory and practice in Language Studies, Vol. 4, No. 8, Finland, pp. 1659-1664,

Xiang, B., Luo, X., and Zho, B. (2013) *Enlisting the Ghost: Modeling Empty Categories for Machine Translation*. Proc. 51st annual meeting of ACL, Bulgaria, pp. 822-831.

Xue, N. and Xia, F. (2000) *The Bracketing Guidelines for The Penn Chinese Treebank 3.0* IRCS-00-08, IRCS, University of Pennsylvania

Yang, Y. and Xue, N. (2010) *Chasing the Ghost: Recovering Empty Categories in the Chinese Treebank*. Proc. 23rd International Conference on Computational Linguistics, Beijing, China, pp. 1382-1390.

Received May 3, 2016 , accepted May 15, 2016

Baltic J. Modern Computing, Vol. 4 (2016), No. 2, pp. 318–330

A Graphical Pronoun Analysis Tool for the PROTEST Pronoun Evaluation Test Suite

Christian HARDMEIER[1], Liane GUILLOU[2]

[1] Uppsala University
[2] Ludwig-Maximilians-Universität München

`christian.hardmeier@lingfil.uu.se, liane.guillou@cis.uni-muenchen.de`

Abstract. We present a graphical pronoun analysis tool and a set of guidelines for manual evaluation to be used with the PROTEST pronoun test suite for machine translation (MT). The tool provides a means for researchers to evaluate the performance of their MT systems and browse individual pronoun translations. MT systems may be evaluated automatically by comparing the translation of the test suite pronoun tokens in the MT output with those in the reference translation. Those translations that do not match the reference are referred for manual evaluation, which is supported by the graphical pronoun analysis tool and its accompanying annotation guidelines. By encouraging the manual examination and evaluation of individual pronoun tokens, we hope to understand better how well MT systems perform when translating different categories of pronouns, and gain insights as to where MT systems perform poorly and why.

Keywords: Evaluation, machine translation, pronouns, graphical interface, manual annotation

1   Introduction

Pronoun translation poses a problem for statistical machine translation (SMT). Despite recent efforts, little progress has been made (Le Nagard and Koehn, 2010; Hardmeier and Federico, 2010; Novák, 2011; Guillou, 2012; Hardmeier, 2014). Most recently, the results of the DiscoMT 2015 shared task on pronoun translation (Hardmeier et al., 2015) revealed that even discourse-aware Machine Translation (MT) systems were unable to beat a simple phrase-based SMT baseline. We believe that there are two important obstacles that currently limit progress in pronoun translation. Firstly, we need to obtain a deeper understanding of the problems that MT systems face when translating pronouns, and of the performance of our systems when faced with these problems. Secondly, we lack evaluation methodologies that specifically target pronoun translation and that are capable of providing a detailed overview of system performance. In this paper, we present a graphical tool and an evaluation methodology for manual assessment and investigation of pronoun translation that address both of these factors.

When dealing with pronouns, many of the fundamental assumptions cherished by the MT community break down. MT researchers routinely rely on automatic evaluation metrics such as BLEU (Papineni et al., 2002) to guide their development efforts. These automated metrics typically assume that overlap of the MT output with a human-generated reference translation may be used as a proxy for correctness. This assumption fails for certain types of pronouns. In particular, it does not hold in the important case of *anaphoric pronouns*, which refer back to a mention introduced earlier in the discourse (an *antecedent*): If the pronoun's antecedent is translated in a way that differs from the reference translation, a different pronoun may be required. One that matches the reference translation may in fact be wrong. In less complex cases, too, the syntactic variability in pronoun translation is generally high even in closely parallel texts, which creates difficulties both for translation modelling and for MT evaluation. We hope that our contribution will make it easier for MT researchers to anchor their decisions in descriptive corpus data and face the full complexity of pronoun translation.

2   The PROTEST Pronoun Evaluation Test Suite

To address the problem of evaluation, Hardmeier (2015) suggests using a test suite composed of carefully selected pronoun tokens which can then be checked individually to evaluate pronoun correctness. In Guillou and Hardmeier (2016) we introduce PROTEST, a test suite comprising 250 hand-selected pronoun tokens exposing particular problems in English-French pronoun translation, along with an automatic evaluation script. The pronoun analysis tool and methodology presented here are specifically designed to be used with the PROTEST test suite. They can be applied to any parallel corpus with (manual or automatic) coreference resolution and word alignments, although pro-drop languages might require changes to the guidelines.

The pronoun tokens in PROTEST are extracted from the *DiscoMT2015.test* dataset (Hardmeier et al., 2016), which has been manually annotated according to the ParCor annotation guidelines (Guillou et al., 2014). The pronoun tokens are categorised according to a range of different problems that MT systems face when translating pronouns. At the top level the categories capture pronoun *function*, with four different functions represented in the test suite[3] (Fig. 1). *Anaphoric* pronouns refer to an antecedent. *Pleonastic* pronouns, in contrast, do not refer to anything. *Event reference* pronouns refer to a verb, verb phrase, clause or even an entire sentence. Finally, *addressee reference* pronouns are used to refer to the reader/audience. At a second level of classification, we distinguish other features like morphosyntactic properties, pronoun-antecedent distance, and different types of addressee reference.

The PROTEST test suite comes with an automatic pronoun evaluation tool, which compares the translation of each pronoun token in the MT output with that in the reference translation. For the purpose of automatic evaluation, pronouns are broadly split into two groups. Anaphoric pronouns must meet the following criteria: The translation of both the pronoun and the head of its antecedent must match that in the reference. For all other pronoun functions, only the translation of the pronoun is considered. Pronoun

---

[3] Some categories in the corpus, e.g. *speaker reference*, were excluded from the test suite to focus on systematic divergences between English and French (Guillou and Hardmeier, 2016).

anaphoric	I have a **bicycle**. **It** is red.
pleonastic	**It** is raining.
event	He lost his job. **It** came as a total surprise.
addressee reference	**You**'re welcome.

Fig. 1. Examples of different pronoun functions

translations that do no match the reference are not necessarily incorrect, but must be manually checked. This is a prime use case of the pronoun analysis tool described here.

3   Use Cases and Interface Design

The PROTEST pronoun analysis tool is intended as a platform for *manual inspection* and *evaluation* of pronoun translation examples in parallel text. Our tool provides the researcher or MT system developer with a focused view of the pronoun translation and its context, and it enables the manual annotation of examples for correctness and other relevant features according to the guidelines detailed in Section 4. On certain occasions, for instance when evaluating major development steps in the system, the system developer may decide to conduct a more thorough evaluation involving external annotators. To cater for this, the tool offers the functionality to prepare batches of examples for annotation, which can then be processed in a special, easy-to-use annotator mode. Annotated batches can be fed back into the master file. A translation overview mode then allows the researchers to gain an overview of all annotations for a specific example.

The core component of the analysis tool is the *translation window*. On its left-hand side, the translation window displays a pronoun in the source language and its translation by a given system. The amount of context shown in the translation window is variable and depends on the pronoun function. In the case of anaphoric pronouns, it includes the sentence(s) that contain the antecedent and the pronoun plus one additional sentence of context. For other pronouns, it just shows the sentence containing the pronoun and the one immediately preceding it. The pronoun and its translation are highlighted in the source text and the translation, as too are the antecedent head and its translation, in the case of anaphoric pronouns.

The right-hand side of the translation window comes in two variants, which we call the *annotation panel* (Fig. 2) and the *overview panel* (Fig. 3). The *annotation panel* (Fig. 2) is used by the developer or by annotators for the task of manually evaluating the translation of the pronouns. During manual evaluation, the annotator is asked to make a yes/no judgement as to whether the pronoun has been correctly translated. These judgements are recorded via radio button groups in the top right-hand corner of the window. In the case of anaphoric pronouns, the correctness of the antecedent translation is evaluated in a separate question.

In addition to these formalised judgements, two additional input elements allow annotators to react flexibly to common annotation issues, to create meaningful annotations for examples that are atypical in some way and to supply additional information. The *tag box* makes it possible to assign tags to an example. The guidelines contain instructions

A Graphical Pronoun Analysis Tool for the PROTEST Test Suite

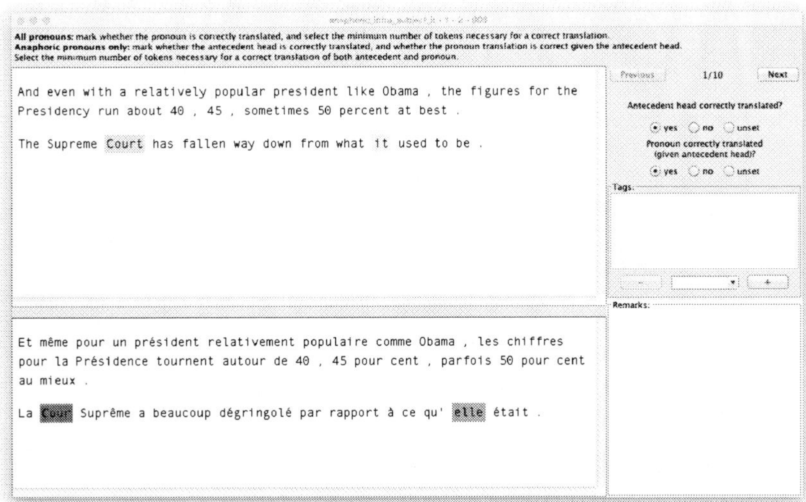

Fig. 2. Translation window with annotation panel

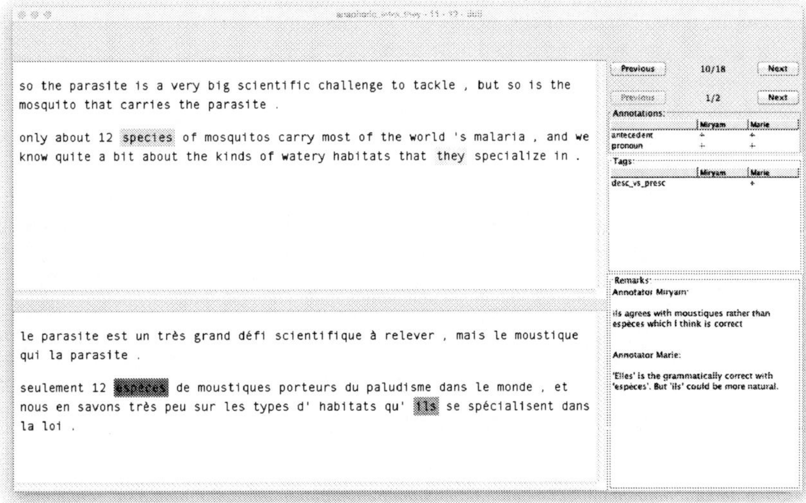

Fig. 3. Translation window with overview panel

on the use of certain tags, and annotators are instructed to be as consistent as possible in their use of tags. The annotation tool does not constrain the tags to a predefined set, allowing annotators to define new tags as the need arises, but provides a drop-down list of existing tags in the corpus to support and encourage consistency. The *remarks* box in the bottom-left corner stores free-form notes about the pronoun translation.

In practical annotation work, we found these two mechanisms extremely useful. Annotation conflicts between our annotators typically arose in borderline cases, where the annotators agreed about their evaluation of the example in principle, but were uncertain about how to encode this according to the formal guidelines. Frequently, they would leave very enlightening comments in the remarks field in those cases, making it easier for us to understand the difficulties they had encountered and the reasoning behind their annotation choices. Moreover, the annotators' free-form comments were very useful as a form of tangible evidence of how they interpreted the guidelines and, consequently, what parts of the guidelines needed to be updated.

In addition to the annotations already discussed, the target text box on the left-hand side of the translation window offers the possibility to click on individual tokens in the translation of the pronoun or, in the anaphoric case, its antecedent to highlight them. We use this functionality to identify, for each example labelled as correct, the minimum set of tokens constituting a correct translation of the pronoun or antecedent. This allows us to distinguish between the tokens making up the core translation and other surrounding tokens that also happen to be word-aligned to the source-language pronoun or antecedent. The annotation guidelines (Section 4) describe the process for assigning judgements and tags to translations, and selecting minimal token sets for correct translations.

Whenever the annotator clicks the "Prev" or "Next" button to navigate to another example, a number of checks are made to detect annotation conflicts such as highlighting tokens in a translation marked as incorrect or failing to highlight tokens in a translation marked as correct. If a conflict is detected, a pop-up dialogue appears, and the annotator has the choice to amend the annotation or to leave it unchanged.

To use and compare annotations created by multiple annotators, the analysis tool offers another view of the translation window, in which the annotation panel is replaced by an overview panel (Fig. 3). The information displayed on this panel is the same as described above, but it shows annotations from multiple annotators simultaneously, and it is not editable. The correctness judgements and tags are shown in tabular form and the remarks field combines notes from all annotators. An additional set of navigation buttons is provided (in the top-right corner) to browse between the tokens highlighted by different annotators.

4   Manual Evaluation Methodology

In this section, we introduce a set of guidelines for manual annotation and evaluation of pronoun translations in the context of our pronoun analysis tool. The aim of the annotation is to assess the ability of MT systems to translate pronouns. It is also possible to use the examples annotated as correctly translated as additional reference translations in conjunction with the automatic pronoun evaluation tool in the PROTEST test suite.

In the annotation, we focus on the correctness of the highlighted pronouns and their antecedents. The correctness of other words in the translated sentences is not considered, except where this makes it impossible to assess the correctness of the pronoun and antecedent head translations. For each example we gather the following information:

- *Overall assessment:* Decide whether or not the pronoun is translated correctly. In the case of anaphoric pronouns, the translation of the pronoun's antecedent head must also be assessed.
- *Token selection:* For those translations marked as "correct", select the minimum set of tokens that constitute a correct translation.
- *Tags:* Certain recurring patterns are marked by assigning *tags*. The set of standard tags and their use is described in Section 4.3.
- *Remarks:* Free-form notes may be added for each example. This function is used to record any information that may be useful in the interpretation or evaluation of the annotations. For example, the annotator may be unsure about the annotation of an example, or may have made assumptions about the interpretation of the text.

Pronoun tokens are annotated according to the general guidelines outlined in Section 4.1. In the case of anaphoric pronouns, additional guidelines apply (see Section 4.2).

4.1 General Guidelines: All Pronouns

The annotator is asked to answer the question: "Pronoun Correctly Translated?". Possible options are "yes" and "no". This question should be answered for all source-language pronouns, regardless of whether they are translated by the MT system. If a pronoun remains untranslated, the annotator should assess whether or not this is a correct translation strategy in this particular case. If the pronoun translation is marked as correct, the next step is to select the *minimum* number of highlighted tokens that constitutes a correct translation of the source-language pronoun.

To enable the use of the annotations as references in an automatic evaluation setting, we emphasise precision over recall and instruct the annotators to reject doubtful cases. We also emphasise natural language use over prescriptive grammar rules in cases where they conflict. In practice the annotators are asked to mark translations as correct only if they feel that the translation is something "natural" that they might say themselves, or that they might expect to hear someone else say. An exception is made for singular addressee reference pronouns, where the correctness decision is made independently of the level of formality ("tu" or "vous") of the French pronoun. The natural level of formality is annotated separately instead (see Section 4.3).

4.2 Anaphoric Pronouns

If the pronoun is anaphoric, it is necessary to consider both the translation of the antecedent head and the pronoun. The *head* of the source-language pronoun's *antecedent* will be highlighted in the interface. If the antecedent head was translated by the MT system, the translations (consisting of one or more tokens) will also be highlighted.

The annotator is first asked to answer the question: "Antecedent Correctly Translated?". Possible options are "yes" and "no". If the antecedent head translation has been marked as correct, the next step is to select the *minimum* number of highlighted tokens that constitutes a correct translation of the source-language antecedent head. To arrive at a truly minimal set, we include noun tokens, but not adjectives or determiners. Multiple tokens may be selected. It is not possible to select tokens that appear outside of the highlighted set of words aligned to the antecedent head in the source.

The annotator is then asked to answer the question: "Pronoun Correctly Translated (given antecedent head)?", again using "yes/no" options. Here a correctly translated pronoun is one that is *compatible* with the translation of the antecedent head, regardless of whether the antecedent head is translated correctly. Compatibility frequently coincides with the notion of morphosyntactic agreement, but it does not always do so. An example of a compatible pronoun-antecedent pair violating morphosyntactic agreement is the use of "singular they" in English to refer to a single person – formally, the pronoun "they" is a plural and does not agree in number with its antecedent, but the use of "they" to refer to singular antecedents is acceptable in English (for example in the case where the gender of the person is unknown) and should therefore be marked as correct. If the pronoun is marked as correct, the minimum number of tokens consisting a correct pronoun translation should be highlighted as in the general case.

4.3 Tags

Tags are used to denote specific recurring patterns, where errors may be present, or to provide additional information that could be useful when interpreting annotations. The following general purpose tags are provided for all pronoun categories.

`bad_translation` is used when the overall sentence translation is so poor that it is not possible to judge whether the translation of the pronoun/antecedent is correct. In this case the example should not be annotated for correctness.

`incorrect_word_alignment` denotes that a pronoun/antecedent translation exists in the translation of the source-language text but is not highlighted due to a problem with the word alignments. In this case the example should not be annotated for correctness.

`noncompositional_translation` is used when the translation as a whole is correct, but the source-language pronoun is aligned to a pronoun with a different function in the target language. A typical example is a referring (event or anaphoric) English pronoun that gets word-aligned to the pleonastic pronoun "il" in the French impersonal construction "il faut" ("it is necessary"). Often such translations are correct, but the French pronoun cannot be said to be a translation of the English one.

`desc_vs_presc` signals a conflict between something that a French speaker might (naturally) say and what French prescriptive grammar rules state.

In the case of anaphoric pronouns, `ant_unsure` indicates uncertainty as to whether the antecedent has been correctly identified in the source language. The antecedents in PROTEST were extracted from manual annotations over the *DiscoMT2015.test* dataset. These annotations are generally of high quality and sometimes the pronoun annotators' doubts are due to the limited context displayed in the pronoun analysis tool, but the possibility of errors in the coreference annotation cannot be completely excluded.

In the specific case of singular, deictic addressee reference pronouns, French makes a distinction between two levels of formality, "tu" and "vous". We view this as a separate problem and do not consider it in the correctness judgements. Instead, the annotators are asked to add one of the tags `politeness_tu`, `politeness_vous` or `politeness_unknown` to each of the examples in this category. The latter tag signals that neither possibility can be ruled out given the available context.

5 Manual Annotation

To demonstrate the use of the pronoun analysis tool for the task of manual annotation, we asked two annotators to annotate a sample of pronoun translations from the DiscoMT 2015 shared task on pronoun translation, an English-to-French MT task. The translations were taken from the official DiscoMT data release (Hardmeier et al., 2016). Both of our annotators are native speakers of French and have a very high standard of English. We gave both of them the same set of 116 pronoun translations produced by MT systems, or taken from the reference translation. The sample set was randomly selected, with the aim of selecting at least 100 pronoun translations from the full set of 1,750 translations, in proportion to the relative size of each pronoun category in PROTEST, and ensuring that at least one translation was included for each category. The full set comprises translations of the 250 pronoun tokens in the test suite, produced by five of the systems submitted to the shared task[4] and the official shared task baseline system, as well as from the human authored reference translation in *DiscoMT2015.test*.

5.1 Results

Table 1 displays the results of the manual annotation of the sample set, completed by two annotators. The "✓" symbol denotes a correct translation, "✗" an incorrect translation and "?" a translation for which no judgement has been provided. Judgements are not provided for bad translations or those with incorrect word alignments.

Inter-annotator agreement scores, calculated using Cohen's Kappa (Cohen, 1960), are displayed in Table 2. Agreement for judgements on antecedent translation are very high, with only one disagreement out of 68 annotations. Agreement is lower for pronoun translations, suggesting that this aspect of the annotation task is more difficult. However, we deem the Kappa score to be high enough to proceed with the annotation of the remaining test suite translations in future work.

Disagreements between two or more annotators can provide a useful starting point for understanding the difficulties of the manual annotation task. Whilst some indication is provided in Table 1, we cannot obtain a complete picture from raw counts alone. To gain a deeper understanding we need to look at the individual pronoun translations and their annotations using the translation window of the pronoun analysis tool (Fig. 3). We can also use the tags and remarks to identify pronoun translations that represent interesting cases. Some examples are discussed in Section 5.2.

---

[4] System A3-108 is omitted due to very poor results in the DiscoMT 2015 shared task evaluation

Category	Count	Pronoun						Antecedent					
		Annotator A			Annotator B			Annotator A			Annotator B		
		✓	✗	?	✓	✗	?	✓	✗	?	✓	✗	?
Anaphoric													
Inter-sentential "it"													
Subject	12	7	3	2	5	5	2	12	0	0	12	0	0
Non-subject	3	2	1	0	1	2	0	3	0	0	3	0	0
Intra-sentential "it"													
Subject	11	10	1	0	10	1	0	11	0	0	11	0	0
Non-subject	8	6	1	1	6	2	0	7	1	0	7	1	0
Inter-sentential "they"	13	9	4	0	8	5	0	13	0	0	13	0	0
Intra-sentential "they"	10	6	4	0	5	5	0	9	0	1	10	0	0
Singular "they"	7	7	0	0	5	1	1	5	2	0	5	2	0
Group "it/they"	4	4	0	0	3	0	1	4	0	0	4	0	0
Event Reference "it"	14	10	4	0	8	6	0	–	–	–	–	–	–
Pleonastic "it"	11	10	1	0	10	1	0	–	–	–	–	–	–
Addressee Reference													
Deictic singular "you"	7	7	0	0	7	0	0	–	–	–	–	–	–
Deictic plural "you"	6	5	0	1	5	1	0	–	–	–	–	–	–
Generic "you"	10	10	0	0	10	0	0	–	–	–	–	–	–
Total	116	93	19	4	83	29	4	64	3	1	65	3	0

Table 1. Annotation results over a sample set of 116 pronoun translations

Judgement	Total Annotations	Disagreements	Kappa Score
Pronoun	116	14	0.69
Antecedent	68	1	0.85

Table 2. Inter-Annotator Agreement Scores

5.2 Discussion

As an example of where the two annotators disagreed, consider Example 1, in which the anaphoric, intra-sentential pronoun "they" refers to "things". The MT system translated the antecedent as "choses" [fem. pl.] and the pronoun as "ils" [masc. pl.]. Both annotators marked the translation of the antecedent as correct, but differed in their judgement of the pronoun. Annotator B marked the pronoun translation as incorrect. Annotator A marked it as correct and added the desc_vs_presc tag, indicating that it is something a French speaker might say, in a very casual manner, despite it being incorrect according to French grammar rules. This difference in descriptive vs. prescriptive grammar highlights a problem that researchers should consider: Whether to be guided by grammar rules or by what is observed in the data, i.e. what people actually say, or how they write.

Example 1.
Source: Yeah, I think many of the **things** we just talked about are like that, where **they**'re really – I almost use the economic concept of additionality, which means that you're doing something that wouldn't happen unless you were actually doing it.

MT Output: Oui, je pense que beaucoup des **choses** que nous avons seulement parlé sont comme ça, où **ils** sont vraiment – j'ai failli utiliser le concept économique de l'additionnalité, ce qui signifie que tu fais quelque chose qui n'arriverait pas si vous étiez réellement le faire.

Another problem for MT systems is the translation of named entities. Both annotators agreed that had the antecedent in the MT output of Example 2 been "Deep Mind" (rather than the literal translation "profond esprit") then the pronoun translation "Ils" [pl.] would have been acceptable, despite not agreeing with the antecedent [sg.].

Example 2.
Source: So I think Deep Mind, what's really amazing about **Deep Mind** is that it can actually – they're learning things in this unsupervised way. **They** started with video games...
MT Output: Je pense donc que l'esprit profond, ce qui est vraiment incroyable **profond esprit** est qu'il peut en fait – ils apprennent des choses dans ce sans supervision. **Ils** ont commencé avec des jeux vidéo ...

Politeness is also a problem for MT systems. In Example 3, the correct translation of the English pronoun "you" requires knowledge of the relationship between the speaker and addressee. Here the annotators commented that it would be unusual for a (modern) French speaker to use the formal "vous" when speaking to their Grandpa.

Example 3.
Source: I mean, I would call him, and I'd be like, "Listen, Grandpa, I really need this camera. **You** don't understand.
MT Output: je compte, je l'appellerais et je serais comme, « listen, Grandpa, j'ai vraiment besoin de cet appareil photo. **vous** ne comprenez pas.

In the set of 116 translations, 8 were marked as noncompositional_translation by at least one annotator, including this example taken from the reference translation:

Example 4.
Source: The big labs have shown that fusion is doable, and now there are small companies that are thinking about that, and they say, it's not that it cannot be done, but **it**'s how to make it cost-effectively.
Reference: Les grands labos ont montré qu'elle était faisable, et maintenant des petites entreprises y pensent et disent : certes, ce n'est pas impossible, mais [**il** faut] que ce soit rentable.

In Example 4, the English pleonastic pronoun "it" is aligned to the French pronoun "il". However, "il faut" (meaning "it is necessary") is a fixed expression and as such, the French pronoun "il" cannot be considered a direct translation of "it". In scenarios such as these, the annotators are instructed to evaluate the translation of the clause instead of the pronoun in isolation. Both annotators marked the translation as correct, which one might expect given that the French translation is taken from the reference. Examples such as this present a problem for both manual and automated evaluation of pronoun translation in MT, which until now has considered pronoun translation at the token level.

6 Related Work

The PROTEST pronoun analysis tool shares some similarities with the interface for the pronoun selection task (Hardmeier, 2014) which has been used by Guillou and Webber (2015) and in the manual evaluation of the DiscoMT 2015 shared task on pronoun translation (Hardmeier et al., 2015). In the pronoun selection task, pronouns in the source-language text are highlighted and their corresponding translations in the MT output are replaced with a placeholder. The role of the human annotator is to select, from a given list of options, which pronoun should replace the placeholder. In this way, the annotator is not biased by the pronoun translation in the MT output. In contrast, our tool presents the annotator with the translation of the pronoun in context and poses questions about its translation. Furthermore, the pronoun analysis tool is not just an annotation interface. It enables researchers to examine translations in detail and to browse and compare translations by different systems, and annotations by one or more annotators.

In spirit, the tool is similar to other user interfaces for manual data inspection such as the `analysis.perl` utility for BLEU score analysis distributed with Moses (Koehn et al., 2007) or the Blast interface for manual error analysis in MT output (Stymne, 2011). Our tool is novel in that it focuses on a specific linguistic problem in translation and links manual inspection and evaluation with a manually selected test suite and the possibility of feeding back the annotations into a semi-automatic evaluation process.

The underlying approach of the automatic evaluation script included as part of PROTEST is similar in its methodology to the ACT metric for assessing the translation of discourse connectives (Hajlaoui and Popescu-Belis, 2013). Like PROTEST, ACT attempts to match translations in the MT output with those in the reference translation and refers mismatches for manual evaluation. ACT, however, is accompanied by neither an interface for, nor guidelines for manual evaluation.

7 Conclusions and Future Work

We have presented a graphical pronoun analysis tool for the PROTEST test suite. It supports the manual evaluation of pronoun translations through manual annotation by one or more annotators. Researchers are provided with the means to manually examine individual pronoun translations and to browse and compare manual annotations. We have also presented a set of annotation guidelines underlying a simple, but useful methodology for manually and semi-automatically evaluating pronouns in MT output. We have tested the use of the tool and the guidelines by annotating a small set of pronoun tokens translated by systems submitted to the DiscoMT 2015 shared task on pronoun translation, and demonstrated the type of insights that this methodology has to offer. A practical conclusion that we have already drawn for our own work is that the problem of translating event pronouns deserves greater attention in future research.

In future work we plan to complete the manual annotation of the translation of all 250 PROTEST pronoun tokens by the DiscoMT 2015 systems. This will provide a set of manually verified translations for use with the automatic evaluation in PROTEST. Both the annotation tool described in this paper and the data sets will be published in the LINDAT data repository.

Acknowledgements

We would like to thank Marie Dubremetz and Miryam de Lhoneux for manually annotating the output of the DiscoMT 2015 systems. This work was funded by the Swedish Research Council under grant 2012-916 *Discourse-Oriented Statistical Machine Translation* (research) and the European Association for Machine Translation (annotation).

References

Jacob Cohen. A Coefficient of Agreement for Nominal Scales. *Educational and Psychological Measurement*, 20(1), 1960.

Liane Guillou. Improving pronoun translation for statistical machine translation. In *Proceedings of the Student Research Workshop at the 13th Conference of the European Chapter of the Association for Computational Linguistics*, pages 1–10, Avignon (France), April 2012.

Liane Guillou and Christian Hardmeier. PROTEST: A test suite for evaluating pronouns in machine translation. In *Proceedings of the Eleventh Language Resources and Evaluation Conference (LREC'16)*, Portorož (Slovenia), May 2016.

Liane Guillou and Bonnie Webber. Analysing ParCor and its translations by state-of-the-art SMT systems. In *Proceedings of the Second Workshop on Discourse in Machine Translation*, pages 24–32, Lisbon, Portugal, September 2015.

Liane Guillou, Christian Hardmeier, Aaron Smith, Jörg Tiedemann, and Bonnie Webber. ParCor 1.0: A parallel pronoun-coreference corpus to support statistical MT. In *Proceedings of the Tenth Language Resources and Evaluation Conference (LREC'14)*, pages 3191–3198, Reykjavík (Iceland), 2014.

Najeh Hajlaoui and Andrei Popescu-Belis. Assessing the accuracy of discourse connective translations: Validation of an automatic metric. In *14th International Conference on Intelligent Text Processing and Computational Linguistics*, page 12. University of the Aegean, Springer, March 2013.

Christian Hardmeier. *Discourse in Statistical Machine Translation*, volume 15 of *Studia Linguistica Upsaliensia*. Acta Universitatis Upsaliensis, Uppsala, 2014.

Christian Hardmeier. On statistical machine translation and translation theory. In *Proceedings of the Second Workshop on Discourse in Machine Translation*, pages 168–172, Lisbon (Portugal), September 2015.

Christian Hardmeier and Marcello Federico. Modelling pronominal anaphora in statistical machine translation. In *Proceedings of the Seventh International Workshop on Spoken Language Translation (IWSLT)*, pages 283–289, Paris (France), 2010.

Christian Hardmeier, Preslav Nakov, Sara Stymne, Jörg Tiedemann, Yannick Versley, and Mauro Cettolo. Pronoun-focused MT and cross-lingual pronoun prediction: Findings of the 2015 DiscoMT shared task on pronoun translation. In *Proceedings of the 2nd Workshop on Discourse in Machine Translation (DiscoMT 2015)*, pages 1–16, Lisbon (Portugal), 2015.

Christian Hardmeier, Jörg Tiedemann, Preslav Nakov, Sara Stymne, and Yannick Versely. DiscoMT 2015 Shared Task on Pronoun Translation, 2016. LINDAT/CLARIN digital library at Institute of Formal and Applied Linguistics, Charles University in Prague. http://hdl.handle.net/11372/LRT-1611.

Philipp Koehn, Hieu Hoang, Alexandra Birch, et al. Moses: Open source toolkit for Statistical Machine Translation. In *Annual Meeting of the Association for Computational Linguistics: Demonstration session*, pages 177–180, Prague (Czech Republic), 2007.

Ronan Le Nagard and Philipp Koehn. Aiding pronoun translation with co-reference resolution. In *Proceedings of the Joint Fifth Workshop on Statistical Machine Translation and MetricsMATR*, pages 252–261, Uppsala (Sweden), July 2010.

Michal Novák. Utilization of anaphora in machine translation. In *Week of Doctoral Students 2011 Proceedings of Contributed Papers, Part I*, pages 155–160, Prague (Czech Republic), 2011.

Kishore Papineni, Salim Roukos, Todd Ward, and Wei-Jing Zhu. BLEU: A method for automatic evaluation of machine translation. In *Proceedings of the 40th Annual Meeting of the Association for Computational Linguistics*, pages 311–318, Philadelphia (Pennsylvania, USA), 2002.

Sara Stymne. Blast: A tool for error analysis of machine translation output. In *Proceedings of the ACL-HLT 2011 System Demonstrations*, pages 56–61, Portland (Oregon, USA), June 2011.

Received May 9, 2016 , accepted May 16, 2016

Baltic J. Modern Computing, Vol. 4 (2016), No. 2, 331-345

Measuring Cognitive Translation Effort
with Activity Units

Moritz SCHAEFFER[1], Michael CARL[2,4], Isabel LACRUZ[3],
Akiko AIZAWA[4]

[1] Johannes Gutenberg University Mainz, An der Hochschule 2 76726 Germersheim, Germany
[2] Copenhagen Business School, Dalgas Have 15, 2000 Frederiksberg, Denmark
[3] Kent State University, 475 Janik Drive, Kent, Ohio 44242
[4] National Insitute of Informatics, 2-1-2 Hitotsubashi, Chiyoda, Tokyo 101-0003, Japan

mschaeffer@uni-mainz.de, mc.ibc@cbs.dk, ilacruz@kent.edu,
aizawa@nii.ac.jp

Abstract

Despite the increased quality of Machine Translation output, human interaction will remain a crucial activity to guarantee the quality of the final translation products. Human-computer interaction in translation will likely be the more successful the more we understand the properties and complementarities of both partners. This paper traces cognitive approaches in machine translation back to the mid-1980s and argues that we now have the technologies available that will allow us to eventually arrive at an in-depth understanding of the human translation processes. It illustrates some of the research methods in empirical translation process research and suggests ngrams of Activity Units for measuring the translation process.

1. Introduction

As a reaction to the then predominant rule-based translation paradigm, Nagao (1984) suggests a cognitive approach to translation, which mimics the human translation process. He states that "[m]an does not translate a simple sentence by doing deep linguistic analysis, rather, [...] first, by properly decomposing an input sentence into certain fragmental phrases ..., then by translating these phrases into other language phrases, and finally by properly composing these fragmental translations into one long sentence." Based on this model, a large number of different example-based MT (EBMT) systems have been developed, which Carl and Way (2003) classify into:
- Pure EBMT: All translation relevant processing takes place at run-time
- Generalizing EBMT: preprocessing of translation templates
- Tree-based EBMT: preprocessing of dependency and phrase-structure trees

As a simulation of the human translation process, and in line with many earlier models of the human translation process (e.g. Nida, 1964), these systems assume that translators proceed:

- Sequentially, in a sentence-by-sentence (or phrase-by-phrase) mode
- Stratificationally, by decomposing – transferring – recomposing

Figure 1 visualises sequences of activities as hypothesized by Nagao's model as successive activities of reading "certain fragmental phrases" of source text words, followed by typing of the corresponding string of TT words. Figure 1 shows such a scenario on the basis of artificial data. The translation progression graph plots the English source text ("the awareness of other hospital staff put a stop") on the left vertical axis and its Spanish translation ("la atencion de otros empleados del hospital puso fin") on the right side. The horizontal axis represents a time line on which the translator's activities, such as keystrokes (black), fixations on words in the source text (blue dots) and words in the target text (green diamonds) are plotted. Figure 1 shows an almost linear fragmented translation production with a 1-to-2 alignment (hospital → del hospital) and a 2-to-1 translation alignment (a stop → fin) and a syntactic re-ordering (hospital staff → empleados del hospital).

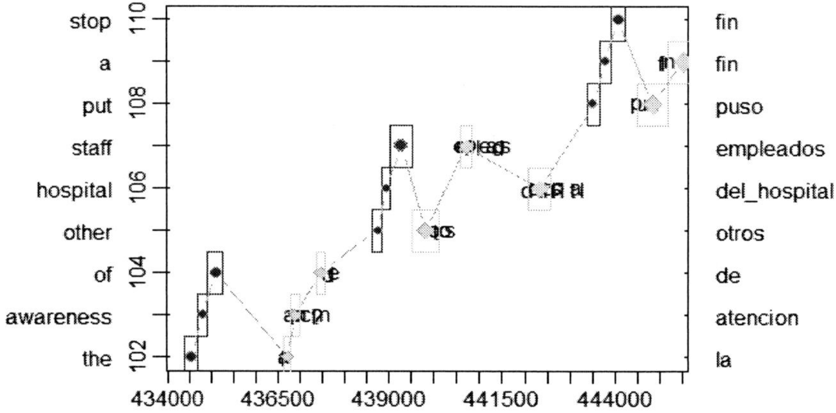

Figure 1. Visualisation of an artificial scanpath exemplifying Nida's / Nagao's sequential / stratificational model of the human translation process.

Translation process research in the past years suggests that translation processes only exceptionally take place in such a linear manner, whereas often iterative and concurrent processes can be observed. However none of the EBMT systems, and for that matter of MT systems in general, are based on actual empirical investigations of the human translation process. The sequential and stratificational nature of the (human) translation and post-editing processes is just taken for granted.

In this paper we present novel methods to analyse empirical translation process data which suggests a more complex picture of the translation process. We look at pauses during typing activity, which have been taken as indicators of cognitive effort in translation and post-editing (Jakobsen, 1998, O'Brien, 2006). On a large data set which was collected in various studies over the past 8 years[1], we compute the pause-word ratio (PWR, Lacruz et al. 2014) which aims at measuring translation difficulties based on the pausing and typing structure. We examine 2101 English → Danish, Spanish, German, Chinese and Japanese translations segments and 1783 English → Spanish, German, Chinese and Japanese post-editing segments, which are extracted from the KTHJ08, BML12, SG12, MS12, ENJA15 and NJ12 studies in the TPR-DB which were produced by 147 different translators with different degrees of translation expertise.

We show that the PWR correlates with a gaze based translation difficult index (TDI) introduced by Mishra et al (2013). Then we suggest Activity Units as a means to analyse in more detail gazing behaviour during text production pauses.

2. The Pause-Word Ratio

A central question in translation and in MT post-editing is related to measuring the cognitive effort involved in the translation production. Lacruz et al. (2014) observe that post-editors proceed in sequences of typing activities interrupted by relatively short pauses, between 300 ms and 2,000ms. Consequently, these authors develop the pause-to-word ratio (PWR), based on the assumption that pauses between keystrokes provide information on cognitive effort, where higher PWR values are associated with more cognitive effort.

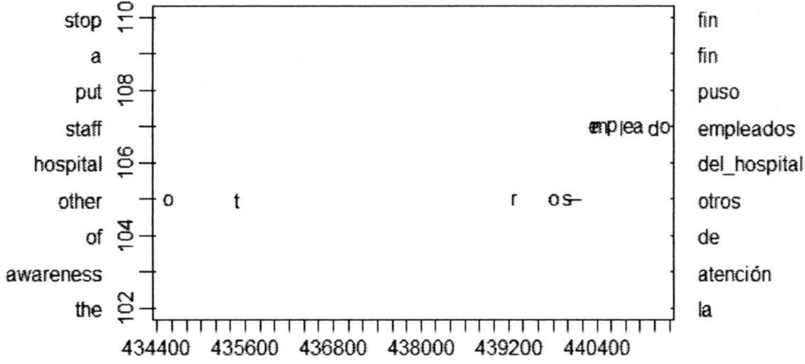

Figure 2. Translation Keystrokes in time

Figure 2 plots a translation progression graph in which a translator produces the translation of English "the awareness of other hospital staff" into Spanish "la atención de otros empleados del hospital"; it shows the distribution of the keystrokes within a

---

[1] The data can be downloaded free of charge from the CRITT TPR-DB the TPR-DB:
https://sites.google.com/site/centretranslationinnovation/tpr-db.
Carl et al (2016) provides a comprehensive introduction to the database and its features.

sequence of approximately 6.7 seconds in which the Spanish translation "otros empleados" (other staff) is typed. There are three longer pauses of approximately 940 ms between the typing of "o" and "t", a pause of 3.8 seconds between the typing of "t" and "r" and a pause of 530 ms between typing "r" and "os empleados". All other inter-keystrokes intervals amount to less than 300 ms.

Sequences of successive keystrokes can be fragmented into segments of coherent text production (i.e. typing bursts), where each production contains at least one keystroke.

The length and duration of a production P depends on the gap of time G between two successive keystrokes: a Production Unit P_i ends if the gap between the last keystroke in P_i and the first keystroke in P_{i+1} exceeds a pre-defined threshold T. The keystrokes of an entire translation session are thus fragmented into successive gaps G_i and typing bursts P_i.

The session initial first gap G_1 can be shorter than the threshold T. A production P contributes to the production of one target text segment TS, and each keystroke K_k in P contributes to exactly one word within the TS. If two successive keystrokes K_k and K_{k+1} are part of two segments TS_t and TS_{t+1}, a unit boundary is inserted so that K_k is the last keystroke in P_i and K_{k+1} is the first keystroke in P_{i+1} even if the gap G_{k+1} between K_k and K_{k+1} is shorter than the threshold T. P_i will be part for the production of segment TS_t and P_{i+1} will be considered part for the production of segment TS_{t+1}. The production of a segment TS is thus made up of p units $\{G_1 , P_1\} \dots \{G_p , P_p\}$. The revision of a segment can lead to non-consecutive typing activities. For instance, a first draft of a segment TS_t may be produced with units $\{G_1 , P_1\} \dots \{G_m , P_m\}$ and a revision of that segment is done at a later stage with units $\{G_{n+1} , P_{n+1}\} \dots \{G_p , P_p\}$ while units $\{G_{m+1} , P_{m+1}\} \dots \{G_n , P_n\}$ are part of one or more other segments. The segment TS_t is thus edited twice. The following features are thus computed for each segment TS:

- *SegInitialGap*: duration of the first gap durations G_1 in TS
- *ProductionGap:* sum of the gap durations G_2 to gap G_p
- *ProductionDur*: sum of the production durations $P_1 \dots P_p$
- *Duration:* production duration of the segment (sum of P and G)
- *ProductionNum*: number 'p' of units $\{G,P\}$ in TS
- *Nedit*: number of revisions of the segment

The above definitions lead to the following equation:

$$Duration = SegInitialGap + ProductionDur + ProductionGap$$

In addition, the *ProductionDur* and the *ProductionGap* are segmented differently according to a thresholds T. Five different thresholds are currently implemented in the TPR-DB, which lead to different values of the **dur*, **gap*, and **num* features, as shown in the Table 1.

Different thresholds segment the keystroke data in different ways, but the translation duration remains the same. That is, the sum of *ProductionDuration + ProductionGap* is identical irrespectively of the thresholds. Thus:

$$Mdur+Mgap = Sdur+Sgap = Pdur+Pgap = Ldur+Lgap = Kdur+Kgap$$

Table 1. Features for different thresholds in the TPR-DB

Unit type	Threshold (T)	Production *dur, gap, num*	PWR
M-Unit	300ms	Mdur, Mgap, Mnum	PWR300 = Mgap / #ST tokens
S-Unit	500ms	Sdur, Sgap, Snum	PWR500 = Sgap / #ST tokens
P-Unit	1000ms	Pdur, Pgap, Pnum	PWR1000 = Pgap / #ST tokens
L-Unit	2000ms	Ldur, Lgap, Lnum	PWR2000 = Lgap / #ST tokens
K-Unit	5000ms	Kdur, Kgap, Knum	PWR5000 = Kgap / #ST tokens

3. The translation difficulty index (TDI)

Mishra et al (2013) develop a Translation Difficulty Index (TDI) which aims at predicting the effort during translation, measured in terms of the sum of ST and TT reading times (TDI score). They show that the TDI score correlates with the degree of polysemy, structural complexity and length of ST segments. They train a Support Vector Machine on observed eye movement data and predicted the TDI score of unseen data during translation on the basis of the linguistic features.

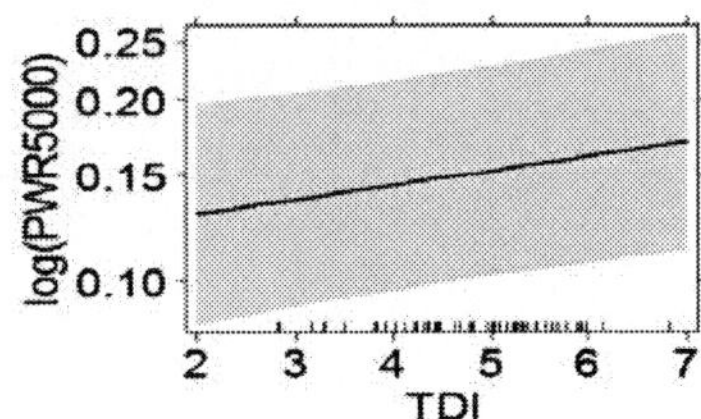

Figure 3. Plot of the effect of TDI on (log) PWR

The prediction was relatively accurate (MSE = 12.88), but to our knowledge, the TDI measure has not been tested on new data. In the next section we test the TDI score for its prediction of the PWR score.

4. Correlation of TDI and PWR

The data used in Mishra et al (2013) were 80 English source sentences translated into Spanish, Danish and Hindi. For the current purpose we use 1476 English sentences translated into Spanish, Danish, Hindi, Chinese, German and Japanese which is a subset of the 2101 segments mentioned in the itroduction (segments with PWR=0 were excluded). These segments include the 80 sentences used by Mishra et al.

For all the analyses in the present study, R (R Development Core Team, 2014) and the lme4 (Bates et al 2014) and languageR (Baayen, 2013) packages were used to perform linear mixed-effects models (LMEMs). To test for significance, the R package lmerTest (Kuznetsova, Christensen, and Brockhoff, 2014) was used.

The LMEM for experiment 1 had the following random variables: item, participant, text and target language. PWR was log transformed because it was not normally distributed. The predictor was the TDI score. TDI had a significant (β=0.056, SE=0.026, t=2.137, p< .05) positive effect on the PWR with a pause threshold of 5000ms (see *Table* 1).

This result validates the TDI as a good predictor of translation effort and it also validates PWR as a good measure of effort during translation and post-editing (Lacruz et al 2014). However, it does not explain what exactly happens during the pauses.

5. Activity Units

The PWR analysis does not explain what happens within the pauses and the TDI score does not differentiate when a translator is looking where on the source or target texts. As

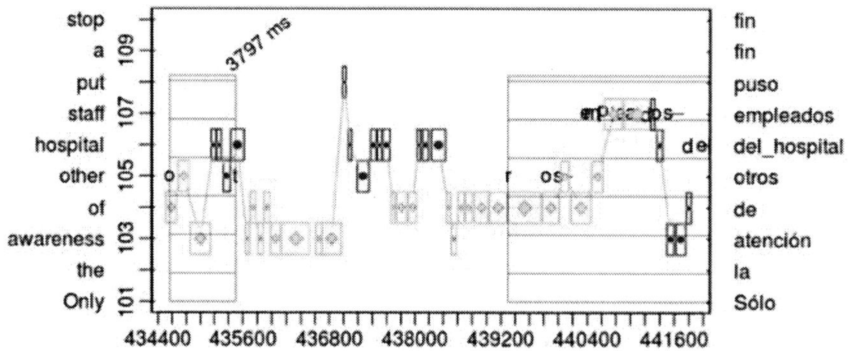

Figure 4. Translation segment of Fig. 1 with keystrokes and fixation data

eye movements are independent from finger movements, there exist several kinds of sequential or concurrent gazing and typing activities which – as we will show - carry important information. As an illustration consider Figure 4 which is a replication of Figure 2 and which shows two typing bursts "ot" and "ros empleados" (in dashed boxes, as generated by the 1000ms threshold). The two Production Units are separated by a 3.8 sec typing pause. The translation progression graph shows, in addition, the gaze behaviour as the eyes move back and forth between the source text (blue dots) and the target window (green diamonds). While the PWR takes into account the pausing information, TDI would predict the sum of the gaze durations. However, both measures ignore how the eyes move across the texts and how the eyes and hands are coordinated: there are concurrent gaze activities on the source or the target text during text production and sequential stretches of source or target reading during the typing pauses, of different length and location. For instance, when typing "ot", the translator monitors the production of "o" in the target text and gazes at the source text while typing "t".

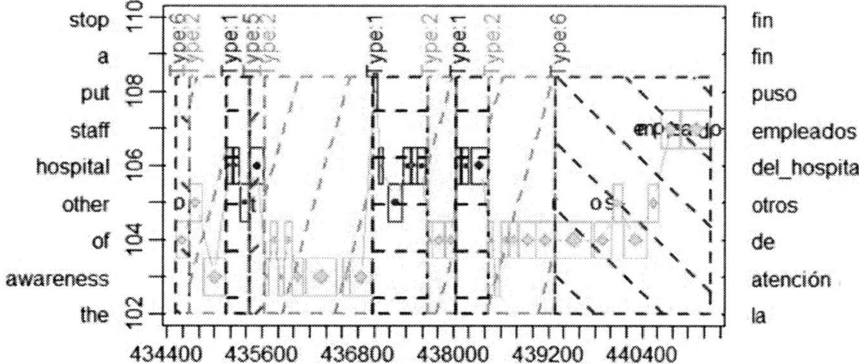

Figure 5. Translation segment of Fig. 4 segmented into ten successive Activity Units

In contrast to the PWR and TDI metrics, Activity Units take this information into account. Similar to (Carl et al, 2016) we make a distinction between 6 different basic types of activities[2]:

- type 1: ST reading
- type 2: TT reading
- type 4: translation typing (no gaze data recorded)
- type 5: ST reading and typing (touch typing)
- type 6: TT reading and typing (translation monitoring)
- type 8: no gaze or typing activity recorded for more than 5 seconds

Figure 5 shows the segmentation of the same data into Activity Units. As can be seen, taking into account the gaze activities allows for a much finer-grained fragmentation of the data into the six types of activity. The first activity in Figure 5 consists of concurrent TT reading (gaze on the translation of word 104) while typing "o", the first letter of the translation for ST word 105 (type 6). In the following typing pause of 940 ms, the eyes first hover over the beginning of the translation of ST words 105 (i.e. the just typed "o") and the translation of word 103 (atención).

---

[2] The Activity Unit of type 7, as suggested in (Carl et al, 2016), which entails concurrent type 1, 2 and 4 behaviour is not assumed here. Instead the activities were split into the six types above.

Table 2. Features which describe the ten Activity Units from Fig. 5

Time	Type	Dur	nKey	nFix	DFix	ScSpan	Turn	SD
434515	6	172	1	1	1	0	0	0
434687	2	469	0	2	2	2	0	1.41
435156	1	281	0	3	2	1	0	0.58
435437	5	203	1	1	1	0	0	0
435640	2	1344	0	8	2	1	3	0.5
436984	1	687	0	6	3	3	1	0.91
437671	2	360	0	3	1	0	0	0
438031	1	422	0	3	1	0	0	0
438453	2	843	0	6	2	1	1	0.41
439296	6	1985	11	7	3	2	2	0.85

This TT reading activity (type 2) is followed by ST reading (type 1) of word 106 (hospital) and 105 (other). The gaze then remains on the source text while "t" is typed which is an activity of type 5. After this, the long pause of 3.7 seconds is structured into five alternating Activity Units of type 2-1-2-1-2 in which the translator seems to develop

Table 3. Correlation matrix for scanpath measures

	nFix	DFix	ScSpan	Turn	SD
Dur	0.71	0.68	0.38	0.72	0.26
nFix		0.83	0.40	0.88	0.25
DFix			0.57	0.87	0.39
ScSpan				0.42	0.93
Turn					0.26

and check a translation strategy for the following noun phrase before, in an activity of concurrent typing and TT monitoring (type 6), "ros empleados" is produced without much hesitation. For each Activity Unit, a number of features are extracted, most of which relate to gaze patterns:

- *Dur*: is the duration in ms of the Activity Unit.
- *nKey*: count of the keystrokes during the Activity Unit.
- *nFix*: number of fixations in the Activity Unit.
- *DFix*: number of different words fixated.
- *ScSpan*: span of the gaze path calculated as difference between largest and smallest word
- *Turn*: moves from regression to progression or vice versa.
- *SD*: standard deviation of median word fixations.

The features *DFix*, *ScSpan*, *Turn* and *SD* describe the linearity of the sequence of fixations in an Activity Unit for which eye movements have been recorded (type 1,2,5 or 6). If *DFix* equals *nFix*, then each word within an Activity Unit has only been fixated once. A large *ScSpan* (scanpath span) occurs if long stretches of text are read, and when the distance between fixated words is large, as indexed by the sequential numbering of words. *SD* is 0 if only one word is fixated. It becomes larger the more words are fixated far away from the median fixated word in a scanpath.

Table 2 shows the extracted features for the 10 units in Figure 5. It shows the starting time and the duration of each of the Activity Units together with the six extracted features.

Table 4. Frequency distributions of bigrams

Bigram	Freq
1_2	0.45
1_5	0.34
1_6	0.20
Total	**0.99**

Correlations between *Dur*, *nFix*, *DFix*, *ScSpan*, Turn and *SD* are relatively high – the longer a coherent reading activity is (*Dur*), the more likely it is that more different words are fixated (*DFix*), resulting in a larger *ScSpan*. It is also more likely that progressions and regressions occur (higher Turn) (see Table 3).

6. Sequences of Activity Units

Martínez-Gómez et al. (2014) cluster sequences of translation events and find that concurrent reading and translation typing correlates with translator experience; i.e. experienced translators are better able to distribute their attention on ST reading and TT production. We investigate ngrams (bigrams and trigrams) of Activity Units to assess fluent translation production and the typical gazing patterns during effortful translation production.

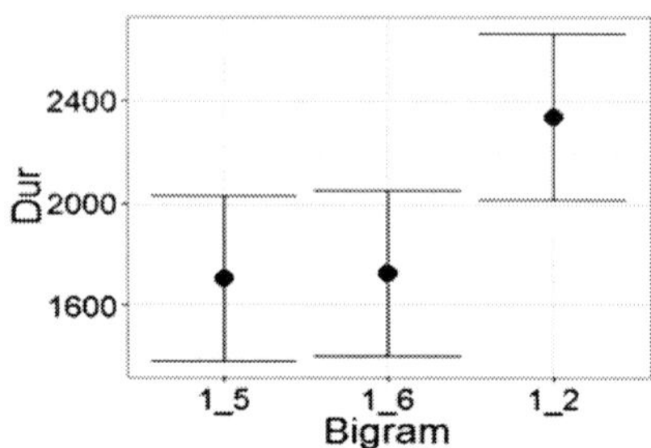

Figure 6. The effect of ST reading duration (Type 1) on subsequent activity (Type 2, 5, 6)

The same data as the one used above was used in this experiment. However, rather than using complete segments, we extract all bigrams and trigrams of Activity Units from the translation drafting phase (Jakobsen 2002) which start with type 1 (ST reading). This resulted in 30,803 Activity Unit bigrams. The three bigrams shown in Table 4 made up more than 99% of the data. Other bigrams (1_4 and 1_8) had a frequency of less than 0.01 and were excluded.

The LMEM for experiment 2 had the following random variables: participant, text and target language. The predictor was the ngram and all of the scanpath measures described above in Table 3 and as measured on the Activity Units of type 1, were entered as dependent variables of the LMEMs. Sliding contrasts were applied to the bigrams. As all scanpath measures correlate, results for the other measures were very similar in size and significance.

There is no significant difference in the duration of Activity Units type 1 followed by either type 5 or 6. However, the difference in *Dur* between bigrams 1_2 and 1_6 was highly significant.

Similarly, the standard deviation (*SD*) from the median word fixation within a scanpath in an Activity Unit of type 1 is lower if the subseqent activity consists of typing. The difference in the *SD* value of Activity Units of type 1 followed by type 5 as compared to those followed by type 6 was relatively small, but highly significant (β = 0.61, SE= 0.14, *t*= 4.28, p< .001). However, the difference between the *SD* of Activity Units of type 1 followed by those of type 2 was much larger as compared to those which were followed by Activity Units of type 6 (β = *1.66*, SE= 0.14, *t*= 11.99, p< .001).

This suggests that the longer and the less linear a scanpath on the ST is, the more likely it is that translators will read the TT immediately after reading the ST. And conversely, the shorter and the more linear a scan path on the ST the more likely it is that translators will start typing immediately after reading the ST.

7. Trigrams of Activity Units

The duration and scanpath linearity of Activity Unit 1 has only an effect on the subsequent activity but not on later units: Trigrams showed a very similar picture to those in bigrams. The frequency distribution of trigrams is shown in Table 5 (trigrams

Table 5: Frequency distributions of Activity Unit trigrams in translation

Trigram	Freq
1_2_1	0.24
1_5_1	0.21
1_2_6	0.18
1_6_2	0.12
1_5_6	0.07
Total	**0.82**

which occurred with a frequency of 4% or less were excluded). Sliding contrasts were applied to the trigrams. There was no significant difference in the SD of Activity Units type 1 for trigrams 1_5_1 and 1_5_6. The difference between trigrams 1_5_2 and 1_5_1 was not significant either. The difference between trigrams 1_6_2 and 1_5_2 was significant (β = 0.83, SE= 0.28, t= 2.97, p< .01). The difference between trigrams 1_2_6 and 1_6_2 was highly significant and relatively large (β = 1.41, SE = 0.19, t=7.53, p< .001). The difference between trigrams 1_2_1 and 1_2_6 was also highly significant, but smaller (β =0.64, SE = 0.16, t=4.06, p< .001). The effect on *Dur* and all other scanpath measures was similar in size and significance, but, more importantly: trigrams containing typing activity in the second place were associated with more linear scanpaths of the initial activity type 1.

Properties of Activity Units of type 1 is therefore restricted to the immediately following Activity Units but has no effect on later activities.

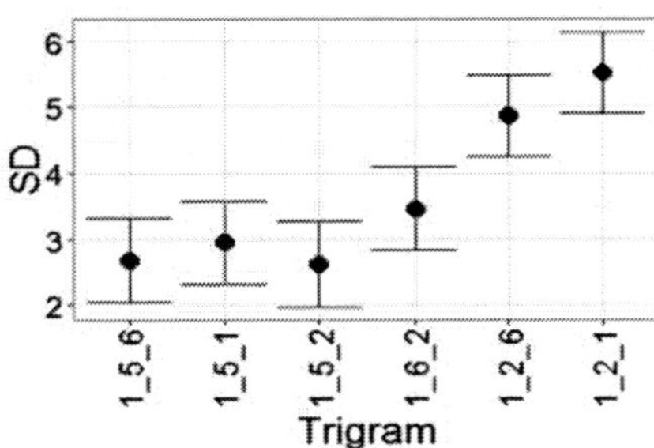

Figure 7. The effect of fixations *SD* during Type 1 activity on next tro subsequent Activity Units

8. PWR and Activity Units in Post- editing

While the previous sections looked at translational behaviour in from-scratch translation, in this section we look into post-editing behaviour. For this investigation we examine all 2101 translations segments and 1783 post-editing segments, as described in the introduction.

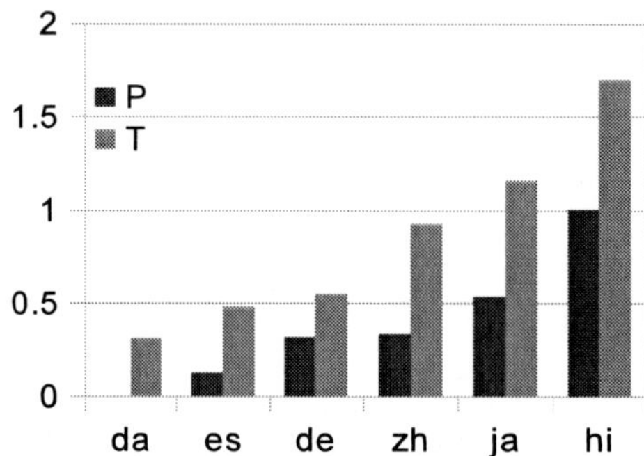

Figure 8. PWR scores for post-editing (P)
and from-scratch translation (T) for different language pairs

1. PWR scores are generally lower during post-editing than during from-scratch translation, indicating a lower cognitive load according to the PWR metric. Figure 8 plots PWR1000 scores, it suggests that the European languages (Danish, Spanish, German) are easier to translate from English than the Asian languages (Chinese, Japanese, Hindi), although the graphs do not take into account the expertise of the translators.

Table 6. Frequency distribution of Activity Unit following Type 1 for post-editing and translation

Bigram	Freq-P	Freq-T
1_2	0.81	0.45
1_5	0.10	0.34
1_6	0.08	0.20
Total	**0.99**	**0.99**

2. The transitions between Activity Units is differently distributed for translation and post-editing. As shown in Table 6, 81% of all the outgoing transitions from 2.

Activity Unit of type 1 during post-editing go to unit of type 2. That is almost twice as much as during translation (see Table 4, which is reproduced for conveniance in Table 6 as column Freq-T). Only in 18% of the cases do post-editors engage in a typing activity after ST reading, as compared to 54% in the translation condition. This suggest that much more reading back-and forth between ST and TT takes place during post-editing than during translation.

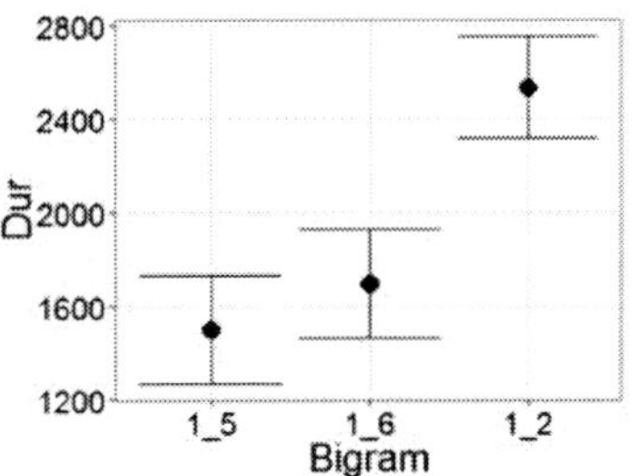

Figure 9. The effect of ST reading duration (Type 1)
on the subsequent Activity Units during post-editing

3. However, it is interesting to note that the relationship between the duration of the ST scanpath and subsequent Activity Units (typing or TT reading) is similar in both translation and post-editing. After an ST reading activity of around 2.5 seconds, translators as well as post-editors are likely to switch to TT reading (Type 2) while for shorter ST reading activities of about 1,5 to 2 seconds, both translators and post-editors are more likely to engage in TT typing.

9. Conclusion

Much of recent investigations in translation process research has sought to identify characteristics of either the ST or the TT in order to predict how difficult it is to process or produce a string of words during translation or post-editing (e.g. O'Brien 2005, Dragsted 2012, Alves and Gonçalves 2013, Schaeffer et al 2016). Lacruz et al (2014) take a different approach and associate pauses in the translation production process (i.e. gaps in typing activities) with cognitive meta-activity. In this paper we investigate the gazing patterns that take place during keystroke pauses to assess what happens during typing pauses that makes translation more or less effortful. Recorded gaze data fills the typing pauses and make it possible to "identify the specific motivation of a particular pause" (Kumpulainen, 2015: p 47). Our research shows that translation processes are much less sequential, (sentence-by-sentence, chunk-by-chunk) and much less stratificational than predicted by earlier translation models (e.g. Nagao, 1984). Rather, we observe iterative translation and revision processes and gazing patterns which indicate earlier and later translation processes (Schaeffer et al, 2016). While there is a substantially higher amount of iteration from ST reading to TT reading during post-editing than during translation, the basic behavioural pattern seems to be similar:

- after a longer and non-sequential scanpath on the ST → translators and post-editors are likely to read the TT
- after a short, sequential and linear scanpath on the ST → translators and post-editors are likely start typing
- properties of the ST reading behaviour only has an impact on the immediately following Activity Unit

References

Alves, F., and Gonçalves, J. L. (2013). Investigating the conceptual-procedural distinction in the translation process. A relevance-theoretic analysis of micro and macro translation units. Target: International Journal on Translation Studies, 25(1), 107–124.
http://doi.org/10.1075/target.25.1.09alv

Baayen, R. H. (2013). "languageR: Data sets and Functions with "Analyzing Linguistic Data: A Practical Introduction to Statistics". Retrieved from
http://cran.r-project.org/package=languageR

Bates, D., Maechler, M., Bolker, B., and Walker, S. (2014). {lme4}: Linear mixed-effects models using Eigen and S4. Retrieved from http://cran.r-project.org/package=lme4

Carl, M., Dragsted, B., Jakobsen, A.-L. (2011) A Taxonomy of Human Translation Styles. In: Translation Journal, Vol. 16, Nr. 2, 2011

Carl, M., Schaeffer M., Bangalore, S. (2016). The CRITT Translation Process Research Database. In: New Directions in Empirical Translation Process Research: Exploring the CRITT TPR-DB. . ed. Michael Carl; Srinivas Bangalore; Moritz Schaeffer. Cham : Springer, p. 13-54

Carl, M., Way, A. (Eds.). (2003). Recent Advances in Example-Based Machine Translation. Text, Speech and Language Technology, Springer Netherlands

Dragsted, B. (2012). Indicators of difficulty in translation — Correlating product and process data. Across Languages and Cultures, 13(1), 81–98.
http://doi.org/10.1556/Acr.13.2012.1.5

Immonen, S. (2006): Translation as a Writing Process: Pauses in Translation versus Monolingual Text Production. In Target 18 (2), 313-335

Jakobsen, A-L. (1998). Logging Time Delay in Translation, LSP Texts and the Translation Process. Copenhagen Working Papers. 73 – 101.

Jakobsen, A-L. (2002). "Translation Drafting by Professional Translators and by Translation Students." In Empirical Translation Studies. Process and product. Edited by Gyde Hansen, 191-204. Copenhagen: Samfundslitteratur

Kumpulainen, M. (2015). On the operationalisation of 'pauses' in translation process research. Translation and Interpreting Vol 7 No 1 (2015)
http://trans-int.org/index.php/transint/article/download/367/183

Kuznetsova, A., Christensen, R. H. B., Brockhoff, P. B. (2014). lmertest: Tests for Random and Fixed Effects for Linear Mixed Effect Models (lmer Objects of lme4 Package). R package version 2.0-6.
Retrieved from http://www.cran.rproject.org/package=lmerTest/

Lacruz, I., Shreve, G. M. (2014). Pauses and Cognitive Effort in Post-Editing.. In Post-editing of Machine Translation: Processes and Applications. Edited by Sharon O'Brien, Laura Winther Balling, Michael Carl, Michel Simard and Lucia Specia

Martínez-Gómez, P., Minocha, A., Huang, J., Carl, M., Bangalore, S., and Aizawa, A. (2014). Recognition of translator expertise using sequences of fixations and keystrokes. Proceedings of the Symposium on Eye Tracking Research and Applications - ETRA '14, 299–302.
http://doi.org/10.1145/2578153.2578201

Mishra, A., Bhattacharyya, P., and Carl, M. (2013). Automatically predicting sentence translation difficulty. *ACL 2013 - 51st Annual Meeting of the Association for Computational Linguistics, Proceedings of the Conference, 2*, 346–351.

Nagao, M. (1984). A Framework of a Mechanical Translation Between Japanese and English by Analogy Principle. In Proc. Of the International NATO Symposium on Artificial and Human Intelligence (pp. 173–180). New York, NY, USA: Elsevier North-Holland, Inc.

Nida, E. A. (1964). Toward a science of translating : with special reference to principles and procedures involved in Bible translating. Leiden: E.J. Brill.

O'Brien, S. (2005). Methodologies for measuring the correlations between post-editing effort and machine translatability. Machine Translation, 19(1), 37–58.
`http://doi.org/10.1007/s10590-005-2467-1`

O'Brien, S. (2006) *Pauses as indicators of cognitive effort in post-editing machine translation output.* Across Languages and Cultures, 7 (1). pp. 1-21. ISSN 1585-1923

R Development Core Team. (2014). R: A language and environment for statistical computing. Vienna, Austria.

Schaeffer, M., Dragsted, B., Kristian Tangsgaard Hvelplund, Laura Winther Balling, Michael Carl. *Word Translation Entropy: Evidence of Early Target Language Activation During Reading for Translation.* In: New Directions in Empirical Translation Process Research: Exploring the CRITT TPR-DB. . ed. Michael Carl; Srinivas Bangalore; Moritz Schaeffer. Cham : Springer, Pages 183-210.

Received May 11, 2016, accepted May 18, 2016

Baltic J. Modern Computing, Vol. 4 (2016), No. 2, 346-353

A Comparative Study of Post-editing Guidelines

Ke HU, Patrick CADWELL

ADAPT Centre, Dublin City University, Glasnevin, Dublin, Ireland

Ke.hu2@mail.dcu.ie, Patrick.cadwell2@mail.dcu.ie

Abstract: With the popular use of machine translation technology in the translation industry, post-editing has been widely adopted with the aim of improving target text quality. Every post-editing project needs to have specific guidelines for translators to comply with, since the guidelines may help clients and LSPs to set clear expectations, and save time and effort for translators. Different organizations make their own rules according to their needs. In this paper, we focus on comparing five sources of post-editing guidelines, and point out their overlaps and differences.

Keywords: translation, light post-editing, full post-editing, post-editing guidelines

1. Introduction

Post-editing has been increasingly researched and implemented by Language Service Providers (LSPs) in recent years as a result of the productivity gains it can bring to translators (Guerberof, 2009; Federico et al., 2012; WEB, a). However, it has been noted that there are no widely accepted general or standard post-editing (PE) guidelines (DePalma, 2013; TAUS, 2016). Since needs vary, it seems that guidelines will never be general or standard. Therefore, this paper is not going to set a general standard to post-editing guidelines (hereafter abbreviated as PE guidelines), but select, review and compare different PE guidelines which are representative (one set of guidelines produced by a resource centre for the translation industry, one by a LSP, and three by scholars). The research mainly focuses on the comparison of five proposals (O'Brien, 2010; Mesa-Lao, 2013; Flanagan and Christensen, 2014; Densmer, 2014; TAUS, 2016).

Since most organizations prefer to keep their PE guidelines for internal use only, we just have access to the ones that have been published, which are not many. Among them, we select the five proposals above as our focus because they have been published recently, are relatively complete and are proposed in terms of two categories: light (rapid or fast) post-editing and full (or heavy) post-editing. For the convenience of comparison, the five selected sets of PE guidelines are general rather than language dependent or aiming at specific contents.

2. Different Levels of Post-editing

According to ISO 17100:2015, post-editing means to "edit and correct machine translation output (ISO, 2015)". Allen (2003) pointed out the distinction between different levels of post-editing. He first explained the determinant factors of the post-editing level and proposed using inbound and outbound translation to categorize the types and levels of post-editing. For the inbound one, there are two levels: MT with no post-editing (for browsing or gisting), and rapid post-editing. For the outbound one, which means the translation is for publication or wide dissemination, the three levels are MT with no post-editing, minimal post-editing and full post-editing. Apart from rapid and full post-editing, the two popular categories, the intermediate category of minimal post-editing was qualified as "fuzzy and wide-ranging (Allen, 2003:304)". He then provided a number of case studies on post-editing as well as the PE guidelines of the European Commission Translation Service (ECTS), some of which were written by Wagner (1985). Wagner's guidelines are general and apply to projects with severe time constraints. Her PE guidelines have been mentioned in the research of O'Brien (2010) and Mesa-Lao (2013). Belam (2003) proposed her "do's and don'ts" PE guidelines under the categories of rapid and minimal post-editing.

Rather than differentiating between guidelines for light and full post-editing, the Translation Automation User Society (TAUS) differentiated between two levels of expected quality, including "good enough" quality, and "human translation quality" (TAUS, 2016). However in this paper, for comparison purposes, we will still regard them as light and full PE guidelines, which are the two most popular post-editing levels.

3. Definitions of Light and Full Post-editing

It can be seen clearly that most people or organizations dealing with translation have very similar views about the two levels of post-editing. For light post-editing, it usually means the quality is good enough or understandable, while for full post-editing, "human-like" is usually the key word. According to TAUS (2016), full post-editing should reach quality similar to "high-quality human translation and revision" or "publishable quality", while light post-editing should reach a lower quality, often referred to as "good enough" or "fit for purpose". As DePalma (2013), founder of Common Sense Advisory, put it:

"Light post-editing converts raw MT output into understandable and usable, but not linguistically or stylistically perfect, text... A reader can usually determine that the text was machine-translated and touched up by a human... Full post-editing, on the other hand, is meant to produce human-quality output. The goal is to produce stylistically appropriate, linguistically correct output that is indistinguishable from what a good human translator can produce." (DePalma, 2013, Online)

Iconic, a MT company based in Dublin, categorizes light and full post-editing by answering three questions: what, when and result (WEB, a). It suggests that light post-editing is for internal dissemination while full post-editing is for wide dissemination or certified documentation.

4. Comparative Studies of PE Guidelines

TAUS established PE guidelines in partnership with CNGL (Centre for Next Generation Localization) in 2010 with the hope that organizations could use the guidelines as a baseline and tailor them for their own purposes as they required. This is the first attempt at publicly available industry-focused PE guidelines. The guidelines start with some recommendations on reducing the level of post-editing required. TAUS highlighted two main criteria that determined the effort involved in post-editing: the quality of the MT raw output and the expected end quality of the content. They then proposed the guidelines according to the different levels of expected quality. Flanagan and Christensen (2014) carried out a research project and tested the TAUS PE guidelines (2010) among translation trainees. Based on the result, they developed their own set of PE guidelines for use in class. They adopted the TAUS guidelines for light post-editing and proposed their tailored guidelines for full post-editing according to the TAUS baseline for translator training purposes. Recently in 2016, TAUS updated their PE guidelines to include a greater amount of detail than the previous set. The updated guidelines have been divided into five parts. In addition to an updated version of the previous guidelines, which constitutes its second part, the other four parts are as follows: evaluating post-editor performance, post-editing productivity, pricing machine translation PE guidelines and about the MT guidelines. For the purposes of this paper, we will only discuss the second part that elaborates on the PE guidelines of different levels. This part is almost a copy of the previous guidelines, but there is one specific difference in that it says "human translation quality" in the caption for the high level post-editing (although it still uses "quality similar or equal to human translation" in the body of the text).

At the 2010 AMTA conference, O'Brien presented a tutorial on post-editing. She first introduced the general PE guidelines of Wagner (1985), then the guidelines on light and full post-editing respectively. Mesa-Lao (2013) restated O'Brien's general PE guidelines in his study. He reported his suggestions on how to decide whether a MT output should be recycled in post-editing or not. He also mentioned the rules of Microsoft (the "5-10 second evaluation" rule and the "high 5 and low 5" rule) on making these decisions in his research.

Although LSPs possess their own tailored PE guidelines, very few have been released online. Lee Densmer, senior manager at Moravia, wrote down her PE guidelines in her blog at the website of Moravia. The guidelines may be her personal opinion but can represent the attitudes of Moravia to some extent. Similarly to Allen (2003), Densmer (2014) listed the determinant factors of post-editing levels. They both believed that the client and the expectation to the level of quality played important roles. Based on their date of publication, we could argue that determinant factors listed by Densmer are more related to modern technology. Let us take TM as an example. While the factors listed by Allen are more traditional, including the time of translation, the life expectancy and perishability of the information, Densmer pointed out that the key phrases for light post-editing were "factual correctness" and "good enough", which are in line with TAUS. She argued that light post-editing was not an easy job for linguists, due to the fact that linguists had to try their best to turn a blind eye to those 'minor' errors. With reference to full post-editing, she indicated that "the effort to achieve human level quality from MT output may exceed the effort to have it translated by a linguist in the first place (Densmer, 2014)", and Iconic (WEB, a) supports this assertion. In the end, she exposed the "shades of grey" which referred to the fact that many clients want the quality of full post-editing with the price and speed of light post-editing.

Inspired by the categories used in the LISA QA Model (Localization Industry Standards Association Quality Assurance Model) and SAE (Society of Automotive Engineers) J2450 translation quality metric, we created Tables 1 and 2 as follows to compare the five proposals of PE guidelines. According to the variables in the left column, we listed all the corresponding requirements of the five proposals. There are some differences in terminology used by authors on PE, but these terms appear to refer to roughly the same concept, such as "accurate" and "correct". If the guidelines did not mention the variable, the cell was left blank.

Table 1. Comparative study of light PE guidelines

LIGHT POST-EDITING	TAUS (2016) (FIANAGAN & CHRISTENSEN, 2014)	O'BRIEN (2010)	MESA-LAO (2013)	DENSMER (2014)
Accuracy	TT communicates the same meaning as ST	Important	Important	Factually accurate
Terminology		No need to research	No need to spend too much time researching if incorrect	Be consistent
Grammar	May not be perfect	Not a big concern	No need to correct unless the information has not been fully delivered	Correct only the most obvious errors
Semantics	Correct			Correct
Spelling	Apply basic rules	Apply basic rules		
Syntax	Might be unusual	Can be ignored	Do not change	
Style	No need		No need	
Restructure	No need if the sentence is correct		No need if can be understood	Rewrite confusing sentences
Culture	Edit if necessary	Edit if necessary		
Information	Fully delivered			
Others	Use as much raw MT output as possible	Textual standards are not important; very high throughput expectation; low quality expectations	No need to change a word if correct	Fix machine-induced mistakes; delete unnecessary or extra machine-generated translation alternatives

From Table 1, it can be seen that all proposals value the accuracy of the message and correctness of semantics by light post-editing, while grammar, syntax and style are not a big concern. O'Brien and Mesa-Lao believe that there is no need to spend too much time researching incorrect terminology, while Densmer contends that terminology should be consistent. TAUS, Flanagan and Christensen, and O'Brien hold that the spelling fixes should be applied with basic rules, and the text should adapt to the target culture. If the sentence is understandable or correct, most proposals express that it should not be restructured. O'Brien clearly points out the quality expectation for light post-editing is low. Densmer emphasizes machine-induced errors and translation alternatives in her guidelines.

Table 2. Comparative study of full PE guidelines

FULL POST-EDITING	TAUS (2016)	O'BRIEN (2010)	FLANAGAN & CHRISTENSEN (2014)	MESA-LAO (2013)	DENSMER (2014)
Accuracy	TT communicates same meaning as ST	Important	Important		Absolutely accurate
Terminology	Key terminology is correct	Key terminology is correct	Key terminology is correct	Apply the term as used in the term database for any incorrect terminology	Consistent and appropriate
Grammar	Correct	Accurate	Correct	Correct	Correct
Semantics	Correct		Correct	Correct	Correct
Punctuation	Correct	Apply basic rules	Apply basic rules		Correct
Spelling	Apply basic rules	Apply basic rules	Apply basic rules		Correct
Syntax	Normal		Correct		Make modifications in accordance with practices for the TL
Style	Fine	Ignore stylistic and textual problems		Not important	Consistent, appropriate and fluent
Restructure			No need if the language is appropriate	No need if the sentence is semantically correct	Rewrite confusing sentences
Culture	Edit if necessary	Edit if necessary	Edit if necessary		Adapt all cultural references
Information	Fully delivered	Fully delivered	Fully delivered		
Formatting	Correct	All tags are present and in the correct positions	Ensure the same ST tags are present and in the correct positions;		Correct (including tagging)
Others	Basic rules apply to hyphenation; human translation quality	Apply basic rules to hyphenation; high throughput expectation; medium quality expectations	Use as much raw MT output as possible; ensure the untranslated terms belong to the client's list of 'Do not translate' terms	No need to change a word if it is correct; accept the repetitive MT output	Perfect faithfulness to the source text; fix machine-induced mistakes; delete unnecessary or extra machine-generated translation alternatives; cross-reference translations against other resources; human translation quality

Regarding full post-editing, TAUS and Densmer expect that the quality should have no difference with human translation, and they emphasize the significance of fine style. However, O'Brien and Mesa-Lao do not agree with a need to pay much attention to the style. They expect the quality after full post-editing be medium rather than equal to translation from scratch. Should the quality after full post-editing be the same as human translation or maintain the traces of machine translation? We can see from Table 2, especially the "Others" row that the resource centre and LSP are more inclined to human translation quality than the scholars. If full post-editing should reach human translation quality, it still remains a question whether full post-editing is more pragmatic than translation from scratch in terms of cost. It is even debatable if post-editing can actually bring productivity gains, which leads to scepticism toward the benefits of post-editing. Guerberof (2009) and Federico et al. (2012) reported productivity gains in their research, while Gaspari et al. (2014) found that post-editing could lead to productivity losses over translation from scratch.

The requirements of the full PE guidelines surpass the considerations of the light PE guidelines in terms of accuracy, semantics and culture in particular. Different from light PE guidelines, most full PE guidelines require the correctness of terminology, grammar, punctuation, syntax and formatting.

5. Conclusions

From this comparative study, we can see that the existing PE guidelines have many overlaps, especially for light post-editing. The main differences lie in the full PE guidelines and concern the requirement for style and the expected quality of the target text, which we believe depends on the use and type of the text.

As we mentioned before, there are no standard PE guidelines. DePalma (2013) contends that clients should share with LSPs exactly what light and full post-editing is to be included before contracting for a job. Densmer (2014) also asserts that the quality levels, throughputs, and expectations must be defined in advance. We agree with their ideas and advise LSPs and their clients to discuss and create their own tailored PE guidelines together beforehand.

In addition to the general PE guidelines above, there are other sources of PE guidelines which are either language-dependent or aim-specific. Such guidelines include, for example, the GALE PE guidelines (WEB, b), PE guidelines with a focus on Japanese (Tatsumi, 2010), ACCEPT's guidelines for monolingual and bilingual post-editing (ACCEPT, 2011), language dependent (English-Spanish) PE guidelines (Rico and Ariano, 2014), PE guidelines for BOLT Machine Translation Evaluation (WEB, c), and PE guidelines for lay post-editors in an online community (Mitchell, 2015).

Acknowledgements

This work is supported by the Science Foundation of Ireland (SFI) ADAPT project (Grant No.: P31021). The authors would also like to thank Dr. Sharon O'Brien for her helpful comments and suggestions.

References

ACCEPT. (2012*). Seminar Material on Post-editing – Edition 2*, available at
  http://cordis.europa.eu/docs/projects/cnect/9/288769/080/deliverables/001-
  D622SeminarMaterialonPostEditingEdition2.pdf

Allen, J. (2003). Post-editing. *Computers and Translations: A Translator's Guide*. 35, 297-317.

Belam, J. (2003). "Buying up to falling down": a deductive approach to teaching post-editing, In:
  Proceedings of MT Summit IX, Workshop on Teaching Translation Technologies and Tools
  (27 Sept. 2003, New Orleans, USA), pp 1-10.

Densmer, L. (2014). *Light and Full MT Post-Editing Explained*, available at
  http://info.moravia.com/blog/bid/353532/Light-and-Full-MT-Post-Editing-Explained

DePalma, D. (2013). *Post-editing in practice*, available at
  http://www.tcworld.info/e-magazine/translation-and-localization/article/post-editing-in-
  practice/

Federico, M., Cattelan, A., Trombetti, M. (2012), Measuring user productivity in machine
  translation enhanced computer assisted translation, In: *Proceedings of the Tenth Conference
  of the Association for Machine Translation in the Americas*, AMTA 2012 (28 Oct. – 1 Nov.
  2012, San Diego, USA).

Flanagan, M., Christensen, T.P. (2014). Testing post-editing guidelines: how translation trainees
  interpret   them and how to tailor them for translator training purposes. *The Interpreter and
  Translator Trainer*, vol. 8, no. 2, pp. 257-275.

Gaspari, F. 2014, Perception vs Reality: Measuring Machine Translation Post-Editing
  Productivity, In: *Proceedings of the Third Workshop on Post-Editing Technology and
  Practice at the 11th Conference of the Association for Machine Translation in the Americas*,
  AMTA 2014 (22-26 Oct. 2014, Vancouver, Canada), pp. 60-72.

Guerberof, A. (2009). Productivity and quality in MT post-editing, In: *Proceedings of MT Summit
  XII-Workshop: Beyond Translation Memories: New Tools for Translators MT*, AMTA 2009
  (26-30 Aug. 2009, Ottawa, Canada).

ISO, *ISO 17100:2015: Translation services – Requirements for translation services*, available at
  http://www.iso.org/iso/catalogue_detail.htm?csnumber=59149

Mesa-Lao, B. (2013). *Introduction to post-editing – The CasMaCat GUI*, available at
  http://bridge.cbs.dk/projects/seecat/material/hand-out_post-editing_bmesa-lao.pdf

Mitchell, L. (2015). The potential and limits of lay post-editing in an online community, In:
  *Proceedings of the 18th Annual Conference of the European Association for Machine
  Translation*, EAMT 2015 (11-13 May. 2015, Antalya, Turkey).

O'Brien, S. (2010). *Introduction to Post-Editing: Who, What, How and Where to Next?* Available
  at http://amta2010.amtaweb.org/AMTA/papers/6-01-ObrienPostEdit.pdf

Rico-Pérez, C., Ariano-Gahn, M. (2014). Defining language dependent post-editing rules: the case
  of the language pair English-Spanish. In O'Brien, S., Balling, L.M., Carl, M., Simard, M.,
  Specia, L., (eds.), *Post-editing of machine translation: processes and applications*.
  Newcastle, pp. 299-322.

Tatsumi, M. (2010). *Post-editing machine translated text in a commercial setting: Observation and statistical analysis*. PhD thesis, Dublin City University, Dublin, Ireland.

TAUS. (2010). *MT Post-editing Guidelines*, available at https://www.taus.net/academy/best-practices/postedit-best-practices/machine-translation-post-editing-guidelines

TAUS. (2016). *TAUS Post-Editing Guidelines*, available at https://www.taus.net/think-tank/articles/postedit-articles/taus-post-editing-guidelines

Wagner, E. (1985). Post-editing Systran - A challenge for Commission Translators, *Terminologie et Traduction*, no. 3, pp. 1-7.

WEB (a). *Post-Edited Machine Translation*. http://iconictranslation.com/solutions/post_edited_mt/

WEB (b). *Post Editing Guidelines for GALE Machine Translation Evaluation*. http://projects.ldc.upenn.edu/gale/Translation/Editors/GALEpostedit_guidelines-3.0.2.pdf

WEB (c). *Post Editing Guidelines for BOLT Machine Translation Evaluation*. http://www.nist.gov/itl/iad/mig/upload/BOLT_P3_PostEditingGuidelinesV1_3_3.pdf

Received May 2, 2016, accepted May 8, 2016

Baltic J. Modern Computing, Vol. 4 (2016), No. 2, pp. 354–360

Dealing with Data Sparseness in SMT with Factored Models and Morphological Expansion: a Case Study on Croatian

Víctor M. SÁNCHEZ-CARTAGENA[1], Nikola LJUBEŠIĆ[2,3], Filip KLUBIČKA[3]

[1] Prompsit Language Engineering, Av. Universitat, s/n. Edifici Quorum III, E-03202, Elx, Spain
[2] Dept. of Knowledge Technologies, Jožef Stefan Institute, Jamova cesta 32, SI-1000, Ljubljana, Slovenia
[3] Dept. of Information and Communication Sciences, University of Zagreb

vmsanchez@prompsit.com, nljubesi@ffzg.hr, fklubicka@gmail.com

Abstract. This paper describes our experience using available linguistic resources for Croatian in order to address data sparseness when building an English-to-Croatian general domain phrase-based statistical machine translation system. We report the results obtained with factored translation models and morphological expansion, highlight the impact of the algorithm used for tagging the corpora, and show that the improvement brought by these methods is compatible with the application of data selection on out-of-domain parallel corpora.

Keywords: data sparseness, factored translation models, morphological expansion

1 Introduction

Data sparseness is a well-known problem that phrase-based statistical machine translation (SMT) systems suffer from when dealing with highly inflected languages, especially
when the highly inflected one is the target language (TL). In these kinds of languages, a
single word (lemma) can have dozens of different inflected forms. Translation performance is hampered because it is difficult to observe all the forms of a given word (in the
different contexts relevant for translation) in the training corpus.

This paper is part of the Abu-MaTran project, where we aim to provide machine
translation support to Croatian, as the official language of a new EU country. Croatian
is a highly inflected language and hence it is affected by data sparseness. For instance,
adjectives inflect for 3 genders, 2 numbers and 7 cases and the *hrLex* Croatian inflectional
lexicon (Ljubešić et al, 2016b) contains 939 unique morphosyntactic description tags.
In this paper, we show how we dealt with that problem in a general-domain English-
to-Croatian phrase-based SMT system by leveraging a Croatian inflectional lexicon
and adapting existing solutions in the literature, namely factored translation models

(Koehn and Hoang, 2007) and morphological expansion (Turchi and Ehrmann, 2011). Sections 2 and 3 respectively describe these solutions, while Section 4 shows that they can be successfully combined with a data selection strategy. The paper ends with a brief description of related approaches and some concluding remarks and future directions.

2 Factored translation models

Factored translation models (Koehn and Hoang, 2007) split the translation of words in the translation of different factors (surface forms, lemmas, lexical categories, morphosyntactic information, etc.). Among the different ways these factors can be combined, we opted for producing a surface form factor and a morphosyntactic description (MSD) factor for each word in the output, and used two different language models (LMs), one operating on surface forms and another one on MSDs. This setup has been reported to be effective (and efficient in terms of decoding time) when the TL is highly inflected but the SL is not (Skadiņš et al., 2010), since it helps the decoder to produce grammatically correct phrases that have not been observed in the training corpus. We considered the following aspects when building our factored phrase-based SMT system.

- Order of the MSD LM. The order of surface-form based LMs is usually set to 5. As the number of different MSDs is several orders of magnitude lower than the number of different surface forms, a greater order can also be considered.
- Corpora tagging algorithm. In order to obtain the MSD factor of the TL side of the parallel corpus and the TL monolingual corpus, a part-of-speech (PoS) tagger is needed. We tested the effect of lexicon constraining in PoS tagging.

2.1 Constrained part of speech tagging

The best performing tagger available for Croatian is a CRF-based tagger (Ljubešić et al, 2016b). While the tagger makes use of the *hrLex* inflectional lexicon (Ljubešić et al, 2016b), the corresponding lexicon entries are not used for constraining the tagger to the potential tags, but just as features. As a result, the number of translations for each SL phrase in a factored system grows when compared to a non-factored phrase-based SMT system: in the system setups described in Section 2.2, the average number of translations per SL phrase in the phrase table of our non-factored system is 2.091. This value grows to 2.119 in the factored system that uses the CRF tagger. Moreover, we observed that the increase in the number of translation options caused by unconstrained tagging is more relevant in frequent SL phrases. For instance, the Croatian surface form *kuća* (*house*) can only be analysed as a feminine, singular, nominative, common noun or as a feminine, plural, genitive, common noun according to the lexicon. However, in our factored system with unconstrained tagging (Section 2.2), we can find 8 phrase table entries whose SL word is *house* and whose TL surface form factor is *kuća*. Additional MSDs include cardinal number, adjective, or proper noun. Since according to some studies (Ling et al., 2012), the presence of redundant phrase translations can hurt translation quality, we also tested a modified version of the tagger in which it only selects the MSDs present in the lexicon.[4] As a result, the average number of translations per SL phrase was 2.111.

---

[4] We post-processed the output of the CRF tagger: for each word tagged with an MSD not present in the lexicon, we replaced it with the most likely one from the lexicon according to a 3-gram

We compared the original and the constrained tagger on the test set traditionally used to evaluate taggers on Croatian: 300 sentences (6306 tokens) from news, general web and Wikipedia domains (Agić and Ljubešić, 2014): constraining the tagger slightly reduces accuracy from 0.9253 to 0.9232.

2.2 Experiments and results

We built our phrase-based SMT system from corpora crawled from the web: we consider them to be the most suitable ones for an open-domain system. In particular, we used *hrenWaC* as parallel corpus (Ljubešić et al., 2016a) and *hrWaC* (Ljubešić and Klubička, 2014) as TL monolingual corpus. The parallel corpus contains 1 166 732 sentences, 32 908 281 English words and 29 199 856 Croatian words. The size of the vocabularies is 605 929 (English) and 888 405 (Croatian): the ratio between them is 1.47, which gives us an idea of the morphological richness of Croatian as compared with English. The monolingual corpus contains 67 403 231 sentences and 1 404 303 868 words. We used Moses[5] with the MIRA tuning algorithm (Watanabe et al., 2007). We estimated a 5-gram surface-form LM from the TL monolingual corpus. Our factored system contains an additional MSD LM estimated from the same monolingual corpus. We experimented with orders 3, 5 and 7 and the two tagging alternatives discussed in the previous section. We used KenLM and Knesser-Ney discounting.[6]

Table 1. Results of the evaluation of factored models. A score in bold means that the system outperforms the plain baseline by a statistically significant margin according to paired bootstrap resampling (Koehn, 2004) ($p = 0.05$, 1 000 iterations).

MSD LM order	constrained tagging	BLEU	TER	METEOR
baseline	-	0.2356	0.6351	0.2119
3	N	**0.2429**	**0.6296**	**0.2152**
5	N	0.2408	0.6327	**0.2142**
7	N	0.2373	0.6352	0.2125
3	Y	**0.2458**	**0.6226**	**0.2167**
5	Y	**0.2432**	**0.6256**	**0.2161**
7	Y	0.2413	**0.6280**	**0.2154**

We tuned the systems with *newstest2012* and evaluated them with *newstest2013*, as Pirinen et al. (2016) did. Table 1 shows the values of the BLEU, TER and METEOR evaluation metrics for the basic phrase-based SMT system and the different factored alternatives. Results show that constraining the tagging brings a consistent improvement (for all evaluation metrics and MSD LM orders), thus confirming the observations by

---

LM of MSDs estimated from the same annotated corpus from which the CRF tagger was trained (Ljubešić et al, 2016b). Words not found in the lexicon were assigned the special tag UNK (this was not done when evaluating tagging accuracy in order to perform a fair comparison with the unconstrained tagger).

[5] http://www.statmt.org/moses/. Corpora were normalized, tokenized and truecased with the tools provided with Moses. Parallel sentences with more than 80 tokens were removed.

[6] https://kheafield.com/code/kenlm/

Ling et al. (2012). Concerning the order of the MSD LM, the best translation quality is obtained for order 3. We observed that, as we increase the value of the order, short-distance agreement deteriorates, but long-distance agreement does not improve. A couple of examples can be found in Table 2. This is probably caused by the fact that the order of the constituents of the sentence is relatively free in Croatian. Thus, it is difficult to predict MSDs in the TL with n-grams that cross constituent boundaries.

Table 2. Example sentences illustrating the difference in local agreement between different orders of the MSD LM. In the first example, the phrase *obične smrt* should be in the genitive case, but it is nominative in the order 7 alternative; in the second example, the adjective *egipatske* should be in neuter gender in order to agree with *društva*, but it is feminine in the order 7 alternative.

	Example 1	Example 2
source	The courage of ordinary death.	[...] respect for the other elements of Egyptian society.
order 3	hrabrost **obične smrti**.	[...] poštovanje za druge elemente **egipatskog društva**.
order 7	hrabrost **obična smrt**.	[...] poštovanja za druge elemente **egipatske društva**.
ref.	hrabrost **obične smrti**.	[...] poštovanja ostalih elemenata **egipatskog društva**.

3 Morphological expansion

Factored systems with an additional MSD LM cannot produce surface forms in Croatian that have not been observed in the training corpus. In order to further mitigate the data sparseness problem, we enhanced our system with morphological expansion. It consists of creating new phrase table entries from existing ones by means of changing values of morphological inflection attributes and inflecting words accordingly. We followed a strategy[7] inspired by Turchi and Ehrmann (2011) but we restricted the process with linguistically motivated rules so as to avoid the need to optimise filtering thresholds. We created new phrase pairs by changing only the TL side of existing phrase pairs, and only for those phrase pairs whose TL side is a single word or a grammatically meaningful phrase. We select, among others, TL phrases that contain a noun, a noun phrase, an adjective, a verb, etc. Then, we generate new phrases with all the possible values of the morphological inflection features not present in English.[8] We added the generated phrase pairs to a new phrase table which is combined with the original one at decoding time by means of independent decoding paths (Koehn and Schroeder, 2007).

We added morphological expansion to the best factored system described in Section 2.2 and repeated the evaluation. In view of the positive results of reducing translation alternatives by constraining PoS tagging, we also evaluated an alternative morphological expansion strategy in which only noun phrases were expanded. Our expansion rules generate only 3 alternatives for them (for nominative, accusative and instrumental cases), while the number of generated entries is higher for verbal phrases and adjectives. Results displayed in Table 3 show that there is not a clear difference between both expansion

---

[7] Implementation is available at: https://github.com/vitaka/morph-xpand-smt

[8] The file with the expansion rules used and some comments can be found at https://github.com/vitaka/morph-xpand-smt/blob/master/tags_29-1-2016-somecases.

strategies, and that morphological expansion is not able to outperform the factored system (the difference is not statistically significant). We performed a manual analysis on the agreement errors found in 40 sentences randomly selected from the test set and found that for only 25% of all the agreement errors proper word forms were not present in the phrase table, out of which only 23% were generated by morphological expansion. Most needed words were not generated because they were not present in the lexicon.

Table 3. Results of the evaluation of morphological expansion.

System	BLEU	TER	METEOR
best factored	0.2458	0.6226	0.2167
+ morph. expansion noun phrases	0.2470	0.6232	0.2174
+ morph. expansion all	0.2460	0.6235	0.2179

4   Combination with data selection

A different way of dealing with data sparseness is to augment the training corpus by selecting the most suitable sentences from out-of-domain data. Pirinen et al. (2016; Section 2.6) followed that strategy and obtained a significant improvement over a plain phrase-based SMT system trained on *hrenWaC* (Table 4 shows the result of evaluating their approach; the evaluation setup defined in Section 2.2 was followed). In order to make the most of the available resources for English–Croatian we combined both approaches: we built a system with factored translation models (following the best setup in Section 2.2) on the parallel corpora obtained as a result of data selection. Results, which are also depicted in Table 4, confirm that both approaches can be successfully combined, allowing us to reach the state-of-the-art system, *Google Translate*.[9]

Table 4. Results of the evaluation of the combination of data selection and the best factored setup. There are not statistically significant differences between that combination and *Google Translate*.

System	BLEU	TER	METEOR
hrenWaC + factored	0.2458	0.6226	0.2167
data selection	0.2576	0.6060	0.2264
Google Translate	0.2673	0.5946	0.2321
data selection + factored	0.2700	0.5963	0.2338

5   Related work

Factored models have been deeply studied by Tamchyna and Bojar (2013), who concluded that automatically searching for the best factored model architecture in a given

---

[9] http://translate.google.com

language pair is not feasible. Successful application of factored models to different language pairs has been already reported by other authors, like Bojar (2007) and Koehn et al. (2010). Regarding morphological expansion, to the best of our knowledge, the approach by Turchi and Ehrmann (2011) is the only one that addresses the expansion of the TL side of the phrase table. Concerning other ways of adding linguistic information to an SMT system, we refer the reader to the survey by Costa-Jussà and Farrús (2014).

6   Conclusions and future work

In this paper, we presented a set of strategies on how to leverage existing Croatian linguistic resources to address data sparseness in a general-domain English-to-Croatian SMT system. Applying factored models showed to be successful. We observed that accuracy of PoS tagging and translation performance are not correlated and that increasing the order of the MSD LM is counterproductive. A combination of factored models and data selection allowed us to build a system that reaches state-of-the-art commercial tools. Improvement obtained with morphological expansion was negligible.

Since most of the agreement errors were not caused by lack of inflected forms in the phrase table, and the best results were obtained with a low-order MSD LM because of the free constituent order in Croatian, hybridisation with an RBMT system that performs full syntactic analysis (Labaka et al., 2014) could further improve the results.

Acknowledgements

Research funded by the European Union Seventh Framework Programme FP7/2007-2013 under grant agreement PIAP-GA-2012-324414 (Abu-MaTran).

References

Agić, Ž., Ljubešić, N. (2014). The SETimes.HR Linguistically Annotated Corpus of Croatian. In *Proceedings of the Ninth International Conference on Language Resources and Evaluation*, Reykjavik, Iceland.

Ondřej Bojar (2007). English-to-Czech factored machine translation. In *Proceedings of the Second Workshop on Statistical Machine Translation*, Prague, Czech Republic.

Costa-Jussà, M. R., Farrús, M. (2014). Statistical machine translation enhancements through linguistic levels: A survey. *ACM Computing Surveys* 46:3.

Koehn. P. (2004). Statistical significance tests for machine translation evaluation. In *Proceedings of the 2004 Conference on Empirical Methods in Natural Language Processing*, Barcelona, Spain.

Koehn, P., Haddow, B., Williams, P., Hoang, H. (2010). More Linguistic Annotation for Statistical Machine Translation. In *Proceedings of the Joint Fifth Workshop on Statistical Machine Translation and MetricsMATR*, Uppsala, Sweden.

Koehn, P., H. Hoang (2007). Factored translation models. In *Proceedings of the 2007 Joint Conference on Empirical Methods in Natural Language Processing and Computational Natural Language Learning* , Prague, Czech Republic.

Koehn, P. and Schroeder, J. (2007). Experiments in domain adaptation for statistical machine translation. In *Proceedings of the Second Workshop on Statistical Machine Translation*, Prague, Czech Republic.

Labaka, G., España-Bonet, C., Màrquez, L., Sarasola, K. (2014). A hybrid machine translation architecture guided by syntax. *Machine Translation*, 28(2):91–125.

Ling, W., Graça, J., Trancoso, I., Black, A. (2012). Entropy-based Pruning for Phrase-based Machine Translation. In *Proceedings of the 2012 Joint Conference on Empirical Methods in Natural Language Processing and Computational Natural Language Learning*, Jeju Island, Korea.

Ljubešić, N., Esplà-Gomis, M., Toral, A., Klubička, F. (2016). Producing Monolingual Web Corpora and Bitext at the Same Time - SpiderLing and Bitextor's Love Affair. In *Proceedings of the Tenth International Conference on Language Resources and Evaluation*, Portorož, Slovenia.

Ljubešić, N., Klubička, F. (2014). {bs,hr,sr}WaC – Web corpora of Bosnian, Croatian and Serbian. In *Proceedings of the 9th Web as Corpus Workshop (WaC-9)*, Gothenburg, Sweden. 29–35.

Ljubešić, N., Klubička, F., Agić, Ž., Jazbec, I. (2016). New Inflectional Lexicons and Training Corpora for Improved Morphosyntactic Annotation of Croatian and Serbian. In *Proceedings of the Tenth International Conference on Language Resources and Evaluation*, Portorož, Slovenia.

Pirinen, T., Rubino, R., Sánchez-Cartagena, V.M., Klubička, F., Toral, A. (2016). *D5.1c Evaluation of the MT systems deployed in the third development cycle*. Automatic building of Machine Translation. FP7-PEOPLE-2012-IAPP project deliverable (http://www.abumatran.eu/?page_id=59).

Skadinš, R., Goba, K., Šics, V. (2010). Improving SMT for Baltic Languages with Factored Models. In *Proceedings of the Fourth International Conference Baltic HLT, Frontiers in Artificial Intelligence and Applications*, Riga, Latvia.

Tamchyna, A., Bojar, O. (2013). No Free Lunch in Factored Phrase-Based Machine Translation. In *Proceedings of the 14th international conference on Computational Linguistics and Intelligent Text Processing - Volume 2*, Samos, Greece.

Turchi, M., Ehrmann, M. (2011). Knowledge Expansion of a Statistical Machine Translation System using Morphological Resources. In *Proceedings of the 12th International Conference on Intelligent Text Processing and Computational Linguistics*, Tokyo, Japan.

Watanabe, T., Suzuki, J., Tsukada, H., Isozaki, H. (2007). Online large-margin training for statistical machine translation. In *Proceedings of the 2007 Joint Conference on Empirical Methods in Natural Language Processing and Computational Natural Language Learning*, Prague, Czech Republic.

Received May 2, 2016 , accepted May 16, 2016

Baltic J. Modern Computing, Vol. 4 (2016), No. 2, pp. 361–367

Collaborative development of a rule-based machine translator between Croatian and Serbian

Filip KLUBIČKA[1], Gema RAMÍREZ-SÁNCHEZ[2], Nikola LJUBEŠIĆ[1,3]

[1] University of Zagreb, Ivana Lučića 3, HR-10000 Zagreb, Croatia
[2] Prompsit Language Engineering, Avenida de la Universidad s/n, ES-03202 Elche, Spain
[3] Jožef Stefan Institute, Jamova cesta 39, SI-1000 Ljubljana, Slovenia

fklubick@ffzg.hr, gramirez@prompsit.com, nljubesi@ffzg.hr

Abstract. This paper describes the development and current state of a bidirectional Croatian-Serbian machine translation system based on the open-source Apertium platform. It has been created inside the Abu-MaTran project with the aims of creating free linguistic resources as well as having non-experts and experts work together. We describe the collaborative way of collecting the necessary data to build our system, which outperforms other available systems.

Keywords: machine translation, collaboration, Apertium, open-source, Croatian, Serbian

1 Introduction

Croatian and Serbian are language varieties and official registers of the pluricentric Bosnian-Croatian-Montenegrin-Serbian (BCMS) language. Although mutually intelligible, the national varieties are standardised differently, and both communities have a high interest to produce documentation that adheres to these standards, if for no other reason, then for the sake of producing standard documents for Serbian, the official language of an EU candidate state. Thus it is sensible to make use of a related language of a recent member state and employ machine translation between these two language varieties to meet this aim.

Creating machine translation (MT) systems for South-Slavic languages, both between themselves and other languages, is also the aim of the Abu-MaTran project.[4] In the first phase of the project, the focus was on MT between English and Croatian, while MT between South-Slavic is the focus of the second phase. The system presented in this paper will be used within the project to increase the amount of English - Serbian parallel data by translating the Croatian side of English-Croatian parallel data to Serbian. It will also be added to another by-product of the Abu-MaTran project - AltLang - a service for translating between language varieties.[5]

---

[4] http://abumatran.eu

[5] http://www.altlang.net

2   Related work

Forcada et al. (2011) and their open-source Apertium platform have shown that, when doing machine translation between language variants or closely-related languages like Spanish and Catalan, a rule-based shallow transfer approach is often sufficient to produce good quality translations. Indeed, work has already been done in building rule based translators from BCMS into Macedonian and Slovene (Peradin et al, 2014). To our knowledge, however, no similar work has been done for the Croatian-Serbian language pair specifically. The only accessible state of the art system for this pair is *Google Translate*,[6] which reaches a BLEU score of 82.27 in the Serbian-Croatian direction. However, the statistical approach that Google uses, which has also been explored in (Popović et al, 2014) but only using small corpora, is not a feasible option for us, as there are not enough parallel corpora available to train SMT systems that can deal with the minute differences between the two languages without introducing additional noise.

Nonetheless, some free linguistic resources were initially available to us: the HBS monolingual dictionary[7] built for other Apertium language pairs like HBS-Macedonian (Peradin and Tyers, 2012) and HBS-Slovene (Peradin et al, 2014), the SETimes news corpora of both Croatian and Serbian[8] and the hrWaC and srWaC web corpora (Ljubešić and Klubička, 2014). This is always an advantage, as both monolingual and bilingual corpora are extensively used to semiautomatically extract knowledge for Apertium such as frequent non-covered entries, bilingual correspondences, rules, development and test sets, and data needed to train statistical part-of-speech taggers.

Considering the amount of available data, coupled with the fact that differences between Croatian and Serbian occur mostly at the level of orthography and lexicon, with only a bit of syntax (limited only to specific structures and verbal tenses), a rule-based approach makes the most sense. We expect a high quality and a more controlled output from such a system, reproducing other Apertium-based success stories such as the Norwegian Nynorsk-Norwegian Bokmål (Unhammer et al, 2006) or Spanish and Aragonese (Cortés et al, 2012) language pairs.

3   Apertium language pair

The structure of the Croatian-Serbian language pair is based on the same structure shared by other Apertium language pairs. This esentially includes two monolingual dictionaries (source and target) which are used as morphological anlysers/generators, one set of morphological tags for the part-of-speech tagger (currently shared by the two languages involved), and two sets of structural transfer rules (one for each translation direction). However, because there is significant overlap in the lexemes of the languages, instead of two separate monolingual dictionaries, there is only one. In addition to pairing lemmas with inflectional paradigms, this monolingual dictionary - called the metadix - explicitly encodes differences between the three language varieties (Bosnian, Croatian, Serbian) with regards to variant-specific lexemes and the reflex of the vowel

---

[6] http://translate.google.com

[7] HBS is the ISO 639-3 code for the macrolanguage covering the three languages in question

[8] http://nlp.ffzg.hr/resources/corpora/setimes/

yat.[9] Furthermore, the language pair includes a bilingual dictionary which explicates lexical differences as one-to-one translations, a shared Hidden Markov Model (HMM) tagger, a transfer module for each translation direction and a transliterator for the cyrilic and latin alphabets.

The basic system on which we started making improvements was produced in only a couple of weeks by extracting relevant components from existing language pairs. In other words, we took the dictionaries from HBS-Slovene, the tagger from the HBS module, a bilingual dictionary created from monolingual entries and the transfer rules for agreement between basic noun phrases. Additionally, the work presented in this paper also kicked off the efforts to enrich the HBS monolingual dictionary, which ran in parallel with our construction of the Croatian-Serbian language pair, and resulted in Apertium's largest lexicon to date, with 97,437 lemmas (Ljubešić et al, 2016).

4 Development

Even though there is considerable overlap, the biggest source of differences between Croatian and Serbian is still the differing lexicon. Thus it was important to construct a large, high-coverage bilingual dictionary. Additionally, transfer rules needed to be defined to account for the few syntactic differences between the languages. Each of these tasks was tackled in two phases - at hands-on Abu-MaTran workshops held in Zagreb and within a course held during the winter semester of 2015/2016 at the University of Zagreb, titled *Selected chapters in Natural Language Processing*.[10]

The approach to including non-experts in the process consisted of creating very focused tasks for data which is needed for each of the Apertium modules based on materials created beforehand, e.g. in the form of precomputed bilingual entries that they had to assess. When possible, user-friendly interfaces or very simple spreadsheets were used to lower the technical barrier. After each task, the contributors were able to see the impact of their collaborative work in the translator's performance almost real-time, which proved to be very motivating. While larger groups could work on dictionary entries (as this is an easy task), only a reduced group worked on writing transfer rules (as this requires an advanced level of technical knowledge).

4.1 Adding bilingual entries

First phase: The first workshop was focused on monolingual and bilingual dictionaries.[11] We automatically produced bilingual candidates from comparable corpora - hrWaC and srWaC (Ljubešić and Klubička, 2014) - by identifying lexemes from the Serbian corpus that, given their frequency in the Croatian corpus, were occurring much more frequently than by chance. The workshop participants validated the candidates and

---

[9] For example, the following lexical entry extracted from the metadix produces either the surface form 'pjevačica' or 'pevačica', depending on the chosen language variant:
<e lm="pjevačica"><i>p</i><par n="e_je__yat"/><i>vačic</i><par n="vodnic/a__n"/></e>

[10] Within this course, students were taught about machine translation and the Apertium framework, among other things.

[11] Materials available at http://www.abumatran.eu/?p=292

added additional linguistic information, such as pointing out parts of speech, morphological differences and translation direction details.[12] This workshop resulted in the addition of approximately 485 new entries in a single day. These entries were additionally checked by experts later on.

Second phase: During a one-semester course, our students collected bilingual data and produced many new entries for the bilingual dictionary using several methods, ranging from running texts of their choice through our translator and filling the bilingual dictionary with the untranslated lexemes, to validating and adding bilingual candidates extracted by using the output of a distributional similarity tool (Fišer and Ljubešić, 2011) applied to texts from the Croatian and Serbian Wikipedia. By the end of the course, the dictionary contained 1694 bilingual entries, which is also its current size.

4.2   Adding rules

First phase: Our second workshop focused on transfer rules[13] from Serbian to Croatian. We automatically extracted rules for Serbian to Croatian (Sánchez et al., 2015) and our workshop participants validated them based on actual examples of these rules, answering the simple question "Is this a valid translation?"[14] We taught them how to formalise the rules and presented them with 100 rules to be validated. The implementation of the rules was done by experts after the workshop. In 1 week we implemented 25 new Serbian to Croatian rules and 10 basic Croatian to Serbian rules.

Second phase: Nearing the end of the course, after adding sufficient bilingual entries, the students were taught about shallow transfer rules. They once again looked into the outputs of the texts they ran through the translator and annotated the syntactic mistakes occurring in the translations. Some of the rules that could be fixed via shallow transfer were added during the course for demonstration purposes, but most were formalised and implemeted as a result of the joint work between a language expert and an Apertium expert during a secondment at Prompsit Language Engineering. At the end of this stage, the number of Serbian to Croatian rules was extended to 99 rules, and Croatian to Serbian to 82, which is the current state of the system. Most of the rules implemented cover a bit of syntax via short-distance word shifting (e.g. there are several verbal constructions involving the *da* particle which differ between the languages in regards to word order and whether the *da* particle is present or not)[15], as well as agreement rules (e.g. if the head noun of a noun phrase changes gender in translation, the premodifying adjectives need to change gender as well).[16]

---

[12] Participants would point out whether the translation of a given lexeme is bidirectional (like *direktorica-direktorka*), just from Croatian to Serbian (like *zabava-žurka*), or just from Serbian to Croatian (like *kasnije-docnije*)

[13] Materials available at http://www.abumatran.eu/?p=418

[14] [SR] Zemlje jugoistočne Evrope trebale bi da suraduju
   [HR] Zemlje jugoistočne Europe trebale bi suradivati

[15] [SR] da li možeš
   [HR] možeš li

[16] [SR] naš brzi računar (masculine)
   [HR] naše brzo računalo (neuter)

4.3 Tagger training

Additional insight gained during the workshops and coursework was that the HBS tagger was in serious need of improvement. The tagger we had at the beginning of the described process was using a constraint grammar, and it was producing many errors, which very palpably hindered the translation process. Fortunately, by the time the bilingual lexicon and transfer rules were extended, we had the newly created hr500k Croatian training corpus (Ljubešić et al, 2016) at our disposal, so we decided to train a statistical tagger[17] based on Hidden Markov Models (Rabiner, 1989) with the tools provided in Apertium. A necessary preprocessing step was to transfer the tags in the training corpus from the MULTEXT-East Morphosyntactic Specifications, revised Version 4[18] to Apertium's notation. This was done by automatically mapping the hr500k training corpus to the Apertium tagset, retaining only sentences with full coverage and splitting this dataset into training and test data. This left us with 145,626 tokens (9,465 sentences) of training data and 7,682 tokens (500 sentences) of test data.

Additionally, a tagset file with ambiguity classes was defined so as to narrow down the tagset as much as possible. This step makes learning the morphological disambiguation process feasible as the amount of training data that would be necessary to observe all the possible sequences of full tags, given the rich morphology of the languages, is many orders higher than the amount of data currently available.

We performed a comparative intrinsic evaluation of both the constraint grammar and statistical tagger on the 500 sentence test dataset. We evaluated both taggers via token-level accuracy. In this setting, the improvement in accuracy was quite substantial: while the old constraint grammar-based tagger had an accuracy of 76%, the new HMM tagger achieved an accuracy of 90.19%.

5 Evaluation

Finally, we perform a comparative evaluation of our system, but we present an evaluation of only the Serbian to Croatian direction as this direction was the initial focus of the development and the other direction was still under development at the moment of presenting these results. We compare our system to the output of *Google Translate*,[19] as this is the current state of the art system. For our baseline we assume that the output is identical to the input, a setup which yields the lowest evaluation scores. Our SMT baseline was constructed by training a phrase-based Moses system on 200k segments from the SETimes parallel corpus, with an additional 2 thousand segments of development data, while we use hrWaC2.0 for building the language model (Ljubešić and Klubička, 2014).

For the evaluation we use a test set consisting of 351 Serbian sentences gathered from newspaper texts that were manually translated into Croatian by students. We evaluate the system with BLEU (Papineni et al, 2006) and TER (Snover et al, 2006). Table 1 shows the results of the evaluation process.

---

[17] It should be noted that even though using the same tagger for both Croatian and Serbian is not ideal, previous experiments (Agić et al., 2013) have shown that only a minor drop in accuracy should be expected from this setting.

[18] https://github.com/ffnlp/sethr/blob/master/mte4r-upos.mapping

[19] Output retrieved on 2016-01-27

	BLEU	TER
baseline	72.66	0.1300
SMT	73.54	0.1255
Google	82.27	0.0873
Apertium	82.97	**0.0782**

Table 1. Results of the MT evaluation. Statistically significantly better results are in bold.

When compared to our baseline systems, the evaluation scores are decidedly positive. When compared to Google's system, we also improve, but the question is whether this improvement is statistically significant. To calculate this we use approximate randomisation with 1000 iterations, and while the reported 0.7 point improvement in BLEU yields a p-value of 0.384, which is too high to prove statistical significance, the improvement in TER by -0.0091 is in fact statistically significant, with a p-value of 0.018. Given that BLEU is known to favour statistical machine translation in its evaluation, it is safe to claim that our system outperforms that of Google.

6 Conclusion

In this paper we present a bidirectional machine translation system between Croatian and Serbian, which was collaboratively developed between the University of Zagreb and Prompsit Language Engineering in the framework of the Abu-MaTran project. To achieve this, we combine Apertium's resources with the University of Zagreb's manpower and resources, taking advantage of our researcher's employment and secondments, as well as hands-on workshops organised as part of our Abu-MaTran activities to get other interested parties to help with the creation of additional necessary linguistic resources.

The result of this work is a system that has been developed in a total of approximately 6 person months (including experiments for semi-automatic extraction of vocabulary and data, work in dictionaries, HMM and implementation of rules, workshop and course materials, training of non-experts and evaluation) and which outperforms the current state of the art. The contribution of this work for the wider community is the release of numerous freely available linguistic tools and resources, as well as the considerable transfer of knowledge between all participating institutions. Additionally, this system opens up the possibility of smoothing the way towards translating official EU documents that are and will be published in Croatian[20] into Serbian, the language of an EU candidate state.

Future work will go into extending the system and further evaluating both translation directions, creating combinations with Bosnian, using it to create synthetic training data, and adding it to AltLang to offer a commercial service that uses the current system to customise content to a specific language variant.

---

[20] E.g. the *acquis communautaire*; EU parallel corpora and translation memories such as DGT (https://ec.europa.eu/jrc/en/language-technologies/dgt-translation-memory); the Special Edition of the EU Official Journal (http://eur-lex.europa.eu/eu-enlargement/hr/special.html)

Acknowledgements

The research leading to these results has received funding from the European Union Seventh Framework Programme FP7/2007-2013 under grant agreement PIAP-GA-2012-324414 (Abu-MaTran) and the Swiss National Science Foundation grant IZ74Z0_160501 (ReLDI).

References

Agić, Ž., Ljubešić, N., Merkler, D. (2013). Lemmatization and morphosyntactic tagging of Croatian and Serbian. In *Proceedings of the Fourth Biennial International Workshop on Balto-Slavic Natural Language Processing*, Sofia, Bulgaria.

Cortés Martínez, J.P., O'Regan, J., Tyers, F.M. (2012). Free/Open Source Shallow-Transfer Based Machine Translation for Spanish and Aragonese. In *Proceedings of the Eighth International Conference on Language Resources and Evaluation*, Istanbul, Turkey.

Fišer, D., Ljubešić, N. (2011). Bilingual Lexicon Extraction from Comparable Corpora for Closely Related Languages. In *Proceedings of the Recent Advances in Natural Langugage Processing Conference*, Hissar, Bulgaria.

Forcada, M.L., Ginestí-Rosell, M., Nordfalk, J., O'Regan, J., Ortiz-Rojas, S., Pérez-Ortiz, J.A., Sánchez-Martínez, F., Ramírez-Sánchez, G., Tyers, F.M. (2011). *Apertium: a free/open-source platform for rule-based machine translation*. Machine Translation. 25(2):127-144

Ljubešić, N., Klubička, F. (2014). {bs,hr,sr}WaC – Web corpora of Bosnian, Croatian and Serbian. In *Proceedings of the 9th Web as Corpus Workshop (WaC-9)*, Gothenburg, Sweden.

Ljubešić, N., Klubička, F., Agić, Ž., Jazbec, I. (2016). New Inflectional Lexicons and Training Corpora for Improved Morphosyntactic Annotation of Croatian and Serbian. In *Proceedings of the Tenth International Conference on Language Resources and Evaluation*, Portorož, Slovenia.

Papineni, K., Roukos, S., Ward, T., and Zhu, W.-J. (2002). BLEU: A method for automatic evaluation of machine translation. In *Proceedings of the 40th Annual Meeting on Association for Computational Linguistics*, Philadelphia, Pennsylvania.

Peradin, H., Tyers, F. (2012). *A rule-based machine translation system from Serbo-Croatian to Macedonian*. Third International Workshop on Free/Open-Source Rule-Based Machine Translation (FreeRBMT 2012).

Peradin, H., Petkovski, F., Tyers, F. (2014). Shallow-transfer rule-based machine translation for the Western group of South Slavic languages. In *Proceedings of the 9th SaLTMiL Workshop on Free/open-Source Language Resources for the Machine Translation of Less-Resourced Languages*, Reykjavik, Iceland.

Popović, M., Ljubešić N. Exploring cross-language statistical machine translation for closely related South Slavic languages. *Language Technology for Closely Related Languages and Language Variants (LT4CloseLang)*, Doha, Qatar.

Rabiner, L. R. (1989). A tutorial on hidden Markov models and selected applications in speech recognition. In *Proceedings of the IEEE*

Sánchez-Cartagena, V.M., Pérez-Ortiz, J.A., Sánchez-Martínez, F. (2015). A generalised alignment template formalism and its application to the inference of shallow-transfer machine translation rules from scarce bilingual corpora. In *Computer Speech & Language*

Snover, M., Dorr, B., Schwartz, R., Micciulla, L., and Makhoul, J. (2006). A Study of Translation Edit Rate with Targeted Human Annotation. In *Proceedings of AMTA*

Unhammer, K., Trosterud, T. (2009). Reuse of free resources in machine translation between Nynorsk and Bokmål. In *Proceedings of the First International Workshop on Free/Open-Source Rule-Based Machine Translation*, Alicante, Spain.

Received May 2, 2016 , accepted May 18, 2016

Baltic J. Modern Computing, Vol. 4 (2016), No. 2, pp. 368–375

Re-assessing the Impact of SMT Techniques with Human Evaluation: a Case Study on English↔Croatian

Antonio TORAL[1], Raphael RUBINO[2], Gema RAMÍREZ-SÁNCHEZ[3]

[1] ADAPT Centre, School of Computing, Dublin City University, Ireland
[2] Universität des Saarlandes, 66123 Saarbrücken, Germany
[3] Prompsit Language Engineering, Avenida de la Universidad s/n, ES-03202 Elche, Spain

`atoral@computing.dcu.ie`, `raphael.rubino@uni-saarland.de`,
`gramirez@prompsit.com`

Abstract. We re-assess the impact brought by a set of widely-used SMT models and techniques by means of human evaluation. These include different types of development sets (crowdsourced vs translated professionally), reordering, operation sequence and bilingual neural language models as well as common approaches to data selection and combination. In some cases our results corroborate previous findings found in the literature, when those approaches were evaluated in terms of automatic metrics, but in some other cases they do not.

Keywords: human evaluation, operation sequence model, bilingual neural language model, data selection

1 Introduction

In the field of statistical machine translation (SMT), when new models and techniques are introduced, it is rather common to assess their performance in terms of automatic metrics solely for just one or a few language pairs. Upon showing significant improvement and being implemented as free/open-source software, some of these techniques become then widely used in the community. In this paper we select a relevant set of such techniques and evaluate the impact they bring by means of a human evaluation.

This paper is part of a wider activity whose goal is to rapidly provide machine translation (MT) for under-resourced languages along with a better insight on how do they work and perform in a way that is meaningful not just for researchers but also for industrial adopters of MT. Our case study is on Croatian given its strategic importance to the EU as the official language of a recent member state. In this work we aim to assess the impact of the components of several SMT systems (English–Croatian in both directions) built for this purpose. To meet this aim, we evaluate, both automatically and manually, each component one at a time. Namely:

1. We assess the impact of using different development sets, produced by professional and amateur translators.
2. Compare the use of three reordering models (word-, phrase-based and hierarchical).
3. Measure the impact of using additional models recently introduced in the SMT pipeline. Specifically, the operation sequence model (OSM) and bilingual neural language models (BiNLM).
4. Assess the impact of different ways to select and combine data sets.
5. Compare our best systems to widely-used commercial systems.

2 Experimental Setting

2.1 MT Systems

SMT systems are trained with Moses 3.0,[4] using default settings unless mentioned otherwise, and tuned with MIRA (Cherry and Foster, 2012). Language models are of order 5 with Kneser-Ney modified smoothing.

The following publicly available parallel corpora are used for training: HrEnWaC 2.0,[5] the DGT Translation Memory,[6] the JRC Acquis,[7] SETimes(Agić and Ljubešić, 2014), TED talks,[8] OpenSubtitles 2013 cleaned (Esplà-Gomis et al., 2014) and SrEnWaC.[9] The last one is a parallel corpus for Serbian–English. The Serbian side is translated to Croatian with a rule-based system in order to get more English-Croatian parallel text.[10] Language models are trained on the hrWaC corpus[11] for Croatian, and on all the available English data for the translation task at WMT15.[12]

The development set consists of multiple translations into Croatian of the first 1,011 sentences from the English side of the WMT2012 test set. Namely, we have 1 translation produced by a professional translator and 2 by amateur translators. The test set consists of the first 1,000 sentences from the English side of the WMT2013 test set, translated into Croatian by a native speaker.

2.2 Evaluation

Each experiment is evaluated both automatically and manually (except the one in Section 3.4). We used the widely used automatic metrics BLEU (Papineni et al., 2002) and

---

[4] https://github.com/moses-smt/mosesdecoder/tree/RELEASE-3.0

[5] http://hdl.handle.net/11356/1058

[6] https://ec.europa.eu/jrc/en/language-technologies/dgt-translation-memory

[7] http://tinyurl.com/CroatianAcquis

[8] http://nlp.ffzg.hr/resources/corpora/ted-talks/

[9] http://hdl.handle.net/11356/1059

[10] https://svn.code.sf.net/p/apertium/svn/staging/apertium-hbs_HR-hbs_SR/

[11] http://nlp.ffzg.hr/resources/corpora/hrwac/

[12] http://www.statmt.org/wmt15/translation-task.html

TER (Snover et al., 2006). Statistical significance is calculated on BLEU scores with paired bootstrap resampling (1,000 iterations and $p = 0.95$).

The human evaluation consists of ranking MT outputs with Appraise.[13] For each experiment 100 randomly selected segments were ranked. All the annotations were carried out by 2 native Croatian speakers with an advanced level of English. The following guidelines were provided to the annotators:

```
Given translations by more than two MT systems, the task is to rank them:
- Rank system A higher (rank1) than B (rank2), if the output of the first
is better than the output of the second.
- Rank both systems equally, A rank1 and B rank1, if the outputs are of
the same quality
- Use the highest rank possible, e.g. if you've three systems A, B and C,
and the quality of A and B is equivalent and both are better than C, then
do: A=rank1, B=rank1, C=rank2. Do NOT use lower rankings, e.g.: A=rank2,
B=rank2, C=rank4.
```

We then derive a human score for each system with the TrueSkill method adapted to MT evaluation (Sakaguchi et al., 2014) following its usage at WMT15.[14] Namely, we run 1,000 iterations of rankings followed by clustering ($p = 0.95$). If two systems are placed in different clusters (column "range" in results' tables) then the one with lower range is considered significantly better.

3 Experiments

3.1 Development Sets

In this experiment we aim to assess the impact of using a development set obtained by professional versus amateur translators. While professional translations should lead to a higher quality data set, its cost is in our case close to an order of magnitude (both in terms of price and time) higher than crowdsourcing. In this sense, Zbib et al. (2013) built MT systems for Arabic–English using development sets that were professionally translated and crowdsourced. They compared tuning with one reference (either professional or crowdsourced) and using both together as multiple references. The latter setup led to the best results. In our experiments we aim to corroborate these results for English-to-Croatian[15] and also compare the use of professional and crowdsourced translations for tuning. Results are shown in Table 1.

Following Zbib et al. (2013), we would expect the combination of both professional and crowdsourced translations to perform better than professional ones, which in turn would be expected to perform better than crowdsourced translations. An interesting question would be whether two crowdsourced translations would perform better than

---

[13] https://github.com/cfedermann/Appraise

[14] https://github.com/mjpost/wmt15

[15] This experiment is run only into Croatian as it is for this language that we have multiple references for the development set.

Table 1. Results (different development sets) for English→Croatian.

System	English→Croatian			
	BLEU	TER	Human	Range
crowd1	0.2362	0.6250	0.110	1-4
crowd2	0.2344	**0.6242**	0.027	1-4
crowd1+2	0.2348	0.6287	-0.109	2-5
prof	0.2273	0.6457	**0.225**	1-4
prof+crowd1+2	**0.2363**	0.6303	-0.253	3-5

one professional translation (Zbib et al. (2013) had only 1 translation of each type) as two crowdsourced translations, in our setup, are 5 times cheaper than one professional translation. The results are mixed: there is no clear winner neither for automatic metrics nor for human evaluation. This may indicate that the impact of the development set in our setup is too small to be of importance.

3.2 Reordering Models

We compare using a word-based reordering model solely (the default in the Moses MT toolkit) to adding two additional models: 1) phrase-based (with the same three orientations as the word-based model: monotone, swap and discontinuous) and 2) hierarchical (with four orientations: non merged, discontinuous, left and right). This combination has been shown to yield the best performance in terms of automatic metrics for English–Chinese and English–Arabic (Galley and Manning, 2008). Here we evaluate it for another language and not only automatically but also manually. Results are shown in Table 2.

Table 2. Results using different reordering models. Best results shown in bold.

System	English→Croatian				Croatian→English			
	BLEU	TER	Human	Range	BLEU	TER	Human	Range
Word-based	**0.2363**	**0.6303**	-0.117	1-2	0.3392	0.5211	**0.168**	1
Three	0.2355	0.6336	**0.117**	1-2	**0.3404**	**0.5202**	-0.168	2

The results are mixed. In terms of automatic metrics, the differences are very small and not significant. According to the human evaluation, the word-based model alone leads to significantly better results than using three models for Croatian-to-English. Although the usual word order is the same in English and Croatian (subject-verb-object, the rich case structure of Croatian makes it a rather free word order language. This may explain the non-conclusive results. The remaining experiments use three reordering models.

3.3 Additional Components

In this experiment we assess the impact brought by two additional components, OSM (Durrani et al., 2011) and BiNLM (Devlin et al., 2014), used both alone and jointly. Results are shown in Table 3.

Table 3. Results using additional components (OSM and BiNLM). Best results shown in bold. †️ indicates that a system is significantly better than the other ones ($p = 0.05$).

System	English→Croatian				Croatian→English			
	BLEU	TER	Human	Range	BLEU	TER	Human	Range
None	0.2355	0.6336	-0.330	3-4	0.3404	0.5202	-0.373	3-4
OSM	0.2408	0.6265	0.231	1-3	0.3460	**0.5088**	**0.207**	1-3
BiNLM	0.2379	0.6310	-0.352	3-4	0.3471	0.5138	0.039	1-4
OSM+BiNLM	**0.2457**†	**0.6198**	**0.452**	1-2	**0.3499**	0.5090	0.127	1-4

OSM results in gains over the baseline consistently, but this is not the case for BiNLM (lower human score into Croatian). The joint use of OSM and BiNLM leads to the best BLEU scores for both directions. Human ranges put OSM+BiNLM and OSM alone on top into Croatian while differences are not significant into English.

3.4 Data Selection and Combination

While the previous experiments used only HrEnWaC as training data, here we consider all available parallel corpora[16] (cf. Section 2.1) and experiment with data selection and combination.

For data selection, we concatenate the parallel corpora and rank their parallel sentences according to the bilingual cross-entropy difference heuristic (Moore and Lewis, 2010; Axelrod et al., 2011). This method was shown to reach state-of-the-art performance for domain adaptation in SMT (Rubino et al., 2014; Banerjee et al., 2015). As in-domain language model we consider SETimes and as out-of-domain a random set of sentences from the concatenated dataset of equal size. We split the ranked sentences into two groups, the top 25% (row "top" in Table 4) and the bottom 75% (rows "bottom"). We then experiment with applying the vocabulary saturation filter (Lewis and Eetemadi, 2013) to the bottom data set (rows "vsf"). Specifically, we drop sentences for which all its words have been seen already at least 10 times (Rubino et al., 2014).

As for combining data sets, we consider concatenation (rows "concat") and linear interpolation (rows "tmc") (Sennrich, 2012) of selected datasets (rows "tmc top bottom") and phrase tables built on the individual parallel corpora (row "7pt").

The systems evaluated in this experiment are built on different amounts of parallel data. Therefore, on top of providing evaluation metrics, we detail the size of each system, in terms of number of sentences in the training parallel corpora (column "%

---

[16] We keep the RMs, OSM and BiNLM trained on HrEnWaC as in this experiment we aim to measure the impact of additional entries in the phrase table.

Sent.")[17] and in terms of number of tokens (measured in millions in column "# token"). Results are shown in Table 4.

Table 4. Results applying data selection and combination. Best results shown in bold.

System	English→Croatian		Croatian→English		% Sent.	# tokens (M)	
	BLEU	TER	BLEU	TER		en	hr
concat	0.2409	0.6178	0.3636	0.4942	100	215.1	176.2
top	0.2487	**0.6115**	0.3679	0.4993	25	81.4	69.7
concat vsf	0.2423	0.6177	0.3640	0.4913	41	117.2	99.2
tmc top bottom	0.2480	0.6120	0.2974	0.5731	100	215.1	176.2
tmc top bottom vsf	**0.2497**	0.6118	0.3646	0.4906	41	117.2	99.2
tmc 7pt	0.2445	0.6147	**0.3721**	**0.4878**	100	215.1	176.2

While most systems outperform the baseline (concatenation of all the corpora), there is no clear winner among them. If one considers a trade-off between translation quality and parallel data size, then systems "top" (trained on 25% of the sentence pairs) and "tmc top bottom vsf" (trained on 41% of the sentence pairs) seem the best choices.

3.5 Comparison to Commercial Systems

Finally, we evaluate our best system[18] against commercial systems available online by Yandex, Microsoft and Google.[19]

Results are shown in Table 5. Google comes on top for both directions, but it is not significantly better than our system (according to the human evaluation), which on its turn is significantly better than both Microsoft and Yandex for English-to-Croatian, and than Yandex only for Croatian-to-English.

Table 5. Results comparing to commercial systems. Best results shown in bold. † indicates that a system is significantly better than the other ones ($p = 0.05$).

System	English→Croatian				Croatian→English			
	BLEU	TER	Human	Range	BLEU	TER	Human	Range
Google	**0.2673†**	**0.5946**	**0.899**	1-2	**0.4099†**	**0.4635**	**0.672**	1-2
Ours	0.2544	0.6081	0.515	1-2	0.3852	0.4819	0.291	1-3
Microsoft	0.2281	0.6263	-0.650	3-4	0.3658	0.5199	0.104	2-3
Yandex	0.2030	0.6801	-0.793	3-4	0.3463	0.5311	-1.306	4

---

[17] This is measured as the percentage of sentences used (taking 100% as the total used in the concatenation).

[18] I.e. system "top" from the previous experiment with reordering models, OSM and BiNLM trained on the "top" dataset.

[19] https://translate.yandex.com/, http://bing.com/translator/ and https://translate.google.com/, respectively. The translations were obtained on December 22nd, 2015.

4   Conclusions

In this paper we have re-assessed the impact brought to SMT systems by a set of widely-used techniques by means of individual experiments for a not very common language pair in the literature: English–Croatian. Namely, we have performed human evaluations on different types of development sets (crowdsourced vs translated professionally), re-ordering models, operation sequence and bilingual neural language models as well as common approaches to data selection and combination. In some cases our results have corroborated previous findings found in the literature, when those approaches were evaluated solely in terms of automatic metrics, but in some other cases they did not.

Acknowledgements

The research leading to these results has received funding from the European Union Seventh Framework Programme FP7/2007-2013 under grant agreement PIAP-GA-2012-324414 (Abu-MaTran).

References

Željko Agić and Nikola Ljubešić. The SETimes.HR linguistically annotated corpus of Croatian. In *Proceedings of LREC*, 2014. ISBN 978-2-9517408-8-4.

Amittai Axelrod, Xiaodong He, and Jianfeng Gao. Domain adaptation via pseudo in-domain data selection. In *Proceedings of EMNLP*, pages 355–362, 2011.

Pratyush Banerjee, Raphael Rubino, Johann Roturier, and Josef van Genabith. Quality estimation-guided supplementary data selection for domain adaptation of statistical machine translation. *Machine Translation*, 29(2):77–100, 2015.

Colin Cherry and George Foster. Batch Tuning Strategies for Statistical Machine Translation. In *Proceedings of NAACL*, pages 427–436, 2012. ISBN 978-1-937284-20-6.

Jacob Devlin, Rabih Zbib, Zhongqiang Huang, Thomas Lamar, Richard Schwartz, and John Makhoul. Fast and Robust Neural Network Joint Models for Statistical Machine Translation. In *Proceedings of ACL*, pages 1370–1380, 2014.

Nadir Durrani, Helmut Schmid, and Alexander Fraser. A joint sequence translation model with integrated reordering. In *Proceedings of ACL*, pages 1045–1054, 2011.

Miquel Esplà-Gomis, Mikel L. Forcada, Nikola Ljubešić, Vassilis Papavassiliou, Prokopis Prokopidis, Sergio Ortiz-Rojas, Tommi Pirinen, Raphaël Rubino, and Antonio Toral. Deliverable D3.1b Acquisition for cycle 2. Technical report, Abu-MaTran project, 2014.

Michel Galley and Christopher D Manning. A simple and effective hierarchical phrase reordering model. In *Proceedings of EMNLP*, pages 848–856, 2008.

William D Lewis and Sauleh Eetemadi. Dramatically reducing training data size through vocabulary saturation. In *Proceedings of WMT*, pages 281–291, 2013.

Robert C. Moore and William Lewis. Intelligent Selection of Language Model Training Data. In *Proceedings of ACL*, pages 220–224, 2010.

Kishore Papineni, Salim Roukos, Todd Ward, and Wei-Jing Zhu. Bleu: a method for automatic evaluation of machine translation. In *Proceedings of ACL*, pages 311–318, 2002.

Raphael Rubino, Antonio Toral, Victor M Sánchez-Cartagena, Jorge Ferrández-Tordera, Sergio Ortiz-Rojas, Gema Ramırez-Sánchez, Felipe Sánchez-Martınez, and Andy Way. Abu-MaTran at WMT 2014 translation task: Two-step data selection and RBMT-style synthetic rules. In *Proceedings of WMT*, 2014.

Keisuke Sakaguchi, Matt Post, and Benjamin Van Durme. Efficient Elicitation of Annotations for Human Evaluation of Machine Translation. In *Proceedings of WMT*, pages 1–11, 2014.

Rico Sennrich. Perplexity minimization for translation model domain adaptation in statistical machine translation. In *Proceedings of ACL*, pages 539–549, 2012.

Matthew Snover, Bonnie Dorr, Richard Schwartz, Linnea Micciulla, and John Makhoul. A study of translation edit rate with targeted human annotation. In *Proceedings of AMTA*, pages 223–231, 2006.

Rabih Zbib, Gretchen Markiewicz, Spyros Matsoukas, Richard M. Schwartz, and John Makhoul. Systematic Comparison of Professional and Crowdsourced Reference Translations for Machine Translation. In *Proceedings of NAACL*, pages 612–616, 2013.

Received May 3, 2016 , accepted May 18, 2016

Baltic J. Modern Computing, Vol. 4 (2016), No. 2, 376-400

Proceedings
of the 19th annual conference
of the European Association
for Machine Translation
(EAMT)

Riga, Latvia, 2016

Projects/Products

TectoMT – a Deep-Linguistic Core of the Combined Chimera MT system

Martin POPEL, Roman SUDARIKOV, Ondřej BOJAR,
Rudolf ROSA, Jan HAJIČ

Charles University in Prague, Faculty of Mathematics and Physics, Institute of Formal and Applied Linguistics, Malostranské nám. 25, CZ-11800 Prague 1, Czech Republic

`{popel,sudarikov,bojar,rosa,hajic}@ufal.mff.cuni.cz`

Abstract. Chimera is a machine translation system that combines the TectoMT deep-linguistic core with phrase-based MT system Moses. For English–Czech pair it also uses the Depfix post-correction system. All the components run on Unix/Linux platform and are open source (available from Perl repository CPAN and the LINDAT/CLARIN repository). The main website is https://ufal.mff.cuni.cz/tectomt. The development is currently supported by the QTLeap 7th FP project (http://qtleap.eu).

TectoMT and Chimera

TectoMT (the deep-linguistic core of Chimera) is an open-source MT system based on the Treex platform for general natural-language processing. TectoMT uses a combination of rule-based and statistical (trained) modules ("blocks" in Treex terminology), with a statistical transfer based on HMTM (Hidden Markov Tree Model) at the level of a deep, so-called tectogrammatical representation of sentence structure. In the Chimera combination, TectoMT is complemented by a Moses PB-SMT system (factored setup with additional language models over morphological tags) and optionally also by an automatic postprocessing (correction) component called Depfix. Chimera can be thus characterized as a hybrid system that combines statistical MT with deep linguistic analysis and automatic post-correction system, which is useful especially for translation into inflectionally rich languages. The three systems are combined serially: TectoMT runs first, then an additional Moses phrase table is extracted from TectoMT's input and output. The additional table is then used in a weighted combination with a large Moses translation table to produce pre-final output. Depfix then re-parses the output (as well as input) and generates the final output based on rules reflecting morphosyntactic properties of the target language.

Chimera was transferred from English Czech to additional three language pairs (English to Dutch, Portuguese and Spanish) within the QTLeap 7th EU project.

References

Dušek, O., Gomes, L., Novák, M., Popel, M., Rosa, R. (2015). New Language Pairs in TectoMT. *Proceedings of the 10th Workshop on Machine Translation*, ISBN 978-1-941643-32-7, ACL, Stroudsburg, PA, USA, 98–104.

Rosa, R., Dušek, O., Novák, M., Popel. M. (2015). Translation Model Interpolation for Domain Adaptation in TectoMT. *Proceedings of the 1st Deep Machine Translation Workshop*, ISBN 978-80-904571-7-1, Charles University in Prague, Faculty of Mathematics and Physics, Institute of Formal and Applied Linguistics, Prague, Czech Republic, 89–96.

Bojar, O., Tamchyna, A. (2015). CUNI in WMT15: Chimera Strikes Again. *Proceedings of the 10th Workshop on Machine Translation*, ISBN 978-1-941643-32-7, ACL, Stroudsburg, PA, USA, 79–83.

WiTKoM - Virtual Sign Language Translator Project

Katarzyna BARCZEWSKA[1], Jakub GAŁKA[1,2], Filip MALAWSKI[1],
Mariusz MĄSIOR[1], Dorota SZULC[1], Tomasz WILCZYŃSKI[1,2],
Krzysztof WRÓBEL[1]

[1]AGH University of Science and Technology, Department of Electronics, Poland
[2]VoicePIN.com Sp. z o. o., Poland

`jgalka@agh.edu.pl`

Abstract. WiTKoM (Virtual Sign Language Translator) is an interdisciplinary research project carried out by AGH University of Science and Technology and VoicePIN.com, which aims to create a Polish Sign Language (PJM, pl. Polski Język Migowy) translator. This work was supported by the Polish National Centre for Research and Development – Applied Research Program under Grant PBS2/B3/21/2013 tilted Virtual sign language translator. Website: www.witkom.info.

Description

WiTKoM is intended to promote the social inclusion. Hearing-impaired people constitute a considerable language minority in Poland. PJM is currently experiencing a renaissance, having 50,000–100,000 users, according to recent statistics. The practical goal of the project is to develop the technology and solutions for communication support for hearing-impaired.

Project WiTKoM consists of various separate elements, responsible for the particular stage of Polish to PJM translation, and statement creation by the signing avatar. Within the project, several developments have been made: know-how, technologies, and automatic PJM translation software. The developed technology includes:

- real-time user-independent gesture recognition system;
- PL–PJM translator, from Polish sentence analysis, through machine translation methods, to avatar transcription system employing HamNoSys;
- mobile application prototype for gesture recognition;
- accelerometer-based sensor glove for gesture motion acquisition;
- computer application for conducting automatic dialogues, module for building and managing dialogue;
- computer application for multi-stream data acquisition and management;
- a rich set of developing tools for conducting researches in the fields of image processing and gesture recognition;
- annotated PJM gesture corpus acquired with RGB and depth cameras;
- Polish-PJM parallel corpus for machine translation research.

WiTKoM project is still in progress. The main focus is currently on the development of continuous statement recognition algorithms and practical use-case deployments.

Multi-Level Quality Prediction with QuEst++

Gustavo H. PAETZOLD, Lucia SPECIA

University of Sheffield, Department of Computer Science
Western Bank, Sheffield, South Yorkshire S10 2TN, United Kingdom

ghpaetzold1@sheffield.ac.uk, l.specia@sheffield.ac.uk

Abstract. We introduce QuEst++: an open-source multi-level Machine Translation Quality Estimation framework. The core of the framework is implemented in Java, and wrappers for a Machine Learning module implemented in Python are provided. QuEst++'s development was funded by the EAMT, as well as by the QT21 and EXPERT projects. The framework is distributed under the BSD license and can be downloaded from: https://github.com/ghpaetzold/questplusplus.

Description

QuEst++ is an extended and improved version of QuEst, a framework for Machine Translation Quality Estimation (Specia et. al., 2013). While the original QuEst framework provides only sentence-level Quality Estimation, QuEst++ is a multi-level framework that combines solutions to word-, sentence- and document-level Quality Estimation in the same pipeline.

QuEst++ is composed of two modules: Feature Extraction and Machine Learning. The Feature Extraction module provides access to 43 word-level features, 148 sentence-level features and 67 document-level features. If certain resources needed for feature extraction are not provided, QuEst++ employs its Automatic Resource Generation routines to produce the resources.

The Machine Learning module offers all the utilities previously included in QuEst, and also an easy-to-use interface to CRFSuite (Okazaki, 2007), which allows for state-of-the-art Conditional Random Field models to be trained. As reported in the WMT 2015 Quality Estimation tasks' results (Bojar et al., 2015), QuEst++ itself performs well as compared to other systems. In addition, it has been used as the basis to create more advanced approaches. More details on QuEst++ can be found in Specia et al. (2015).

References

Specia, L., Paetzold, G., Scarton, C. (2015). Multi-level Translation Quality Prediction with QuEst++. In *ACL-IJCNLP 2015 System Demonstrations*, 115–120, Beijing.
Bojar, O., Chatterjee, R., Federmann, C., Haddow, B., Huck, M., Hokamp, C. Koehn, P., Logacheva, V., Monz, C., Negri, M., Post, M., Scarton, S., Specia, L., Turchi, M. (2015). Findings of the 2015 Workshop on Statistical Machine Translation. In *WMT*, 1–46, Lisbon.
Specia, L., Shah, K., De Souza, J. G., & Cohn, T. (2013). QuEst-A Translation Quality Estimation Framework. In ACL 2013, 79-84, Sofia.
Okazaki, N. (2007). CRFsuite: A Fast Implementation of Conditional Random Fields (CRFs). URL http://www. chokkan. org/software/crfsuite.

Apertium: A Free/Open-Source Platform for Machine Translation and Basic Language Technology

Mikel L. FORCADA[1] and Francis M. TYERS[2]

[1] Departament de Llenguatges i Sistemes Informàtics, Universitat d'Alacant, Alacant
[2] HSL-fakultehta, UiT Norgga árktalas universitehta, Romsa

`mlf@dlsi.ua.es, francis.tyers@uit.no`

Abstract. Apertium is a free/open-source platform for rule-based machine translation which was started in 2005. The Apertium community is using it to build machine translation systems for a variety of language pairs, especially, but not only, for related-language pairs, where shallow transfer suffices to produce good quality translations. Apertium is also being used to develop monolingual language processors for these languages. We present the Apertium platform: the translation engine, the encoding of linguistic data, and the tools developed around the platform.

Description

Apertium (wiki.apertium.org, Forcada et al. 2011) is a free/open-source platform for machine translation (MT), providing a shallow-transfer rule-based MT engine, data (dictionaries, rules) for more than 40 language pairs, and a wide variety of software to manage, convert and exploit the data and run the engine in a variety of environments. Apertium is also the free/open-source community developing it since 2005.

Apertium is built as a pipeline in which the source text is gradually converted into target text. The pipeline contains, among others, filters to handle markup, finite-state morphological analysers and generators using both a native format and the Helsinki Finite-State Toolkit (HFST) one, part-of-speech taggers using Constraint Grammar, hidden Markov Models, and sliding-window classifiers, and shallow-transfer rules capable of identifying, transforming and reordering syntactic chunks. These components may also be used for other human-language technologies besides MT.

Apertium is also available in several end-user products: apps for Android smartphones and tablets, a plugin for the OmegaT computer-aided translation environment, and a number of stand-alone applications for desktops. It also powers the multilingual open-content management environment, Wikimedia Content Translation, used to translate Wikipedia articles.

Finally, Apertium is both a research and a business platform, enabling reproducibility and transferability of results and successful marketing of MT products and services.

References

Forcada, M. L., Ginestí-Rosell, M., Nordfalk, J., O'Regan, J., Ortiz-Rojas, S., Pérez-Ortiz, J. A., Sánchez-Martínez, F., Ramírez-Sánchez, G. and Tyers, F. M. (2011) Apertium: a free/open-source platform for rule-based machine translation. Machine Translation 24(1) 1–18

BabelDr: A Web Platform for Rapid Construction of Phrasebook-Style Medical Speech Translation Applications

Pierrette BOUILLON, Hervé SPECHBACH

FTI/TIM, Geneva University, Geneva, Switzerland
Hôpitaux Universitaires de Genève, Geneva, Switzerland

Pierrette.Bouillon@unige.ch, Herve.Spechbach@hcuge.ch

Abstract. BabelDr (http://babeldr.unige.ch/) is a joint project of Geneva's Faculty of Translation and Interpretation (FTI) and University Hospitals (HUG), that has been active since July 2015. The goal is to develop methods that allow rapid prototyping of medium-vocabulary web-enabled medical speech translators, with particular emphasis on languages spoken by victims of the current European refugee crisis. A demonstrator system freely available on the project site translates spoken French medical examination questions into four languages.

BabelDr (http://babeldr.unige.ch/) is a joint project of Geneva University's Faculty of Translation and Interpretation (FTI/TIM) and Geneva University Hospital (HUG), active since July 2015 under funding from "La fondation privée des HUG". The goal is to develop methods that allow rapid prototyping of medium-vocabulary web-enabled medical speech translators, with particular emphasis on languages spoken by migrants. The application can be characterised as a flexible speech-enabled phrasebook (Rayner et al 2015). Semantic coverage consists of a prespecified set of utterance-types (around 2000 in the current version), but users can use a wide variety of surface forms when speaking to the system. Each utterance-type is associated with a canonical source-language version, which is rendered into the target languages by suitably qualified translation experts. The central design goals are to ensure that a) translations are completely reliable, b) the bulk of the work can be performed directly by translation experts, with minimal or no involvement from language engineers, c) speech recognition performance is excellent for in-coverage data and adequate even for new users, d) new versions of the live app can be quickly deployed over the web, enabling rapid updating of coverage in response to requests from medical staff, e) new target languages can easily be added, enabling flexibility in the face of changing patient demographics. A demonstrator system freely accessible at http://babeldr.unige.ch/demos-and-resources/ translates French into Spanish, Italian, Arabic and Tigrinya.

References

Rayner, M. et al. (2015). Helping Domain Experts Build Phrasal Speech Translation Systems. Proceedings of the Workshop on Future and Emerging Trends in Language Technology, Sevilla, Spain, pages 1-12.

SCATE – Smart Computer Aided Translation Environment

V. VANDEGHINSTE[1], T. VANALLEMEERSCH[1], L. AUGUSTINUS[1],
J. PELEMANS[1], G. HEYMANS[1], I. VAN DER LEK-CIUDIN[1],
A. TEZCAN[2], D. DEGRAEN[3], J. VAN DEN BERGH[3], L. MACKEN[2],
E. LEFEVER[2], M. MOENS[1], P. WAMBACQ[1], F. STEURS[1],
K. CONINX[3], F. VAN EYNDE[1]

[1]University of Leuven – Departments of Linguistics, Computer Science, and Electronical
Engineering; [2]Ghent University – LT3; [3]Hasselt University - EDM

`scate-board@ccl.kuleuven.be`

Abstract. The SCATE project aims at improving translators' efficiency through improvements in translation technology, evaluation of computer-aided translation, terminology extraction from comparable corpora, speech recognition accuracy, and work flows and personalised user interfaces. It is funded by IWT-SBO[*], project nr. 130041. http://www.ccl.kuleuven.be/scate/

Envisaged Project Results

We present the envisaged results of SCATE, now the project is mid-term, with two more years to go.

We have surveyed and observed translators with respect to the following aspects: human-machine interaction in post-editing, human acquisition of domain knowledge and terminology, and workflow usage and interface personalization. We are researching different computer-aided translation (CAT) technologies, such as syntax-based fuzzy matching and concordancing, tools for speedier and more consistent collaborative translation, automated term extraction methods from comparable corpora, and integrated models and domain adaptation for speech as a post-editing method. Concerning MT Technology, we are working on syntax-based transduction, taxonomy-based confidence estimation metrics and speech translation. For these purposes, we have developed the following resources: a taxonomy of MT errors and manually annotated corpus of MT errors. Concerning the user interface, we are developing new approaches towards visualisation of translation features and towards flexible user interfaces. By the end of the project, we intend to integrate most of these aspects in a demonstration system that translates from English to Dutch.

We are interested in feedback from language service providers and translators: what do you consider useful and interesting – how can we improve your translation environment?

---

[*] The Flemish Agency for Innovation through Science and Technology, Strategic Basic Research.

HimL: Health in My Language

Barry HADDOW, Alex FRASER

Ludwig Maximilian University of Munich

`fraser@cis.lmu.de`

Abstract. HimL (www.himl.eu) is a three-year EU H2020 innovation action, which started in February 2015. Its aim is to increase the availability of public health information via automatic translation. Targeting languages of Central and Eastern Europe (Czech, German, Polish and Romanian) we aim to produce translations which are adapted to the health domain, semantically accurate and morphologically correct. The project is coordinated by Barry Haddow (University of Edinburgh) and includes two additional academic partners (Charles University and LMU Munich), one integration partner (Lingea) and two user partners (NHS 24 and Cochrane).

Description

In HimL we aim to deploy and evaluate machine translation systems for the public health domain, addressing domain adaptation, semantic accuracy and target morphology. The systems are used to tramslate content for NHS 24 (Scotland's national telehealth organisation) and Cochrane (an international NGO that produces systematic reviews of healthcare topics). The project has now been running for over a year, and we have already developed the first release of our translation systems and used them to translate the user partner websites. To build these systems, we have collected a large and diverse training set and are analysing the performance of existing domain adaptation techniques in combining these resources, as well as investigating the use of neural models in domain adaptation. We have been developing our corrective approaches to morphology handling, using machine learning to provide language independence, as well as extending the two-step approach to morphology to handle a wider range of phenomena, and new language pairs. For improved semantic accuracy we have experimented with using semantic roles to make sure important information is not lost, as well as developing methods to remove semantically incorrect translations from the model, and analysing the problems that arise in the translation of negation. The goal of semantic accuracy is supported by our development of new human and automatic semantic evaluation measures based on the UCCA (universal conceptual cognitive annotation) framework.

Acknowledgements

This project has received funding from the European Union's Horizon 2020 research and innovation programme under grant agreement No 644402.

OPUS – Parallel Corpora for Everyone

Jörg TIEDEMANN

Department of Modern Languages, University of Helsinki, 00014 Helsinki, Finland

`jorg.tiedemann@helsinki.fi`

Abstract. Abstract. OPUS is a large collection of freely available parallel corpora that we provide in various formats and packages. All data sets are completely aligned at the sentence level for all possible language pairs. OPUS covers over 200 languages and language variants with a total of about 3.2 billion sentences and sentence fragments containing over 28 billion tokens. The collection contains data from various sources and domains and each sub-corpus is provided in common data formats to make it easy to integrate them in research and development. OPUS also provides tools and on-line interfaces for exploring parts of the collection and is continuously growing in terms of size and coverage.

Description

Parallel data sets in OPUS[1] are freely available and cover various domains. The largest collections (in terms of volume) come from political and administrative sources such as the European Commission and user-provided movie subtitles in various languages. Other sources include software localisation, multilingual news providers, translated descriptions of medical products, religious texts and multilingual wikis and other websites. OPUS is organised by source and one of the main principles of the collection is to preserve the original data structures (file structure, formatting, meta-data) as much as possible. The goal of our project is to make the collection applicable as widely as possible. Currently, OPUS comprises 3.2 billion sentences with over 28 billion tokens in total. An important principle is complete sentence alignment for all language pairs, thus, supporting even low-density languages and unusual combinations. There are bitexts such as Arabic–Korean or Indonesian–Latvian with over one million translation units among the 12,572 language pairs with their 10.8 billion translation units in total. We provide the data in standalone XML and stand-off alignment (as its native format) but also commonly used formats such as TMX and aligned plain Unicode text. The latest edition of OPUS contains parallel sentences extracted from Wikipedia and a significantly extended collection of movie subtitles, now also including intra-lingual alignments of alternative translations. Furthermore, we also provide word alignments and phrase-tables for statistical machine translation (SMT) ready to be used in common SMT toolboxes. A subset of our data is also available via on-line search interfaces. Feedback and contributions are welcome.

---

[1] http://opus.lingfil.uu.se

Integration of Machine Translation Paradigms

Marta R. COSTA-JUSSÀ

TALP Research Center, Universitat Politècnica de Catalunya, Barcelona

`marta.ruiz@upc.edu`

Abstract. Machine Translation (MT) is a highly interdisciplinary and multidisciplinary field since it is approached from the point of view of engineering, computer science, informatics, statistics and linguists. The goal of this research project is to approach the different profiles in the MT community by providing a new integrated MT paradigm which mainly includes linguistic technologies and statistical algorithms.

Description

The proposed new paradigm in this project provides solutions to current MT challenges such as unknown words, reordering and semantic ambiguities. The project focuses on three of the most spoken languages: Chinese, Spanish and English. These language pairs do not only involve many economic and cultural interests, but they also include some of the most relevant MT challenges such as morphological, syntactic and semantic variations. This project is funded under FP7-PEOPLE-2011-299251-IOF MarieCurie International Outgoing Fellowship[1]. The project duration is from 2012-12-07 to 2016-07-08. The project coordinator center is Universitat Politècnica de Catalunya (UPC, Barcelona) and the supervisor is Prof. José A. R. Fonollosa. The host institution has been the Institute for Infocomm Research (I2R, Singapore) and the corresponding supervisors were Prof. Haizhou Li and Dr. Rafael E. Banchs. The MarieCurie Researcher is Dr. Marta R. Costa-jussà. See a complete list of the project publications[2].

References

Costa-jussà, M. R. How much Hybridization does MT Need? *Journal of the Association for Information Science and Technology*, 6(10), 2015

Costa-jussà, M. R. and Centelles, J. Description of the Chinese-to-Spanish RBMT System Developed with a Hybrid Combination of Human Annotation and Statistical Techniques. *ACM Transactions on Asian and Low-Resource Language Information Processing*, 15(1), 2016

Costa-jussà, M. R and Fonollosa, J.A.R. Character-based Neural MT Proc. of ACL, 2016

---

[1] http://www.costa-jussa.com/projects/ongoing/imtrap/
[2] http://www.costa-jussa.com

STAR Transit & STAR MT:
Morphologically Generated Additional Information for Improving MT Quality

Nadira HOFMANN

STAR Group, Wiesholz 35, 8262 Ramsen, Switzerland

nadira.hofmann@star-group.net

Abstract. As an experienced developer of language processing solutions, STAR Group applies its proven technologies to MT training: Transit's morphological support for 80+ languages is used to extract inflected terminology from dictionaries and reference material without any additional effort. This additional input for the engine training noticeably improves the MT quality – especially in morphologically rich languages.

Description

For STAR's MT system STAR MT, validated customer-specific dictionaries are used for MT training. However, dictionaries contain terms in canonical forms, while text corpora predominantly contains inflected forms. A large proportion of the terminological potential would remain untapped if engines were only trained with canonical forms.

This is where STAR's experience pays off: The TMS Transit offers morphological terminology support for over 80 languages -- not just simple stemming, but using linguistic expertise mapped out in rules that have been tried and tested throughout years.

As a result, inflected forms in the source and target language of a bilingual body of text are reliably identified and used to enrich the training material. This additional information is particularly valuable for the quality of the MT because it is validated twice: Customer-validated canonical forms that are retrieved from the dictionary along with their inflected forms that are actually used in the validated translation memory.

With this approach, STAR MT benefits from Transit's existing and proven morphological technology to create terminology that offers added value without investing any time. In practice, this brings about significant improvements in quality: For a customer-specific German-French engine, an additional 17% of terminology was extracted and the BLEU score increased by 1.1 points. The translations that are created from this were clearly selected as preferred translations by the translators who carried out the manual evaluation of the sentence BLEU lists.

References

Pinnis, M. (2015). Dynamic Terminology Integration Methods in Statistical Machine Translation, Proceedings of the 18th Annual Conference of the European Association for Machine Translation, 89-96.

AltLang: an Automatic Converter between Varieties of English, Spanish, French and Portuguese

Gema RAMÍREZ-SÁNCHEZ

Prompsit Language Engineering, Av. de la Unversitat s/n, 03202, Elx, Alacant, Spain

`gramirez@prompsit.com`

Abstract. AltLang is a rule-based automatic converter for language varieties. It deals with differences in spelling, lexicon and local grammar along with numeric, style and punctuation conventions. It is available for varieties of English, Spanish, French and Portuguese. AltLang is based on the GNU GPL-based free/open-source technologies of the Apertium platform, and is offered as a service by Prompsit. It can be tested through an online application at www.altlang.net.

Description

AltLang is a rule-based automatic converter for language varieties. It aims at minimising the effort required to generate content in different varieties of the same language by automatically replacing controlled existing differences between them. AltLang can convert between American and British English, Canadian and European French, Latin American and European Spanish and Brazilian and European Portuguese with high accuracy. The technology behind AltLang comes from the free/open-source Apertium platform (Forcada et al. 2011). Data for dictionaries and rules have been semi-automatically adapted from two main sources: Apertium data and freely available or client-owned bilingual corpora. AltLang's knowledge grows through continuous contributions from clients and testers. AltLang gives priority to user-defined vocabulary and translation memories: vocabulary is input as a simple two-column spreadsheet and translation memories are supported through standard TMX files. AltLang reports basic statistics about the conversions (number of words and characters in source and target and number of substitution, shifts, insertions and deletions). It also shows the individual changes performed to a document with a convenient colouring. All these features allow the user to have full control over the behaviour of AltLang. It deals with a wide range of file formats including some interchange and localization ones (.xliff, .po). It can be used through an API, AltLang's web application and is available in other third-party tools such as the MateCat translation platform. Prompsit offers customisation services for AltLang to add new languages, new language varieties or domain-adaptation.

References

Forcada, M. L.; Ginestí-Rosell, M.; Nordfalk, J.; O'Regan, J.; Ortiz-Rojas, S.; Perez-Ortiz, J. A.; Sanchez-Martínez, F.; Ramírez.-Sánchez, G.; and Tyers, F. M. (2011). Apertium: a free/open-source platform for rule-based machine translation; Machine Translation, 25(2):127–144.

iEMS – Interactive Experiment Management System for Machine Translation

Pēteris ŅIKIFOROVS

`p@mak.id.lv`

Abstract. Interactive Experiment Management System (Interactive EMS or iEMS) is an experiment management system with a graphical user interface for designing and running statistical machine translation experiments. It is written in JavaScript and runs in all modern desktop browsers with no installation. iEMS produces a script that can be used to train a complete machine translation engine from scratch. There is an optional backend that can be used to launch and configure virtual servers on the Amazon Web Services cloud for running experiments. It is an open-source project licensed under the Apache 2.0 license. The development of iEMS is supported by the European Association for Machine Translation (EAMT). Project website: https://github.com/pdonald/iems

Description

Training a statistical machine translation engine consists of many steps. There are experiment management systems like Moses EMS and eman that help manage all these steps. However, their configuration is stored in text files which makes it is difficult to visualize the order of execution and adding or modifying steps may require diving into application code.

iEMS is an interactive experiment management system with a graphical user interface that aims to make it easy to design and run machine translation experiments from scratch. The main objective of the project is to have very little friction to get started. It is a single-page application written in JavaScript intended to run in modern desktop browsers without any setup.

In the application, there are several predefined tools that represent various steps in machine translation training that can be dragged and dropped onto a design surface. They can be linked together to set the order of execution. Tools can be grouped which allows quick swapping one set of tools with another.

There is also a backend that allows the user to run their experiments. The experiments can be run on a local host via the secure shell SSH or a new virtual server can be launched to run them on the Amazon Web Services cloud with a single click. Both regular (only pay for what you use) and spot (cheaper but can be terminated at any time) types of virtual servers are supported. Docker, a tool for automating the deployment of software inside Linux containers, is used for provisioning which means it is not necessary to compile or install dependencies for machine translation tools and setting up the server for use takes very little time.

The project is still in development. Its development is supported by the European Association for Machine Translation.

KantanLQR: A Platform for Human Evaluation of Machine Translation Output to Drive Engine Rapid Improvement

Laura CASANELLAS LURI

KantanMT, Invent Building, Dublin City University, Glasnevin, Dublin 9, Ireland

Laurac@kantanmt.com, Tonyod@kantanmt.com

Abstract: KantanLQR is a quality review tool dedicated to making human evaluation of machine translation (MT) faster, seamless and more efficient. Its final goal is to dramatically reduce the time of engine re-training. It is a tool aimed to project managers (PMs) and reviewers. It is part of the KantanMT suite of tools and includes comprehensive error typology based on industry standards that can be customized to address the needs of each specific project. Some of the functionalities include automatic workflow and report creation, as well as sophisticated visuals produced in real time. KantanLQR is cloud-based and does not require any software instalments or license, only a monthly subscription. www.kantanmt.com.

Description

KantanLQR technology removes the need of static forms by offering an automated workflow that can be customized to the dynamic character of quality definition and the industry requirements of fast, simple and customizable tools. Up until now the industry would have used different forms depending on the type of evaluation required; for instance, evaluation of an output that will be used for gisting should focus on *usability* and does not require a complex form that includes error typology, whereas a project with the goal of producing full post-edited publishable content will require something more comprehensive. KantanLQR provides this type of flexibility. With the use of this platform, the linguistic skills of the reviewers assigned to the project are maximized, as they can focus on the review and post-editing of the MT segments without being overburdened with complex interfaces.

This tool is designed for both reviewers and PMs to automate the review workflows involved in improving the quality and translation fidelity of their customized KantanMT engines. It will reduce the time required to quality review the MT engines by as much as 50% and it will improve team collaboration and workflow management. KantanLQR is based on the concept that the best MT solution is the one that can be intelligently customized and improved. The gains are twofold: the quality of the MT output is checked and assessed following specific quality requirements that have been set up by the PM, and the linguistic edits and feedback can be used to further retrain the engine.

As this process is automated, it reduces time. Segments are distributed among reviewers who work using the error typology that have been customized for the project. Results are tracked in real time and progress is easily monitored. The outcome becomes a radiography of an engine at a glance, as the report containing data gathered from all reviewers involved is displayed in a highly visual manner.

PangeaMT v3 – Customise Your Own Machine Translation Environment

Alexandre HELLE, Manuel HERRANZ

Pangeanic BI-Europe SL, Av de las Cortes Valencianas, 26-5 Of. 107, 46015 Valencia, Spain

a.helle@pangeanic.com, m.herranz@pangeanic.com

Abstract. PangeaMT is the tool developed by Pangeanic in 2010 to automate translation processes. Pangeanic, together with the Computer Science Institute (ITI) of Valencia has completed the development of PangeaMT v3 platform as part of the Spanish national project "COR: FAST AND EFFICIENT TRANSLATION MANAGEMENT TOOL" with funding from the Spanish research organization CDTI, dependant from the Ministry of Economy. PangeaMT (http://pangeamt.com/) is based on Moses and it runs on GNU/Linux.

Customized Machine Translation

PangeaMT is a full machine translation environment. Pangeanic was the first LSP in the world to make commercial use of a Moses version with it as reported in the FP7 Euromatrixplus[1] project and earlier at AMTA (Yuste 2010). The platform is capable of processing large translation volumes and manage training datasets. It is ideal for companies, corporations and institutions that produce large amounts of documentation. It can be used to train engines with the client's own previously translated material and terminology, overcoming some of Moses limitations. Clients are free to create and retrain engines with new material. Thanks to its interfaces, the system can accept calls from external systems to translate digital and web content, or from CAT (Computer Assisted Translation) tools to improve translator's productivity.

PangeaMT has now reached version 3. New features include the use of monolingual data managed by the user to train different language models at will, further improvements in machine translation customisation and hybridisation. Version 3 also offers new interface connections, custom-built hybridisation techniques which can easily be expanded, and even a choice of translation engines (Moses, Apertium and third-party services) and algorithms if required for particular language pairs.

References

Yuste, E. et al. (2010) PangeaMT – putting standards to work... well. In Proceedings of The Ninth Conference of the Association for Machine Translation in the Americas – AMTA 2010, Denver. Available at: amta2010.amtaweb.org/AMTA/papers/4-04-HerranzYusteEtal.pdf

---

[1] http://www.euromatrixplus.net/moses-decoder/

Interlingual Translation in the Grammatical Framework (GF)

Aarne RANTA, Krasimir ANGELOV, Thomas HALLGREN,
Prasanth KOLACHINA, Inari LISTENMAA

Department of Computer Science and Engineering, Chalmers University of Technology and
University of Gothenburg, 41296 Gothenburg, Sweden

{aarne,krasimir,hallgren,prasanth.kolachina,inari}@cse.gu.se

Abstract. Grammatical Framework (GF) is a grammar formalism for *multilingual grammars*, where many languages share a common *abstract syntax*. The abstract syntax can be used as a translation interlingua. GF was initially designed for domain-specific controlled language systems, but it has in recent years scaled up to wide-coverage translation as well. GF is an open-source project with a world-wide community that has created grammars for over 30 languages. Fifteen of these languages are currently included in a wide-coverage translator, which is available in the GF cloud and also as a mobile app, the GF Offline Translator, with a compact size that fits in a mobile phone. We plan to demo both kinds of systems in the conference.

Description

Interlingual grammar-based translation is probably as far from the current mainstream as an MT approach can be. However, it is a natural choice in controlled language applications, where a translator can work much like a compiler with multiple source and target languages and a shared abstract syntax. The original purpose of GF[1] was to make it easy to build such systems, by providing powerful engineering techniques and a general-purpose resource grammar library (RGL), which takes care of morphology and surface syntax.

Scaling up GF to wide-coverage translation is made possible by *layered interlinguas*, where deeper analysis levels (with narrower coverage) are backed up by shallower levels (with wider coverage). The interlingual grammar is combined with a *multilingual linked lexicon* (bootstrapped from open sources such as Wiktionary and Wordnet) and equipped with *statistical ranking* (based on treebanks) to select the best translations.[2,3]

---

[1] GF homepage: http://www.grammaticalframework.org/

[2] Available as GF cloud translator: http://cloud.grammaticalframework.org/wc.html,
  an Android app: https://play.google.com/store/apps/details?id=org.grammaticalframework.ui.android
  and an IOS app: https://itunes.apple.com/us/app/gf-offline-translator/id1023328422?mt=8

[3] This project is currently funded by REMU (Vetenskapsrådet): http://remu.grammaticalframework.org/

Domain-Specific Multilingual Translation for Producers of Information

Aarne RANTA, Krasimir ANGELOV, Markus FORSBERG,
Thomas HALLGREN

Digital Grammars AB, Framnäsgatan 23, 41264, Gothenburg, Sweden

{aarne,krasimir,markus,thomas}@digitalgrammars.com

Abstract. Producers of multilingual information (webpages, manuals, etc) often need not solve the general problem of "translating anything", but can stay content with a more limited system, which however must be accurate. One way to do this is to define a *semantic interlingua*, which exactly fits the content to be translated. It has turned out that *algebraic datatypes*, and the way they are used in compilers to encode *abstract syntax*, are useful for this purpose. The grammar formalism Grammatical Framework (GF) was originally designed to support this kind of systems. While much of the current research in GF is focused on scaling it up to general-purpose translation, the creation of domain-specific systems has become a routine task, which is commercially exploited by the start-up company Digital Grammars AB. In the conference, we plan to show a demo of the tools for building such systems, as well as some actual systems built for customers.

Description

If we divide translation into the phases of *analysis* (of the source) and *generation* (of the target), we can identify some of the hardest problems as having to do with the analysis phase: in particular, *ambiguity* and *unexpected input*. The most radical solution to these problems is to *eliminate* them whenever possible. This is what *natural language generation* (NLG) is about: the source of documents in all target languages is *structured data*, such as databases or logical formulas. However, in real applications, such data is not always available in a clean form, but must be extracted from unstructured sources, typically from text. *Translation*, in this perspective, is NLG fed by parsing a source language. In GF, generation and parsing are defined simultaneously, since GF grammars are reversible.[1]

The mission of Digital Grammars AB[2] is to build high-quality documentation systems (either pure NLG or with translation) tailored for customers' needs. The technique enables both automatic and interactive translation, and is available for over 30 languages. Depending on the domain and on the work invested in building the system, we can reach publication quality (which is needed in real-time documentation) or come close to it (in which case we provide tools that support interaction; the system indicates confidence levels and displays translation alternatives with their semantic analyses). The product can be delivered in the form of batch translation jobs, as a web service, and as mobile (speech-enabled) applications.

[1] GF: http://www.grammaticalframework.org/
[2] Digital Grammars AB: http://www.digitalgrammars.com/

The EXPERT Project: Training the Future Experts in Translation Technology

Constantin ORĂSAN

Research Group in Computational Linguistics, University of Wolverhampton, Wulfruna St.,
Wolverhampton, WV1 1LY, United Kingdom

c.orasan@wlv.ac.uk

Abstract. The EXPERT project (http://expert-itn.eu) is an Initial Training Network (ITN) supported by the People Programme (Marie Curie Actions) of the European Union's Framework Programme (FP7/2007-2013) under REA grant agreement no 317471. By appointing 15 fellows to work on related projects, the project aims to train the next generation of world-class researchers in the field of data-driven translation technology.

1. Description

This project presentation gives a brief overview of the EXPloiting Empirical appRoaches to Translation (EXPERT) project, an FP7 Marie Curie ITN in the field of translation technology. The purpose of the project is two-fold: to train 15 fellows to become future leaders in the field, by enabling them to pursue well-defined research projects, organising dedicated training events and enabling intersectoral and transnational secondments, and to advance the state of the art in data driven translation technologies.

The EXPERT project runs between 1st October 2012 and 30th September 2016, and is delivered by a consortium coordinated by University of Wolverhampton, UK and which contains five other academic partners: University of Malaga, Spain; University of Sheffield, UK; Saarland University, Germany; Dublin City University, Ireland and University of Amsterdam, Netherlands, as well as three industrial partners: Pangeanic, Spain; Translated, Italy and Hermes, Spain. In addition, the consortium benefits from the contribution of four associated partners: WordFast, France; Etrad, Argentina; Unbabel, Portugal and DFKI, Germany.

The appointed researchers are working on 15 individual, but related, projects which aim to improve the state of the art from five different directions: the user perspective, data collection and preparation, incorporation of language technology in translation memories, the human translator in the loop, and hybrid approaches to translation. To date, the project has produced over 120 high-quality publications and delivered three consortium wide training events. More details can be found in (Orasan et al. 2015).

References

Orasan, C.; Cattelan, A.; Corpas Pastor, G.; van Genabith, J.; Herranz, M.; Arevalillo, J; Liu, Q.; Sima'an, K.; Specia, L. (2015) The EXPERT Project: Advancing the State of the Art in Hybrid Translation Technologies. In Proceedings of Translating and the Computer 35, London, UK

Amplexor MTExpert - Machine Translation Adapted to the Translation Workflow

Alexandru CEAUSU, Sabine HUNSICKER, Tudy DROUMAGUET

AMPLEXOR International, Luxembourg, Luxembourg

Alexandru.Ceausu@amplexor.com, Sabine.Hunsicker@amplexor.com,
Tudy.Droumaguet@amplexor.com

Abstract. MTExpert is AMPLEXOR's proprietary machine translation (MT) system based on state-of-the-art statistical and linguistic algorithms, easily integrated with existing linguistic assets, delivering quality results tailored to different communication objectives.

Description

AMPLEXOR MTExpert is a fully automated MT service based on the Moses open-source platform with *language-specific linguistic optimizations* (Ceausu and Hunsicker, 2014), as well as *terminology integration* and *format handling*. The available MT engines include specialised MT domains, as well as customisable MT engines adapted to a particular content type.

MTExpert provides translation for *specialised and generic MT language domains* for most European languages, Chinese, Japanese and Arabic. It includes domains ranging from the EU official publication domain to the technical domain or life sciences. Existing translation engines can be *customised* to a particular content type, based on existing language assets like translation memories or terminology databases.

MTExpert *confidence score* can automatically estimate the reliability of the machine translated content, for a better quality and cost-benefit assessment. The confidence score can be fine-tuned for each translation workflow using the feedback from translators (Hunsicker and Ceausu, 2015).

System integration into standard translation / post-editing processes is achieved using flexible interfaces such as CAT system plugins that allow a flexible threshold definition for the application of MT, e.g. for words in segments below a defined match quality. The output of MT is used as additional linguistic resource for translators and post-editors who can work in their usual translation environment.

References

Hunsicker, S., Ceausu, A. (2015) Machine Translation Quality Estimation Adapted to the Translation Workflow. Translating and the Computer 36: 133-136

Ceausu, A., Hunsicker, S. (2014) Pre-ordering of phrase-based machine translation input in translation workflow. LREC 2014: 3589-3592

Abu-MaTran: Automatic building of Machine Translation

Antonio TORAL[1], Sergio ORTIZ_ROJAS[2], Mikel FORCADA[3],
Nikola LJUBESIC[4], Prokopis PROKOPIDIS[5]

[1]ADAPT Centre, School of Computing, Dublin City University, Ireland
[2]Prompsit Language Engineering SL, Spain
[3]Departament de Llenguatges i Sistemes Informatics, Universitat d'Alacant, Spain
[4]Faculty of Humanities and Social Sciences, University of Zagreb, Croatia
[5]Athena Research and Innovation Center, Greece

`atoral@computing.dcu.ie`

Abstract. We present the current status of Abu-MaTran (http://www.abumatran.eu), a 4-year project (January 2013–December 2016) on rapid development of machine translation for under-resourced languages. It is funded under Marie Curie's Industry-Academia Partnerships and Pathways 2012 programme. This is a consortium-based project with 5 partners (4 academic and 1 industrial).

Description

Abu-MaTran seeks to enhance industry–academia cooperation as a key aspect to tackle one of Europe's biggest challenges: multilingualism. We aim to increase the hitherto low industrial adoption of machine translation (MT) by identifying crucial cutting-edge research techniques, making them suitable for commercial exploitation. We also aim to transfer back to academia the know-how of industry to make research results more robust. We work on a case study of strategic interest for Europe: MT for the language of a new member state (Croatian) and related languages. All the resources produced are released as free/open-source software, resulting in effective knowledge transfer beyond the consortium.

At EAMT 2016 we will present a selection of the latests developments of the project: (i) state-of-the-art statistical and rule-based MT systems for South-Slavic languages based on free/open-source software, web crawled and publicly available data and linguistic knowledge, (ii) a novel tool for massive crawling of parallel and monolingual data from the Internet's top level domains and (iii) outcomes of the project's transfer and dissemination activities, e.g. MT hybridisation and web crawling for industry uses, rapid data creation for rule-based MT systems and establishment of a national linguistics Olympiad. All the resources developed within the project are freely available[1] and the MT systems deployed can be tested online.[2]

---

[1] http://www.abumatran.eu/?page_id=351

[2] http://translator.abumatran.eu/

TraMOOC (Translation for Massive Open Online Courses): Providing Reliable MT for MOOCs

Valia KORDONI, Lexi BIRCH, Ioana BULIGA, Kostadin CHOLAKOV,
Markus EGG, Federico GASPARI, Yota GEORGAKOPOULOU,
Maria GIALAMA, Iris HENDRICKX, Mitja JERMOL,
Katia KERMANIDIS, Joss MOORKENS, Davor ORLIC,
Michael PAPADOPOULOS, Maja POPOVIĆ, Rico SENNRICH,
Vilelmini SOSONI, Dimitrios TSOUMAKOS,
Antal van den BOSCH, Menno van ZAANEN, Andy WAY

Humboldt Universität zu Berlin (Coordinator, Germany), Dublin City University (Ireland),
University of Edinburgh (UK), Ionian University (Greece), Stichting Katholieke Universiteit
(Radboud University, Netherlands), EASN-Technology Innovation Services BVBA (Belgium),
Deluxe Media Europe Ltd (UK), Stichting Katholieke Universiteit Brabant (Tilburg University,
Netherlands), Iversity GMBH (Germany), Knowledge 4 All Foundation LBG (UK)

`info@tramooc.eu`

Abstract. TraMOOC is a 3-year EU-funded Horizon 2020 collaborative project that started in February 2015 (ICT-17-2014: Cracking the language barrier; project reference: 644333) which aims at providing reliable MT for MOOCs. The main outcome of the project will be a high-quality semi-automated MT service for all types of educational textual data available on a MOOC platform. The service will support nine European languages, in addition to Russian, and simplified Chinese. Progress may be monitored via the official project website at TraMOOC.eu, which is updated regularly with publications, news, and public deliverables.

TraMOOC: Reliable MT for Massive Open Online Courses

Language barriers constitute major impediments to sharing massive open online courses (MOOCs) with all peoples and in the attempt to educate all citizens. The EU-funded TraMOOC (Translation for Massive Open Online Courses) project aims at tackling this major issue by developing high-quality MT for all types of text included in MOOCs (e.g. assignments, tests, presentations, lecture subtitles, blog text) from English into eleven languages (DE, IT, PT, EL, DU, CS, BG, HR, PL, RU, ZH). The core of the TraMOOC platform will be open-source with some premium add-on services, enabling the integration of any MT solution in the educational domain, for any language. The project is conducting a major crowdsourcing drive, creating more training and evaluation data, while also performing comparative evaluations of phrase- and syntax-based SMT systems and state-of-the-art neural network MT engines, using standard metrics of fluency and adequacy, along with more detailed error taxonomies.

Modern MT: A New Open-Source Machine Translation Platform for the Translation Industry

U. GERMANN[1], E. BARBU[2], L. BENTIVOGLI[3], N. BERTOLDI[3],
N. BOGOYCHEV[1], C. BUCK[1], D. CAROSELLI[2], L. CARVALHO[4],
A. CATTELAN[2], R. CATTONI[3], M. CETTOLO[3], M. FEDERICO[3],
B. HADDOW[1], D. MADL[1], L. MASTROSTEFANO[2], P. MATHUR[3],
A. RUOPP[4], A. SAMIOTOU[4], V. SUDHARSHAN[4],
M. TROMBETTI[2], J. van der MEER[4]

[1] University of Edinburgh, 10 Crichton Street, Edinburgh EH8 9AB, United Kingdom
[2] Translated srl, Via Nepal, 29, 00144 Rome, Italy
[3] Fondazione Bruno Kessler, Via Sommarive, 18, 38123 Povo, Italy
[4] TAUS B.V., Oosteinde 9, 1483 AB De Rijp, Netherlands

`ugermann@inf.ed.ac.uk`

Abstract. *Modern MT* (`www.modernmt.eu`) is a three-year Horizon 2020 *innovation action* (2015–2017) to develop new open-source machine translation technology for use in translation production environments, both fully automatic and as a back-end in interactive post-editing scenarios. Led by Translated srl, the project consortium also includes the Fondazione Bruno Kessler (FBK), the University of Edinburgh, and TAUS B.V. *Modern MT* has received funding from the *European Union's Horizon 2020 research and innovation programme* under Grant Agreement No645487 (call ICT-17-2014).

Project Description

Modern MT aims to improve the state of the art in open source machine translation software by developing cloud-ready software that offers

- A **simple installation** procedure for a ready-to-go, REST-based translation service.
- **Very fast set-up times** for systems built from scratch using existing parallel corpora (e.g., translation memories). The goal is to process incoming data at approximately the speed at which it is uploaded.
- **Immediate integration of new data** (e.g., from newly post-edited MT output). Rebuilding or retuning the system will not be necessary.
- **Instant domain adaptation** by considering translation context beyond the individual sentence, without the need for domain-specific custom engines.
- **High scalability** with respect to throughput, concurrent users, and the amount of data the system can handle.

A first version of the software is available at `https://github.com/ModernMT/MMT`.

Modern MT is also actively **collecting and curating parallel data** for internal use and public release from web crawls and contributions from translation stakeholders, to improve MT quality for everyone.

MODERN: Modeling Discourse Entities and Relations for Coherent Machine Translation[*]

A. POPESCU-BELIS[1], J. EVERS-VERMEUL[4], M. FISHEL[3],
C. GRISOT[2], M.GROEN[4], J. HOEK[4], S. LOAICIGA[2], N.Q. LUONG[1],
L. MASCARELL[3], T. MEYER[1], L. MICULICICH[1], J. MOESCHLER[2],
X. PU[1], A. RIOS[3], T. SANDERS[4], M.VOLK[3], S. ZUFFEREY[4]

[1] Idiap Research Institute, 1920 Martigny, Switzerland
[2] University of Geneva, Department of Linguistics, 1211 Genève 4, Switzerland
[3] University of Zürich, Institute of Computational Linguistics, 8050 Zürich, Switzerland
[4] Utrecht University, Utrecht Institute of Linguistics, 3512 JK Utrecht, The Netherlands

andrei.popescu-belis@idiap.ch

Abstract. The MODERN project addresses coherence issues in sentence-by-sentence statistical MT, by propagating across sentences discourse-level information regarding discourse connectives, verb tenses, noun phrases and pronouns.

The goal of the MODERN project is to model and detect word dependencies across sentences, and to study their use by MT systems (MT), in order to demonstrate improvements in translation quality over state-of-the-art statistical MT, which still operates on a sentence-by-sentence basis. Three types of text-level dependencies are studied: referring expressions such as noun phrases and pronouns [4], discourse relations signaled by discourse connectives or implicit ones [1, 3], and verb tenses [2].

The overall approach of MODERN is to study the discourse-level phenomena from a theoretical perspective, but also using corpus-based approaches, in order to derive acceptable labels, features for automatic labeling, and training/test data. The automatic labeling systems are designed and combined with phrase-based statistical MT systems using factored models. The improvement in translating the respective phenomena is evaluated using specific automatic metrics or human evaluators.

MODERN started in 2013, building upon the COMTIS project started in 2010, with studies on English, French, German, Italian, Dutch, Arabic and Chinese. The main corpora used are Europarl, WIT3 (transcripts of TED talks), and Text+Berg (Swiss Alpine Club yearbooks).

References

1. Hoek J. et al., "The role of expectedness in the implicitation and explicitation of discourse relations", *Proc. of the 2nd DiscoMT workshop*, Lisbon, 2015.
2. Grisot C., *Temporal reference: empirical and theoretical perspectives*, PhD, UniGe, 2015.
3. Meyer T., *Discourse-level features for statistical machine translation*, PhD, EPFL, 2015.
4. Pu X., Mascarell L. et al., "Leveraging Compounds to Improve Noun Phrase Translation from Chinese and German", *Proc. of the ACL Student Session*, Beijing, 2015.

* MODERN is supported by the Swiss NSF, see www.idiap.ch/project/modern/.

Digital Curation Technologies (DKT)

Georg REHM, Felix SASAKI

DFKI GmbH, Language Technology Lab, Alt-Moabit 91c, 10559 Berlin, Germany

georg.rehm@dfki.de, felix.sasaki@dfki.de

Abstract. Digital Curation Technologies ("Digitale Kuratierungstechnologien", DKT) is a project that involves four Berlin-based SMEs (ART+COM AG, Condat AG, 3pc GmbH and Kreuzwerker GmbH) and DFKI GmbH (Language Technology Lab). The two-year action started in Sept. 2015 and aims at supporting digital curation processes, carried out by knowledge workers, through robust, precise and modular language and knowledge technologies. We combine these into workflows for the efficient processing, creation and dissemination of digital content. DFKI contributes language and knowledge technology components, including MT, and develops them further. Together with our partners, DFKI develops a platform for digital curation technologies, which offers services such as, e.g., translation, search, analytics, re-combination and summarisation. DKT is supported by the German Federal Ministry of Education and Research, Wachstumskern-Potenzial (no. 03WKP45). Details: http://www.digitale-kuratierung.de.

Description

The curation of digital content is a complex, knowledge- and time-intensive process in which authors or editors work, analyse, process and integrate highly heterogeneous data, content and media modules from disparate sources into a new content product that has a specific focus and communicative purpose. Among the processes involved are the selection, summarisation, classification, internationalisation, analysis, reordering, restructuring, and visualisation of various types of content. At the same time we need to bear in mind the continuously growing speed at which new information is coming in, the quantity and number of sources as well as of information pieces to be processed. The DKT SME partners contribute their respective sector-specific expertise (e.g., interactive showrooms, museums, television stations, newsrooms). In DKT we build showcases that demonstrate how language and knowledge technologies can be used in these typical digital curation workflows. The technologies contributed to DKT by DFKI belong to three areas: *semantic analysis* (e.g., information extraction), *semantic generation* (e.g., semantic story telling) and *multilingual technologies*, i.e., robust, adaptable MT components and integration of different monolingual or multilingual data and knowledge sources (including linked open data and standardised workflow data) for the sector-specific curation workflows. MT is used both for inbound and outbound translation (i.e., documents to be published). We also plan to incorporate MT engine improvement from user feedback. For the platform, we focus in particular the following features: fully integrated, robust, precise and scalable components with open interfaces in order to be efficiently embedded in sector-specific curation workflows; easy access to the cloud platform; application-oriented sector-technologies with high usability.

CRACKER – Cracking the Language Barrier.
Selected Results 2015/2016

Georg REHM

DFKI GmbH, Language Technology Lab, Alt-Moabit 91c, 10559 Berlin, Germany

`georg.rehm@dfki.de`

Abstract. CRACKER is a Coordination and Support Action (ref. 645357; 01/2015–12/2017), funded by the EU. The consortium consists of seven partners: DFKI GmbH (DE); Charles Univ. in Prague (CZ); ELDA (FR); FBK (IT); R.C. "Athena" (GR); Univ. of Edinburgh (UK); Univ. of Sheffield (UK). Details are available at http://www.cracker-project.eu.

Description – Summary and Selected Results 2015/2016

The European MT research community is experiencing increased pressure for rapid success – from the political frameworks of the EU, but also from the business world. CRACKER pushes towards an improvement of MT research by implementing the successful example of other disciplines where massively collaborative research on shared resources – guided by interoperability, standardisation, challenges and success metrics – has led to important breakthroughs. The nucleus of this new R&D&I strategy is the group of projects funded through the call H2020-ICT-2014 topic 17, that is supported by CRACKER in coordination, evaluation and resources as well as in community building activities. CRACKER builds upon, consolidates and extends initiatives for collaborative MT research supported by earlier EU-projects.

In terms of selected results (2015/2016), a large number of evaluation tasks are now jointly organised by the IWSLT and WMT workshops. WMT went from five tasks in 2015 to ten tasks in 2016. IWSLT featured automatic speech recognition tasks (English, German), and spoken language translation and MT tasks involving English, German, French, Chinese, Czech, Thai, and Vietnamese. After a successful MT Marathon 2015 the event will again take place in Prague in September 2016, covering lectures, labs, projects, and tools. CRACKER co-organises, with the project QT21, an LREC 2016 Workshop on Translation Evaluation, bringing together representatives from language service providers and researchers working on high-quality MT, SMT and human evaluation. Resource sharing in CRACKER builds upon and extends the open resource exchange infrastructure META-SHARE. Its new version restructures the relevant content and aggregates it into one place; it also includes improved search as well as an updated licensing module. In terms of community building and outreach, CRACKER organised META-FORUM 2015 (and co-organised the Riga Summit 2015) and prepared, with the project LT_Observatory, a Strategic Agenda – an updated version will be presented at META-FORUM 2016 (Lisbon, July 4/5). CRACKER is also the main driver behind the emerging "Cracking the Language Barrier" federation of European organisations and projects working on technologies for multilingual Europe.

AUTHOR INDEX

Association for Computational Linguistics
209 N. Eighth Street
Stroudsburg, Pennsylvania 18360

ISBN 978-1-5108-3185-8